BROADCASTING AND DEVELOPMENT COMMUNICATION

BROADCASTING AND DEVELOPMENT COMMUNICATION

Law, Policy and Action Plan

VED PRAKASH GANDHI

KANISHKA PUBLISHERS, DISTRIBUTORS
NEW DELHI-110 002

KANISHKA PUBLISHERS, DISTRIBUTORS
4697/5-21A, Ansari Road, Daryaganj
New Delhi -110 002
Phone : 2327 0497
(M) : 9810041277, 9654296751
E-mail : kanishka_publishing@yahoo.co.in
kanishkabooks@gmail.com

Broadcasting and Development Communication: Law, Policy and Action Plan

First Published 2008

Edition-2023

ISBN : 978-81-7391-046-5

Rs. 1500

PRINTED IN INDIA

Published by Madan Sachdeva for Kanishka Publishers, Distributors, 4697/5-21A, Ansari Road, Daryaganj, New Delhi-110002, Typeset by Sunshine Graphics, Delhi, and Printed at G.S. Printers, Delhi.

Preface

This book titled "Broadcasting and Development Communication: Law, Policy and Action Plan" covers the theme in the broadest possible way. Besides introducing the subject areas of media, communication and broadcasting, this book specially focuses on mass-media and development communication. Various dimensions of broadcasting in India are discussed in detail. Similarly, the impacts of broadcasting on rural progress is dealt in brief. India's information technology: law and action plan are covered with requisite details on cyber laws, IT action plan Target ITEX-50 and National Task Force on IT and Software Development. The Broadcasting Services Regulation Bill is described with focus on elements of proposed draft of 2006. This book also provides readers with an overview of laws and policies regarding India's broadcasting operations. Views and opinions of the Indian Broadcasting Regulation Forum on such matters are provided in detail. Guidelines regarding broadcasting content regulation in India are given. Also, report of the National Task Force on Information Technology and Software Development regarding the introduction of Conditional Access System (CAS) is documented in great detail. Also, rules and regulations, including penal provisions are discussed for running illegal television channels in violation of the down-linking guidelines in Cable/DTH services. India's media and broadcast policies at present and in coming future are analysed briefly.

In sum, this book can serve the purpose of a sourcebook on Indian broadcasting and development communication system. For additional readings and future research on the topic, a detailed bibliography is provided herein. This book is user-friendly and will help readers understand the Indian situation on the said subject in a complete way.

Ved Prakash Gandhi

Contents

1

Media, Communication and Broadcasting: An Introduction

MEDIA

Media may refer to various aspects

In Communication

- Print media—communications delivered via paper or canvas
- Electronic media—communications delivered via electronic or electromechanical energy
    - Multimedia—communications that incorporate multiple forms of information content and processing.
    - Hypermedia—media with hyperlinks.
- Published media—any media made available to the public
    - Mass media—all means of mass communication
        - Broadcast media—communications delivered over mass electronic communication networks.
        - News media—mass media focused on communicating news.

In Data Storage

- Recording media—devices used to store information
    - Digital media—electronic media used to store information.

In Art

- Media (arts)—materials and techniques used by an artist to produce a work.

In Biology

- Growth media—objects in which micro-organisms or cells can experience growth.
- Tunica media—the middle layer of the wall of a blood vessel.

In Astronomy

- Kaus Media—a star system in the constellation Sagittarius.

In Geography

- Media or Medea—the realm of the Medes.
- Media, Pennsylvania.
- Media, Illinois.

MASS MEDIA

Mass media is a term used to denote, as a class, that section of the media specifically conceived and designed to reach a very large audience such as the population of a nation state. It was coined in the 1920s with the advent of nationwide radio networks, mass-circulation newspapers and magazines, although mass media was present centuries before the term became common.

The term *public media* has a similar meaning. It is the sum of the public mass distributors of news and entertainment across mediums such as newspapers, television, radio, broadcasting and text publishers. The concept of mass media is complicated in some internet media as now individuals have a means of potential exposure on a scale comparable to what was previously restricted to select group of mass media producers. These internet media can include personal web pages, podcasts and blogs.

The mass media audience has been viewed by some commentators as forming a mass society with special characteristics, notably atomization or lack of social connections, which render it especially susceptible to the influence of modern mass media techniques such as advertising and propaganda. The term "MSM" or "mainstream media" has been widely used in the blogosphere in discussion of the mass media and media bias.

Etymology and Usage

Media (the plural of "medium") is a truncation of the term *media of communication,* referring to those organized means of dissemination of fact, opinion, entertainment, and other information, such as newspapers, magazines, out-of-home advertising, cinema films, radio, television, the World Wide Web, books, CDs, DVDs, video-cassettes, computer games and other forms of publishing. Although writers currently differ in their preference for using *media* in the singular ("the media is...") or the plural ("the media are..."), the former will still incur criticism in some situations. Academic programmes for the study of mass media are usually referred to as mass communication programmes.

An individual corporation within the mass media is referred to as a Media Institution.

The term "mass media" is mainly used by academics and media-professionals. When members of the general public refer to "the media" they are usually referring to the mass media, or to the news media, which is a section of the mass media.

Sometimes mass media (and the news media in particular) are referred to as the "corporate media." Other references include the "mainstream media" (MSM). Technically, *mainstream media* includes outlets that are in harmony with the prevailing direction of influence in the culture at large. In the United States, usage of these terms often depends on the connotations the speaker wants to invoke. The term "corporate media" is often used by leftist media critics to imply that the mainstream media are themselves composed of large multinational corporations, and promote those interests (see e.g., Fairness and Accuracy in Reporting; Herman and Chomsky's "A Propaganda Model"). This is countered by the right-wing media critics with the term "MSM", the acronym implying that the majority of mass media sources are dominated by leftist powers which are furthering their own agenda.

The more recent term 'Drive-by Media' has been popularized by conservative talk-show host Rush Limbaugh in response to the proposed transfer of operations of several U.S. ports to Dubai Ports World.

History

Types of drama in numerous cultures were probably the first mass-media, going back into the Ancient World. The first printed book known is the "Diamond Sutra", printed in China in 868 AD, and it is often suspected that books were printed earlier. Movable clay type was invented in 1041 in China. However, due to the slow spread to the masses of literacy in China, and the relatively high cost of paper there, the earliest printed mass medium was probably European popular prints from about 1400. Although these were produced in huge numbers, very few early examples survive, and even most known to be printed before about 1600 have not survived. Johannes Gutenberg printed the first book on a printing press with movable type in 1453. This invention transformed the way the world received printed materials, although books remained too expensive really to be called a mass-medium for at least a century after that.

Newspapers developed around from 1605, with the first example in English in 1620; but they took until the nineteenth century to reach a mass-audience directly.

During the 20th century, the growth of mass media was driven by technology that allowed the massive duplication of material. Physical duplication technologies such as printing, record pressing and film duplication allowed the duplication of books, newspapers and movies at low prices to huge audiences. Radio and television allowed the electronic duplication of information for the first time.

Mass media had the economics of linear replication: a single work could make money proportional to the number of copies sold, and as volumes went up, units costs went down, increasing profit margins further. Vast fortunes were to be made in mass media. In a democratic society, independent media serve to educate the public/electorate about issues regarding government and corporate. Some consider the concentration of media ownership to be a grave threat to democracy.

Timeline

c1400 : Appearance of European popular prints.

1453 : Johnannes Gutenberg prints the Bible, using his printing press, ushering in the Renaissance.

1620 : First newspaper (or *coranto*) in English.

1825 : Nicéphore Niépce takes the first permanent photograph.
1830 : Telegraphy is independently developed in England and the United States.
1876 : First telephone call made by Alexander Graham Bell.
1878 : Thomas Alva Edison patents the phonograph.
1890 : First juke box in San Francisco's Palais Royal Saloon.
1890 : Telephone wires are installed in Manhattan.
1895 : Cinematograph invented by Auguste and Louis Lumiere.
1896 : Hollerith founds the Tabulating Machine Co. It will become IBM in 1924.
1897 : Guglielmo Marconi patents the wireless telegraph.
1898 : Loudspeaker is invented.
1906 : The Story of the Kelly Gang from Australia is world's first feature length film.
1909 : RMS Republic, a palatial White Star passenger liner, uses the Marconi Wireless for a distress at sea. She had been in a collision. This is the first "breaking news" mass media event.
1912 : Air mail begins.
1913 : Edison transfers from cylinder recordings to more easily reproducible discs.
1913 : The portable phonograph is manufactured.
1915 : Radiotelephone carries voice from Virginia to the Eiffel Tower.
1916 : Tunable radios invented.
1919 : Short-wave radio is invented.
1920 : KDKA-AM in Pittsburgh, United States, becoming the world's first commercial radio station.
1922 : BBC is formed and broadcasting to London.
1924 : KDKA created a short-wave radio transmitter.
1925 : BBC broadcasting to the majority of the UK.
1926 : NBC is formed.
1927 : The Jazz Singer: The first motion picture with sounds debuts.
1927 : Philo Taylor Farnsworth debuts the first electronic television system.
1928 : The Teletype was introduced.
1933 : Edwin Armstrong invents FM Radio.

1934 : Half of the homes in the U.S. have radios.
1935 : First telephone call made around the world.
1936 : BBC opened world's first regular (then defined as at least 200 lines) high definition television service.
1938 : *The War of the Worlds* is broadcast on October 30, causing mass hysteria.
1939 : Western Union introduces coast-to-coast fax service.
1939 : Regular electronic television broadcasts begin in the U.S.
1939 : The wire recorder is invented in the U.S.
1940 : The first commercial television station, WNBT (now WNBC-TV)/New York signs on the air.
1948 : Cable television becomes available in the U.S.
1951 : The first colour televisions go on sale.
1957 : Sputnik is launched and sends back signals from near earth orbit.
1959 : Xerox makes the first copier.
1960 : Echo I, a U.S. balloon in orbit, reflects radio signals to Earth.
1962 : Telstar satellite transmits an image across the Atlantic.
1963 : Audio cassette is invented in the Netherlands.
1963 : Martin Luther King gives "I have a dream" speech.
1965 : Vietnam War becomes first war to be televised.
1967 : Newspapers, magazines start to digitize production.
1969 : Man's first landing on the moon is broadcast to 600 million people around the globe.
1970s : ARPANET, progenitor to the internet developed.
1971 : Intel debuts the microprocessor.
1972 : Pong becomes the first video game to win widespread popularity.
1975 : The MITS Altair 8800 becomes the first pre-assembled desktop computer available on the market.
1976 : JVC introduces VHS videotape—becomes the standard consumer format in the 1980s and 1990s.
1980 : CNN launches.
1980 : New York Times, Wall Street Journal, Dow Jones put news database online.
1981 : The laptop computer is introduced by Tandy.
1982 : Philips and Sony put the Compact Disc on the

Japanese market. It arrives on the U.S. market early the following year.

1983 : Cellular phones begin to appear.

1984 : Apple Macintosh is introduced.

1985 : CD-ROMs begin to be sold.

1985 : Pay-per-view channels open for business.

1991 : World-Wide Web (WWW) publicly released by Tim Berners-Lee at CERN.

1993 : CERN announces that the WWW will be free for anyone to use.

1995 : The Internet grows exponentially.

1996 : First DVD players and discs are available in Japan. Twister is the first film on DVD.

1999 : Napster contributes to the popularization of MP3.

Purposes

Mass media can be used for various purposes:

- Advocacy, both for business and social concerns. This can include advertising, marketing, propaganda, public relations and political communication.
- Enrichment and education.
- Entertainment, traditionally through performances of acting, music, and sports, along with light reading; since the late 20th century also through video and computer games.
- Journalism.
- Public service announcements.

Claimed Inherent Negative Characteristics of Mass Media

Another description of Mass Media is central media meaning they emanate from a central point, the same identical message to numerous recipients. It is claimed this forces certain intrinsic constraints on the kind of messages and information that can be conveyed such as: an inability to transmit tacit knowledge, a focus on the unusual and sensational rather than a restatement of wisdom, the promotion of anxiety and fear to sell the newspaper/channel etc. inability to deal with complex issues so a need to simplify.

This view of central media can be contrasted with lateral media such as e-mails networks where messages are all slightly different a spread by a process of lateral diffusion.

Journalism

Journalism is a discipline of collecting, analyzing, verifying, and presenting information regarding current events, trends, issues and people. Those who practice journalism are known as journalists.

News-oriented journalism is sometimes described as the "first rough draft of history" (attributed to Phil Graham), because journalists often record important events, producing news articles on short deadlines. While under pressure to be first with their stories, news media organizations usually edit and proof-read their reports prior to publication, adhering to each organization's standards of accuracy, quality and style. Many news organizations claim proud traditions of holding government officials and institutions accountable to the public, while media critics have raised questions about holding the press itself accountable.

Public Relations

Public relations is the art and science of managing communication between an organization and its key publics to build, manage and sustain its positive image. Examples include:

- Corporations use Marketing Public Relations (MPR) to convey information about the products they manufacture or services they provide to potential customers to support their direct sales efforts. Typically, they support sales in the short and long-term, establishing and burnishing the corporation's branding for a strong, ongoing market.
- Corporations also use public relations as a vehicle to reach legislators and other politicians, seeking favourable tax, regulatory, and other treatment, and they may use public relations to portray themselves as enlightened employers, in support of human-resources recruiting programmes.
- Non-profit organizations, including schools and universities, hospitals, and human and social service agencies, use public relations in support of awareness programmes, fund-raising programmes, staff recruiting, and to increase patronage of their services.

- Politicians use public relations to attract votes and raise money, and, when successful at the ballot box, to promote and defend their service in office, with an eye to the next election or, at career's end, to their legacy.

Forms

Electronic media and print media include:

- Broadcasting, in the narrow sense, for radio and television.
- Various types of discs or tape. In the 20th century, these were mainly used for music. Video and computer uses followed.
- Film, most often used for entertainment, but also for documentaries.
- Internet, which has many uses and presents both opportunities and challenges. Blogs and podcasts, such as news, music, pre-recorded speech and video.
- Publishing, in the narrow sense, meaning on paper, mainly via books, magaziness, and newspapers.
- Computer games, which have developed into a mass form of media since devices such as the PlayStation 3, Xbox 360, and the Wii broadened their use.

Audio Recording and Reproduction

Sound recording and reproduction is the electrical or mechanical recreation and/or amplification of sound, often as music. This involves the use of audio equipment such as microphones, recording devices and loudspeakers. From early beginnings with the invention of the phonograph using purely mechanical techniques, the field has advanced with the invention of electrical recording, the mass production of the 78 record, the magnetic wire recorder followed by the tape recorder, the vinyl LP record. The invention of the compact cassette in the 1960's, followed by Sony's Walkman, gave a major boost to the mass distribution of music recordings, and the invention of digital recording and the compact disc in 1983 brought massive improvements in ruggedness and quality. The most recent developments have been in digital audio-players like the Apple iPod.

An album is a collection of related audio tracks, released together to the public, usually commercially.

The term record album originated from the fact that 78 RPM Phonograph disc records were kept together in a book resembling a photo album. The first collection of records to be called an "album" was Tchaikovsky's *Nutcracker Suite*, release in April 1909 as a four-disc set by Odeon records. It retailed for 16 shillings—about £15 in modern currency.

A music video (also promo) is a short film or video that accompanies a complete piece of music, most commonly a song. Modern music videos were primarily made and used as a marketing device intended to promote the sale of music recordings. Although the origins of music videos go back much further, they came into their own in the 1980s, when Music Television's format was based around them. In the 1980s, the term "rock video" was often used to describe this form of entertainment, although the term has fallen into disuse.

Music videos can accommodate all styles of film-making, including animation, live action films, documentaries, and non-narrative, abstract film.

Broadcasting

Broadcasting is the distribution of audio or video signals (programmes) to a number of recipients ("listeners" or "viewers") that belong to a large group. This group may be the public in general, or a relatively large audience within the public. Thus, an Internet channel may distribute text or music world-wide, while a public address system in (for example) a workplace may broadcast very limited *ad hoc* soundbites to a small population within its range.

The sequencing of content in a broadcast is called a schedule. With all technological endeavours a number of technical terms and slang are developed.

Television and radio programmes are distributed through radio broadcasting or cable, often both simultaneously. By coding signals and having decoding equipment in homes, the latter also enables subscription-based channels and pay-per-view services.

A broadcasting organization may broadcast several programmes at the same time, through several channels (frequencies), for example, BBC One and Two. On the other hand, two or more organizations may share a channel and each use it during a fixed part of the day. Digital radio and digital television may also transmit multiplexed programming, with several channels compressed into one ensemble.

When broadcasting is done via the Internet the term webcasting is often used. In 2004, a new phenomenon occurred when a number of technologies combined to produce podcasting. Podcasting is an asynchronous broadcast/narrowcast medium, with one of the main proponents being Adam Curry and his associates the Podshow.

Broadcasting forms a very large segment of the mass media. Broadcasting to a very narrow range of audience is called narrowcasting. The term "broadcast" was coined by early radio engineers from the mid-western United States.

Film

Film is a term that encompasses motion pictures as individual projects, as well as the field in general. The origin of the name comes from the fact that photographic film (also called *filmstock*) has historically been the primary medium for recording and displaying motion pictures. Many other terms exist—*motion pictures* (or just *pictures* or "picture"), *the silver screen, photoplays, the cinema, picture shows, flicks*—and commonly *movies.*

Films are produced by recording people and objects with cameras, or by creating them using animation techniques and/or special effects. They comprise a series of individual frames, but when these images are shown rapidly in succession, the illusion of motion is given to the viewer. Flickering between frames is not seen due to an effect known as persistence of vision—whereby the eye retains a visual image for a fraction of a second after the source has been removed. Also of relevance is what causes the perception of motion; a psychological effect identified as beta movement.

Film is considered by many to be an important art form; films entertain, educate, enlighten and inspire audiences. The visual elements of cinema need no translation, giving the motion picture a universal power of communication. Any film can become a worldwide attraction, especially with the addition of dubbing or subtitles that translate the dialogue. Films are also artifacts created by specific cultures, which reflect those cultures, and, in turn, affect them.

Internet

The Internet (also known simply as "the Net" or "the Web") can be briefly understood as "a network of networks." Specifically, it is the world-wide, publicly accessible network of interconnected computer networks that transmit data by packet switching using the standard Internet Protocol (IP). It consists of millions of smaller domestic, academic, business, and governmental networks, which together carry various information and services, such as electronic mail, online chat, file transfer, and the interlinked web pages and other documents of the World-Wide Web.

Contrary to some common usage, the Internet and the World-Wide Web are not synonymous: the Internet is a collection of interconnected *computer networks,* linked by copper wires, fiber-optic cables, wireless connections etc.; the Web is a collection of interconnected *documents,* linked by hyperlinks and URLs. The World-Wide Web is accessible via the Internet, along with many other services including e-mail, file sharing and others described below.

Toward the end of the 20th century, the advent of the World-Wide Web marked the first era in which any individual could have a means of exposure on a scale comparable to that of mass media. For the first time, anyone with a web-site can address a global audience, although serving to high levels of web traffic is still relatively expensive. It is possible that the rise of peer-to-peer technologies may have begun the process of making the cost of bandwidth manageable. Although a vast amount of information, imagery, and commentary (i.e., "content") has been made available, it is often difficult to determine the authenticity and reliability of information contained in web pages (in many cases, self-published). The invention of the Internet has also allowed breaking news stories to reach around the globe within minutes. This rapid growth of instantaneous, decentralized communication is often deemed likely to change mass media and its relationship to society. "Cross-media" means the idea of distributing the same message through different media channels. A similar idea is expressed in the news industry as "convergence". Many authors understand cross-media publishing to be the ability to publish in both print and on the web without manual conversion effort. An increasing number of wireless devices with mutually incompatible data and screen formats make it even more difficult to achieve the objective "create once, publish many."

Publishing

Publishing is the industry concerned with the production of literature or information—the activity of making information available for public view. In some cases, authors may be their own publishers.

Traditionally, the term refers to the distribution of printed works such as books and newspapers. With the advent of digital information systems and the Internet, the scope of publishing has expanded to include websites, blogs and the like.

As a business, publishing includes the development, marketing, production, and distribution of newspapers, magazines, books, literary works, musical works, software, other works dealing with information.

Publication is also important as a legal concept; (1) as the process of giving formal notice to the world of a significant intention, for example, to marry or enter bankruptcy, and; (2) as the essential pre-condition of being able to claim defamation that is, the alleged libel must have been published.

Book

A book is a collection of sheets of paper, parchment or other material with a piece of text written on them, bound together along one edge within covers. A book is also a literary work or a main division of such a work. A book produced in electronic format is known as an e-book.

In library and information science, a book is called a monograph to distinguish it from serial publications such as magazines, journals or newspapers.

Publishers may produce low-cost, pre-proof editions known as galleys or 'bound proofs' for promotional purposes, such as generating reviews in advance of publication. Galleys are usually made as cheaply as possible, since they are not intended for sale.

A lover of books is usually referred to as a bibliophile, a bibliophilist, or a philobiblist, or, more informally, a bookworm.

A book may be studied by students in the form of a book report.

It may also be covered by a professional writer as a book review to introduce a new book. Some belong to a book club.

Magazine

A magazine is a periodical publication containing a variety of articles, generally financed by advertising and/or purchase by readers.

Magazines are typically published weekly, biweekly, monthly, bimonthly or quarterly, with a date on the cover that is in advance of the date it is actually published. They are often printed in colour on coated paper, and are bound with a soft cover.

Magazines fall into two broad categories: consumer magazines and business magazines. In practice, magazines are a subset of periodicals, distinct from those periodicals produced by scientific, artistic, academic or special interest publishers which are subscription-only, more expensive, narrowly limited in circulation, and often have little or no advertising.

Magazines can be classified as:

- General interest magazines (e.g. Frontline, India Today, The Week, etc.).
- Special interest magazines (Women's, Sports, Business, Scuba Diving, etc.).

Newspaper

A newspaper is a publication containing news and information and advertising, usually printed on low-cost paper called *newsprint*. It may be general or special interest, most often published daily or weekly. The first printed newspaper was published in 1605, and the form has thrived even in the face of competition from technologies such as radio and television. Recent developments on the Internet are posing major threats to its business model, however. Paid circulation is declining in most countries, and advertising revenue, which makes up the bulk of a newspaper's income, is shifting from print to online; some commentators, nevertheless, point out that historically new media such as radio and television did not entirely supplant existing media.

Software Publishing

A software publisher is a publishing company in the software industry between the developer and the distributor. In some companies, two or all three of these roles may be combined (and indeed, may reside in a single person, especially in the case of shareware).

Software publishers often license software from developers with specific limitations, such as a time limit or geographical region. The terms of licensing vary enormously, and are typically secret.

Developers may use publishers to reach larger or foreign markets, or to avoid focussing on marketing. Or publishers may use developers to create software to meet a market need that the publisher has identified.

Video and Computer Games

A computer game is a computer-controlled game. A video game is a computer game where a video display such as a monitor or television is the primary feedback device. The term "computer game" also includes games which display only text (and which can therefore theoretically be played on a teletypewriter) or which use other methods, such as sound or vibration, as their primary feedback device, but there are very few new games in these categories. There always must also be some sort of input device, usually in the form of button/joystick combinations (on arcade games), a keyboard and mouse/trackball combination (computer games), or a controller (console games), or a combination of any of the above. Also, more esoteric devices have been used for input. Usually there are rules and goals, but in more open-ended games the player may be free to do whatever they like within the confines of the virtual universe.

The phrase interactive entertainment is the formal reference to computer and video games. To avoid ambiguity, this game software is referred to as *computer and video games* throughout this article, which explores properties common to both types of game.

In common usage, a "computer game" or a "PC game" refers to a game that is played on a personal computer. "Console game" refers to one that is played on a device specifically designed for the use of such, while interfacing with a standard television set. "Video game" has evolved into a catchall phrase that encompasses the aforementioned along with any game made for any other device, including, but not limited to, mobile phones, PDAs, advanced calculators, etc.

Contrast with Non-mass Media

Non-mass or "personal" media (point-to-point and person-to-person communication) include:

- Speech
- Gestures
- Telephony
- Postal mail
- Some uses of the Internet
- Some Interactive media.

MEDIA AND DEVELOPMENT COMMUNICATION

In media studies, the subject of *Media and Development Communication* introduces the structure of mass communication, processes and effects of media, different aspects of development and communication, communication technologies, print and electronic cornucopia, emerging interactive media, communication research methodology, theories of media and society, rural development and communication strategies.

They affect changes at all levels in society and culture, trade and commerce, politics and government and other areas of life.

PRINTING

Printing is a process for production of texts and images, typically with ink on paper using a printing press. It is often carried out as a large-scale industrial process, and is an essential part of publishing and transaction printing.

History of Block Printing

Block Printing in China

Woodblock printing on paper, whereby individual sheets were pressed against wooden blocks with the text and illustrations carved into them, was first recorded in China in the Tang Dynasty, although as a method for printing patterns on cloth the earliest surviving examples from China date to before 220, and from Egypt to the 6th or 7th centuries.

In the Tang Dynasty, a Chinese writer named Fenzhi first mentioned in his book "Yuan Xian San Ji" that the woodblock was used to print Buddhist scripture during the Zhenguan years (627-649 A.D.). The oldest known Chinese surviving printed work is a woodblock-printed Buddhist scripture of Wu Zetian period (684-705 A.D.); discovered in Tubofan, Xinjiang province, China in 1906, it is now stored in a calligraphy museum in Tokyo, Japan. The oldest surviving documented printed book, a copy of the Buddhist Diamond Sutra, is dated 848 AD, but a recent excavation at a Korean pagoda may have unearthed an even earlier Buddhist text dating to AD 750-751. In the modern Chinese historiography, printing is considered one of the Four Great Inventions of ancient China.

In a memorial to the throne in 1023, Northern Song Dynasty China, it recorded that the Central Government at that time used copperplate to print the paper money also the copper-block to print the numbers and characters on the money, now-a-days we can find these shadows from the Song paper money. Later in the Jin Dynasty, people used the same but more developed technique to print paper money and formal official documents, the typical example of this kind of movable copper-block printing is a printed "check" of Jin Dynasty in the year of 1215.

Block Printing in Europe

Block printing came to Christian Europe as a method for printing on cloth, where it was common by 1300. Images printed on cloth for religious purposes could be quite large and elaborate, and when paper became relatively easily available, around 1400, the medium transferred very quickly to small woodcut religious images and playing cards printed on paper. These prints were produced in very large numbers from about 1425 onwards.

Around the mid-century, *block-books*, woodcut books with both text and images, usually carved in the same block, emerged as a cheaper alternative to manuscripts and books printed with moveable type. These were all short heavily illustrated works, the best sellers of the day, repeated in many different block-book versions: the Ars moriendi and the Biblia pauperum were the most common. There is still some controversy among scholars as to whether their introduction preceded or, the majority view, followed the introduction of movable type, with the range of estimated dates being between about 1440-1460.

The volume of Joseph Needham's *Science and Civilization in China* dealing with paper and printing has a chapter that suggests that "European block printers must not only have seen Chinese samples, but perhaps had been taught by missionaries or others who had learned these un-European methods from Chinese printers during their residence in China." But he also admitted that the "only evidence of European printing transmitted from China is a lack of counter evidence."

Movable Type Printing

Movable type allowed for a much more flexible processes than hand copying or block printing.

In East Asia

For a description of

- the oldest surviving metal type
- early books printed with such metal type
- the oldest surviving movable metal print book printed in Korea in 1377
- the Korean font casting process as recorded by Song Hyon in the 15th century
- problems due to the nature of the Chinese language.

Movable type printing was first invented in 1041 by Bi Sheng in China. Sheng used clay type, which broke easily, but Wang Zhen later carved a more durable type from wood.

The transition from wood type to metal type occurred during the Goryeo Dynasty of Korea and is credited to Chwe Yun-Ui.

Movable type, though known in China, was not extensively used there until the European-style printing press was introduced in relatively recent times.

East Asian printing technology may possibly have diffused into Europe through the trade routes from China through India or the

Arabic world, although there is no evidence. The lack of known intermediaries and profound technical differences in detail indicate that Gutenberg's invention of movable type was done independently.

In Europe

Johann Gutenberg, of the German city of Mainz, developed European printing technology in 1440, with which the classical age of printing began. Also, Johann Fust and Peter Schöffer experimented with him in Mainz. Genealogically, all modern movable type printing can be traced back to a single source, Gutenberg's printing press which he derived from the design of long known agricultural presses. East Asian style movable type printing, which was based on laborious manual rubbing and which had been scarcely used, practically died out after the introduction of European style printing in the 19th century.

Gutenberg is also credited with the introduction of an oil-based ink which was more durable than previously used water-based inks. Having worked as a professional goldsmith, Gutenberg made skillful use of the knowledge of metals he had learned as a craftsman. Gutenberg was also the first to make his type from an alloy of lead, tin, and antimony, which was critical for producing durable type that produced high-quality printed books, and proved to be more suitable for printing than the clay, wooden or bronze types used in East Asia. To create these lead types, Gutenberg used what some considered his most ingenious invention, a special matrix wherewith the moulding of new movable types with an unprecedented precision at short notice became feasible. Within a year after his B42, Gutenberg also published the first coloured prints.

Gutenberg's invention of the printing press revolutionized communication and book production leading to the spread of knowledge. Rapidly, printing spread from Germany by emigrating German printers, but also by foreign apprentices returning home. A printing press was built in Venice in 1469, and by 1500 the city had 417 printers. In 1470 Johann Heynlin set up a printing press in Paris. In 1473 Kasper Straube published the Almanach Cracoviense ad annum 1474 in Kraków. In 1476 a printing press was developed in England by William Caxton. The Italian Juan Pablos set up an imported press in Mexico City in 1539. Stephen Day was the first to build a printing press in North America at Massachusetts Bay in 1628, and helped establish the Cambridge Press.

Printing Houses

Early printing houses (near the time of Gutenberg) were run by "master printers." These printers owned shops, selected and edited manuscripts, determined the sizes of print runs, sold the works they produced, raised capital and organized distribution. Some master printing houses became the cultural centre for literati such as Erasmus.

- *Print shop apprentices*: Apprentices, usually between the ages of 15 and 20, worked for master printers. Apprentices were not required to be literate, and literacy rates at the time were very low, in comparison to today. Apprentices prepared ink, dampened sheets of paper, and assisted at the press. An apprentice who wished to learn to become a compositor had to learn Latin and spend time under the supervision of a journeyman.
- *Journeyman printers*: After completing their apprenticeships, *journeyman* (so-called from the French "journée" for day) printers were free to move employers. This facilitated the spread of printing to areas that were less print-centred.
- *Compositors*: Those who set the type for printing.
- *Pressmen*: The person who worked the press. This was physically labour intensive.

The earliest-known image of a European, Gutenberg-style print shop is the *Dance of Death* by Matthias Huss, at Lyon, 1499. This image depicts a compositor standing at a compositor's case being grabbed by a skeleton. The case is raised to facilitate his work. The image also shows a pressman being grabbed by a skeleton. At the right of the printing house a bookshop is shown.

Financial Aspects

Court records from the city of Mainz document that Johannes Fust was, for some time, Gutenberg's financial backer.

By the sixteenth century jobs associated with printing were becoming increasingly specialized. Structures supporting publishers were more and more complex, leading to this division of labour. In Europe between 1500 and 1700 the role of the Master Printer was dying out and giving way to the bookseller—publisher. Printing during this period had a stronger commercial imperative than previously. Risks associated with the industry however were substantial, although dependent on the nature of the publication.

Bookseller publishers negotiated at trade fairs and at print shops. Jobbing work appeared in which printers did menial tasks in the beginning of their careers to support themselves.

1500—1700: Publishers developed several new methods of funding projects.

1. *Cooperative associations/publication syndicates*: A number of individuals shared the risks associated with printing and shared in the profit. This was pioneered by the French.
2. *Subscription publishing*: Pioneered by the English in the early 17th century. A prospectus for a publication was drawn up by a publisher to raise funding. The prospectus was given to potential buyers who signed up for a copy. If there were not enough subscriptions the publication did not go ahead. Lists of subscribers were included in the books as endorsements. If enough people subscribed a reprint might occur. Some authors used subscription publication to bypass the publisher entirely.
3. *Installment publishing*: Books were issued in parts until a complete book had been issued. This was not necessarily done with a fixed time period. It was an effective method of spreading cost over a period of time. It also allowed earlier returns on investment to help cover production costs of subsequent installments.

The *Mechanick Exercises*, by Joseph Moxon, in London, 1683, was said to be the first publication done in installments.

Publishing trade organizations allowed publishers to organize business concerns collectively. Systems of self-regulation occurred in these arrangements. For example, if one publisher did something to irritate other publishers he would be controlled by peer pressure. Such systems are known as cartels, and are in most countries now considered to be in restraint of trade. These arrangements helped deal with labour unrest among journeymen, who faced difficult working conditions. Brotherhoods predated unions, without the formal regulations now associated with unions.

In most cases, publishers bought the copyright in a work from the author, and made some arrangement about the possible profits. This required a substantial amount of capital in addition to the capital for the physical equipment and staff. Alternatively, an author who had sufficient money would sometimes keep the copyright himself, and simply pay the printer for the production of the book.

Eighteenth Century Innovations

At the end of the eighteenth century there were several remarkable innovations in the graphic techniques and those that were utilized to make their materials. Bewick developed the method of using engraving tools on the end of the wood. Senefelder discovered lithography. Blake made relief etchings.

Nineteenth Century Innovations

Early in the nineteenth century Stanhope, George E. Clymer, Koenig and others introduced new kinds of type presses, which for strength surpassed anything that had previously been known.

Modern Printing Technology

In 2006, there are approximately 30,700 printing companies in the United States, accounting for $112 billion, according to the *2006 U.S. Industry & Market Outlook* by Barnes Reports. Print jobs that move through the Internet made up 12.5 per cent of the total U.S. Printing market last year, according to research firm InfoTrend/CAP Ventures.

Books and newspapers are printed today using the technique of offset lithography. Other common techniques include:

- *flexography* used for packaging, labels, newspapers
- *relief print* (mainly used for catalogues)
- *screen printing* from T-shirts to floor tiles
- *rotogravure* mainly used for magazines and packaging
- *inkjet* used typically to print a small number of books or

packaging, and also to print a variety of materials from high quality papers simulate offset printing, to floor tiles; Inkjet is also used to apply mailing addresses to direct mail pieces

- hot wax *dye transfer*
- *laser printing* mainly used in offices and for transactional printing (bills, bank documents). Laser printing is commonly used by direct mail companies to create variable data letters or coupons, for example.

Gravure

For this process, the image to be printed is made up of small holes sunk into the surface of the printing plate. The cells are filled with ink and the excess is scraped off the surface, then a rubber-covered roller presses paper onto the surface of the plate and into contact with the ink in the cells. The printing plates are usually made from copper and may be produced by engraving or etching.

Gravure printing is used for long, high-quality print runs such as magazines, mail-order catalogues, packaging, and printing onto fabric and wall-paper. It is also used for printing postage stamps and decorative plastic laminates, such as kitchen worktops.

Digital Printing

Printing at home or in an office or engineering environment is sub-divided into:

- small format (up to ledger size paper sheets), as used in business offices and libraries
- wide format (up to 3' or 914 mm wide rolls of paper), as used in drafting and design establishments.

Some of the more common printing technologies are:

- *line printing*, where pre-formed characters are applied to the paper by lines
- *daisy wheel*, where pre-formed characters are applied individually
- *dot-matrix*, which produces arbitrary patterns of dots with an array of printing studs

- *heat transfer*, like early fax machines or modern receipt printers that apply heat to special paper, which turns black to form the printed image
- *blueprint*, and related chemical technologies
- *inkjet*, including bubble-jet—where ink is sprayed onto the paper to create the desired image
- *laser*, where toner consisting primarily of polymer with pigment of the desired colours is melted and applied directly to the paper to create the desired image.

Vendors typically stress the total cost to operate the equipment, involving complex calculations that include all cost factors involved in the operation as well as the capital equipment costs, amortization, etc. For the most part, toner systems beat inkjet in the long run, whereas inkjets are less expensive in the initial purchase price.

Professional digital printing (using toner) primarily uses an electrical charge to transfer toner or liquid ink to the substrate it is printed on. Digital print quality has steadily improved from early colour and black and white copiers to sophisticated colour digital presses like the Xerox iGen3, the Kodak Nexpress and the HP Indigo Digital Press series. The iGen3 and Nexpress use toner particles and the Indigo uses liquid ink. All three are made for small runs and variable data, and rival offset in quality. Digital offset presses are called direct imaging presses; although these receive computer files and automatically turn them into print-ready plates, they cannot insert variable data.

Small press and fanzines generally use digital printing or more rarely xerography. Prior to the introduction of cheap photocopying the use of machines such as the spirit duplicator, hectograph, and mimeograph was common.

PRINTING PRESS

The printing press is a mechanical printing device for making copies of identical text on multiple sheets of paper. It was invented in Germany by the Goldsmith and printer Johannes Gutenberg in 1445. Printing methods based on Gutenberg's printing press spread rapidly throughout first Europe and then the rest of the world, replacing most block printing and making it the sole progenitor of modern movable type printing. Printing's effect on civilization has often been discussed in terms of the effect of the "printing press" on civilization—a rhetorical device, which alludes to the pivotal role of the printing press in the global spread of printing.

Movable type printing, which allowed individual characters to be arranged to form words, is a separate invention from the printing press. In what is regarded as an independent invention, movable type printing as we know it today was invented in Germany by Gutenberg in the 1440s, although the first known invention was in China by Bi Sheng between 1041 and 1048.

Invention of the Printing Press

Johannes Gutenberg is credited with inventing the first printing press, although there are several local claims for the invention of the printing press in other parts of Europe, including Laurens Janszoon Coster in the Netherlands and Panfilo Castaldi in Italy. Screw presses for olives and wine were known in Europe since Roman times; presses for the binding of manuscript books were also in use. Gutenberg was the first to convert the concept for printing uses. Gutenberg's use of mechanical presses, along with other innovations of his, made printing from the start a proto-industrial process with a far greater printing output than with manual work.

Having previously worked as a professional goldsmith, Gutenberg also made skillful use of the knowledge of metals he had learned as a craftsman. He was the first to make his type from an alloy of lead, tin, and antimony, which was critical for producing durable type that produced high-quality printed books, and proved to be more suitable for printing than the clay, wooden or bronze types used in East Asia. To create these lead types, Gutenberg used what some considered his most ingenious invention, a special matrix enabling the moulding of new movable types at short notice and with unprecedented precision.

In the Gutenberg Bible, Gutenberg made a trial of coloured printing for a few of the page headings, present only in some copies. (Albert Kapr, "Johannes Gutenberg", Scolar 1996, p. 172)

A later work, the Mainz Psalter of 1453, presumably designed by Gutenberg but published under the imprint of his successors Johann Fust and Peter Schoeffer, had elaborate red and blue printed initials. (Kapr, p. 203). Gutenberg is also credited with the introduction of an oil-based ink which was more durable than the previously used water-based inks. As printing material he used both vellum and paper, the latter having been introduced in Europe somewhat earlier from China by way of the Arabs, who had a paper mill in operation in Baghdad as early as 794.

Method of Using the Gutenberg-style Printing Press

The parts of the printing press:

- The frame—immovably braces and supports the two moving parts.
- The carriage assembly—carries the type and paper in and out of the impression assembly.
- The impression assembly—pushes (or presses) the paper onto the inked type.

The Printing Process:

1. Buy the paper. Paper from the same lot will give the resulting book a uniform look.
2. Arrange the paper into stacks of 250 sheets. These are called tokens and are the units for calculating a pressman's work. Most book editions are in multiples of 250 copies.
3. The night before printing, wet the stack of paper and let it stand under a heavy weight. This helps the paper to absorb ink.
4. Make register by loading the forme into the carriage assembly on the press stone so that when the paper was printed on one side and then flipped over and printed on the other side, the pages printed squarely on top of each other. Press points on the tympan were adjusted to hold the paper in position.
5. Paste one sheet of paper to the tympan to serve as a guide to positioning the sheets of paper to be printed.
6. Paste another sheet of paper to the frisket, print the first forme on it and cut out the areas where text appears. This will protect the white areas of the sheet from dirt and ink.
7. The beater inks the type in the forme (called beating the forme) using two ink balls—leather-covered pads of horsehair or wool with handles. Ink rollers were not invented until after the hand-press era.
8. The puller lays the sheet of clean paper to be printed onto

the tympan and then lowers the frisket onto it.

9. The beater folds the tympan, paper, and frisket down onto the forme.
10. The puller runs the front end of the carriage assembly under the impression assembly by turning the rounce.
11. The puller pulls on the bar to force the platen down onto the tympan, thereby pressing the paper onto the inked forme. When he releases the bar, the platen will spring back.
12. The rounce is turned again to pull the second half of the forme under the platen and the platen is lowered again.
13. Release the bar to lift the platen and turn the rounce to pull the carriage assembly out from under the impression assembly.
14. Unfold the carriage assembly to remove the printed sheet.
15. Repeat this procedure from step 8 for each sheet in the stack.

The same procedure was followed for printing the second side of the sheet, positioning the sheet on the already-adjusted points. Printing the second side is called perfecting. In the sixteenth century, the first side of the sheet was printed in the morning and the second side was printed in the afternoon. In the eighteenth century, one side was done on one press and the other side was done on another press.

Two pressmen could print 250 sheets an hour, going from step 8 to step 15 in about fifteen seconds but according to McKenzie, they seldom did. A full press-crew was two men—a puller and a beater, and often a boy to put on fresh ink.

Impact of Printing

Effects of Printing on Culture

The impact of printing is comparable to the development of writing and the invention of the alphabet or the internet, as far as its effects on the society. Printing did not achieve a position of total dominance, and handwritten manuscripts continued to be produced, and the continuing influences of the printed word and oral communication on each other meant that no one form of communication could dominate.

Printing also was a factor in the establishment of a community of scientists who could easily communicate their discoveries, which had previously been communicated by personal letters, helping to bring on the scientific revolution. Also, although early texts were printed in Latin, books were soon produced in common European vernaculars, leading over several centuries to the decline of the Latin language as the medium of scholarly communication.

Because of the printing press, authorship became more meaningful and profitable. It was suddenly important who had said or written what, and what the precise formulation and time of composition was. This allowed the exact citing of references, producing the rule, "One Author, one work (title), one piece of information" (Giesecke, 1989; 325). Before, the author was less important, since a copy of Aristotle made in Paris would not be exactly identical to one made in Bologna. For many works prior to the printing press, the name of the author was entirely lost.

Because the printing process ensured that the same information fell on the same pages, page numbering, tables of contents, and indices became common, though they previously had not been unknown. The process of reading was also changed, gradually changing over several centuries from oral readings to silent, private reading. And obviously, the availability of printed materials led to a continuing rise in the literacy level, revolutionizing education.

It can also be argued that printing changed the way Europeans thought. With the older illuminated manuscripts, the immediate visual emphasis was on the images and the beauty of the page. Early printed works emphasized principally the text and the line of argument. In the sciences, the introduction of the printing press marked a move from the medieval language of metaphors to the adoption of the scientific method.

In general, knowledge came closer to the hands of the people, since printed books could be sold for a fraction of the cost of illuminated manuscripts. There were also more copies of each book available, so that more people could discuss them. Within 50-60 years, the entire library of "classical" knowledge had been printed on the new presses (Eisenstein, 1969: 52). The spread of works also led to the creation of copies by other parties than the original author, leading to the formulation of copyright laws. Furthermore, as the books spread into the hands of the people, Latin was gradually replaced by the national languages. This development was one of the keys to the creation of modern nations.

Some theorists, such as McLuhan, Eisenstein, Kittler, and Giesecke, see an "alphabetic monopoly" as having developed from printing, removing the role of the image from society. Other authors stress that printed works themselves are a visual medium. Certainly, modern developments in printing have revitalized the role of illustrations.

The Art of Book Printing

For years, book printing was considered a true art form. Typesetting, or the placement of the characters on the page, including the use of ligatures, was passed down from master to apprentice. In Germany, the art of typesetting was termed the "black art" in allusion to the ink-covered printers. It has largely been replaced by computer typesetting programmes, which make it possible to get similar results with less human involvement. Some practitioners continue to print books the way Gutenberg did. For example, there is a yearly convention of traditional book printers in Mainz, Germany.

Printing in the Industrial Age

The Gutenberg press was much more efficient than manual copying, and as testament to its effectiveness, it was essentially unchanged from the time of its invention until the Industrial Revolution, some three hundred years later. The "old style" press (as it was termed in the nineteenth century) was constructed of wood and could produce 240 impressions per hour of simple work using a well experienced two-man crew.

The invention of the steam powered press, credited to the German inventors Friedrich Koenig and Andreas Friedrich Bauer in 1812, made it possible to print over a thousand copies of a page per hour.

Koenig and Bauer sold two of their first models to *The Times* in London in 1814, capable of 1,100 impressions per hour. The first edition so printed was on November 28, 1814. They went on to perfect the early model so that it could print on both sides of a sheet at once. This began the long process of making newspapers available to a mass audience (which in turn helped spread literacy), and from the 1820s changed the nature of book production, forcing a greater standardization in titles and other metadata. Their company Koenig & Bauer AG is still one of the world's largest manufacturers of printing presses today.

Their press was improved by Applegath and Cooper. The press is built-up from a large flat inking table (A) which moves regularly back and forth, the form (B) on the table holds the type. The paper travels clockwise round a large cloth covered cylinder, the impression roller (C), and is pressed against the table. The ductor roller (D) rotates and so draws ink from the attached reservoir. The ink passes from the ductor roller to the vibrating roller (E), this moves, on its arms, in a regular motion between the ductor roller and the table. The ink is spread thinly and evenly by the distributing rollers (F) and then, as the table moves, passes onto the inking rollers (G). The axles of the inking rollers rest in grooves, allowing them to rise and fall, they are also position at a slight angle to the table to improve ink distribution. As the table continues to move the form passes alternately under the inking rollers, twice, and then under the impression roller.

Later on in the middle of the 19th century the rotary printing press (invented in 1833 in the United States by Richard M. Hoe) allowed millions of copies of a page in a single day. Mass production of printed works flourished after the transition to rolled paper, as continuous feed allowed the presses to run at a much faster pace.

Also, in the middle of the 19th century, there was a separate development of jobbing presses, small presses capable of printing small-format pieces such as billheads, letterheads, business cards, and envelopes. Jobbing presses were capable of quick set-up (average make-ready time for a small job was under 15 minutes) and quick production (even on treadle-powered jobbing presses it was considered normal to get 1,000 *impressions per hour* [iph] with one pressman, with speeds of 1,500 iph often attained on simple envelope work). Job printing emerged as a reasonably cost-effective duplicating solution for commerce at this time.

Later inventions in this field include the following:

- Lithography
- Offset printing
- Desktop publishing
- Electronic publishing (on CD-ROM or online)
- Computer printer
- Composing stick

MASS COMMUNICATION

Mass communication is the term used to describe the academic study of various means by which individuals and entities relay information to large segments of the population all at once through mass media.

In the United States, many university journalism departments evolved into schools or colleges of mass communication or "journalism and mass communication," as reflected in the names of two major academic organizations. In addition to studying practical skills of journalism, public relations or advertising, students also may major in "mass communication" or "mass communication research." The latter is often the title given to doctoral studies in such schools, whether the focus of the student's research is journalism practice, history, law or media effects. Departmental structures within such colleges may separate research and instruction in professional or technical aspects of newspaper and magazine publishing, radio, television and film. Mass communication research includes media institutions and processes, such as diffusion of information, and media effects, such as persuasion or manipulation of public opinion.

With the Internet's increased role in delivering news and information, mass communication studies—and media organizations—have increasingly focused on the convergence of publishing, broadcasting and digital communication.

The academic mass communication discipline historically differs from media studies and communication studies programmes with roots in departments of theatre, film or speech, and with more interest in "qualitative," interpretive theory, critical or cultural approaches to communication study. In contrast, many mass communication programmes historically lean toward empirical analysis and quantitative research—from statistical content analysis of media messages to survey research, public opinion polling, and experimental research.

Interest in "New Media" and "Computer Mediated Communication" is growing much faster than educational institutions can assimilate it. So far, traditional classes and degree programmes have not been able to accommodate new paradigm shifts in communication technologies. Although national standards for the study of interactive media have been in place since the mid-nineties, course work in these areas tends to vary significantly from university to university.

Graduates of Mass Communication programmes work in a variety of fields in traditional news media and publishing, advertising, public relations and research institutes.

Such programmes are accredited by the Accrediting Council on Education in Journalism and Mass Communication (ACEJMC). The Association for Education in Journalism and Mass Communication (AEJMC) is the major membership organization for academics in the field, offering regional and national conferences and refereed publications.

The International Communication Association (ICA) and National Communication Association (formerly the Speech Communication Association) include divisions and publications that overlap with those of AEJMC, but AEJMC historically has stronger ties to the mass communication professions in the United States.

BROADCASTING

Broadcasting is the distribution of audio and/or video signals which transmit programmes to an audience. The audience may be the general public or a relatively large sub-audience, such as children or young adults.

There are wide variety of broadcasting systems, all of which have different capabilities. The smallest broadcasting systems are institutional public address systems, which transmit verbal messages and music within a school or hospital, and low-powered broadcasting systems which transmit radio stations or television stations to a small area. National radio and television broadcasters have nationwide coverage, using retransmitter towers, satellite systems, and cable distribution. Satellite radio and television broadcasters can cover even wider areas, such as entire continents, and Internet channels can distribute text or streamed music worldwide.

The sequencing of content in a broadcast is called a schedule. As with all technological endeavours, a number of technical terms and slang have developed. A list of these terms can be found at list of broadcasting terms. Television and radio programmes are distributed through radio broadcasting or cable, often both simultaneously. By coding signals and having decoding equipment in homes, the latter also enables subscription-based channels and pay-per-view services.

The term "broadcast" was coined by early radio engineers from the mid-western United States. Broadcasting forms a very large segment of the mass media. Broadcasting to a very narrow range of audience is called narrowcasting.

Business Models of Broadcasting

There are several dominant business models of broadcasting. Each differs in the method by which stations are funded:

- in-kind donations of time and skills by volunteers (common with community broadcasters)
- direct government payments or operation of public broadcasters
- indirect government payments, such as radio and television licenses
- grants from foundations or business entities
- selling advertising or sponsorships
- public subscription or membership
- fees charged to all owners of TV sets or radios, regardless of whether they intend to receive that programme or not (an approach used in the UK).

Broadcasters may rely on a combination of these business models. For example, National Public Radio, a non-commercial network within the United States, receives grants from the Corporation for Public Broadcasting (which in turn receives funding from the U.S. Government), by public membership, and by selling "extended credits" to corporations.

Recorded Broadcasts and Live Broadcasts

One can distinguish between recorded and live broadcasts. The former allows correcting errors, and removing superfluous or undesired material, rearranging it, applying slow-motion and repetitions, and other techniques to enhance the programme. However, some live events like sports telecasts can include some of the aspects including slow motion clips of important goals/hits etc., in between the live telecast.

American radio network broadcasters habitually forbade pre-recorded broadcasts in the 1930s and 1940s, requiring radio programmes played for the Eastern and Central time zones to be repeated three hours later for the Pacific time zone. This restriction was dropped for special occasions, as in the case of the German dirigible airship *Hindenburg* at Lakehurst, New Jersey in 1937. During World War II, pre-recorded broadcasts from war correspondents were allowed on U.S. radio. In addition, American radio programmes were recorded for playback by Armed Forces Radio stations around the world.

A disadvantage of recording first is that the public may know the outcome of an event from another source, which may be a spoiler. In addition, pre-recording prevents live announcers from deviating from an officially-approved script, as occurred with propaganda broadcasts from Germany in the 1940s and with Radio Moscow in the 1980s.

Many events are advertised as being live, although they are often "recorded live" (sometimes this is referred to as "live-to-tape"). This is particularly true of performances of musical artists on radio when they visit for an in-studio concert performance. This intentional blurring of the distinction between live and recorded media is viewed with chagrin among many music lovers. Similar situations have sometimes appeared in television.

Distribution Methods

A broadcast may be distributed through several physical means. If coming directly from the studio at a single radio or TV station, it is simply sent through the air chain to the transmitter and thence from the antenna on the tower out to the world. Programming may also come through a communications satellite, played either live or recorded for later transmission. Networks of stations may simulcast the same programming at the same time, originally via microwave link, and now mostly by satellite.

Distribution to stations or networks may also be through physical media, such as analogue or digital videotape, CD, DVD, and sometimes other formats. Usually these are included in another broadcast, such as when electronic news gathering returns a story to the station for inclusion on a news programme.

The final leg of broadcast distribution is how the signal gets to the listener or viewer. It may come over the air as with a radio station or TV station to an antenna and receiver, or may come through cable TV or cable radio (or "wireless cable") via the station or directly from a network. The Internet may also bring either radio or TV to the recipient, especially with multicasting allowing the signal and bandwidth to be shared.

The term "broadcast network" is often used to distinguish networks that broadcast an over-the-air television signal that can be received using a television antenna from so-called networks that are broadcast only via cable or satellite television. The term "broadcast television" can refer to the programming of such networks.

BROADCAST LICENSE

A *broadcast license* is a specific type of spectrum licence that grants the licensee the right to use a portion of the radio frequency spectrum in a given geographical area for broadcasting purposes.

Licensing is typically performed by government agencies, providing a mechanism both for managing the limited resource of radio frequency spectrum and for implementing prevailing public policy, such as policies regarding concentration of media ownership.

Management of technical specifications, such as those implemented in broadcast television systems, is normally undertaken as a part of broadcast licensing in each country.

Economics

Originally, broadcast licenses were issued for only a nominal payment, but work by economist Ronald Coase developed a theory that broadcast licenses in a spectrum that was limited had high economic value, which could and should be paid for on the open market. Increasingly, spectrum licenses are offered via spectrum auctions.

External Links

Regulators

- Australian Communications and Media Authority http://www.acma.gov.au/
- Radio Spectrum Management New Zealand http://www.rsm.govt.nz/
- Ofcom *United Kingdom* http://www.ofcom.org.uk/

- Federal Communications Commission *United States* http://www.fcc.gov/

PUBLIC POLICY

Public policy is a course of action or inaction chosen by public authorities to address a problem. Public policy is expressed in the body of laws, regulations, decisions and actions of government. Policy analysis may be used to formulate public policy and to evaluate its effectiveness. Many public policy analysts earn Ph.D., Master of Public Policy and Master of Public Administration degrees in public policy schools, while others earn specialized degrees, such as an M.Ed., for specializing in educational policy or an MSW for specializing in social welfare policy.

Various Definitions

According to William Jenkins in *Policy Analysis: A Political and Organizational Perspective* (1978), a Public Policy is "a set of interrelated decisions taken by a political actor or group of actors concerning the selection of goals and the means of achieving them within a specified situation where those decisions should, in principle, be within the power of those actors to achieve." Thus, Jenkins understands Public Policy making to be a process, and not simply a choice.

According to Thomas Birkland in *An Introduction to the Policy Process* (2001), there is a lack of a consensus on the definition of public policy. Birkland outlines a few definitions of public policy:

- *Clarke E. Cochran, et al.*: "The term public policy always refers to the actions of government and the intentions that determine those actions."
- *Clarke E. Cochran, et al.*: "Public policy is the outcome of the struggle in government over who gets what."
- *Thomas Dye*: Public policy is "Whatever governments choose to do or not do."
- *Charles L. Cochran and Eloise F. Malone*: "Public policy consists of political decisions for implementing programmes to achieve societal goals."
- *B. Guy Peters*: "Stated most simply, public policy is the sum of government activities, whether acting directly or through agents, as it has an influence on the life of citizens."

Birkland indicates that the elements common to all definitions of public policy are as follows:

- The policy is made in the name of the "public."
- Policy is generally made or initiated by Government.
- Policy is interpreted and implemented by public and private actors.
- Policy is what the government intends to do.
- Policy is what the government chooses not to do.

History of Public Policy

According to Birkland:

> While the study of politics has a long history, the systematic study of public policy, on the other hand, can be said to be a twentieth century creation. It dates, according to Daniel McCool, to 1922, when political scientist Charles Merriam sought to connect the theory and practices of politics to understanding the actual activities of government, that is public policy."

New Zealand Law Journal page 91; May 20, 1947: Article by L.F. Moller, B.C.L., B.Litt, (Oxon), LL.B. (N.Z.) *Some Aspects of the Doctrine of Public Policy*. Lord Mansfield used the name "public policy" for the first time in a case, Holman *v.* Johnson, 2 Bing. 229; 130 E.R. 294. The principle of public policy then was, ex dolo malo non-actio. No court will lend its aid to a man who founds his cause of action upon an immoral or an illegal act.

Public Policy and Science

Michael Crichton said:

> As the twentieth century drew to a close, the connection between hard scientific fact and public policy became increasingly elastic. In part this was possible because of the complacency of the scientific profession; in part because of the lack of good science education among the public; in part, because of the rise of specialized advocacy groups which have been enormously effective in getting publicity

and shaping policy; and in great part because of the decline of the media as an independent assessor of fact.

Philip Handler, former president of the National Academy of Sciences (1969-1981), said that "Scientists best serve public policy by living within the ethics of science, not those of politics. If the scientific community will not unfrock the charlatans, the public will not discern the difference—science and the nation will suffer."

Types of Public Policy

- Crime policy
- Domestic policy
- Education policy
- Energy policy
- Environmental policy
- Foreign policy
- Healthcare policy
- National defense policy
- Public policy (law)
- Sex policy
- Social policy
- Social welfare policy

FEDERAL COMMUNICATIONS COMMISSION: A CASE STUDY

The *Federal Communications Commission (FCC)* is an independent United States Government agency, created, directed and empowered by Congressional statute.

The FCC was established by the Communications Act of 1934 as the successor to the Federal Radio Commission and is charged with regulating all non-Federal Government use of the radio spectrum (including radio and television broadcasting), and all interstate telecommunications (wire, satellite and cable) as well as all international communications that originate or terminate in the United States. It is an important factor in US telecommunication policy. The FCC tookover wire communication regulation from the Interstate Commerce Commission.

The FCC's jurisdiction covers the 50 states, the District of Columbia and U.S. possessions.

Organization

The FCC is composed of five Commissioners appointed by the President and confirmed by the Senate for five-year terms, except when filling an unexpired term. The President designates one of the Commissioners to serve as Chairman. Only three Commissioners may be members of the same political party. None of them can have a financial interest in any Commission-related business.

As the Chief Executive Officer of the Commission, the Chairman delegates management and administrative responsibility to the Managing Director. The Commissioners, Michael Copps, Jonathan Adelstein and Robert M. McDowell.

Bureaus

The Bureaus' responsibilities include processing applications for licenses and other filings, analyzing complaints, conducting investigations, developing and implementing regulations, and participating in hearings.

Consumer and Governmental Affairs

The Consumer and Governmental Affairs Bureau (CGB) develops and implements the FCC's consumer policies, including disability access. CGB serves as the public face of the FCC through outreach and education, as well as through their Consumer Centre, which is responsible for responding to consumer inquiries and complaints. CGB also maintains collaborative partnerships with state, local, and tribal governments in such critical areas as emergency preparedness and implementation of new technologies.

Enforcement

The Enforcement Bureau (EB) is responsible for enforcement of provisions of the Communications Act, 1934, FCC rules, FCC orders, and terms and conditions of station authorizations. Major areas of enforcement that are handled by the Enforcement Bureau are consumer protection, local competition, public safety and homeland security.

International

The International Bureau (IB) develops international policies in telecommunications, such as coordination of frequency allocation and orbital assignments so as to minimize cases of international electromagnetic interference involving U.S. licensees. The International Bureau also oversees FCC compliance with the International Radio Regulations and other International Agreements.

Media

The Media Bureau (MB) develops, recommends and administers the policy and licensing programmes relating to electronic media, including cable television, broadcast television, and radio in the United States and its territories. The Media Bureau also handles post-licensing matters regarding direct broadcast satellite service.

Wireless Telecommunications

The Wireless Telecommunications Bureau (WTB) handles nearly all FCC domestic wireless telecommunications programmes, policies, and outreach initiatives. Wireless services include: *amateur radio; cellular networks; paging; Personal Communications Service*; and Part 27 Wireless Communications Services (WCS) such as Advanced Wireless Serices (AWS) and fixed, mobile, and broadcast services on the 700 MHz Band.

Wireline Competition

The Wireline Competition Bureau (WCB) develops policy concerning wireline telecommunications. The Wireline Competition Bureau's main objective is to promote growth and economical investments in wireline technology infrastructure, development, markets and services.

Parking Safety and Homeland Security Bureau

A priority of the Chairman Kevin Martin administration is the establishment of the Public Safety and Homeland Security Bureau within the FCC. The Bureau has yet to be established; trade reports indicate, however, that the organization of the new Bureau is in its final stages.

Offices

The FCC's Offices provide support services to the Bureaus. Even though the Bureaus and Offices have their individual functions, they regularly join forces and share expertise in addressing FCC issues.

Administrative Law Judges

The Office of Administrative Law Judges (OALJ) is responsible for conducting hearings ordered by the Commission. The hearing function includes acting on interlocutory requests filed in the proceedings such as petitions to intervene, petitions to enlarge issues, and contested discovery requests. An Administrative Law Judge, appointed under the Administrative Procedure Act, presides at the hearing during which documents and sworn testimony are received in evidence, and witnesses are cross-examined. At the conclusion of the evidentiary phase of a proceeding, the presiding Administrative Law Judge writes and issues an Initial Decision which may be appealed to the Commission.

Communications Business Opportunities

The Office of Communications Business Opportunities (OCBO) promotes telecommunications business opportunities for small, minority-owned, and women-owned businesses. To this end, OCBO works with entrepreneurs, industry, public interest organizations, individuals, and others to provide information about FCC policies, increase ownership and employment opportunities, foster a diversity of voices and viewpoints over the airwaves, and encourage participation in FCC proceedings.

Engineering and Technology

The Office of Engineering and Technology (OET) advises the Commission concerning engineering matters. Its chief role is to manage the electromagnetic spectrum, specifically frequency allocation and spectrum usage. OET conducts technical studies of advanced phases of terrestrial and space communications and administers FCC rules regarding radio devices, experimental radio services, and industrial, scientific and medical equipment.

OET also organizes the Technical Advisory Council, a committee of FCC advisors from major telecommunication and media corporations.

In addition, the OET operates the Equipment Authorization Branch, which is tasked with overseeing equipment authorization for all devices using the electromagnetic energy from 9KHz to 300GHz. OET maintains an electronic database of all Certified equipment which can be easily accessed by the public.

General Counsel

The Office of General Counsel serves as the chief legal advisor to the Commission. The General Counsel also represents the Commission in litigation in United States federal courts, recommends decisions in adjudicatory matters before the Commission, assists the Commission in its decision-making capacity and performs a variety of legal functions regarding internal and other administrative matters.

Inspector General

The Office of the Inspector General (OIG) recommends policies to prevent fraud in agency operations. The Inspector General recommends corrective action where appropriate, referring criminal matters to the United States Department of Justice for potential prosecution.

Legislative Affairs

The Office of Legislative Affairs (OLA) is the FCC's liaison to the United States Congress, providing lawmakers with information about FCC regulations. OLA also prepares FCC witnesses for Congressional hearings, and helps create FCC responses to legislative proposals and Congressional inquiries. In addition, OLA is a liaison to other Federal agencies, as well as state and local governments.

Managing Director

The Office of the Managing Director (OMD) is responsible for the administration and management of the FCC, including the agency's budget, personnel, security, contracts and publications.

Media Relations

The Office of Media Relations (OMR) is responsible for the dissemination of Commission announcements, orders, proceedings, and other information per media requests. OMR manages the FCC Daily Digest, website and Audio Visual Centre.

Secretary

The Office of the Secretary (OSEC) oversees the receipt and distribution of documents filed by the public through electronic and paper filing systems and the FCC Library collection. In addition, OSEC publishes legal notices of Commission decisions in the Federal Register and the FCC Record.

Strategic Planning and Policy Analysis

The Office of Strategic Planning and Policy Analysis (OSP), essentially a think tank within the FCC, identifies policy objectives for the agency. OSP works closely with the FCC Chairman and is responsible for monitoring the state of the communications industry to identify trends, issues and overall industry health. OSP acts as expert consultants to the Commission in areas of economic, business and market analysis. The Office also reviews legal trends and developments not necessarily related to current FCC proceedings, such as intellectual property law, the Internet, and electronic commerce. Previously OSP was called the Office of Plans and Policy (OPP). Robert Pepper, currently with CISCO was the Chief of OPP from 1989 until 2005.

Workplace Diversity

The Office of Workplace Diversity (OWD) develops policy to provide a full and fair opportunity for all employees, regardless of non-merit factors such as race, religion, gender, colour, age, disability, sexual orientation or national origin, to carry out their duties in the workplace free from unlawful discriminatory treatment, including sexual harassment and retaliation for engaging in legally protected activities.

History

Communications Act of 1934

In 1934, Congress passed the Communications Act, which abolished the Federal Radio Commission and transferred jurisdiction over radio licensing to a new Federal Communications Commission. Title III of the Communications Act contained provisions very similar to the Radio Act of 1927, and the new FCC largely took over the operations and precedents of the FRC.

Report on Chain Broadcasting

In 1940, the Federal Communications Commission issued the "Report on Chain Broadcasting." The major point in the report was the breakup of NBC (See National Broadcasting Company), but there were two other important points. One was network option time, the culprit here being CBS. The report limited the amount of time during the day, and what times the networks may broadcast. Previously a network could demand any time it wanted from an affiliate. The second concerned artist bureaus. The networks served as both agents and employees of artists, which was a conflict of interest the report rectified.

Consolidation Permissivity, Indecency Crackdowns

The inauguration of Ronald Reagan as President of the United States in 1981 marked the beginning of a shift in the FCC towards a decidedly more permissive stance. Monopoly regulations were relaxed so far as to be practically irrelevant, and remaining restrictions were laxly enforced. A substantial portion of other regulations were repealed, such as guidelines for minimal amounts of non-entertainment programming in 1985. In addition, the Fairness Doctrine was removed in 1987. This deregulation has led to the rapid rise in the channel selection offered by broadcast alternatives such as cable television. It has also led to greater concentration of media ownership.

In the early 2000s, the FCC began stepping up censorship and enforcement of indecency regulations again, most notably following the Janet Jackson "wardrobe malfunction" that occurred during the halftime show of Super Bowl XXXVIII. However, the FCC's regulatory domain with respect to indecency remains restricted to the public airwaves, notably VHF and UHF television and AM/FM radio.

On June 15, 2006, President George W. Bush signed into law the Broadcast Decency Enforcement Act of 2005 sponsored by Senator Sam Brownback, a former broadcaster himself, and endorsed by Congressman Fred Upton of Michigan who authored a similar bill in the United States House of Representatives. The new law stiffens the penalties for each violation of the Act. The Federal Communications Commission will be able to impose fines in the amount of $325,000 for each violation by each station, which violates decency standards. The legislation raises the fine by a tenfold increase.

FCC Commissioners since Inception in 1934

Current Commissioners

Chairman Kevin Martin (FCC) (R-NC), Commissioner Michael Copps (D-WI), Commissioner Jonathan Adelstein (D-SD), Commissioner Deborah Taylor Tate (R-TN), Commissioner Robert M. McDowell(R-VA).

Past Commissioners

A complete list of Commissioners is available on the FCC website. Notable commissioners have included:

- Dean Burch (AZ)
- Richard E. Wiley (IL)
- James H. Quello (MI)
- Charles Ferris (MA)
- Alfred Sikes (MO)
- William E. Kennard (CA)
- Michael K. Powell.

Regulatory Powers

The Federal Communications Commission has one major regulatory weapon, revoking licenses, but short of that has little leverage over broadcast stations (see FCC MB Docket 04-232). It is reluctant to do this since it operates in a near vacuum of information on most of the tens of thousands of stations whose licenses are renewed every eight years (previously, every three years). Broadcast licenses are supposed to be renewed if the station meets the "public interest, convenience, or necessity." The Federal Communications Commission rarely checks except for some outstanding reason; burden of proof would be on the complainant. Fewer than 1 per cent of station renewals are not immediately granted, and only a small fraction of those actually denied.

The Federal Communications Commission also licenses amateur radio operators and stations, and does use its power to fine amateur radio operators who flagrantly violate its rules. It also licenses commercial operators who operate and repair certain *radiotelephone*, television, *radar*, and *Morse code* radio stations. In recent years it has also licensed people who maintain or operate GMDSS stations. While the FCC maintains control of the written and Morse testing standards, it no longer administers the exams, having delegated that function to private organizations.

Note: Similar authority for regulation of U.S. Government radio communications is vested in the President who has delegated it to National Telecommunications and Information Administration (NTIA).

Spectrum Auctions

Beginning in 1994, commercial spectrum has been allocated via competitive auctions rather than the previous method of "best public use." This was a cumbersome bureaucratic process in which competitors attempted to show that they were most capable of making best public use of the license they wished to obtain. The structure and licenses available in each auction are determined by vote of the Commission, with the licenses awarded to the highest bidders. Auctions are usually conducted on a simultaneous multiple-round basis, with all offered licenses being auctioned at the same time. Auctions proceed in bidding rounds of decreasing duration until no more bids are received. Revenues are deposited in the US Treasury to be spent by Congress.

The FCC has been criticized for awarding a Digital TV (DTV) channel to each holder of an analog TV station license without an auction, as well as trading auctionable spectrum to Nextel to resolve public safety interference problems. Nonetheless, in 2009, all analog terrestrial broadcast licenses in the U.S. will be terminated, with terrestrial television subsequently available only from the digital channels.

Criticisms

The FCC has been criticised on many fronts, both for being too restrictive and too permissive in its regulation.

On the issue of broadcast indecency, the FCC has taken heat from right wing conservatives and family-oriented groups for not sufficiently censoring and restricting sexually explicit and violent material to which the groups believe children should not be exposed (a Family Viewing Hour was instituted in the 1970s and then discontinued).

In the actions taken against broadcasters, the FCC is frequently criticized for violating the First Amendment guarantee of Freedom of Speech, both directly by censorship and enforcement action sometimes alleged to be politically motivated, and indirectly by the general intimidation that FCC action allegedly creates, particularly with the U.S. Congress considering multiplying fines exponentially.

The FCC considered requiring all broadcasters to retain copies of all broadcasts for up to three months (FCC MB Docket 04-232). One critique of this proposal is that this action would wipe out smaller broadcasters because of the enormous expense of having to purchase new equipment with the necessary features for content storage and the need for facilities to store content.

Low-power broadcasting has also been a source of contention, as the FCC has set the power limits very low, while allegedly making it nearly impossible for anyone except large corporations or large non-profit organizations to obtain a license. Although Stephen Dunifer won a case versus the FCC, few others have successfully argued against the Commission.

Cable outlets, such as Cartoon Network's Adult Swim, are not governed by the FCC and generally do much less editing. How much is usually determined by the outlet's standards and practices department.

Another critique is that the Commission has historically been dominated by lawyers, often from the telecommunications industry, due to the FCC's direct effects on commerce and public policy. This is in stark contrast to other technically-focused government agencies, such as the Nuclear Regulatory Commission, which is often populated by engineers and physicists.

The FCC is also criticized by "Family Guy" in the episode PTV when Lois say to Peter that call the FCC for censuring Peter's Station (PTV) and Peter sing the "FCC Song."

The FCC is also often criticized by Amateur Radio operators for rule changes affecting the Amateur Radio Service, or for its perceived lack of enforcement of violations within the service and in general.

While the FCC, under much criticism, has been tightening its control and censorship of broadcast television, neither the FCC nor any other regulatory body has the authority to censor the internet, allowing broadcasters to use the internet as a source for their unedited creative expression. In December 2006, NBC and "Saturday Night Live" posted an uncensored video on the NBC website and YouTube under the headings "Special Treat in a Box" or "Special Christmas Box." The censored version of the video played on NBC's Saturday Night Live, and was bleeped (censored) sixteen times. Lorne Michaels, the creator and executive producer of "Saturday Night Live," predicted that other shows and networks, time and money permitting, would surely follow NBC's lead in making available material that was deemed not ready for prime time, or even late night.

The NBC show Studio 60 on the Sunset Strip had a story line where the FCC was fining the fictional NBS network an absurd amount of money for a obscenity said by a U.S. Marine during a live news broadcast in Afghanistan. They badmouth the FCC for being upset for a real life reaction of an near death incident in wartime being accidentally picked up in a required News broadcast. (The FCC requires that Educational programming be provided for free by networks in exchange for the right to broadcast over the airwaves.) The problem becomes worse when they give them the option of losing the fee in exchange for a five second delay of live news feeds. This form of censorship that is becoming used enforced more and more by the real life FCC. The show points out that this practice is an attack on the First Amendment rights of the press, and states that it is destroying the credibility of the Networks as well as pushing news to other forms of mediums.

Controversy

Unreleased Reports

2003 Study of Commercial Radio Concentration

In 2003, the FCC Media Bureau produced a draft report analyzing the impact of deregulation in the radio industry. The report stated that from March 1996 through March 2003, the number of commercial radio stations on the air rose 5.9 per cent while the number of station owners fell 35 per cent. The concentration of ownership followed a 1996 rewrite of telecommunications law that eliminated a 40-station national ownership cap.

The report was never made public, nor have any similar analyses followed, despite the fact that radio industry reports were released in 1998, 2001 and 2002. In September 2006, Senator Barbara Boxer, who had received a copy of the report, released it.

2004 Study of Television Media Concentration

In 2004, the FCC ordered its staff to destroy all copies of a draft study by Keith Brown and Peter Alexander, two economists in the FCC's Media Bureau. The two had analyzed a database of 4,078 individual news stories broadcast in 1998, showed local ownership of television stations adds almost five and one-half minutes of total news to broadcasts and more than three minutes of "on-location" news.

The conclusion of the study was at odds with FCC arguments made when it voted in 2003 to increase the number of television stations a company could own in a single market. (In June 2004, a federal appeals court rejected the agency's reasoning on most of the rules and ordered it to try again.)

In September 2006, Senator Barbara Boxer, who had received a copy of the report "indirectly from someone within the FCC who believed the information should be made public," wrote a letter to FCC Chairman Kevin Martin, asked whether any other commissioners "past or present" knew of the report's existence and why it was never made public. She also asked whether it was "shelved because the outcome was not to the liking of some of the commissioners and/or any outside powerful interests?" Boxer's office said if she does not receive adequate answers to her questions, she will push for an investigation by the FCC inspector general.

Action by FCC Chairman

In a letter in response to Senator Boxer, FCC Chairman Martin said, "I want to assure you that I too am concerned about what happened to these two draft reports." The letter also said "I have asked the inspector general of the FCC to conduct an investigation into what happened to these draft documents and will cooperate fully with him." Martin added that he was not chairman at the time the reports were drafted, and that neither he nor his staff had seen them.

NSA Wiretapping

When it emerged in 2006 that AT&T, BellSouth and Verizon may have broken U.S. laws by aiding the National Security Agency in possible illegal wiretapping of its customers, Congressional representatives called for an FCC investigation into whether or not those companies broke the law. The FCC declined to investigate, however, claiming that it could not investigate due to the classified nature of the programme—a move that provoked the criticism of members of Congress.

> "Today the watchdog agency that oversees the country's telecommunications industry refused to investigate the nation's largest phone companies' reported disclosure of phone records to the NSA," said Rep. Edward Markey (D-Mass.) in response to the decision. "The FCC, which oversees the protection of consumer privacy under the Communications Act of 1934, has taken a pass at investigating what is estimated to be the nation's largest violation of consumer privacy ever to occur. If the oversight body that monitors our nation's communications is stepping aside then Congress must step in."

Doraemon

The character "Broadband" (FCC Kids Zone) looks like Doraemon, a popular manga character in Japan. Doraemon was created for print in magazines in 1969, which makes Doraemon predate the FCC's character. According to Japanese news media, both Shogakukan (copyright manager) and Fujiko-production (owner of the copyright) have warned the FCC over the alleged copyright infringement, but so far there has been no answer.

Diversity

With the major demographic shifts occurring in the country in terms of the racial-ethnic composition of the population, where 9 of the 10 largest cities, for example, now have "majority minority" populations, the FCC has also been criticized for ignoring the issue of decreasing racial-ethnic diversity of the media. This includes charges that the FCC has been watering down the limited affirmative action regulations it had on the books, including no longer requiring stations to make public their data on their minority staffing and hiring. In the second half of 2006, groups such as the National Hispanic Media Coalition, the National Latino Media Council, the National Association of Hispanic Journalists, the National Institute for Latino Policy, the League of United Latin American Citizens (LULAC) and others held town hall meetings in California, New York and Texas on media diversity as its affects Latinos and other communities of colour. They documented widespread and deeply-felt community concerns about the negative effects of media concentration and consolidation on racial-ethnic diversity in staffing and programming. *El Diario-La Prensa*'s editorial on media diversity. At these Latino town hall meetings, the issue of the FCC's lax monitoring of obscene and pornographic material in Spanish-language radio and the lack of racial and national-origin diversity among Latino staff in Spanish-language television were other major themes.

FCC-Broadcasting Tower Database

The FCC-Database of broadcasting towers is a very useful tool to get information about the height and year of built of broadcasting towers in the USA. Nevertheless this database contains no information about the structural types of towers. The FCC-Database does not contain information about the height of towers used for non-broadcasting purposes like NDBs, LORAN-C transmission towers or VLF transmission facilities of the US-Navy, or from towers not used for transmission at all like the BREN-Tower.

2

Dimensions of Broadcasting in India

TV RADIO, RADIO AND TELEVISION: NATIONAL AND GLOBAL SCENARIO

Broadcasting

Governmental Broadcasting Agencies

- *DD-Doordarshan India*: India's national, regional, local, and cable networks, government controlled.
- Ministry of Information and Broadcasting.

News Agencies

- Antara.
- Reuters India.

Industry News

- Exchange-media.com.

Television

National Television Networks

- *India*: Television Broadcasting.

Television Broadcasting Services

- Siti Cable.

Television Related Websites

- *Indian Cable TV*: Online community for cable TV operators in India.
- *Indian Television.com*: An online information resource on the Indian television industry. Provides information, news and market research.
- *Satellite and Cable TV India.*

Radio

National Radio Networks

- *AIR (All India Radio) (Akashvani)*: India's main radio broadcasting network, government operated, with one national service, 100+ regional, and 70+ local stations.

Radio Broadcasting Parent Companies

- *Prasar Bharati (Broadcasting Corporation of India)*: Autonomous parent corporation of All India Radio and Doordarshan.

Radio Stations on the Web

- *India*: Local Radio/Television Stations on the Web.

Shortwave Broadcasters

- All India Radio External Service: AIR's shortwave external service in several languages.
- BBC—Hindi Service.
- BBC—Tamil Service.
- *DD India*: International Service of Doordarshan.

RADIO, TELEVISION AND CINEMA

In the United States of America, the beginning of radio was made as early as in 1909. A station in San Jose, California, started broadcasting announcements and phonograph music. But regular and systematic broadcasting began only in 1920. Thereafter, the expansion was fast in the USA and other countries. Before long there was a huge network of radio broadcasting almost in every country. In India, like in many other countries, amateurs were the first to start broadcasting. The Radio club of Mumbai, broadcast its first programme in June, 1923. In November 1923, the Kolkata Club went on the air. The Chennai Radio Club started broadcasting on 31 July, 1924 with a 40 watt transmitter. Later, it broadcast with a 200 watt transmitter, for 2½ hours very evening. But it closed down due to financial difficulties. The Chennai Corporation re-started the broadcast service in 1930.

Organised broadcasting in India was started by the Indian Broadcasting Company (IBC) in 1927. Mumbai and Kolkata stations were inaugurated in July and August, 1927. The first radio programme journal India Radio Times was started on July 15, 1927. Its name was later changed to The India Listener and again to Akashvani.

IBC was a financial failure in spite of a loan from the government. It went into liquidation and was closed down in March, 1930. Under pressure from the radio-set declares, programmers and the general public, the government took over the Mumbai and Kolkata stations in April, 1930. The Indian Broadcasting Service was formed. Those were the days of worldwide depression. The government too faced financial difficulties. Even otherwise, it was not very enthusiastic about broadcasting. So, it ordered the closure of the Indian Broadcasting Service on October 10, 1931. Representations and agitations compelled the government to reverse the orders of November 23, 1931. The Government doubled the duty on radio sets.

In 1932, the British Broadcasting Corporation (BBC) started an Empire Service. The number of receiving sets, which were all imported doubled in less than two years. This resulted in an increase in the Government's income from license fees. The increase in import duty on radio sets and components of the radio sets also enhanced the government's revenue. Broadcasting now become financially viable. It was decided to start a radio station in Delhi. It actually went on the air on January 1, 1936. The BBC loaned the services of Lionel Fielden who became the Controller of Broadcasting. (Today the radio chief is called Director General.) He persuaded the government to realise the potential of broadcasting and allot more money to the service. In his autobiography. The Natural Bent, he writes about financial problem and red-tapism. He also gives an interesting account of how he could persuade the then Viceroy to adopt the name All India for the broadcasting service. The name was adopted from June 8, 1936.

Fielden got together a group of devoted young people. With the help of these and of Goyder, his Chief Engineer, he started short-wave service in 1938, to cover the entire country. Lucknow station went on air on April 2, 1938, and Chennai on June 16, 1938. In 1939, the Tiruchi station into being. The same year the External Service Division at Delhi started.

A.S. Bokhari, another dynamic administrator, took over from Fielden to become the first Indian Director General. He was the chief during all the war years and thereafter till the partition. A new Broadcasting House was built on Parliament Street, New Delhi. On June 3, 1947, Lord Mountbatten (the Viceroy), Jawaharlal Nehru and Mohd. Ali Jinnah made historic broadcasts on the partition of India. In the midnight on August 14-15, Nehru broadcast his famous speech "Tryst with Destiny". It is preserved in the AIR archives.

Following the country's partition, six radio stations came to the share of India (Mumbai, Kolkata, Delhi, Tiruchi, Lucknow and Chennai). When the princely states become a part of India, five more stations (Hyderabad, Aurangabad, Baroda, Mysore and Trivandrum) were taken over by AIR. During the First Five Year Plan (1951-56) much development of broadcasting took place. In 1952, the first National Orchestra was set up with Pundit Ravi Shankar as its conductor. Regional news bulletins in Hindi and Marathi were started in 1953 from Lucknow and Nagpur respectively. The first National programme of Talks too went on the air in 1953. In 1955, the first Radio Sangeet Sammelan was broadcast.

Dr. B.V. Keskar, the Minister for Information and Broadcasting (1953-61), did a lot for Indian classical music. He also brought eminent writers, poets, musicians and playwrights on contract as Producers. Finances for broadcasting for the Second Plan (1956-61) were creased four times against finances in the First Plan. In 1957, Vividh Bharati, an All India Radio Variety Programme Service, was started at Mumbai. It provided light entertainment with a generous dose of film music. Over the years, it has become a very popular service. The service was started to cataract the increasing popularity of Radio Ceylon's commercial service. It has succeeded very well in its aim.

1957 also saw the start of an Inter-station Programme Exchange unit at Delhi. An annual folk music festival, "Songs of National Builders", was started in 1958 but it was short-live. The scheme of Radio Rural forums was implemented in 1959, for two-way communication with rural listeners. In 1960, Jawaharlal Nehru's speech at the UN was directly relayed from New York. By 1961, radio covered 55 per cent of the population and 37 per cent of the area. The Third Five Year Plan (1962-66) saw much expansion of medium wave broadcasting. As many as 26 transmitters were added to Air stations for broadcasting Vividh Bharati Programmes. In addition, two independent transmitters were installed at Chandigarh and Kanpur. By 1966, 54 station covered 70 per cent of the population and 52 per cent area.

A committee on Broadcasting and Information Media was set up in 1964 under the Chairmanship of A.K. Chanda. It gave its report in 1966. It recommended separation of radio and television with the two independent corporations. It was not accepted by the government then. The separation ultimately came about 1976 and the TV set up was called Doordarshan. Another recommendation was for the starting of a commercial service was started from Vividh Bharati in 1967.

A 9-point code for broadcasters, introduced in 1969, prohibits the following: criticism of friendly countries; attack on religion or communities; anything obscene or defamatory; incitement to violence or anything against maintenance of law and order; aspersions against the integrity of the President, Governors and Judiciary; attack on a political party by name; anything amounting to contempt of court; hostile criticism of any state of the Centre; anything showing disrespect to the constitution or advocating change in the constitution by violent means, but advocating changes in a constitutional way should not be debarred.

In 1969, a new channel "Yuva Vani" was started at Delhi. The sponsored programmes on the commercial service were introduced in 1970 and the Sanskrit news bulletins were introduced in 1974. Earlier, in 1971, the highest AIR station was set up at Leh. In the same year, the first satellite link was established.

In 1977, the Janata Government appointed a Working Group headed by B.G. Verghese, to suggest an autonomous set up for AIR and Doordarshan. The Group recommended in 1978 the creation of a National Broadcast Trust or Akash Bharati to look after both radio and TV. A bill to create the recommended Trust, was introduced in 1979. The recommendations of the Working Group, however were much diluted in the Bill. Eventually the bill lapsed when the Janata Government went out of power.

The Janata Government also introduced party election broadcasts for the first time in 1977, on the eve of assembly election in several states.

By 1980, radio covered about 90 per cent of the population and over 78 per cent of the area in the country. Expenditure on radio broadcasting in the First Plan (1951-56) was just over 2 crores. By the 7th Plan (1985-90) it increased to 700 crores. In 1991, we had 102 full-fledged radio stations which were production centres. The number of broadcasting centres, which included relay centre, was 205. The population covered was 97.5 per cent. Area covered was 91 per cent. The number of transmitters was over 300. This number included short wave and VHP (very high frequency) or FM (Frequency Modulation) transmitters. National AIR channel via satellite was started in May, 1988.

Vividh Bharati programmes are broadcast from 32 centres including two short wave transmitters at Mumbai and Chennai. They are relay Centre with low-power transmitters. They broadcast taped or pre recorded programmes. The tapes are sent to the various centre much in advances.

The External Services Division broadcasts programmes in 24 languages (17 foreign and 7 Indian) for a total of 75 hours daily. A special weekly programme is prepared and is broadcast through foreign radio stations in UK, USA and Canada. These programmes are meant for a large number of Indians living in these countries.

Several stations broadcast educational programmes for schools (schools broadcasts), twice or thrice a week. The duration generally is 30 minutes. Unfortunately one about 20 thousand schools out of 7 lac schools have their own radio sets. Only about 40 per cent schools actually listen to school broadcasts. They do not too have the listen period in their regular time-table.

Some stations help the Directorates of Correspondence Courses with University broadcasts. "Yuv Vani" provides the youth (15-30 years) with a channel to express themselves and for their talents to blossom.

Communication process is a two-way process. Unless there is feedback, the quality of effectiveness of broadcasts cannot be known. For this purpose AIR started an Audience Research Wing in 1946. But in 1952, after six years, the wing was closed. Some critics say that it was closed because the finding of the Research Wing were not very pleasant for the bosses. In mid-sixties the

Audience Research cell was set up again. Unfortunately, it does not have adequate staff. The staff is also not very well trained. Some other means of getting feedback are letters from the listeners, staff meetings (daily) of stations and newspaper media columns.

Radio now covers almost the entire population of India. It has a great ability to inform, educate and entertain the people. It can be made effective as an agent for development, especially in the rural areas. Rural areas do not have as many facilities for information, education and communication as the urban areas have. It remains a very relevant medium in India, like in other developing countries. This is so because about 40 per cent people in India are below the poverty line. Many are able to afford only a radio set or a transistors. TV sets are out of their reach. That is why, in a poor country like India, TV is called an elite medium which only the rich can afford.

Here, about half the populations is illiterate, Radio, being a medium of the spoken word uses conversational, simple and direct language. This can be easily understood even by illiterate folks. The effectiveness of radio can be gauged from the fact that its Rural Programme has been able to help the farmers in agricultural work. Varieties of grain or fertilizer popularized by the radio are commonly known as "radio seeds" or "radio khad".

But to be fully effective, radio must come out with new categories of programmes and new styles of presentation. It should encourage the formulation of Radio Forums or Clubs. Through these, radio should associate the people, the target audience with very aspect of programmes. In this way, there will be audience participation which surely leads to the success and effectiveness of radio. Radio stations should also go local. There should be at least one radio station in each district. The station should take care of the felt needs of the local communities. Small stations can involve the local communities in the total production process. That way the local people will have a sense of belonging to the radio and its broadcasts.

FM (frequency modulation) should be strengthened to provide reception without noise and disturbance. Feedback needs to be strengthened. Fair systematic research along can yield truthful findings. Feedback for external services broadcasts should be obtained in a more meaningful way. These services are important for our nationals sitting far away from home. Their thirst for home news and cultural needs to be adequately satisfied. External services are also important for projecting the Indian culture and situation correctly and effectively in foreign countries.

Experiments in TV broadcasting started in the USA in the twenties of this century. But the available equipment did not scan the picture effectively. In the next five years came certain inventions like the picture tube, electronics camera and TV sets. They made it possible for NBC (National Broadcasting Co.) in the thirties to set up a TV station in New York. BBC too started a TV station in London.

The Second World War halted the expansion of TV. But immediately after the war TV broadcasting started expanding in the USA and other Western countries. By 1948, there were 48 TV stations in 25 cities and two million TV sets in the USA. Within 10 years, 512 stations were sending programmes to 5 crore sets, Canada, Japan and European countries were also making brisk progress. Satellite revolutionised TV broadcasting from 1962. In that year appeared the first satellite called the Early Bird. In 1965 came Intelsat, a big international communication system. Another such system, Intersputnik was added in 1971. Today, more than 125 countries have their earth stations linked to satellites. Thirty-five satellite systems have brought the people and nations of the world much nearer. In the seventies, computer technology made possible a 2-way communication between the transmitting stations and receiving households. Then came audio visual cassettes and the video tape recorder and player. They were followed by closed-circuit TV, cable TV, pay-phone TV and now Direct Broadcasting System (DBS). In DBS broadcasting, you do not need even a receiving station. Programmes can be transmitted direct to the TV sets.

The latest broadcasting technology has not yet reached several Third World countries in Asia, Africa and Latin America. There is a gap between the rich and the poor countries in this respect. That is why UN observed 1983 as the World Communications Year, to narrow down this gap.

Television came to India rather late, on September 15, 1959. For years the debate went on whether a poor country like India could afford TV. It was feared that TV might alienate us from our cultural roots, that it might spread a consumerist culture. Consumerism would increase the hunger for comforts and luxuries.

It might increase frustration and lead to social conflict between the rich and the poor. But manufactures, businessmen, educational institutions continued to make strong demands for TV in India. UNESCO offered a grant of twenty thousand dollars to buy community sets. The USA also offered some equipments. Philips India offered a transmitter at a low price. Ultimately, the Government yielded. It set up a TV station at Delhi on an experimental basis. The declared aim was to discover what TV could achieve in community development and formal education.

The transmission could cover an area of 40 km in and around Delhi. Programmes were beamed twice a week. Each programme was of 20 minutes duration. The viewers were members of 180 tele-club. These club were provided free TV sets for community viewing by UNESCO. Programmes were beamed from an improvised studio at Delhi. UNESCO conducted a survey in 1961 and its conclusion was that TV did make "some impact." On pressure from public and TV set manufacturers, internment programmes were started on August 15, 1965.

The first rural programme "Krishi Darshan" was started from Delhi on the Republic Day, January 26, 1967. This programme was received by farmer-members of 180 village tele-club in Delhi, U.P. and Haryana.

Daily TV transmission was increased from one to one and half hours and to two hours on Sundays on August 15, 1968, On 3rd December 1971, the first English news bulletin was introduced. In 1972 (October) the inauguration of the Mumbai TV centre came about. In 1973, Srinagar and Amritsar Kendras started relaying programmes from Mumbai that year. Kolkata, Chennai and Lucknow TV centre were set up in 1975. So, we can see that the real expansion of TV in India came about in the seventies. For example, the number of TV sets, all of which were imported was 22,000 in 1975. In 1975, the number shot to over one lakh. What is even more important is that now the Indian sets are available in the market.

In 1975, the Satellite Instructional Television Experiment (SITE) was conducted. It made a deep impact on the country and the world. The one year SITE exercise proved to India itself that it was ready for the satellite television. In 1967, a UNESCO study was conducted in India on satellite TV's use in the country. The study concluded that India can and should use satellite for national development. Accordingly, our Department of Atomic energy entered into an agreement with the National Aeronautic and Space Administration (NASA) of USA for the loan of a satellite for one year. The satellite called ATS 6 was provided free of cost from August 1, 1975, to July 31, 1976, for SITE.

Educational programmes were broadcast direct from a satellite to the TV sets for the first time. Direct satellite transmission means that it does not pass through the relay station. The SITE programmes were revived by 2400 villages in six states—Andhra Pradesh, Bihar, Karnataka, Madhya Pradesh, Orissa and Rajasthan. An additional 25000 villages and towns in these states received these programmes through earth transmitters.

The daily 4 hours programmes were on education, agriculture, health and family planning. The satellite provided for two video channel and two audio channels, so that various programmes could be telecast only in two languages at one time. According to surveys conducted by the Indian Space Research Organisation (ISRO) and others, the experiment had a fair though not complete success. Commercial service on TV was started on January 1, 1976. Advertisers had to be allowed in because TV is a "Supreme Salesman". But a code for Advertisers was framed. Every advertisement had to be in accordance with the code. It could not be offensive. It could not hurt the normal, aesthetic and religious sentiments of the people. It could not be obscene and could not encourage violence or social conflict.

On April 6, Doordarshan was separated from All India Radio or Akashvani. Now Doordarshan, like AIR, got a directorate of its own, with its own Director General as the chief. But both AIR and Doordarshan continued to be under the Ministry of Information and Broadcasting. There had been great demand from the opposition parties to be given time on the electronic media. They strongly criticised the ruling party for using these powerful media of mass communication for their own political ends. It was for the first time in 1977 that the opposition shared time with the ruling party for election campaign. It was a step forward for the growth of a healthy democracy.

The Janata Party was the first non-Congress party to come into power at the Centre in 1977. It appointed a Working Group to find out how best Doordarshan and AIR could be freed from the government control and made autonomous. Opposition parties has always been against the government control of the electronic media. So now that they were in power, they wanted to show their commitment to his conviction. They did so by appointing the Working Group. The Group is popularly called the Verghese Group since the Chairman of the 12-member group was B.G. Verghese.

The Group submitted its reports in March 1978. It recommended a single autonomous National Broadcast Trust (NBT). It suggest that such an independent, impartial and autonomous Trust could be made by an Act of Parliament, National Broadcast Trust or Akash Bharati would look after the working of the both AIR and Doordarshan. It did not recommend two separate corporations for radio and TV. Because of their different nature, they would be two unit no doubt, but at the apex level these two units would be integrated under the care of a single Trust.

There would be Licensing Board to issue License to franchise stations for institutions like the universities. These franchise stations could have their own transmitters for specific proposes. No commercial advertising would be allowed on the educational channel. Their license would be renewable every three years. The Group also recommended the setting up of a Complaints Boards, selected by the Chief Justice of India. This Board would deal with the complaints of unfair treatment of persons, subjects, events etc., by AIR or Doordarshan.

The Trust would be responsible to the Parliament through its budget, annual reports, auditor's reports, reports of the Complaints Board and the Licensing Board.

The Controller General of Broadcasting (CGB), the chief of radio and TV broadcasting would provide a link between the trustees and the entire broadcasting organisation.

The year 1980 saw the start of the National Programmes of Music and Dance. The basic aims of radio and TV are to provide information, education and entertainment. It is also their responsibility to preserve and promote our culture and heritage. It is to fulfill this aim that Doordarshan started these National Programmes. The idea of National Programmes was already existing at AIR. The National Programme for the whole of India began on TV on August 15, 1982. In 1982, Doordarshan took to colour transmission August 15. Then occurred two significant events in the development of Indian TV. In November 1982, the Asian Games were efficiently covered through colour transmission.

The way the TV personnel handled this huge task was appreciated widely in India and abroad. In March 1983, Doordarshan covered the Non-Aligned Meet (NAM) held in Delhi. This was another feather in the cap of Doordarshan.

The first domestic satellite was launched in 1982. This satellite, INSAT 1-A, was placed in orbit but it could not become operational. India's second satellite, INSAT 1-B, was launched in August 1983. This made TV programmes available to much larger segment of our population, it also improved the quality of broadcasts. The year 1984 was very important for our TV. The first sponsored serial, Humlong went on the air in July. Higher Education TV (HETV), produced by the University Grants Commission, was started. Doordarshan celebrated its silver jubilee and Delhi Kendra's second channel started.

Before our own Humlong, we imported serials, sitcoms (situation comedies), soap operas and similar other programmes. The name soap opera is given to sentimental, sob-and-sigh dramatic serials. Such serials first appeared on the Radio in 1920s in America. They were sponsored by soap sellers and their sentimental stuff was mainly meant for women. Broadcasts like 'The Fox' 'Sorry', 'I Love Lucy' and 'Star Trek' were all imported. The imports came mainly from the USA and Germany. Our Indian soap operas took their inspiration from Mexico and achieved great success with its soap operas like 'Come With Me' and 'Come Along with Me'. The first was meant to encourage adult literacy. The later attempted to popularise family planning. The project of Humlong was inspired by these Mexican soap operas. The serial was on the air for 156 weeks. It became very popular with the viewers. Actors become TV personalities. This soap opera was sponsored by Food Specialities that launched Maggi noodles in the market. The sales of noodles increased enormously, especially in urban India. Educational TV (ETV) was started in 1961 from Delhi. The broadcasts, to start with were, for science teachers and students of Delhi schools. Later, they covered larger areas and more subjects. ETV was then extended to other *kendras* like Mumbai, Kolkata, Chennai and Srinagar. The service was also made available to higher secondary schools.

We have already noted that the Verghese Group recommended franchise stations for the University to prepare and broadcast their own programmes. Such programmes for higher education were started by the University Grants Commission (UGC) in 1984, UGC set up an ISAT Cell at Jamia Millia Islamia, New Delhi, to co-ordinate programmes prepared at different university. The UGC transmission for higher education was called Countrywide Classroom.

Several Audio-Visual-Research Centres (ADRCs) and Educational Media Research Centres (EMRCs) were set up in different parts to produce programmes. The programmes are meant to supplement the old and old formal process of education. They also try to promote the interest of students in seeking knowledge outside the syllabi. The morning Transmission was introduced in 1987. The late night feature film project was also introduced that year. Besides a weekly news bulletin for the deaf and dumb was launched. In 1988, Kolkata and Chennai got a second channel, INSAT-IC was also launched. In 1989 came the Afternoon transmission. In 1990, INSAT-ID was launched. In 1993, Doordarshan started five Metro Channel, including music, sports, entertainment channels. They were started under pressure from the foreign channels like the Hong Kong based Star TV and the US based CNN. We must acknowledge three important things that happened in the 1980s eight is. One was the Joshi Report on TV. The second was the video boom and the third was the appearance of Cable TV.

The Joshi Committee on Software for TV set up under the Chairmanship of P.C. Joshi, gave its report in 1985. The report is called "An Indian Personality for Television". The report criticised Doordarshan for concentrating mostly on the North for its programme content. It also criticised TV's attitude to made broadcasts predominantly in Hindi. The Committee said that Doordarshan has not been able to achieve its aim of becoming a medium of public service and social education. The reason was that it did not have functional freedom.

The Joshi Committee recommended the setting up of a National Doordarshan Council. Its aim would be (1) to review and guide Doordarshan's performances, (2) to act as a guardian of functional and professional autonomy, (3) to act like Press Council to examine complaints of unfairness against the medium. The Committee also recommended decentralisation of Doordarshan. Local stations at district level should be set up to involve the local communities in the process of programme production. Every village must have at least one community viewing set, and the Audience Research Unit should be strengthened. Viewers should be encouraged to give views freely so that the organisation becomes democratic in its programming.

The Committee did not ask for an autonomous corporation for Doordarshan. But it asked the organisation to find its roots in the rich Indian heritage and develop a strong Indian personality. Only then shall we be able to fight the foreign invasion of the Indian Skies.

When you go around any city or town, you find that many individuals possess Video Cassette Records (VCR) or Video Cassette Players (VCP). It appears like a situations of a video boom. Why only in cities and towns, even comparatively well off villages in many states like Punjab, Karnataka, Kerala, Maharashtra seem to have a situation of that kind. Even the northeastern states have not been left behind. The video seems to be even more active when you come across video parlours, video clubs, video restaurants and video buses. Video has become a profitable business proposition. It is shown to a fair number of people who are charged tickets. And this activity of video playing and watching activity continue till late in the night.

Video boom in India came in the early eighties, especially after the Asiad in 1982. No confirmed figures are available for the number of video players in India. Similarly, correct figures are not available for the number of people who watch video daily. Figures for players very from one to four million and for watchers from one to two million daily. Estimates and surveys have been made by advertisement agencies, cinema organisation and individuals. They have used different methods. So naturally the figures differ. For example, the number of video parlours ranges between 50,000 and two lakhs, according to different estimates.

Films are transferred to the tapes or cassettes illegally. Several "blue" (absence or not in good taste) film are also obtained in this manner. Cassettes are also obtained illegally from Dubai and Hong Kong. The government amended the Cinematograph Act. It was made illegal to screen or show films without a certificate from the Central Board of Film Certification. In spite of the amendment, the video business continued. It is rather difficult to catch hold of very video criminal.

One reason why people gather in video restaurants and

parlours that cinema theatres are not enough even in towns and several cities. Villages have only mobile make-shift in cinema theatres. Video parlours cash in the hunger of the people for watching films. Another reason is that people do not have to stand for long in queues to buy tickets. It is quality convenient to a parlour and buy a ticket easily. Also the price of entry into the parlour is reasonable.

For the parlour owners too, things seem convenient. They do not have to contract a theatre for showing films. They can screen films at their shop or in a room of their house. And the cost of the video is fast recovered. They can also rent out the video players at fairly high rates at night till the early hours of the morning or till they themselves will require it for their group of customers.

The cassettes are not very costly for the businessmen. One cassette costs anywhere between 100 and 150 rupees, depending on its quality. All sorts of cassettes are today available from T-series and Gold to the National Film Development Corporation cassettes. The NFDDC cassettes have foreign film prints too. The video owner uses one cassette several times. Many a times a film is copied from a copy. That is why many video cassettes are poor in quality.

Video has affected the film producers and theatre owners. People, who can see a movie on video, have stopped going to the cinema theatre. Illegal screening of films on video without paying any royalty to the producer or distributor means a loss to the latter. That is why cinema producers, film makers, distributors and exhibitors have joined hands to demand laws and action against illegal video operators. Cable TV is another significant development. It has spread in a big way, especially during the 1990s, cable was there earlier too, in metro cities like Mumbai. Cable has been operating in Mumbai and other metres for almost ten years. But in the past two years cable TV has invaded much smaller cities.

Cable TV is operated by linking the viewers' TV sets through cables to a common antenna. It is operated through a dish antenna and from a control room. The dish antenna, placed in a particular angle, can catch signal from broadcasting services like Doordarshan or foreign services like Star TV, CNN, BBC, MTV, Prime Sports, Pakistan TV etc. These broadcasts can be relayed through cable to individual customers of a cable TV operator. He also provides what is generally called 'domestic service or TV'. In this service, he shown films or other programmes like Pakistani tele-play, according to the demands of his customers. The Customers are charged installation fee to lay-cable. After this they are charged a monthly fee. This fee, generally various from Rs. 50 to 200 per month the fee or the rent would depend on the cost or providing the services, quality of the service, number of channels made available to customers and the customers capacity to pay. Cable TV is fast becoming popular. By paying say, one hundred rupees a month you can get five to eight or even more channels. On the top of it you also get one or two movies in the domestic service provided by the Operator. And these movies the customers can get on demand. Video and cable TV are now increasingly being used by political parties, especially during elections. Industrialists, businessmen and professionals like doctors, architects and consultants have also started using these media. Several video news magazines like India Today's News Track, Stardust's Starbuzz and former Union Minister, Harmohan Dhawan's Third Eye give a round-up of even news. Their cameras go when Doordarshan's cameras do not go. These magazines probe subjects which are not taken up by Doordarshan. Their coverage and comments tend to be bolder and deeper. Sometimes, of course, they can indulge in what is called "yellow" journalism (cheap, Sentimental).

Our TV, like all TV services abroad, offers a wide variety of programmes. These programmes are generally divided into general audience and special audience broadcasts. In the first category are included programmes of general interest like news, current affairs, films, light music, film songs, Chitrahaar, tele-plays, serials, soap operas. In the second category are included broadcasts for particular section of the population. For example, youth programmes, women's broadcasts, children's films and other children's telecasts, quiz shows, interviews, discussion, documentaries on particular subjects, features, docu-features, sports educational TV (ETV), Countrywide classroom, classical music etc. We have also now Intent Service, which was introduced in Delhi in 1985. It now broadcasts information on airlines, transport, railway services, stock exchange, cultural engagements, tourist services, current affairs, sports. This information is made available from the Second Channel of Delhi Kendra. Our TV has made some contribution no doubt but there is much left to be desired. It has provided internment to the viewers. It has brought films in their drawing rooms. It has served the farmers by informing them of new methods and techniques of agriculture, horticulture, poultry and villages industry. It has also traded to spread awareness about our great epics, about women's condition and role, about political processes like elections. It has made people aware of what is happening beyond India. ETV (educational TV) and HETV (Higher Education) have also imparted education to schools, college and university students in an informal way.

But our TV has not 'been able to do several other important things. It has not been impartial and fearless in reporting political developments. Its current affair programmes could have been an important platform for political education for the general public. It also not been as efficient as required in reporting the national and international news—in respect of neither speed nor of analysis. It is too much dependent on news agencies. After all it is a medium of immediacy, of "here and now". TV in Indian not proved to be an effective medium for social change, and development. TV has a great potential tc change a traditional society into a modern society. It has been contented to be a medium for internment. There has been a great predominance of film-based programmes on its screen. Its failure to promote and popularise our cultural heritage can be clearly seen. It has not been able to develop for itself what could be called a unique Indian personality. In short, it has not been able to change the traditional attitudes of people. Nor has it been able to change its own attitude of moving leisurely, behaving like a government organisation. It has been much too loyal to the government, forgetting its responsibility towards the people as a medium of mass communication.

ALL INDIA RADIO (AIR) NETWORK

It is hardly possible to exaggerate the role which radio can play in our society. With seventy per cent of our people illiterate and with most of them living in rural areas, radio has been the most important and most effective medium for providing information and stimulating new attitudes wherever it has reached. Communication by word of mouth alone had been possible until radio was used to spread the word. The difficulties faced by All India Radio were formidable; a vast country, with a huge population speaking numerous languages, and a varied pattern of social and economic development, living in villages, some of which are isolated for months on account of geographical, climatic and other reasons. Besides, the chronic inadequacy of capital resources, of equipment and manpower posed the kind of challenge which could only be met by zeal and enthusiasm, both were available in plenty in AIR's pioneering days.

But forty-four years after the start of organised broadcasting, radio listening is still very restricted in spite of the extension of the radio network. Why? Because the zeal and enthusiasm have been weakened by the absence of a long-term communication policy on the basis of which the extension of the network could be properly planned. Such a policy, taking into account the priorities and the available resources, would have provided the guidelines for development appropriate to the country's needs. In the absence of such policy, the expansion has been hesitant, short-sighted and out of step with listeners' demands and requirements. Impromptu decisions, often taken in haste, have led to the present stagnation and lack of balance in the network.

The First Plan of development, drawn up in 1945, was quite correctly based on a medium-wave service for the entire country. This involved putting up one or more fairly powerful transmitters in each linguistic and cultural area which had not, until then, been adequately served by AIR's medium-wave service. But because the cost of the installations was rather high, and because political considerations demanded that stations should be completed more or less simultaneously, to avoid charges of neglect of some areas and partiality towards others, the government decided to instal 'pilot' stations with transmitters of one kilowatt or even less power and make-shift studios with the minimum of staff and equipment. It was decided that once these were all installed they would gradually be replaced by more powerful transmitters and permanent studio and, offices.

In 1951, at the start of the First Five Year Plan, a primary service on medium-wave was available to about twenty per cent of the population. By the end of the Second Plan, by 1960, fifty-six per cent of the population and thirty-seven per cent of the country's area was covered by a medium-wave service. In the rest of the country, people had to make-do with a short-wave service from a few centres or with a poor grade medium-wave service from a distant transmitter.

The rate of growth has continued to be slow. Even in 1984, a reliable medium-wave service can reach only ninety per cent of the population and seventy-eight per cent of the area of India. This is in spite of 85 broadcasting centres, but there are only 25,000,000 radio sets of which only about 5,000,000 are in the countryside where 450,000,000 people live. So, in fact, radio serves not more than 20 per cent of the people and most of them live in the cities.

There are still considerable parts of the country which get no service at all or a very unreliable short-wave service. But as all radio sets do not have short-wave bands those who cannot afford these more expensive sets are, in fact, denied a service of any kind.

When to this limitation is added the restriction of language, the reach of AIR's services is still further reduced for there are large linguistic minorities in most States of the Indian Union who are not content to listen to programmes from their regional centre in the language of the majority. Their demand for a service, or at least a partial service in their own language, cannot be met without many more transmitters to provide alternative channels for the different languages.

It is not as though AIR has not heeded the demand for such services. At some stations where more than one channel is available it provides programmes in more than one language, as in the case of Delhi, Mumbai, Chennai and a few others, even if there is only a nominal service in some of the languages. Dialects, even those spoken by millions of people, can also be served only nominally. In Awadhi and Bhojpuri, to take two major dialects of Hindi, there are just a few programmes of music from Lucknow; in Kumaoni and Maithili there are programmes of less than three hours per week from Lucknow and Patna.

This incomplete coverage in terms of area, population and language has retarded the growth of listening in the country. After 1968, the annual rate of increase in licences has fallen steadily. We have only twenty-five million households with radios in the country.

The production figures of radio receivers tell the same story. Between 1960 and 1970 or so the demand for sets was greater than the supply but since 1970 the annual increase in the sales of radio sets, which was between forty per cent and fifty per cent in 1968 and 1969, was reduced to thirty per cent in 1970 and seven per cent in 1971. Even the cheaper single-band medium-wave receivers are not much in demand. This is disappointing because the green revolution had inspired hopes that there would be a spurt in the demand for sets from rural areas and manufactures had expanded their capacity to meet it. There are only about five million domestic receivers outside the towns and about ninety thousand community receivers for eight per cent of the population. Even according to the out of date UNESCO standard, there should be 110,00,000 receivers in India for a population of six hundred and fifty million. There is therefore a vast potential market for sets; why does it not materialise?

To set things right, the first and most urgent need is to decide the nature and extent of the service to be provided in the next ten years. As a poor country, beset with numerous problems crying out for solution, we cannot afford to give the people the variety and quality of broadcasting which more affluent countries can afford. With limited resources we can only hope to fulfil targets over a period of time according to well-considered priorities. While there can be no unanimity on such priorities and it would be impossible to satisfy all the different competing demands, it should be possible for a group of professional broadcasters and persons experienced in communication to advise and assist the Planning Commission and the Government to draw up a plan for development which would be professional in content. Several ideas aired in the past few years require to be examined on the basis of reliable data and research. The National Council for Mass Communication, which is discussed in a later chapter, would be an appropriate body to take up this assignment.

Whatever, the policy prescribed, certain, ingredients are essential in any plan for AIR's development. Firstly, it must be accompanied by plans for the production of a cheap radio set. It is quite clear that there will be no increase in listening in the towns unless a set is available for less than Rs. 120 which is the price of the cheapest reliable set today.

Such a set is also required for growth of listening in rural areas because it is now admitted that the scheme for community listening has outlived its utility and there is talk of subsidising the sale of low-cost receivers to increase and popularise domestic listening in the countryside. In the present economic conditions it would hardly be possible to subsidise millions of receivers. The solution lies in allowing the manufacture of a cheap set which would be within the means of even a family of landless labourers. How this can be done was discussed in the Report of the Committee on Broadcasting and Information Media.

Increase in listening also depends on an expansion of the services in regional languages from the regional transmitters of AIR. These must, in as short a time as possible, cover the entire population. This may require the installation of some more transmitters but, as far as possible, it should be achieved by strengthening the existing transmitters. A smaller number of powerful transmitters is easier and more economical to manage than a lager number of low-power ones. Besides, powerful transmitters would ensure that the signal is strong enough to provide satisfactory reception on low-priced sets.

The regional services of AIR can only use the language of the majority of people in the State. Any attempt to broadcast programmes for linguistic minorities would lead to fragmentation of the programme pattern which can satisfy no one. For some years we cannot afford to serve those who live in a State in which their mother-tongue is not the language of the majority.

The regional service should be a comprehensive service of entertainment and information catering for all the different groups of listeners who can be reached in the language of the State. Thus programmes for children, women, students and youth should find a place in each day's programme plan.

A policy plan for development must decide on whether the rural or the urban community must take precedence. Till now, the urban listener has received far more attention although in the cities people have access to other media, such as the press and the cinema. It seems only proper that the present urban bias in the planning of programmes should give place to more attention and resources being devoted to programmes for rural listeners. The limited time, one to two hours per day, for which such programmes are broadcast is only one of the problems. Still more unsatisfactory is the content of the programmes. Broadcasting can only help in development if radio and TV are accessible to the people. Instead of local broadcasts of immediate concern to the rural community in local languages and dialects, the programmes are broadcast from one centre for a whole State as large and variegated as Andhra Pradesh or Uttar Pradesh. Such programmes are often irrelevant for large areas of the State and cannot attract any listening. The only solution is a local radio service. Even in countries in which the gulf between the city and the village is not as wide as in India, local radio stations are being set up where they did not exist earlier. The regional service such as we have at present, or such as could be organised around one transmitter in a State, neglects the needs of our vast agricultural population. Though the music, news, talks and other items broadcast in the regional service would be available to all listeners, the agriculturist needs programmes of education and instruction which cannot be broadcast from one centre in a State in which climate, soil, crops, and other conditions vary from district to district. The local transmitter would also put out programmes of interest to rural women and youth and for part of the time could relay news and light entertainment from the Vividh Bharati or regional service. Unfortunately, the Planning Commission has provided for only 6 local stations in the 6th Plan whereas there should be at least 300.

The Vividh Bharati service of light entertainment should continue though it needs to be reorganised to constitute a proper service instead of being mainly based on film music. Listening in the countryside would increase if the Vividh Bharati service could be made available on medium wave. At present it is broadcast on short wave to cover a substantial area of the country, and on low-power medium-wave transmitters, located in thirty-one towns, each of which serves a limited area of about 16 km radius. It has been noticed that the demand for sets in a rural area increases as soon as it comes within the range of a medium-wave Vividh Bharati transmitter. The present thirty-one low-power medium-wave transmitters need to be replaced by a few of higher power, so located as to serve the entire country. The low-power transmitters can then be used to carry classical music, talks and discussions in English, serious radio features and other programmes for which there is a small but articulate audience mainly in the towns. These transmitters can also be used for the programmes for industrial workers and other groups living in cities. Some of these transmitters can also be moved to form art of the local radio service for agriculturists.

The lack of foreign exchange and resources in general has prevented the setting up of as many studios, transmitters, auxiliary centres and Vividh Bharati centres as are required to provide a good service. For every Five Year Plan the funds sanctioned for AIR have been much less than AIR asked for. This is partly because broadcasting is not given a high priority and, more so, because the decisions are not taken by professional broadcasters but the generalist civil servants of the government. It is also a measure of the failure of AIR to convince the Government of India of the importance of broadcasting in the process of development.

The Planning Commission has provided approximately 0.25 per cent of the total outlay for broadcasting. It has been argued that at least one per cent of the total should be made available for the development of broadcasting. But even the allocations are not spent to achieve the best possible results. This is because until recently the plans were made for each five-years period. This is far too short a span. Considering the time taken to implement many of the projects and to take into account the progressive changes in the needs of listeners, the time span of fifteen to twenty years would be more appropriate. Only long-term policies would make such planning possible.

AIR and the other authorities concerned have been much too easily satisfied with token achievements. For example, to provide a worthwhile service for each of the tribes on our north-east frontier may require many more studios and transmitters than we can afford. The choice, then, is to have no service at all, or a satisfactory service in English, Hindi, and one or two of the major dialects. But this requires a firm decision on the part of the political leadership which is not available because whatever the decision it would be unpopular with some of the tribes; so, the compromise of broadcasting in five dialects from Gauhati, eight from Dibrugarh, ten from Imphal and thirteen from Kohima for ten minutes in each tribal dialect once or twice a week. The service does not and cannot attract any listening and scarce funds are thus wasted merely to sustain a claim that there is broadcasting to most of the tribes in the region.

Incorrect decisions of this kind were sometimes the result of haste to meet the deadlines laid down by the Planning Commission. AIR was sometimes given a week in which to revise its proposals to reduce the total outlay by half. This could not allow careful thought or the collection of relevant information or sufficient consultation between engineers, programme officers and such audience research personnel as AIR has. But incorrect decisions were also the result of a wrong approach to planning on the part of non-professional civil servants in AIR and in the Ministry of Information and Broadcasting. The Minister of the day would direct the thinking about the nature of the development plans for the next five years along the lines he desired. Every time with the change of Minister there was a change in policy and a re-allotment of priorities. Thus a scheme given top priority by one minister might be downgraded to such an extent that it might not be taken up for ten years after it was officially approved. Likewise, top priority would be given to a scheme which had not even been considered before a particular Minister expressed interest in it.

The awkward and irrational location of certain AIR transmitters is the result of such non-professional zeal to bestow favours on certain areas or cities. For example, when the coverage for Kerala was under examination it was suggested that transmitters in Trivandrum and Calicut would not serve the entire State adequately but political considerations demanded that Calicut must have a transmitter. When many listeners complained that they could not hear the programmes from either centre a third transmitter had to be installed hurriedly at Trichur.

Planning under such conditions was bound to be erratic. The development of technical resources such as the installation of a transmitter became a matter of patronage and so the programme output had to be fitted to the technical facilities available instead of first considering the requirements of listeners and then providing the technical facilities to meet their needs. Such non-professional interference in making and implementing plans for development was the outcome of the absence of a communication policy.

Certain wasteful procedures and practices can also be traced back to the absence of long-term policies and plans, such as the use of high-power short-wave transmitters for the broadcast of news from Delhi. Thus news in Oriya, for example, goes out on two high-power transmitters just for the Cuttack transmitter to relay it for listeners in Orissa. Correct planning would have given priority to the laying of permanent telephone lines between Delhi and all AIR centres so that all news bulletins and programmes like 'Spotlight' and 'Current Affairs', nation-wide broadcasts by the President or Prime Minister, and national programmes of music and talks could be fed on such lines to the stations concerned. This would also have ensured satisfactory reception all over the country. The present short-wave radio link makes listening difficult in several areas.

Or, to take another example, if a satisfactory medium-wave coverage for Vividh Bharati required the installation of a small number of high-power transmitters which had to be imported, because we did not make them, and if foreign exchange was not available, the decision was to set up many low-power (one kilowatt) transmitters which were available locally but which could serve only a small part of the country. Worse still, since AIR does not have a network of transmitters for the Vividh Bharati service, the thirty-one individual centres have to be fed with tape-recordings of the entire day's programmes of about 12½ hours per day made several days in advance at the Vividh Bharati headquarters. The labour involved in making so many copies, in dispatching them by post, in collecting them at the other end, in returning the tapes to headquarters so that they may be used again, add up to an exorbitant expense which must by now have exceeded the cost, which seemed prohibitive in 1957, of installing a few high-power transmitters to make the service available all over the country. Economy can only be measured in the long-term but a department of government is bound by the rigidity of the annual budget.

The expense involved in providing a minimum service on these lines can be spread over some years. The regional service is already well-provided and only a few pockets require additional or higher-power transmitters. The present twenty-five auxiliary centres can be used for the local radio service but at least two hundred more would be necessary to serve the entire agricultural population. Some Vividh Bharati transmitters can be shifted for the local service but, in any case, low-power transmitters made in India cost only Rs. 1,50,000. The expensive part of this package plan is the installation of high-power medium-wave to be imported and installed at a cost of about Rs. 40,00,000 each. Since the commercial service, which already earns Rs. 18 crore per annum, would, as an all-India service, earn much more, the expense could be met.

With this basic service every listener will have what he needs for entertainment and for instruction and information. In course of time alternative channels at stations can be considered provided that by then TV does not make radio expendable.

Once a plan of development to meet the essential needs of listeners is drawn up, it would be necessary for a committee or body of experts in electronics engineering to advise on the equipment to be used; the power of the medium-wave transmitters needed for the Vividh Bharati service and the nature of the transmitters best suited for local broadcasting, whether AM (Amplitude Modulation) or FM (Frequency Modulation), VHF (Very High Frequency) or UHF (Ultra High Frequency), taking into account the costs not only of the equipment but also of the different types of radio receivers which may be required to receive signals from the transmitters. The expected development of TV would also have to be kept in minds as certain transmitters can be used for TV signals as well as radio.

Ultimately there is no substitute for clear thinking to make a satisfactory plan of development. Expert committees may suggest what they think best but if the government, that is the Planning Commission, the Ministry of Information and Broadcasting and the Cabinet as a whole, which in theory is responsible for each plan, does not give the correct lead the plans will continue to be patchy, fulfilling short-term objectives at the expense of long-term goals. The aims and objectives of broadcasting should be the guiding factor and not the ways and means position at any given time. If resources are wanting the development can be spread over a longer period but it is wasteful, in the extreme, to adopt temporary palliatives which have to be scrapped entirely in due course. The government's hesitation in making long-term commitments has already cost us dear and retarded the growth of radio and TV. And when government does, occasionally, commit itself, the inadequate delegation of powers to the Director-General of All India Radio prevents the implementation of the schemes.

INDIAN RADIO: AN INTRODUCTORY OVERVIEW

Radio broadcasting is a Government of India monopoly under the Directorate General of All India Radio—established in 1936 and since 1957 also known as Akashvani—a government-owned, semi-commercial operation of the Ministry of Information and Broadcasting. From only six stations at the time of independence, All India Radio's network had expanded by the mid-1990s to 146 AM stations plus a National Channel, the Integrated North-East Service (aimed at tribal groups in northeast India), and the External Service. There are five regional headquarters for All India Radio: the North Zone in New Delhi; the North-East Zone in Guwahati, Assam; the East Zone in Kolkata; the West Zone in Mumbai; and the South Zone in Chennai.

The government-owned network provides both national and

local programmes in Hindi, English, and sixteen regional languages. Commercial Radio services in India, which were inaugurated in 1967, are provided by Vividh Bharati Service, headquartered in Mumbai. Vividh Bharati, which accepts advertisements, broadcasts from thirty-one AM and FM stations in the mid-1990s.

India has an extensive network of medium wave and shortwave stations. In 1994, there were eighty-five FM stations and seventy-three shortwave stations that covered the entire country. The broadcasting equipment is mostly Indian made and reaches special audiences, such as farmers needing agroclimatic, plant protection, and other agriculture-related information. The number of radio receivers increased almost five-fold between 1970 and 1994, from around 14 million to nearly 65 million. Most radios are also produced within India.

The foreign broadcast service is a function of the External Services Division of All India Radio. In 1994 seventy hours of news, features and entertainment programmes were broadcast daily in twenty-five languages using thirty-two shortwave transmitters. The principal target audiences are listeners in neighbouring countries and the large overseas Indian community.

Terrestrial Radio, India

FM Radio

91.0 Radio City Bangalore—Bangalore (Karnataka) IN
91.9 Gyan Vani—Coimbatore (Tamil Nadu) IN
91.9 Radio Mirchi—Ahmedabad (Gujarat) IN
92.5 Go—Mumbai (Maharashtra) IN
93.9 Radio Mirchi—Pune (Maharashtra) IN
98.3 Radio Mirchi—Delhi (Delhi) IN
98.3 Radio Mirchi— Mumbai (Mumbai) (Maharashtra) IN
98.3 Radio Mirchi—Chennai (Chennai) (Tamil Nadu) IN
98.3 Radio Mirchi—Kolkata (Kolkata) (West Bengal) IN
98.4 Radio Mirchi—Indore (Madhya Pradesh) IN
102.6 AIR FM Rainbow—Delhi (Delhi) IN
105.6 Gyan Vani—Delhi (Delhi) IN.. *educational*
105.6 Gyan Vani—Mumbai (Mumbai) (Maharashtra) IN.. *educational*

105.6	Gyan Vani—Lucknow (Uttar Pradesh) IN.. *educational*
105.8	Suryan FM—Chennai (Chennai) (Tamil Nadu) IN
105.8	Suryan FM—Coimbatore (Tamil Nadu) IN
106.4	AIR FM Gold—Delhi (Delhi) IN
106.8	Suryan FM—Tirunelveli (Tamil Nadu) IN
107.4	Gyan Vani—Allahabad (Uttar Pradesh) IN.. *educational*
107.6	Gyan Vani—Bangalore (Karnataka) IN.. *educational*

AM Radio

666 100kW	AIR Radio Delhi A—Delhi (Delhi) IN
819 200kW	AIR Radio Delhi B—Delhi (Delhi) IN
1215	AIR National Channel I rep.—Delhi (Delhi) IN
1368 10kW	AIR Radio Delhi C—Delhi (Delhi) IN
1566 1000kW	AIR National Channel—Nagpur (Maharashtra) IN

Internet Radio, India

Internet Radio

Web Radio	DD India
Web Radio	Dishant.Com Radio
Web Radio	EBC Radio
Web Radio	India Radio
Web Radio	IndiaStereo.. hindi/Pakistani music
Web Radio	Mehfil Remixes.. Bollywood remixes
Web Radio	Nazrana Radio
Web Radio	Radio of India
Web Radio	Radio Xiaos Hits.. Bollywood hits
Web Radio	Radio Xiaos Remixes.. Bollywood remixes
Web Radio	Rza Radio.. Hindi Bhangra remixes
Web Radio	TeluguFM. Hindi music
Web Radio	Thenisai—Ar Rahman.. CHR-Tamil movie hits Tamil
Web Radio	Thenisai—Ilaiyaraja.. CHR-Tamil movie hits Tamil
Web Radio	Thenisai—Oldies.. oldies Tamil
Web Radio	Thenisai—Tamil FM.. CHR-Tamil pop Tamil
Web Radio	Vishwabharti.. news/talk/info

Shortwave Radio, India

Shortwave Radio

BBC Aajkal Service
BBC Hindi Service
BBC Tamil Service
BBC Vivechna Service

TELEVISION IN INDIA

Television service is available throughout the country. Broadcasting is a central government monopoly under the Ministry of Information and Broadcasting, but the only network system, Doordarshan, also known as TV1, accepts advertisements for some programmes. Doordarshan, established in 1959 and a part of All India Radio until 1976, consists of one national network and seven regional networks. In 1992, there were sixty-three high-power television transmitters, 369 medium-power transmitters, seventy-six low-power transmitters, and twenty-three transposers. Regular satellite transmissions began in 1982 (the same year colour transmission began).

By 1994 some 6 million people were receiving television broadcasts via satellite, and the number was expected to increase rapidly throughout the rest of the decade. Cable television was even more prolific, with an estimated 12 to 15 million subscribers in 1994. Besides Doordarshan, Zee TV—an independent station broadcasting from Mumbai since 1992—uses satellite transmissions. In fact, because Doordarshan is the only network that is permitted to broadcast television signals domestically, Zee TV and other entrepreneurs broadcast their Indian-made videotapes via foreign transmitters. Other networks joining the fray are Cable News Network (CNN—starting in 1990); Asia Television Network (1991); Hong Kong-based Star TV (1991); Jain TV, near Mumbai (1994); EL TV, a spinoff of Zee TV in Mumbai (1994); HTV, an affiliate of the *Hindustan Times* in New Delhi (1994); and Sun TV, a Tamil-language service in Chennai (1994). In a communications breakthrough in July 1995, Doordarshan agreed, for a US $1.5 million annual fee and 50 per cent of advertising revenue when it exceeds US $1.5 million, to allow CNN to broadcast twenty-four hours a day via an Indian satellite.

Doordarshan offers national, regional, and local service. The number of television sets increased from around 500,000 in 1976 to 9 million in early 1987 and to around 47 million in 1994; increases are expected to continue at around 6 million sets per year. More than 75 per cent of television sets were black and white models in 1992, but the proportion of colour sets is increasing annually. Most television sets are produced in India.

ALL INDIA RADIO: PROFILE, RESOURCES AND SERVICE OFFERED

- *AIR* Resources—a Technology Centre under AIR for marketing the vast resources of *Prasar Bharati* (The Broadcasting Corporation of India).
- *Prasar Bharati* one of the largest broadcast facilities set up in its two organisations—All India Radio (AIR) and Doordarshan (DD) catering to one billion people.
- *AIR Resources* provides total solution for Broadcasting, audio, video and tele-communication needs by pooling from *Prasar Bharati's* vast reservoir of resources in the form of Infrastructure, Human Resources and Technical Expertise in the field of broadcasting and related areas.
- *AIR Resources* is open to commercial opportunities and Revenue Earning ventures in the field of broadcasting covering planning, installation, operation and maintenance of broadcast facilities.

Achievements

- Signed an agreement on 2nd August, 2001 with IGNOU to provide turn-key solutions for setting up 40 FM stations for Gyan Vani Channels in the country (consultancy, implementation, maintenance and operation).
- IGNOU's Gyan Vani Stations in Allahabad and Coimbatore became operational on 7th November, 2001 and 14th January, 2002.
- AIR time on Bangalore station of AIR was given on licence fee basis to IGNOU.
- Another 12 stations are in various stages of commissioning.
- Signed an agreement on 9th October, 2001 with M/s Music

Broadcast Pvt. Ltd. for sharing Prasar Bharati Infrastructure at AIR, Lucknow.

- MBPL's City Radio became operational in December 2001.
- Harness inner strengths of the organisation to identify, develop and consolidate its resource base.
- Generate revenue by taking profitable venture in the field of broadcasting, computers and communications.
- To provide world class consultancy services and undertake turn key jobs in the specialised field of broadcast engineering and related areas.
- To facilitate growth of Indian Broadcasting sector by optimal utilization of Broadcasting facilities and resources.
- To become premier national and global provider of broadcast transmission infrastructure and related services.
- To initiate appropriate measures and develop business opportunities to undertake profitable projects and activities in broadcasting sector.
- To allow other broadcasters/telecom providers to use Prasar Bharati hardware/ software infrastructure by charging licence fee/usage fee.
- To provide consultancy and services to various broadcasting organizations, private companies, telecom service providers, ISPs etc.
- To undertake system design, integration with existing infrastructure, drawing of specifications, costing, formulation of proposals and other related works for the clients.
- To undertake installation, operation and maintenance of broadcasting facilities.

Infrastructure: Studio set-ups, transmitters, Terrestrial and Satellite Linking system, lands and buildings.

Manpower: Core team to do basic work of consultancy, soliciting business, technical design. Draws the staff from *Prasar Bharati* to execute projects and activities.

Prasar Bharati Technical Infrastructure

Radio and TV—Broadcasting Facilities

All India Radio

Broadcast Centres	207
Transmitters	321
External Services Transmitting Centres	19
Studios	193
Studio to Transmitter Links	122
Satellite Uplinking Captive Earth Stations	20
Receive Radio/TV Networking Ferminals	350

Doordarshan

Programme Production Centre	49
Transmitters	1223
Satellite uplink stations Mobile uplink and News Gathering Vans	21

Management

- *AIR Resources'* set up and managed on the lines of profit centres in a corporate entity under AIR.
- At apex level CEO, *Prasar Bharati* assisted by an empowered committee consisting of Engineer-in-Chief (AIR), Financial Advisor, Head AIR Resources.
- Head AIR Resources, responsible for implementation of projects and fulfilling commitments to the clients.

Achievements

- Taken up the job of providing turn-key solution to Indira Gandhi National Open University (IGNOU) in setting up FM transmitter at 40 places in the country. This included planning, system design, formulation of specifications and installation of the transmitters at 40 locations.
- The Prasar Bharati has signed an agreement with M/s Music Broadcast Pvt. Ltd. for sharing Prasar Bharati's infrastructure viz. land, building and tower at AIR, Lucknow on licence fee basis.
- AIR resources is in consultation with Bureau of Police Research and Development, Ministry of Home Affairs to enhance the standards of police performance by providing training support through AIR's Broadcast media.

- AIR resources is in consultation with other private broadcasters to provide consultancy and use of Prasar Bharati infrastructure for setting up their FM transmitters in metro and other cities.

Use of Prasar Bharati hardware/software infrastructure by charging licence fee/ usage charges.

Consultancy services including feasibility studies, turn-key jobs and operations and maintenance in the specialised fields of:

- *Terrestrial Broadcasting for Radio and Television*: This includes the frequency planning, coverage planning, system design, installation and commissioning, operation and maintenance of terrestrial broadcast networks.
- *Satellite Broadcasting*: This includes planning and system design, execution of operation of fixed and mobile (SNG) uplink and down-link systems using both analogue and digital technologies.
- Studio systems including interior design, acoustics, state-of-the-art, studio and post-production equipment.
- Data Broadcasting and Internet broadcasting.
- Acoustics and audio video system for theatres, auditoriums and conference halls:
    - Selling of air time on broadcast transmitters.
    - Availability of programmes from its large and rich archives.
    - Production services and software generation.
    - On site and institutional training in various disciplines of broadcasting.
- Software development and content packaging.

Key objectives in every project undertaken are:

- Flexible, state-of-the-art and cost effective solution to every customers unique requirement.
- Emphasis on total professional approach, on schedule completion of projects and customer satisfaction.
- High quality and cost-effective operation and maintenance support.
- Consultancy and advice in selection of appropriate equipment in customers best interest.

RECOMMENDATIONS OF FM RADIO COMMITTEE

Licensing Process

The Committee is of the view that the open auction bid process was not suitable for auctioning of the frequencies and it did not yield the desired results. Various legal challenges were raised in connection with the open auction bid process followed in case of Phase I of the liberalization of FM broadcasting. The Committee recommends that adoption of tender process for radio licenses is more suitable for the following reasons:

1. It is a standard and simple process followed by the Government in numerous sectors whereby sufficient experience has been garnered. The process is also judicially well-recognised.
2. It is an internationally well-accepted process.[1]
3. It is the preferred process, specifically for broadcast licenses. It is one of the prescribed processes in case of auction of spectrum licenses in Australia and is also followed in the United Kingdom. The European Community recommendation on Independent Broadcast Regulator also envisages a tender process for broadcast licenses.

The License process shall consist of the following rounds:

(*a*) The first round should be the pre-qualification round and only bidders complying with the financial and technical eligibility criteria specified in the tender documents and as certified through a viability/sensitivity study by an Eligible Financial Institution/Bank should qualify for the next round. The security for participating in this stage should be the earnest money deposit as specified in the tender document. The security amount should be in line with Phase I tender document.

---

1. It is the standard process in international competitive bidding recognized and elaborated upon in a number of International Instruments like the WTO Agreement of Government Procurement; UNCITRAL Model Law on the Procurement of Goods (Under Article 18 tendering is the preferred mode of procurement), World Bank Guidelines on Procurement etc.

(*b*) After the pre-qualification stage, the financial bids of the qualified applicants should be opened at a notified time and place to determine the Entry Fees.

The bid license amount must be based on the business plan and the security for the same should be in the form of an irrevocable, unconditional and confirmed bank guarantee for the full amount of the quoted license fees. The bank guarantee shall be the security for the period from the date of application till the date of payment in full of the entry fees (i.e., the date of allocation of frequency).

In the tender process the entry fees could naturally be different for each bidder. The number of highest bidders that equal the number of frequencies available, would automatically win the frequencies at each centre (e.g., if there are seven frequencies available at a centre, the seven highest bidders would be allotted the frequencies).

Immediately upon award of the bid, 25 per cent of the entry fees should be payable and the frequency should be allocated only upon payment of the balance amount of the entry fees.

License Fees

The fixed annual license fee (that escalates annually at the rate of 15 per cent) determined by the auction procedure in Phase-I of FM Licenses for Private Broadcasters has proved to be unviable. In such a scenario, migration to a one-time entry fees plus revenue sharing model, as in the case of cellular licenses (Telecom) in India, is the most suitable option.

Entry fees: The Committee recommends that the entry fees should be determined by a competitive bid process that will reflect the true market value of the frequency.

Revenue Share: In light of the fact that:

- The Tenth Plan has also envisaged a revenue share mechanism in radio.
- The revenue sharing arrangement has been tried in a number of instances in India (like Telephones/Major ports etc.) and in the media sector as well (in case of DTH).
- Revenue understatement may be a cause of concern in the case of large public utilities. But radio is comparatively a small local industry with much smaller capital investment

and revenue flows. The only form of revenue in the radio industry is in the nature of advertising and opportunities of revenue understatement are therefore much less in comparison to an infrastructure industry like electricity or oil.

- Detailed guidelines have been formulated in relation to related party transactions in Accounting Standard 18 of the Institute of Chartered Accountants of India.
- Internationally the revenue share model is used in spectrum allocation (as in Australia) and broadcast licenses.

The Committee recommends a revenue share of 4 per cent of gross revenue.[1] This revenue share shall be subject to review by a committee every five years and may be increased/decreased, depending on the then prevailing market conditions. Such revision, covered under the agreement, will not be considered as a change in law.

Duration of License

The duration of the licenses in Phase-I of the award of FM broadcast license was fixed at ten years and no extensions were permissible on any grounds whatsoever. Internationally, the initial period of license is lower (e.g., in Canada the period is seven years,[2] in UK it is eight years). However, in most countries, renewal of the licenses is permitted, which taken together with the original license period, would mean that the term of the license extends more than 10 years (e.g., in Canada renewals of license for terms not exceeding seven years is permitted[3] while in UK licenses are renewable for one term not exceeding eight years, after the completion of the first eight years of license).

The Committee recommends that the license would be valid for a period of 10 years from the date of grant of operational license

1. The revenue share percentage suggested by industry players varies in the range of 2-3 per cent of gross revenue. On the other hand, the revenue share percentage suggested in Ernst and Young Report is in the range of 3-5 per cent.
2. Section 9 (b) of the Broadcasting Act, 1991.
3. Section 9 (d) of the Broadcasting Act, 1991.

by WPC, as in the case of Phase-I. The Committee also recommends that the renewal of license be permitted, for a further period of five years, subject to satisfactory performance by the licensee and provided that no default has occurred during the license period. This assessment and recommendation for renewal of license will be made by the independent regulator to the Government, once the regulator is in place.

Multiple Licenses in a City

In Phase-I the licensees were not permitted to own multiple frequencies in the same city. The recent trend internationally is towards abolition of such restrictions, as evident in (say) the Canadian Commercial Radio Policy, 1998. Due to non-viability of market in the Indian context, the restriction on multiple licenses in the same centre needs to be reviewed, without loosing sight of the potential for monopolies/oligopolies.

Therefore, the Committee recommends that:

(*a*) The number of frequencies that an entity, directly or indirectly, may hold in a particular centre be restricted to 3 or 33 per cent of the total licenses available in the centre, whichever is less.

(*b*) No entity shall hold more than one frequency (license) for news and current affairs in any one centre.

(*c*) Further, such additional licenses should be permitted only if the total number of frequencies available in a centre to establish a broadcast station (including frequencies in Phase-I) is equal to or more than six.

Total Number of Frequencies that an Entity May Hold: Containing Monopoly

The total number of frequencies that an entity may hold, directly or indirectly, nationally in each phase should not be more than 25 per cent of the total number of frequencies being tendered during the phase.[1] The bidder should at the time of submitting a bid furnish a declaration to the effect that it shall not accept bids for more than 25 per cent of the frequencies offered in any phase.

1. Similar restrictions obtain internationally e.g., in UK.

An undertaking should be said to be in a dominant position, if it holds more than 25 per cent of the total operationalised licenses in the country and in the event of abuse of dominance by such dominant undertakings, the Government or the regulator, as the case may be, should have the power to order the sale of the licenses, through a tender process, to other undertakings that are not connected in any manner whatsoever, with any dominant undertaking. This condition of reserving the right of the Government or the regulator (as the case may be) to break up a monopoly, should be part of the tender documents so as to minimize the chances of litigation.

The content plan for each separate frequency at the same centre being bid for, by the same bidder must be different to ensure wider availability of choices to the listeners.

The licensees would neither be permitted to network among the multiple channels in one center, nor would they be allowed to network with another licensee in the same centre.

Each license should constitute a separate undertaking and licensees should maintain separate accounts for each frequency allocated to them. It should be the endeavour of each licensee to properly segment the expenditure with reference to each license in accordance with the applicable accounting standards or guidelines issued by Institute of Chartered Accountants of India.

Networking

Networking or chain broadcasts means simultaneous transmission of programmes by various broadcast stations (transmitters). Licensees in Phase-I were not permitted to Network except on important occasions with the prior permission of the Government.

In light of the fact that networking can significantly reduce the Capital Expenditure and Operating Expenditure of a broadcast station (especially in small cities), we recommend that networking be permitted. We believe that the market mechanism will ensure differentiation of content reflecting listener's choice.

Please note that Networking be permitted only amongst the broadcast stations of the same entity and not across the licensees. Furthermore, networking should not be permitted in the same city.

News and Current Affairs

Phase-I licensees were not permitted to broadcast news and current affairs. The Committee recommends that the restriction on news and current affairs should be lifted and the committee strongly recommends that the AIR Code of Conduct and the applicable industry codes should be strictly followed. The violation of any aspects of these codes would result in the immediate revocation of the license.

Co-location

Co-location, in this particular context, is the term used to mean locating the transmitting set ups of various broadcasters of a particular city in the same premises and sharing the common tower. This term gathers more significance in the situations of lesser frequency separation between the channels allotted for the same city. The basic idea behind co-location is that the Effective Radiated Power (ERP) of all the channels would be nearly the same and since they are located at the same site, they will be attenuated similarly with the distance thus maintaining the same protection between the channels.

In this context, following observations are made:

1. Co-location in metro cities was mandatory in Phase-I. The objective was to increase the availability of frequencies by spacing them 400 kHz instead of 800 kHz.
2. Most of the representations received by the Committee have opposed co-location due to the following reasons:
   (*a*) For co-location purpose, it is necessary for private broadcasters to form a consortium.
   (*b*) It is very difficult to form a consortium of private broadcasters competing with each other.
   (*c*) If a private broadcaster backs out, his share of cost on common infrastructure would have to be borne by the remaining ones.
   (*d*) Private broadcasters have to bear substantial cost on studio-transmitter link as in co-location case, the studio set up would mostly be at a different location.
   (*e*) There are number of other operational difficulties.

In view of the above difficulties expressed by the private broadcasters, it is recommended that co-location may not be made mandatory in Phase-II.

Reserve Entry Fees

In Phase-I, the Government divided the centres (cities where frequencies were offered to private bidders) in five categories for the purposes of license fee: A+ (reserved license fee Rs. 125 lacs), A (reserved license fee Rs. 100 lacs), B (reserved license fee Rs. 75 lacs), C (reserved license fee Rs. 50 lacs) and D (reserved license fee Rs. 20 lacs).[1]

In light of the following:

> Internationally (e.g., in case of Spectrum Allocation in Australia) the Government is free to determine a reserve price in case of scarce resources like frequencies so that due to imperfections, the market does not grossly undervalue the frequencies. In Phase-I also, some licenses were granted to the bidders at the reserve price, as there were no other applicants. Even internationally, instances wherein there is only one bidder for a particular frequency are quite common.

However, the purpose of such reserve price is again not meant for revenue maximization but only to prevent gross undervaluation. Reserve price must be objectively calculated on pre-published criteria in the light of alternate and probable uses of the frequency. It should necessarily reflect the lowest permissible price.

The Committee recommends that the historical reserve price of Phase-I be followed. The Government can consider revising the reserve price in subsequent regimes.

Foreign Investment

The Committee is in favour of a simplified foreign investment regime for radio.

We recommend that the following safeguards be introduced in the license agreement:

1. FDI up to 26 per cent should be permitted in FM broadcasting (news as well as entertainment).
2. While calculating the 26 per cent limit on FDI, the foreign

1. Section 1 of the Tender Documents.

holding component, if any, in the equity of the Indian shareholder companies of the licensee should be duly factored in on a pro rata basis to determine the total foreign holding in the licensee.[1] The equity held by the largest Indian shareholder group should be at least 51 per cent of the equity excluding equity held by public sector banks and public financial institutions.

3. 75 per cent of the directors of the licensee, the Chief Executive Officer of the licensee and/or head of the channel and all key executives and editorial staff of the channel must be resident Indians appointed by the licensee without any reference on or from any other company for all news channels. For all entertainment channels exception to the above could be made for 'People of Indian Origin' cardholders/NRIs for the position of key executives and editorial staff. This facility will not be available to channels providing any kind of news. It should be obligatory on the part of the licensee to inform the Ministry in writing before effecting any alteration in the foreign shareholding pattern or in the shareholding of the largest Indian shareholder and/or in the CEO/Board of Directors. Further, the licensee should be liable to intimate the Ministry the details of any foreigners/NRIs employed/engaged by it for a period exceeding 60 days. Further, there should be a bar on direct/indirect outsourcing of content to foreign parties.
4. The licensee should be required to make disclosures of any shareholders agreements, loan agreements and such other agreements that are finalized or proposed to be entered into. Subsequent changes to the said agreements should be permitted only with the prior approval of the Ministry. Further, the licensee should not be permitted to raise loans from foreign entities for all news channels beyond the proportion of foreign equity allowed. (In other words, for Licensees putting out news, up to 26 per cent of their total equity can be taken as loans from foreign sources and no more).
5. In the light of the aforementioned changes to the FDI policy,

---

1. See revised eligibility criteria Clause (b) and (d).

in respect of FM broadcasting, the existing licensees should be required to effect the necessary amendments to their Memorandum of Association and Articles of Association and relevant agreements no later than two months from the date of migration of their licenses from Phase-I to Phase-II.

Increase in Number of Frequencies for Private FM Broadcasts

Committee is of the view that the released frequencies for Phase-II of liberalization of FM transmission will include unutilized spectrum in Phase-I after migration.

The spectrum being a scarce resource nas to be used rationally, efficiently and optimally by all.

The Committee strongly recommends that as the market develops and gathers the required momentum, Government should release additional frequencies in subsequent phases of liberalization, so as to boost further growth of the market.

The Committee is of the opinion that some other available frequencies may be more effectively utilized for the purposes of educational broadcasts by IGNOU. It has been brought to the notice of the Committee that during the last few years AIR is in the process of migrating high quality music programmes like Vividh Bharati from MW to FM. The possibility of availing these MW transmitters from AIR for the purposes of educational broadcasts by IGNOU requires serious consideration. This would address the issue of costs as IGNOU will not have to incur heavy expenditure on building broadcast infrastructure because AIR facilities could be used by IGNOU at a reasonable cost. This arrangement would lead to the best possible use of spectrum and release of additional frequencies.

Non-Commercial Channels

The PBS (Public Broadcast Service in the USA) model and the BBC model for non-commercial channels are widely followed abroad, where the programmes are funded by various organisations.

The Committee proposes a similar model wherein, out of the 4 per cent revenue share that the Government would receive from the FM broadcasters, 1 per cent point of the revenue share should be set apart as a separate fund dedicated for the purpose of developing the non-commercial channels (related to a wide range of areas such as culture and heritage of India, public health etc.). The resources which will accumulate in this fund will be sought by private broadcasters to develop non-commercial channels and programmes, in accordance with the directions of a Committee of eminent personalities of the nation formed by the Government. The funds should be disbursed through transparent rules and regulations framed for this purpose by the esteemed Committee. There would be a yearly audit of the broadcaster and the audit report would be presented to the Committee.

Such non-commercial channels will be initially required in all A+, A and B category towns, followed by its expansion in other cities in the future.

Considering the fact that the number of commercial channels are already limited, it is suggested that additional frequencies be released at the earliest for the above non-commercial channels.

Niche Channels Through Fiscal Incentives

The Committee is of the view that it is possible to help the market process in the direction of development of niche channels. In this respect the Committee recommends the following:

In every city, certain frequencies should be reserved for niche channels to be tendered separately with a low reserve fee and low revenue share percentage. Detailed terms and conditions may be prescribed to ensure that such channels are exclusively developed for niche programming and no partial niche programming be allowed.

The Committee feels that such niche channels will be initially required in A+, A and B category towns, followed by its expansion in other cities in future. The Committee also strongly urges the Government to consider releasing additional frequencies to encourage such niche channels.

Foreign Satellite Broadcast

Presently, Government of India has a policy on uplinking of TV channels. The following two major benefits have accrued from this policy:

(*a*) Outflow of foreign exchange has been curtailed since the uplinking is done from the Indian soil instead of foreign countries.

(*b*) Government is able to enforce a code of conduct for the TV channels.

In the absence of similar policy on the uplinking of Radio channels in the country, valuable foreign exchange outflow is taking place and the Government is unable to enforce any code of conduct on Satellite radio channels.

In view of the above, it is recommended that Government should come out with a policy on uplinking of satellite radio channels and downlinking process, so that the forex outflow could be curtailed and a code of conduct could be enforced.

Migration

For the purposes of migration to the new regime, 24th July 2003 (the day of appointment of this Radio Broadcast Policy Committee) shall be taken as the "Cut-off Date" from which the rights and obligations under the new regime will be applicable to the players. Rights accrued and Liabilities incurred till the Cut-off Date shall be governed by the old regime.

The Committee is of the opinion that operationalisation of license or at least a serious attempt at operationalisation should be the criterion for distinguishing between serious licensees and not so serious ones. Therefore, the following should be entitled to migrate to the new regime:

(*a*) Successful bidders that have operationalised the license and have paid the license fees till date. From the cut off date all fees paid shall be adjusted (but not refunded) against the new system of revenue share.

(*b*) Successful bidders that operationalised the license but later due to non-viability of business defaulted in payment of license fees.

(*i*) They will have to pay the original license fees due till the Cut-off Date.

(*ii*) Defaults in the original license fee that was to be due, after the cut off date, are to be ignored.

(*iii*) Payment will be treated as one time entry fee.

(*c*) In case of delay in operationalisation due to co-location, those who are operating under "deemed operationalisation", should be granted a revised deadline, either to co-locate by say December 31, 2003 or set up independent facilities by say March 31, 2004. On completing either of the above, they shall be entitled to migrate to the Phase-II licensing system. Till the point of operationalisation, they will be governed by the old regime.

The Committee strongly recommends that there should not be any blacklisting of bidders for new licenses on the basis of their default in Phase-I, as the Phase-I was characterized by acute market and regulatory imperfections that rendered the market unviable. Also, the Committee appeals to all bidders who have gone to court to withdraw their litigations and take advantage of the new Phase-II regime.

Import Duty

In this sector, almost all the broadcasting equipments are imported and none of them are manufactured domestically. To make the economics more viable, the Committee suggests that the import duty on the broadcast equipment be brought in line with that of the Telecom sector.

Code of Conduct

The Committee suggests that broadcast by private broadcasters must not, inter alia contain the following (as per the AIR code):

- Criticism of friendly countries.
- Attack on religion or communities.
- Anything obscene or defamatory.
- Incitement to violence or anything against maintenance of law and order.
- Anything amounting to contempt of court.
- Aspersions against the integrity of the President, Governors and Judiciary.
- Attack on political party by name.
- Hostile criticism of any State or the Centre.
- Anything showing disrespect to the Constitution or advocating change in the Constitution by violent means, but advocating changes in the constitutional way should not be debarred.

AIR code and the advertising code to be looked at as per current scenario and appropriate changes can be made, if required.

Shift of IGNOU (Educational Broadcast) to Medium Wave and Availing of MW Transmitters from AIR

In Phase-I of liberalization of FM broadcasting one frequency in each of the forty cities was reserved for educational broadcast by IGNOU. However, so far IGNOU has been able to operationalise only 10 FM stations. It appears that due to limits on availability of funds IGNOU may not be in a position to operationalise all these frequencies. On account of paucity of spectrum it is not advisable to allocate FM frequencies for educational broadcasts.

The Committee is of the opinion that some other available frequencies (like medium wave) may be more effectively utilized for the purposes of educational broadcasts by IGNOU. It has been brought to the notice of the Committee that during the last few years AIR is in the process of migrating high quality music programmes like Vividh Bharati from MW to FM. The possibility of availing these MW transmitters from AIR for the purposes of educational broadcasts by IGNOU requires serious consideration. This would address the issue of costs as IGNOU will not have to incur heavy expenditure on building broadcast infrastructure because AIR facilities could be used by IGNOU at a reasonable cost. This arrangement would lead to the best possible use of spectrum.

Broadcast Regulator

The radio industry in India is in a nascent stage of growth. However, as the market develops a number of legal and social issues (like content regulation, networking regulation etc.) as well as technological issues [like digital radio broadcasting (terrestrial/ satellite) subscription radio channels etc.] are likely to arise in relation to radio. The market competitive forces may not always work in harmony and sometimes may require reconciliation of competing interests. Therefore, as the industry develops it will require maintenance of an appropriate regulatory environment through an autonomous regulator.

The Committee in this respect shares the views and the

concerns of the Hon'ble Supreme Court as reflected in the case of *Secretary, Ministry of Information and Broadcasting vs. Cricket Association of Bengal,*[1] wherein it was observed that the Central Government should establish an independent autonomous public authority representative of all sections and interests in the society to control and regulate the use of airwaves.

The Committee therefore, recommends the constitution of an independent broadcast regulator.

The Committee would like to clarify that the Broadcast Regulator should provide and maintain appropriate regulatory environment to foster market led growth rather than seek to supplant and substitute market forces through regulation. The main objective of the Broadcast Regulator should be to seek proper enforcement of rules and regulations and its actions should primarily be complaint driven.

We suggest to the Ministry of Information and Broadcasting that pending the creation of a Regulator (which is likely to take time, requiring Parliamentary approval), a non-statutory Committee be set up which has Terms of Reference similar to what the Regulator would have. (We understand that the formal creation of SEBI was preceded by such a Committee).

Penalty for Non-Operationalisation of Awarded Licenses

The Committee strongly recommends that after being awarded the license, it is mandatory for licensee to operationalise the license within a maximum period of one year. If the licensee does not operationalise the license within one year from the date of the award, the Government, as a condition of the license, will forfeit the license and re-tender it in public interest.

COMMUNITY RADIO BROADCASTING IN INDIA

With the advent of community broadcasting, a whole new exciting world awaits listeners in far-flung areas where radio listening revolves around community centres. The proposed community radio serves to bring small groups together through their own

8. (1995), 2 SCC 161.

participation to reflect their day-to-day concerns. The community will participate by creating contents of the programmes for its own people. This narrow broadcasting does not require big transmitters. Community radio of the future will strive to bring people together through interaction. Like teleconferencing, the listeners will be able to talk to each other through the radio network using small wireless sets. This will help in business activities of the particular district or a village where the artisan will know his prospective buyer for his wares.

At present, however, programmes will be created for the listeners in the community and reflect what is relevant for their needs and aspirations. The community in these areas is well-knit. There is always a collective response to all radio programmes as the listeners generally assemble at one place where they listen to radio programmes, discuss and react. This turns into public service broadcast because it is here that the aspirations of the people can be fulfilled. To achieve this, the programmes have to be drawn up with a foresight keeping in mind the priorities of varied areas so that people can easily identify themselves with the programmes.

Out of the existing network of All India Radio, the Frequency Modulation, commonly known as the FM, technique of the radio wave has a distinct advantage. The Medium Wave and Short Wave suffer from the disadvantage of deteriorating sound quality with the increase in distance. The FM provides stereo quality and is ideal for short-range broadcasts. In the far-flung rural areas where the availability of power supply is unreliable, the FM is ideally suited for community broadcast for dissemination of information, education and entertainment. The Working Group on the 10th Plan has recommended future expansion of radio, primarily in the FM mode. To supplement the broadcasting by All India Radio, the Government, in July 1999, approved private participation in FM broadcasting.

After offering licences to private FM broadcasting in 40 cities through 110 channels for commercial broadcasting, the Government has decided to offer private licences to the established educational institutions and organizations having their own campus and residential schools. At present, AIR has 133 FM transmitters covering more than 21 per cent of area and about 31 per cent population of the country. Private licences for FM broadcasting have been offered in 40 cities for 110 channels for setting up 10 kW radio transmitters, except in four metro cities where the capacity could be between 10 to 20 kW. These private channels are already operating in Delhi, Mumbai, Kolkata, Chennai, Bangalore, Indore, Ahmedabad, Pune and Lucknow. Next in the line are Patna, Bhuvaneswar, Cuttack, Jabalpur, Coimbatore, Tirunelveli and Vishakhapatnam. The number of channels will provide plurality of choice to the listeners leading to improvement in the quality of programmes.

To start with, programmes on the community radio service will focus on issues relating to education, health, environment, agriculture and rural and community development. The Government expects these programmes to be popular if done innovatively done to sustain the listeners' interest.

This service is expected to provide a platform for students and teachers to give expression to their creative talent in producing programmes and in socio-cultural cohesion of the masses at the local level. The licencees will not be allowed to broadcast any news, current affairs programmes, election and political broadcasts. They will also not be allowed to air any advertisement of sponsored programmes.

The Government is aware of the need to safeguard the radio stations from being misused for undesirable propaganda against national interest and safety and security of the country. Therefore, in the first phase, the Government has given licenses to only the selected and established educational institutions in the country for community broadcasts. For the sake of credibility, the licensees will ensure that nothing is included in the programme that goes against good taste and decency. The code of conduct rules out anything obscene, defamatory and innuendos. The licencees will also ensure that there is nothing that amounts to contempt of court or by casting aspersions on the integrity of the President or the judiciary.

The programme code will almost be the same as for All India Radio. It would strive to promote national integration, religious harmony, scientific temper and Indian culture.

The applicant will be permitted only one licence valid for three years and the licensee will provide service on free-to-air basis. No channel will be permitted for commercial purposes. The Government will have the right to inspect broadcast facilities and reserve the right to take over the entire services or network or revoke or suspend the license in the interest of national security.

The licensee will ensure that all foreign personnel likely to be appointed as employees or consultants obtain security clearance from the Government. The licensee will be expected to furnish a bank guarantee to ensure timely performance of the licensee agreement and failure to start the services within the stipulated period can result in cancellation of license and forfeiture of the bank guarantee.

The people are likely to immensely benefit from community radio because of its inter-active nature and low costs of broadcasting.

Radio as a communication medium plays an important role in the nation's socio-cultural, political and economic development. It has the unique advantage of being receivable through low cost, battery operated, and mobile receiving sets, affordable for almost everyone, even in the rural areas. With appropriate strategies, radio can expand its reach to sparsely populated areas and remote corners of the country.

Concept

There are three options for expansion of radio network viz: (*i*) the commercial broadcast model, (*ii*) public service broadcast route and (*iii*) the community radio. While each of these modes helps in enhancing coverage, there could be clashes of interest particularly in the share of target audience and content. A commercial radio station is market driven and therefore its objective is to gain as much market share as possible, expand business and take competitive initiatives in the public service domain. Public service broadcasting, on the other hand, concentrates on content for education, information and entertainment with the broad objective to address the concerns of a large and varied listener group and it generally accords lower priority to commercial considerations. Community radio, as distinct from public service broadcasting, serves to bring small communities together, focuses on the common man's day-to-day concerns and helps in realizing local aspirations. In this sense, it aims to contribute to the lives of the local community by creation of content by the people and for the people of that community.

Policy on Community Radio Broadcasting

In December 2002, the Government announced a policy for the

Grant of Community Radio Licenses to educational institutions and organizations to be identified/selected, in accordance with the prescribed eligibility conditions and on the terms and conditions given in the Guidelines for the grant of licenses for Community Radio Stations.

Under the terms of this policy, Community Broadcasting Licenses can be granted to well-established educational institutions/organizations, recognized by the Central Government or the State Government. These will include the universities and institutes of technology/management and residential schools.

Community radio is expected to focus on issues relating to education, health, environment, agriculture, rural and community development. The contents are to be confined to social, cultural and local issues and the format, subject, presentation and language must reflect and exude the local flavour and fragrance.

Period of License

License will be granted for 3 years.

Fees

Since community radio broadcasting has to operate on non-commercial basis, no license fee is being charged. The licensee will be required to furnish a Bank Guarantee for a sum of Rs. 50,000 only, to ensure performance of the license agreement. The licensee will, however, be required to pay spectrum usage fee, as determined by the Wireless Advisor in WPC Wing of Ministry of Communications.

Benefits

- (*i*) Enhancing participation of the people in the development process.
- (*ii*) Capacity building in rural areas, through education.
- (*iii*) Providing opportunities to the people to upgrade their skills and enhance their creative talents.
- (*iv*) Preserving and promoting the traditional wisdom, knowledge and skills, thereby helping to promote and project the local language, arts, craft, culture and traditions.
- (*v*) Bring within easy reach of the rural population, topical

information in areas of agriculture, social welfare, education, health and environment.

(*vi*) Help in creating rural networks for the rural cottage and village industry.

Selection Procedure

Through open advertisement in a transparent manner from eligible educational institutions/organizations. The intending educational institutions need to apply for license, in the prescribed application form, in accordance with the guidelines for grant of licenses for Community Radio Stations.

Power and Cost of Community Radio

Maximum 50 watt transmitter power permitted with an antenna height of 30 meters above ground covering an area of about 5-10 km radius. One-time capital investment is estimated at around Rs. 8-10 lakh.

Execution of Project

Educational institutions can set up the Radio Station on their own or with the help of All India Radio or BECIL (Broadcast Engineering Consultants India Ltd.), a wholly owned PSU of this Ministry.

Inter-Ministerial Clearances Prior to Grant of Letter of Intent/ License

- Ministry of Home Affairs.
- Wireless Planning and Coordination (WPC), Ministry of Communications and Information Technology.
- Ministry of Human Resource Development.

Safeguards

1. Adherence to programme code of All India Radio. News and Current Affairs, election and political broadcasts are prohibited.
2. Government can revoke/terminate/suspend license, in case of violation of the terms and conditions of license.
3. Bank Guarantee of Rs. 50,000 to ensure timely performance.

4. To prevent overlap with private FM, the community radio stations will be non-commercial ventures—advertisements or sponsored programmes prohibited.
5. Preservation of records for 6 months, by the licensee.

Frequency

License will be issued in the shared frequency band from 87.5 to 100 MHz. However, in the event of frequency not being available in this band, the exclusive broadcast band of 104 to 108 MHz may also be considered, as in case of private FM broadcasters. The frequency band from 100 to 104 MHz, earmarked exclusively for the use of AIR, Prasar Bharati, will not be disturbed.

Implementation of the Decision on Community Radio

1. A public notice, inviting applications for grant of licenses for setting up Community Radio Stations has been issued, which has appeared in various daily newspapers, in the first fortnight of February, 2003.
2. The Ministry has received 55 applications from various educational institutions including universities, which are under active consideration in consultation with other Ministries.
3. WPC, Ministry of Communications and IT has earmarked frequencies to 17 applicants and accordingly letter of intent has been issued to 12 applicants whose applications have been cleared by Ministry of Home Affairs and Human Resource Development.
4. Country's first Community Radio Station has become operational since 1st February, 2004 at Anna University, Chennai, after grant of license by Ministry of Information and Broadcasting.

The Constraints

Though the idea was holistic and the approach positive, yet there were some apprehensions. One apprehension was regarding the ability and willingness of the educational institutions to come forward for the social cause of upliftment of the society and the communities at large. Another area of concern was in the context of the present security scenario of the country and the pluristic nature of our society. The issues of sustainability and the arithmetic of cost economics are equally important. The technical issues like efficient spectrum management; proper bandwidth usage and the receiver technologies hold the key to the growth of community radio in India. Last, but not the least is the need for the self-regulation and observance of the code of conduct for the content of the programmes to be broadcast.

Need for Policy Reforms

Incidentally, the present policy on community radio contained the element of mid-term course correction. To address the above issues, it is logical to attempt such a mid-term correction now. A Workshop on Community Radio provides a platform to share the experiences of other countries and organizations and to come out with a policy framework that takes into account all the issues raised above.

Ministry of Information and Broadcasting therefore proposes to organize a workshop on Community Radio in collaboration with UNDP and UNESCO, who can bring in the perspective of international experience in tackling such issues.

Purpose of the Workshop

To study and share the experience of other key stakeholders about successful community radio frameworks and practices as well as to identify and brainstorm on key issues of concern while formulating a national policy framework on Community Radio in India.

Organisers

Ministry of Information and Broadcasting with the support of UNDP, UNESCO, AIR, BECIL and PRIA.

Key Objectives

Effective policy instruments and regulatory mechanisms for India.

Issues to be Addressed

- Eligibility criteria—Broad basing the existing policy beyond educational institutions to other well-established social organizations working in the field of community development.

- Technical Issues—spectrum usage, band width, receiver technologies and value added services like radio browsing and convergence of technology etc.
- Procedures to ensure public notice and intervention concerning licenses and systems of public accountability.
- Programme content.
- Capacity Building for content generation.
- Linkage to local development planning.
- Security—the present day scenario and the possible safeguards.
- Sustainability and costs—various business models including sponsorship etc.
- Self-regulation/code of conduct—the need for self-restraint and shouldering the responsibility for self-regulation.

Participants

- Government of India: Ministry of Home Affairs, Ministry of Information and Broadcasting, Ministry of Defence, Ministry of External Affairs, Ministry of Environment and Forests, Ministry of Human Resource Development, Ministry of Communication and Information Technology, Ministry of Rural Development, Ministry of Agriculture, Ministry of Health and Family Welfare, Ministry of Social Justice and Empowerment, Ministry of Tribal Affairs.
- All India Radio, Prasar Bharati, IIMC.
- Multilateral and bilateral organizations: UNESCO, UNDP, UNICEF, UNFPA, DfID and World Bank.
- NGOs: Population Foundation of India, PRIA, KMVS, NFI, VOICES, Kalpvriksh, DDS and SWRC.
- Academics and experts working on CR.

Resource Persons

- Legal and policy experts—policy instruments and modalities of regulation.
- Practitioners—different models, addressing key concerns.

CITIZENS' CHARTER

This Charter is a declaration of our mission, values and standards and our commitment to achieve excellence in formulation and implementation of policies and procedures of this Ministry in order to strike a balance between the commercial needs and benefit of the public at large.

Our Services/Activities

- We play an effective role in empowerment of people by providing free flow of information through the mass communication media consisting of radio, television, films, press, publication, advertising and traditional modes of dance and drama.
- We cater to the vital needs of communication and entertainment of all sections of the Society.
- We are responsible for formulation of policies, rules, regulations and laws relating to information, broadcasting and film sectors.
- We interact with our foreign counterparts with a view to further international co-operation in the fields of broadcasting, films and print media.

Our Commitment

- Carry out tasks with integrity and judiciousness, courtesy and understanding, objectivity and transparency, promptness and efficiency.
- All officers/staff available during office hours.
- Speedy and timely redressal of grievances by creating friendly environment.
- Simplification and rationalization of the system for the beneficiaries under various welfare schemes.
- Transparency in working by creating an Internet based system.
- Simplification of procedure for reports and returns.
- Progressive increase in use of e-governance as a measure for improving efficiency of the Ministry.

Our Expectations

We expect Media Units, Attached and Subordinate Offices, PSUs under the control of the Ministry of Information and Broadcasting to be prompt and reasonable in discharging their duties and to be true and honest in furnishing information to us.

Media Units, Autonomous Organisations and Public Sector Undertakings

Media Units

Press Information Bureau (PIB)

- Acts as a nodal agency of the Government for disseminating information to the print/electronic media on government policies, programmes, initiatives and achievements through press releases, photographs, press conferences, interviews, press tours etc.
- Provides accreditation facility to media persons to enable them easy access to information from the Government sources.

Research Reference and Training Division (RR&TD)

- Functions as an information-serving agency for Ministry of Information and Broadcasting, its media units and their field offices.
- Serves as an information bank as well as an information feeder service to the media units to help in their programming and publicity campaigns.
- Studies trends in Mass Communication Media and maintains a reference and documentation service of Mass Communication.
- Provides background, reference and research materials and other relevant facilities relating to mass communication.
- Looks after the training aspect of the Indian Information Service (IIS) officers in collaboration with the Indian Institute of Mass Communication.
- It publishes annually "Reference Annual India".

Publications Division (PD)

- Publishes and sells books and journals at affordable prices on India's art and culture, land and people, biography, flora and fauna, ancient wisdom, works of reference, books for children.

- Some of the important journals published by the Division include Yojana, Kurukshetra, Employment News, Aajkal, Bal Bharati etc.
- Publishes speeches of prominent leaders.
- Published the largest series on Father of our Nation—"The Collected Works of Mahatma Gandhi"—in 100 volumes in English, out of which 87 volumes have been published in Hindi.
- Publishes the biographies of personalities in Hindi, English and Regional languages under Builders of Modern India (BMI) series who contributed to the growth and development of Modern India.

Photo Division

- Prepares photographs both in black and white and colour on the subjects pertaining to the growth and social changes in the country for documentation and for internal and external publicity on behalf of the Government of India.
- Supplies photographs on payment to non-publicity organisations and general public under Competitive pricing scheme.

Registrar of Newspapers for India (RNI)

- Verifies and approves titles of newspapers, registers them, checks and establishes circulation claims.
- Circulation claims of individual papers and Journals are also taken up on demand.
- Publishes *PRESS IN INDIA* containing detailed information on print media.
- Issues eligibility certificates for import of foreign and purchase of indigenous newsprint from specified mills as well as essentiality certificates for import of printing machinery etc., for use by registered publications.

Directorate of Field Publicity (DFP)

- Plays pivotal role in national cohesion and development

with the active involvement of people belonging to different strata of society, especially the weaker sections by using a variety of communication modes including group discussions, public meetings, seminars, symposia and competitions of various kinds.

- Organizes publicity campaign on women's empowerment, healthcare, prevention of diseases, awareness of AIDS, population hazards, promotion of blood donation etc.

Song and Drama Division (S&DD)

- Organises Information Communication Techonology activities in hilly, tribal, desert, sensitive and border areas.
- Organises sound and light shows and presenting theatrical shows on national/social themes in consultation with nodal Ministry.
- Caters entertainment requirements of the Armed Forces in most inhospitable and remote border areas.

Directorate of Advertising and Visual Publicity (DAVP)

- Acts as the primary multi-media advertising agency of the central government.
- Caters information and education to the people, both rural and urban, about the government's policies and programmes and motivates them to participate in development activities.
- Endeavours to make aware the common mass about the national integration and communal harmony, rural development programmes, health and family welfare, women empowerment, girl child upliftment, population control, new economic measures, small savings, consumer affairs, literacy, employment, AIDS, Income Tax, Defence, Environment, energy conservation, handicraft etc.

Films Division

- Educates and motivates people for their active support and participation in the implementation of national programmes to uplift the national image and to project the national heritage.

- Produces documentaries, short films, animation films and newsmagazines having significance in the field of information, communication and integration.

Directorate of Film Festivals (DFF)

- Provides platform for the best in Indian cinema by organizing the National Film Awards, the Indian Panorama and the International Film Festivals of India every year.
- Promotes cultural understanding and friendship at international level.
- Makes latest trends in world cinema accessible to the public within the country.

National Film Archive of India (NFAI)

- Traces, acquires and preserves for posterity, the heritage of Indian cinema.
- Classifies documents data and undertakes research relating to films.
- Acts as a centre for dissemination of film culture.

Central Board of Film Certification (CBFC)

- Responsible for certifying the films produced in India as well as outside the country suitable for public exhibition.
- Gives four categories of certificates "U" for unrestricted public exhibition, "A" for public exhibition restricted to adults only, "UA" for unrestricted public exhibition with parental guidance for children below the age of 12 and "S" for exhibition to restricted audience such as doctors etc. These certificates are issued through the Regional Offices of the Board located at Bangalore, Kolkata, Chennai, Cuttack, Guwahati, Hyderabad, Mumbai, New Delhi and Thiruvananthapuram.
- Appeal against the decision of the Board lies with the Film Certification Appellate Tribunal.

Autonomous Organisations: Prasar Bharati

All India Radio (AIR)

- AIR's network provides radio coverage to 97.3 per cent of

the population and reaches 90 per cent of the total area of the country. It comprises the National Channel, Regional Stations, Local Radio Stations, Vividh Bharati Centres, FM Stereo Service, External Services and North-Eastern Services.

- Educates, entertains and provides information for enrichment of lives of the people.
- Provides information through news and current affairs programmes and entertainment through Music—devotional, classical (Indian & Western) Folk/Pop/Light, Film songs etc.
- Provides live service on the Internet on a regular 24 hours basis for coverage of AIR programmes to all parts of the world including USA and Canada, where signals of AIR External Service are not received adequately.

Doordarshan (DD)

- One of the largest broadcasting organisations in the world in terms of the infrastructure of studios and transmitters, the variety of software and the vastness of the viewership.
- Accessible to more than 87 per cent of population of the country through a network of nearly 1044 terrestrial transmitters and 19 channels—two All India Channels, 11 Regional Languages Satellite Channels (RLSC), four State Networks (SN), an International Channel and a Sports Channel. About 46 Doordarshan Studios are producing TV software.
- On DD-1 National programmes, Regional programmes and Local programmes are carried on time-sharing basis. Metro Entertainment Channel carries Network programmes from Delhi and also Single-Metro Programmes from the four metro cities.
- The Regional Languages Satellite channels have two components—The Regional service for the particular state relayed by all terrestrial transmitters in the state and additional programmes in the Regional Language in prime time and non-prime time available only through cable operators.

Press Council of India (PCI)

- A statutory autonomous body established for the purpose of preserving the freedom of the press, and of maintaining and improving the standards of newspapers and news agencies in India.
- Deliberates on the complaints received either by the press or against the press and is empowered to make observation in respect of conduct of any authority including the Government.
- If it is considered necessary, it can warn, admonish or censure the newspaper, news agency, the editor or the journalist or disapprove the conduct of the editor or the journalist. The decision of the Council cannot be questioned in any court of law.

Film and Television Institute of India (FTII)

- Member of the International Liaison Centre of Cinema and TV School (CILECT).
- Provides latest education and technological experience in the art and technique of film-making and television production.
- Provides in-service training to officers of all grades of Doordarshan.
- Provides excellent exposure to the faculty and students of film and television with the latest digital and broadcast grade production set up.

Satyajit Ray Film and Television Institute (SRFTI)

- Imparts practical and theoretical training in all aspects of film and television programme conception and production including introduction to allied fields.
- Grants certificates, diplomas, honours diplomas and such other certificates, advanced diplomas as may be instituted by the Governing Council to the trainees on successful completion of prescribed courses of study.
- Co-ordinates the activities of education and skill development in the field of film and television programme conception and production.

Indian Institute of Mass Communication (IIMC)

- Runs courses with the objective to produce well-equipped communication professionals sensitive to needs of changing mass communication scenario.
- Conducts short-term specialized courses to meet the professional training needs of media personnel working in the Central/State Governments and Public Sector Organisations.
- Organizes seminars, symposia and conferences on various themes of communication with a view to contributing better understanding of communication in the context of India and other developing countries.
- Provides consultancy services on request to Central/State Government Departments and Public Sector Undertakings, and helps in designing and organizing training and research programmes related to Development communication.
- Publishes seminar reports, research studies, teaching material and books related to various aspects of communication.
- Publishes the quarterly journals like *Communicator in English & Sanchar Madhyam in Hindi* based on the Institute's academic works as well as on major issues in the field of communication.

Children's Film Society, India (CFSI)

- Provides value-based entertainment to the children and young people through the medium of films.
- Organizes Mini Film Festivals and CFSI's International Children's Film Festivals.

Public Sector Undertakings

Nation Film Development Corporation Limited (NFDC)

- Plans, promotes and organizes an integrated and efficient development of the Indian Film Industry keeping in view the economic policy and objectives laid down by the Government from time to time.

- Encourages the concept of low-budget films, quality contents and thematic values by funding/producing.

Broadcast Engineering Consultants India Limited (BECIL)

- Provides consultancy services in the field of Acoustics, Audio, Video, MMDS, Digital Satellite Contribution links etc.
- Executes several turn key jobs such as design/installation of Sound Reinforcement System, Audio Announcement Management System for Airports, integration and supply of Satellite Receiving Terminal, design and installation of Video Compression System for satellite uplink in India as well as abroad.
- At present, the company is run by a Board of Directors.

Prominent Schemes/Services Meant for Citizens Provided by the Various Media Units of Ministry of Information and Broadcasting are Given in the Following Table:

Name of the Media Unit/Organisation Under Ministry of Information and Broadcasting	*Schemes/Services Provided to the Citizens*
(1)	*(2)*
Film and Television Institute of India	Teaching/Training Courses in Film and Television
Indian Institute of Mass Communication	Teaching Courses in Jornalism, Advertising and Public Relation
Children's Film Society of India	Production of feature films, TV Serials and Short Films Purchase of Films Dubbing and subtitling of films
Prasar Bharati (Doordarshan)	Commercial Bookings, Sponsered Programmes and Commissioned Programmes
National Film Development Corporation	Film Finance and Production Import and Distribution of Films in India Export of Films Technical Services for Pre/Post-Production of Films Cine Artist Welfare Fund Panorama Films
Press Information Bureau	Accredition to Media Representatives

(*Contd.*)

(1)	*(2)*
Publications Division	Production and Sale of Books on Art, History, Culture etc. Publication and Sale of Journals viz. Employment News: Yojna, Kurukshetra, Aajkal and Bal Bharati Production and Sale of CDs on Collected Works of Mahatma Gandhi
Registrar of Newspapers for India	Title Verification Registration of Newspapers Verification of Circulation Claims Issue of eligibility certificate for import of Newsprint Issue of essentiality certificate for import of printing machinery and allied material.
Directorate of Advertising and Visual Publicity	Empanelment of Printers Empanelment of Producers for Audio Video productions Empanelment of Newspapers/Periodicals for the purpose of release of advertisements Empanelment of Outdoor Publicity Agencies
Films Division	Sale of Stock Shots Sale of Video Cassettes of Films Produced by Films Division Entering of Agreements with the Theatre Owner for Screening of Approved Films Lending of Video Theatres and Premises of Gulshan Mahal on Rental Basis Conducting of Biennial International Film Festival for Documentary, Short and Animation Films Hiring of Equipments at Prescribed Rates Loaning of Print Films Made by Films Division to Schools/Colleges, Societies for Non-Commercial Exhibitions

(*Contd.*)

(1)	(2)
Directorate of Film Festivals	Participation of Film Makers in the India Panorama Section of Internation Film Festival of India Participation of Film Makers in the National Film Awards Hiring of Sirifort Auditoria for the public on rental basis for events
Song and Drama Division	Registration of Private Cultural Troupe and Empanelment of Performing and Back Stage Artistes.

Redressal of Grievances

This Ministry is sensitized to redress grievances received from public and employees directly or through Department of Administrative Reforms and Public Grievances in a responsible and effective manner through the following:

- A Grievance Cell under the chairmanship of Joint Secretary (Administration) has been set in the Main Ministry.
- Complaint Committee has been constituted to deal with the complaints of sexual harassment of female employees in the Ministry of Information and Broadcasting.
- Similar Cells have been set up in all the attached and subordinate offices.
- Citizen's Charter has been formulated by all the Media Units/Autonomous Organisation/Public Sector Undertakings under the control of this ministry.
- E-mail address of the Grievances Cell of the Ministry has already been registered for grievance monitoring. The e-mail address of the Public Grievance Cell is: jsp@sb.nic.in.

The Citizen's Charter will be reviewed annually for further improving our response to the public.

Time Frame of Redressal of the Grievances

Sl. No.	*Subject*	*Time*
1.	Issue of acknowledgement/interim reply to the petitioner	2 weeks
2.	Forwarding of the grievances/petition to the concerned authority	2 weeks
3.	Final disposal of transferred/referred cases by the concerned Ministry/Department/State and time limit for informing the position of the outcome	3 months
4.	Cases referred to Complaint Committee on "Sexual Harassment of Women at workplace"	3 months

Information Facilitation Counter

An Information Facilitation Centre has been set up for providing the following services to the public:

- Receive the public, reply to their queries and direct them to concerned Officer / Section.
- Provide information regarding various schemes and procedures through brochures, booklets, reports etc.
- Forms that are to be utilised for various procedures are made available.
- Provide information regarding the functioning of the Ministry.

Ministry of Information and Broadcasting—Important Telephone Numbers

Main Secretariat

1.	Minister of Information and Broadcasting, 'A' Wing, Shastri Bhawan, New Delhi–110001.	011-2338 4782/2338 4340/ 2338 6892
2.	Minister of State, Information and Broadcasting, 'A' Wing, Shastri Bhawan, New Delhi–110001.	011-23381074/2338 4894
3.	Secretary, 'A' Wing, Shastri Bhawan, New Delhi–110001.	011-2338 2639
4.	Joint Secretary (Admn. & PG), Room No. 657, 'A' Wing, Shastri Bhawan, New Delhi–110001.	011-2338 3857
5.	Director (C) & Chairperson of Complaint Committee on "Sexual Harassment of Women at Workplace", Room No. 556, 'A' Wing, Shastri Bhawan, New Delhi–110001.	011-2338 4484
6.	Deputy Secretary (Admn.) & Liaison Officer for SC/ST, Room No. 553, 'A' Wing, Shastri Bhawan, New Delhi–110001.	011-2338 5592

Grievance Officers of Media Units, Autonomous Organisations and PSUs

1.	Director of Programmes (PP&D), Directorate General: All India Radio, Room No.115, Akashwani Bhawan, Sansad Marg, New Delhi-110001.	011-2342 1542
2.	Deputy Director General (Admn.), Directorate General: Doordarshan, Room No. 510, Doordarshan Bhawan, Mandi House, New Delhi-110001.	011-2338 2093
3.	Additional Principal Information Officer, Press Information Bureau, Room No. 113(a), 'A' Wing, Shastri Bhawan, Dr. Rajendra Prasad Marg, New Delhi–110001.	011-2338 2127
4.	Regional Director, Directorate of Advertising and Visual Publicity, Room No. 16, 3rd Floor, PTI Building, Sansad Marg, New Delhi–110001.	011-2371 787
5.	Joint Director (Admn.), Publications Division (DPD), Room No. 122, Patiala House, Tilak Marg, New Delhi–110001.	011-2307 3015
6.	Deputy Press Registrar, Office of the Registrar of Newspapers for India, West Block-8, Wing No. 2, R.K. Puram, New Delhi–110066.	011-2610 6251
7.	Joint Director (M), Directorate of Field Publicity, East Block IV, Level III, R.K. Puram, New Delhi–110066.	011-2610 4475
8.	Deputy Director (S&L), Song & Drama Division, Room No. 929, Soochna Bhawan, C.G.O. Complex, Lodi Road, New Delhi–110003.	011-2436 3509
9.	Joint Director, Research, Reference and Training Division, Room No. 402, 'B' Wing, Shastri Bhawan, Dr. Rajendra Prasad Marg, New Delhi-110001.	011-2338 4844
10.	Director, Photo Division, Soochna Bhawan, C.G.O. Complex, Lodi Road, New Delhi–110003.	011-2436 2384
11.	Chief Producer, Films Division, Films Bhawan, 24 Dr. Gopalrao Deshmukh Marg, Mumbai–400026.	022-2386 4633
12.	Chairman, Central Board of Film Certification, Bharat Bhavan, 91E, Walkeshwar Road, Mumbai–400006.	022-2363 1048
13.	Deputy Director (Admn.), Directorate of Film Festival, Siri Fort Cultural Complex, August Kranti Marg, New Delhi–110049.	011-2649 9370
14.	Deputy Director-cum-Curator, National Films Archive of India, Law College Road, Pune-411004.	0952-5659487

(*Contd.*)

15.	Professor of Music, Film and Television Institute of India, Law College Road, Pune–411 004.	020-543 0416 Extn. 277
16.	Administrative Officer, Children's Film Society, India, Films Division Complex, 24, Dr. Gopalrao Deshmukh Marg, Mumbai–400026.	022-2380 8592
17.	Manager, National Film Development Corporation Limited, "Discovery of India", Nehru Centre, Dr. Anne Besant Road, Worli, Mumbai–400018.	022-2492 9096
18.	Registrar, Indian Institute of Mass Communication, Aruna Asaf Ali Marg, JNU New Campus, New Delhi–110007.	011-2610 9268/ 2618 9925
19.	Deputy Secretary, Press Council of India, Faridkot House (Ground Floor), Copernicus Marg, New Delhi–110001.	011-238 1726
20.	Registrar, Satyajit Ray Film & Television Institute, E.M. Bye Pass Road, P.O. Panchsayar, Kolkata–700094.	033-2432 8355
21.	Controller of Accounts, Principal Accounts Office, Tropical Building, Connaught Circus, New Delhi-110001.	011-23323151
22.	Director (Operation & Marketing), Broadcast Engineering Consultants India Limited, B-1, Sector-31, Noida–201301 (UP).	0120-245 8034

Broadcasting Policy and Administration

All matters relating to radio and television broadcasting within the Union including regulation of the use of All India Radio and Doordarshan by recognised national and regional political parties during elections to the Lok Sabha and State Assemblies and procedure to be followed by the official electronic media during periods of national mourning on the demise of a high dignitary.

The enunciation and implementation of the law relating to radio and television broadcasting in India by private Indian companies or Indian nationals.

Broadcast Monitoring and Administration of the Prasar Bharati (Broadcasting Corporation of India) Act, 1990 (25 of 1990).

All matters relating to the Indian Broadcasting (Programme) Service and the Indian Broadcasting (Engineering) Service until they are handed over to Prasar Bharati.

Cable Television Policy

Cable Television Networks (Regulation) Act, 1995 (7 of 1995).

Radio

All business connected with All India Radio embracing news services in the home programmes, programmes for the foreign countries and Indians overseas, radio journals, research in the field of broadcasting engineering, monitoring of foreign broadcasts, programme exchange and transcription services, supply of community receiving sets to State Governments under the community listening scheme, etc.

Development of Radio Broadcasting throughout the Union, installation and maintenance of Radio Stations and Transmitters and operation of broadcasting services.

Doordarshan

Exchange including cultural exchange of television programmes.

Development of television throughout the Union, including installation, maintenance and operation of television programme production centres and Transmitters, and operation of television services.

Promotion of production of television programmes outside Doordarshan.

Films

Legislation under entry 60 of the Union List, viz., 'Sanctioning of Cinematograph films for exhibition'.

Administration of the Cinematograph Act, 1952 (37 of 1952).

Import of feature and short films for theatrical and non-theatrical viewing.

Export of Indian films, both feature and short films.

Import of unexposed cinematograph films and various types of equipment required by the film industry.

All matters relating to film industry, including developmental and promotional activities thereto.

Promotion of good cinema by institution of State awards for films produced in India and assistance through the National Film Development Coporation Limited.

Production and distribution of documentaries and newsreels and other films and film strips for internal and external publicity.

Preservation of films and filmic materials.

Organisation of International Film Festivals in India and participation of India in International Film Festivals abroad.

Organisation of Film Festivals under Cultural Exchange Programmes.

Film society movement.

Advertising and Visual Publicity

Production and release of advertisements on behalf of the Government of India.

Press

Presentation and interpretation of the policies and activities of the Government of India through the medium of the press.

Advising Government on information problems relating to the Press, keeping Government informed of the main trends of public opinion as reflected in the Press and liaison between Government and the Press.

Publicity to and for the Armed Forces.

General conduct of Government relations with the Press excluding the administration of Sections 95 and 96 of the Code of Criminal Procedure, 1973 (2 of 1974).

Administration of the Press and Registration of Books Act, 1867 (25 of 1867) relating to Newspapers.

Administration of the Press Council Act, 1978 (37 of 1978).

Allocation of Newsprint to Newspapers.

Publications

Production, sale and distribution of popular pamphlets, books and journals on matters of national importance for internal as well as external publicity, with a view to imparting to the general public at home and abroad upto date and correct information about India.

Research and Reference

To assist the Media Units of the Ministry of Information and Broadcasting in collection, compilation and preparation of material involving research into published works, etc.

Building up of a compendium of knowledge on important subjects and to prepare guidance and background notes on current and other topics for the use of the Media Units of the Ministry.

Miscellaneous

Publicity for the policies and programmes of Government of India.

Administration of Journalists Welfare Fund.

Financial assistance to distinguished musicians, both vocal and instrumental, dancers and dramatists who have contributed substantially to the success of All India Radio and other units of the Ministry or their survivors in indigent circumstances.

All matters relating to the Asia-Pacific Broadcasting Union, Commonwealth Broadcasting Association and the Non-Aligned News Agency Pool.

Cadre management of the Indian Information Service (Groups 'a' and 'b').

Attached and Subordinate Organisations

(*a*) All India Radio.
(*b*) Doordarshan.
(*c*) Press Information Bureau.
(*d*) Directorate of Advertising and Visual Publicity.
(*e*) Publications Division.
(*f*) Office of the Registrar of Newspapers for India.
(*g*) Central Board of Film Certification.
(*h*) Films Division.
(*i*) Directorate of Film Festivals.
(*j*) National Film Archives of India.
(*k*) Directorate of Field Publicity.
(*l*) Song and Drama Division.
(*m*) Research, Reference and Training Division.
(*n*) Photo Division.
(*o*) Principal Accounts Office.
(*p*) Central Monitoring Service.

Autonomous Organisations

(*a*) Film and Television Institute of India, Pune.
(*b*) Satyajit Ray Film and Television Institute, Kolkata.
(*c*) Children Film Society of India.
(*d*) Indian Institute of Mass Communication.
(*e*) Press Council of India.
(*f*) Federation of Film Society of India.

Public Sector Undertaking

National Film Development Corporation Limited.
Broadcast Engineers Consultants (India) Limited.

3

Broadcasting for Rural Progress

The role of television and radio in education has been discussed in the previous section insofar as school children and university students are concerned. Similar claims are made for the part the electronic media can play in adult education though, in recent years, there is a growing awareness that broadcasting by itself can achieve little.

Social science has shown that broadcasting and other mass media can provide information, and affect listeners' tastes but by themselves they cannot change attitudes which lead to positive action. The mass media cannot win against traditional attitudes unless they are reinforced by personal influence. In all developing societies where traditions die hard broadcasting, controlled and run by educated, urban people has been less important in communications information and ideas to the villages than traditional village leaders and even bazaar gossip.

If broadcasting is used to support inter-personal communication it proves very effective, and, in several cases, man-to-man communication must have the help of broadcasting to be effective.

The media can bring timely information directly to people; they can inform them of new methods and devices and give them incentives to act in new ways. In the sphere of social reform, radio and television programmes can encourage socially progressive practices and attitudes in respect of marriage, child rearing, health and hygiene. They can also create the urge for a higher standard of living which can lead, firstly, to greater productivity, by the employment of modern techniques in agriculture and home industries, and, secondly, to more favourable attitudes to saving and investment in productive items and a reduction in wasteful expenditure on traditional ceremonies. So though broadcasting cannot do any of the essential tasks of village level workers, agriculture extension officers, malaria spraying teams or family planning and medical personnel, without it development plans and programmes would continue to suffer delays caused by lack of basic knowledge in the villages.

In the course of the last forty years, since rural broadcasting began, many farmers and their families scattered over the entire country have come to depend on AIR for information and entertainment. In some parts of the country the broadcasts have succeeded in changing agricultural practices to the advantage of the individual farmer and the country's agricultural production. Such success encourages one to hope that radio can be an agent for change and progress if properly used.

But while, in theory, the claims of broadcasters are valid it is in practice that the lofty aims are unfulfilled because of a variety of factors. From our own experience and that of other societies which have attempted to use radio and television for purposes other than entertainment, it is now acknowledged that certain conditions must be met if such broadcasts are not to fail.

The very first of these is that priorities must be clearly laid down. With scarce resources it is essential to concentrate on the most important targets and ignore others until such time as they can be considered. The primary consideration is to ensure that the benefits of whatever investment the community makes flow to the section of people who need them most. In this respect AIR's rural programmes have not been effective. Women and Harijans have not been allowed in many villages to be present when the community listening set is on. Studies show that it is only the middle-level farmers who derive benefit from the programmes. The illiterate find them too difficult to follow.

Perhaps the most important condition for success is the proper organisation of listening. When AIR started rural broadcasting radio sets were too expensive for individual farmers to own and listening at community sets alone was possible. Even today though one-band sets are available for about Rs. 120 they are well beyond the means of landless labourers and poor artisans.

As at present, State Governments buy, instal and maintain community receivers with the help of grants from the Union Government. Local communities also pay a small share of the cost. There are about 70,000 community receivers in all. Apart from the limited number of villages provided with sets there is the problem of maintenance. Most villages are unelectrified and battery operated sets have to be installed. The replacement of batteries and other repairs require on organisation which most States have not been able to achieve. In the States which have managed to set up a fairly efficient organisation the cost is extremely heavy as may be expected when government undertakes such an operation. The Vidyalankar Committee found that as many as 50 per cent of the total number of sets were not functioning on any given day.

It is not only the malfunctioning of sets that has made the scheme unworkable. People in the villages find it irksome to go to the *Panchayatghar* or the *Chaupal*, or wherever the set is installed, after a day's hard work to listen to the rather dull programmes to which the community sets are pretuned. They would rather listen on a neighbour's private set to Vividh Bharati.

The failure of community listening has been evident for a long time but AIR has been unable to scrap it and replace it with some more effective way of reaching the villages. The only alternative is to allow farmers and their families to listen in their homes to programmes of entertainment and education. This would be possible if the price of a radio set were within the means of the average farmer. The Report of the Committee on Broadcasting and Information Media has discussed at length the reasons for the high cost of radio sets in India and suggested how it can be brought down by reducing or abolishing taxes and duties now levied by government.

Experience has shown that broadcast programmes must be used in coordination with other media of communication to get results. Whether in adopting new agricultural practices or in accepting the idea of family planning, the broadcasts have to be reinforced by personal contacts with local opinion leaders and those who have accepted and adopted the new ideas and practices. Such contacts must be institutionalised by forming groups or forums in which new ideas can be discussed. But coordination of this kind requires great flexibility. Rigid institutions and organisations which cannot experiments with a variety of methods of reaching a desired goal cannot hope to succeed in using new technological devices.

In 1959 AIR started Radio Forums. It was felt that with the organisation of such Forums the rural programme would have a greater impact. The Forums were modelled on the Farm Radio Forums of Canada. They are organised listening groups of fifteen to twenty persons who listen together at a community set to bi-weekly programmes, directed specially to them, as part of the Rural Programme. After the broadcast the farmers are expected to discuss the information and suggestions contained in the programmes and to decide on a plan of action. It was believed that such action oriented discussion in the villages would result in many innovations being accepted which, otherwise, would not.

But the Forums too have become moribund. After the first flush of enthusiasm the collective listening has dwindled and with it the plans for action. No one knows how many are active though each State has a chief organiser of Forums to organise its activities in collaboration with the district officials.

The reasons for the failure of the Forums are not far to seek. AIR lacked the resources to operate so ambitious a programme covering the whole country. The villages lacked the leadership to conduct the discussions intelligently and effectively and AIR could not be expected to provide. The machinery for carrying the reactions of the Forums to the programme planners was weak. In Canada the Forums were the joint responsibility of the Canadian Broadcasting Corporation, the Canadian Broadcasting Federation of Agriculture and the Canadian Association for Adult Education. While the broadcasts were the responsibility of the broadcasting organisation, the other two provided the money for running offices to look after the Forums. A very elaborate system was evolved of planning the broadcast discussions and for reporting the findings. Unfortunately AIR could not afford anything like this organisation. Without a close contact between the radio station and the Forums their success was only partial at best.

Besides, it has been found that only forums with a homogenous membership can be successful. It is the farmers in the age-group 30-50 with a middle-school level education who are most keen on listening to radio programmes which would help them to improve their productivity and thus their standard of living. The poor and illiterate farmer fails to derive any benefit from the broadcasts. For him personal contact with the village level worker is the only effective medium for changing his ideas, attitudes and practices.

With the growth of TV, programmes for rural viewers around the TV centres have been started. They go out for thirty minutes or so twice or thrice a week. What has been their impact? The introduction of Krishidarshan in 1967 from Delhi for eighty villages around the capital was mentioned in the chapter on the growth of TV. It contains agricultural instruction for fifteen minutes thrice a week. There is also some suitable entertainment.

The first point of interest is that from the start of the programme only half the members of the teleclubs turned up to watch it and since then the number has steadily declined. Non-members also watch the programmes in limited numbers. In all there is an audience of ten to twenty persons. About a third of the total number of farmers in the village never watch Krishidarshan. Yet as many as four hundred people turn up to watch films and 'Chitrahar'. Why? The surveys indicate that the programmes are unsuitable. While some viewers understand technical language, English words and metric measures as many as 90 per cent of the women said they could not follow them. Secondly, TV sets are not kept in working order. A study in 1970 by ISRO found that on 13 per cent of the days when Krishidarshan is broadcast the sets were not working because of electric failure, minor flaws which could not be repaired, the operator was not available, and so forth. On the question of persuading farmers to adopt new techniques the studies are inconclusive.

Another study in Maharashtra produced similar findings. Out of about 250 villages with TV sets in the Pune district, fifty were visited during a period of one-and-a-half years from 1977-79. Most of them were revisited at least once during the same period to see if there was any change. It was found that TV sets were put on Sundays, Saturdays and Thursdays, on which dates film based programmes are telecast. Monday, Wednesdays and Fridays a special rural programme is telecast, but does not reach the villagers, as the sets are not put on. The rural chunk from Pune is rarely seen or heard by the community viewers. On the other hand, 'Chhaya Geet' and feature films are never missed.

When the custodians of the sets were asked why there was such poor attendance, they blamed the Gram Panchayats. But the plain fact is that no one is interested in the TV programmes meant for development. It can be assumed that the same pattern prevails in all the villages in the Pune district.

Obviously the custodians are not playing their part. They should inform Doordarshan why the rural programmes is not popular. It is not difficult to guess why.

Rural programmes have a very low priority in the output of a TV centre. Out of the entire programme in the month only 4 per cent is devoted to the rural viewer. All the rest are programmes for urban viewers. While the policy declared by the government is to make TV a rural medium, 96 per cent of the programmes are for the urban rich in languages which rural people cannot understand.

Even the 4 per cent broadcast for rural viewers are of agricultural achievements by the big farmers. There is very little of such topics as health, nutrition, sanitation, which would greatly help in improving life in the villages. Moreover, the programmes are all in the from of talks and discussions. Drama, folk music, folk dance, which would sustain interest are never attempted because they would cost money and would involve too much time being spent on them. In view of this, it is not surprising that the village viewer finds the programmes dull and irrelevant, and the TV set is turned off.

Obviously, the potential of TV could be realised only if the programmes are based on the needs of those they profess to serve in language which the people can understand.

It is also obvious that if TV is to be used as a medium for education and instruction, the custodians of community sets must be given a course in the mode of using the TV programmes. There should also be weekly briefs sent to the custodians about programmes to be telecast in the coming week or two. These could be inserted between some film based programmes so as to ensure that the custodians would be watching the screen.

Adequate investment of funds is essential for the success of broadcasts for education and development. If funds are spread too thinly over a variety of projects none is likely to succeed. Because technical equipment is more or less a fixed charge, the danger is that programme material will be starved of funds, but the best technical devices are of no avail of the messages they carry are vague, dull and ineffective.

The greatest weakness, in trying to manage with inadequate funds, arises in respect of personnel. Underdeveloped societies suffer from a shortage of qualified people in almost all fields. If inadequate remuneration keeps out the best qualified people, programme planning, production and presentation will be dull and therefore unsuccessful. Training of personnel assumes considerable importance in these circumstances, and the training cannot be of a general nature. It has to be related to the specific programme activity involved, because the requirements for educating children are not the same as those for instructing village women or farmers. Besides technicians it is necessary to train TV instructors and monitors for villages, field representatives versed in the techniques employed in the programmes, staff experts to recruit people, and research working and evaluators.

Continuous audience research is necessary to ensure the success of such programmes. Before they are launched there must be some form of pre-testing to ensure that the language, the format, the time, the duration, are appropriate. After they are launched the reactions of the audience have to be assessed periodically and regularly. If this had been done by AIR, the results of several of its educational and instructive programmes would have been far more rewarding. Research and evaluation are usually starved of funds. This is false economy in every sense.

Although rural broadcasts have been put out since 1936 there has been no systematic evaluation because AIR has no funds for such research. A few limited studies here and there are all there is to go on.

TV programmes for rural viewers have received more attention—the impetus came from SITE and the glamour of TV attracts many students of social science, communication and so forth.

It is now recognised the world over that educational broadcasts must use the local language and idiom and must be planned to meet local needs. It is not possible to centralise, even at the State capital, the planning and preparation of instructional material, whether for adults of children, if it is to be relevant in terms of the listeners' linguistic, cultural, social and religious background. The careful preparation of such material is one of the most important conditions for the success of the project. Without an interested, responsive human receiver at the other end no message can be learned or accepted. Nothing is less effective and more boring than a poorly produced educational programme.

Unfortunately, AIR has not, for a variety of reasons, been able to broadcast programmes for the rural community which are of local interest and this, combined with the weaknesses of the community listening scheme, is mainly responsible for the limited impact of its programmes.

From the start of rural broadcasting, programmes have been broadcast from the regional stations of AIR to cover an entire State or large areas in a State. Starting with broadcasts from Peshawar for the N-WFP, the Delhi station introduced in 1936.

As new station came up the same pattern was repeated and continues more or less unchanged to this day. The programmes contain news and the broadcasts are, for many in the rural areas, the only source of news, market and weather reports, which are useful for the farming community. Entertainment in the form of folk music and film music and plays are popular. But it is difficult to say how effective the instructional content of the programmers has been. Research has been haphazard and very limited. Such findings as are available indicate that radio is behind other media in influencing farmers to adopt new techniques of farming. Demonstration and personal contact with village level workers are far more important than listening to the radio.

To some extent this because the programmes are not always very lovely even though some of them are very good; to some extent, because in the absence of satisfactory organisation and coordination, the broadcasts are not accompanied by or followed up by personal visits by village level workers or agricultural extension workers; and to some extent because the content of most programmes is of general interest and not related specifically to the needs of the farming community.

Realising this in 1966, AIR initiated Farm and Home broadcasts. At AIR headquarters and at several station Farm and Home Units have been formed to provide information and advice on fertilisers, pesticides, implements, seeds and other items of interest to farmers through the rural programmes of stations located in the intensive agricultural development areas.

It was necessary to give farmers intensive education and assistance in adopting the improved practices in their own fields. The broadcasts differed from the earlier ones because they gave technical information, for day-to-day farming operations, which was supplied by specialists and extension workers and was related to the needs of small farming communities in the vicinity of the stations. The Units were also required to record discussions and interviews with farmers for broadcast in the rural programmes and to obtain from them suggestion for the future planning of the broadcasts.

As a result of staff shortages the intention of broadcasting programmes which were mostly field-based has not been fulfilled.

The high cost of petrol makes it still more difficult to collect recordings from the villages and so the programmes will continue to be mainly studio-based, consisting of talks by "experts". All the same, some studies reveal that the Farm and Home Broadcasts are popular with semi-educated farmers who listen to the agricultural advice they obtain as it helps them to increase productivity and earn more from their farms.

The title "Farm and Home" would imply that the Units must give some thought to the home in urban and rural areas and to the women who run these homes but, in fact, this side of their activity has been neglected. The broadcast of programmes in health and hygiene in the rural programme can of course be heard by women as well as men but it has been noticed that women do not go to the community listening sets when the men are collected there and they find the evening hour inconvenient. Special programmes for rural women are broadcast once or twice a week during the rural programme for thirty minutes from some stations but not from all. There are no funds either to increase their frequency or to extend the broadcast to every station.

With "Farm and Home" broadcasts it could be said that AIR has taken the first step towards broadcasting material of local interest to small farming communities in place of the omnibus programmes it has broadcast hitherto, but unless the broadcast of programmes shifts to the districts the programmes cannot be "local" in the proper sense.

Even countries which do not have to make a massive effort for development are turning to local radio. The UK started some years ago but the USA has had local broadcasting for many years. Every small town has its own station. It is an Australia that such local station have been set up with the primary aim of serving the rural community. The new station were "expected to combine popular programming with fostering a greater public awareness of local affairs and involvement in the community."

Ordinary citizens were expected to acquire a new and effective channel for their views, demands and grievances. The stream of local news would keep people informed about the issues and policies affecting their lives, supplemented by special investigations into particular matters of local concern. There would be a permanent arena for discussion and debate about local issues. Its local news service, always seen as a key element in its output, would contribute greatly progress towards local democracy.

Everywhere it is now recognised that the development of centralised systems of mass communication is useless unless regional and local systems of communication are developed. Such local systems have to reflect local life but also show how local problems are connected with events in the community of the State, the country and even the world.

In India we have found that programmes broadcast from regional stations in the language or dialect most widely spoken by rural people in that State leaves many listeners unapproached. With the diversity of languages in our country there may have to be programmers in half a dozen languages or dialects in any one State.

One centralised programme is irrelevant to the needs of many parts of the State. Farmers like programmes which tell them what to do and how to do it in the form of informal conversations or questions and answers. Such broadcasts can only be planned and transmitted locally for each homogeneous agricultural region with a common language, common crop, similar weather conditions, marketing facilities and so forth. The farmers' preference for field-based programmes has been noted earlier. This cannot be met from the studios of the regional station. Nor can the stations afford the transport for covering all the distracts for such field-based programmes. A local radio station could get farmers and others to come to it for recording their views, suggestions and questions.

Small-scale television has become possible in technological terms with the development of VTR Portapak units and time-base correctors which enable language video to be used for making programmes away from a studio, for editing and transmission at minimum cost.

On the other hand, the technical standards adopted nationally and internationally tend towards ever higher technical and production standards. These call for high-cost sophisticated equipment, which implies a minimum capital cost per station, and reliance on network programming. The service area has to be large enough to justify the station's existence or make a profit. But the resulting service area is too large to allow a station adequately to reflect the needs of small communities within it.

Fifteen years ago, the Committee on Information and Broadcasting popularly known as the Chanda Committee, studied the failure of communication with the rural people. It found that there were few listeners for the rural programmes and this was mainly because the local needs of the vast audience of about 450 million people, living in 550 thousand villages, had not and could not be met by a conventional urban based, professionally staffed broadcasting system. It concluded that two important, radical changes were needed in the reception and broadcast of programmes for the rural people.

First, the community listening scheme must be abandoned as Governments in the various States of the Indian Union had failed to organise and operate the scheme satisfactorily. Listening in rural areas should move from the community set to the village home through one-band radio receivers which could be made much cheaper by adopting the correct industrial and fiscal policies.

Secondly, the broadcast of the programmes must be over low-power transmitters located in the countryside at the headquarters of each of India's 400 districts, each serving about one or two million people. This would ensure that the programmes would be relevant to the specific problems of people in comparatively small areas. Such station would allow centrally planned messages about development to be modified or added to as may be appropriate for each community. They would provide for local inputs without which centrally-planned messages fail to evoke the desired response.

The duration of the daily service would depend on local needs but if programmes for farmers and their families are to be meaningful they must be for at least three or four hours a day, at times most convenient for the community, and should provide information and advice relevant to the needs. Programmes would vary from district to district but some massage would be common to all. The Government's plans for promoting family planning, for improving sanitation and health, for increasing agricultural productivity, for non-formal education for adults, for literacy and basic education for children, for stimulating innovation and enterprise in traditional and new crafts, for discouraging custom and attitudes which hinder economic and social progress, all these and others would find a place in the broadcasts.

News could be prepared specially at each local station to satisfy local interest. The present news bulletins in the rural services of AIR are not tailored to rural requirements either in terms of language or content. Operators of small town radio stations in the USA, Australia and elsewhere find that comprehensive local news coverage is the single most attractive programme which makes listeners forsake the national networks in favour of their local station. Village folk are interested in district developments and the activities of the Taluka Panchayat Samiti and not in those of the remote Legislative Assemblies and the even-remoter Lok Sabha. They want news of development work in co-operation, rural industries, irrigation, the construction of village roads, a new bus service, personalised stories of achievements of individual farmers, problems of land-holders and agricultural labourers, irrigation rates, and all those things that affect their lives. A local station can collect such news from district officials, panchayats, social workers, teachers, traders, and others and also give timely warning of flooding of roads, breakdowns in the bus service, and so forth.

Local broadcasting alone can ensure co-ordination with district authorities and with extension services to guarantee follow-up action and to make available the inputs discussed in the programmes. It is hardly possible, at the State capital, for AIR to plan programmes in consultation with extension workers and to effect coordination with district personnel in the veterinary, agriculture, forestry, health and other departments.

The local station must appeal to voluntary effort. In place of professional standards and bureaucratic rules and regulations there has to be a unofficial atmosphere and a spirit of experimentation. The programmes should be initiated by the community and the staff has to be small and flexible as it used to be even in the old established broadcasting stations in their pioneering days. This would make it possible for one or two professional broadcasters to run a station with the help of local volunteers. Village extension workers, young people, women, the elderly, those with little or no formal education, could all be employed as volunteers with, possibly, a small honorarium. The main duty of the professional staff would be to train the volunteers and coordinate their work.

When rural people begin to communicate within their community they acquire self-confidence which encourages them to articulate their own needs and those of their community.

It would be unrealistic to expect that community stations could be run by the established broadcasting organisation which caters for the population as a whole. The objectives and methods are so different that any attempt to combine the services will most certainly hinder the growth of the community stations.

These would have to be quite different from the conventional broadcasting station in India and elsewhere with its sophisticated and expensive equipment. The technology employed has to be the simplest and most economical: a low-power transmitter; one or two improvised studios, without complicated equipment; mobile, light-weight type-recorders and playback equipment; a bicycle or two to supplement public transport; a good radio receiver to receive news and programmes of entertainment to be relayed from one of the urban centres. High technical standards would have to be abandoned. Who, then, should be responsible for community radio?

The ownership and control of each station by the local community, as in the United States or Canada, may not be possible in India and other developing societies for some time because of the poverty of the people. But if local stations are to yield results, decisions on programmes and policies must be made by the listeners and the volunteers, assisted by the professional staff, while the ownership of the stations may be diversified. Such stations can be set up by any group or institution and can be licensed by the government on certain conditions. These would ensure that the station is to be used in the community's interest, that it would provided a certain amount of educational and instructive programming and so forth. A local authority, an agricultural university, a co-operative society, a band of social workers or educationists, and many other such groups of citizens could be allowed to operate community stations. At present the Government of India, like many other governments, has a monopoly of broadcasting and refuses permission to start even closed-circuit radio and television services.

The question of finance is difficult. Some funds could be obtained from advertising appropriate items of rural consumption such as bicycles, tortures, radio sets, clothing, soap, detergents, disinfectants, nutritious food stuffs, simple drugs and so forth. As the stations would help to achieve several national goals in education, health, family planning, and economic development, it would be quite appropriate for government to provide funds at least for the capital investment in transmitters and equipment. If such funds are made available through a properly constituted authority it could supervise their use. To prevent government interference in the work of the authority and of the community stations the funds would have to be allotted to the authority for several years at a time, through the Finance Commission or some such body. The authority itself should not interfere in the day-to-day working of the stations.

If the community radio station is to be a community effort the authority should not establish stations without a demand from the community and a promise of its active involvement; it can stimulate such interest and guide the efforts of the local community or suitable organisations to set up a station; it can help to obtain the required capital and the professional staff but, for the rest, it should be responsible only for the overall performance of the station which can be reviewed at the time of renewing the license.

This is looking too far in to the future. The immediate need is to encourage the starting of independent local stations wherever some individuals or organisations are capable of doing so with some financial assistance. Experiments with different kinds of control, staffing and financing should be allowed to find out which mix would be the most rewarding. All India Radio is going in for local stations—six have been sanctioned by the Planning Commission during the Sixth Plan—these should co-exist with a few independent ones until, after some years' experience, all the local stations can be brought under one authority which could then organise the extension of the service to every district in India where the people are willing to give voluntary service for their community station.

It is a question of priorities. If the Government of India is convinced that communication with the people and their willing cooperation is essential for progress and national development, the money and the equipment can be found to take radio to the people.

Finally, the relative merits of radio and TV must be assessed in respect of every programme of this type. There is a growing feeling in India and outside that radio is being neglected even for tasks it can perform as well as if not better than TV, and at considerably lower cost. Nearly 80 per cent of our population can be served by radio if an abundant number of cheap radio sets is made available. While there are already over 200 million radio receivers, we produce about two million each year. There are already 70,000 community receivers and 20,000 schools sets, too few for a country of our size but certainly far more than the TV sets and service we can expect to provide for some years to come.

A telecommunication system to serve the less developed countries effectively must be cheap and reliable and should not require highly sophisticated maintenance and operating personnel. It should function even without an elaborate infrastructure of a stable electric supply, good roads and a network of microwave cable. We have the infrastructure for radio technology; we do not have it for TV and will not have it for decades. In other developing countries TV has remained an entertainment for the rich. Experience in Algeria, Brazil and other Third World countries shows that when sophisticated technology is introduced into a static tradition-bound social environment, it does not work.

Of course, there are some things TV can do better but surely the cost factor is important for a poor country like ours. The point is that serious cost-benefit studies must be undertaken before it is decided which medium to use for any purpose.

Without attempting any such studies the Government of India has decided that TV would be more effective than radio. If 500,000 villages are to be provided with TV sets how much will it cost? Radio sets on the other hand, which cost ten times less, can be provided in every village though the proper thing to do is to reduce their cost or subsidise their sale so that private sets can spread throughout the village homes.

To provide radio programmes for village we need about 400 low-power district transmitters—all of which can be produced in India. Local TV transmitters would cost a fortune. But, say the protagonists of TV, we do not need local TV transmitters—the satellite will take TV programmes everywhere. And that brings us up against the question whether, where TV is to be used, it should be through satellite or through terrestrial stations.

Although INSAT (1A) is no longer available, INSAT (1B) has become operative from August 1983 and presumably the plans for the use of INSAT (1A) will be carried forward. In the chapter on the Growth of TV, the use of satellite technology has been discussed in general. Here its utility for broadcasts for the rural community is assessed. According to the plans announced by the Minister for Information and Broadcasting, a one hour programme will be broadcast daily for a few hundred direct receiving sets which will be increased to 2,000 by the end of the Sixth Plan. There would be 2,000 community viewing sets.

To begin with, the Ministry of I & B had intended to provide 1,00,000 DRS—the least required to justify the claim that the satellite would revolutionise life in the village of India but financial constraints reduced the number of 8,000 by the end of the Sixth Plan 8,000 out of 500,000 villages.

There are far more serious problems, first of all, the difficulty of providing suitable and effective programmes for rural audiences through a satellite have to be examined. Apart from experience in other parts of the world, our own SITE showed up certain glaring shortcomings of satellite communication.

Due to the extremely limited time available for TV programmes and with only two channels, the rural programmes, even for only a few villages, can only be of half-an-hour's duration per day in the language of the area. The remaining half hour is in Hindi. Hardly sufficient to sustain interest.

"Secondly, the programmes made at two or three centres at Hyderabad, Cuttack and Nagpur for six villages in six different States could not cater to the special needs of the different groups of villages. During SITE it was found that programmes prepared in Delhi in Hindi for villages in Rajasthan, Bihar and Madhya Pradesh failed to make any impact. This is because our village folk speak in dialect and not the language of the city.

Thirdly, the cost of satellite communication cannot be justified if the village audience finds the programmes irrelevant.

Fourthly, there was the difficulty of maintenance of the Direct Reception TV sets. Although the Indian Space Research Organisation was responsible for their maintenance, there were frequent breakdowns. What will the position be when the State Governments or local bodies are made responsible for the maintenance of the sets? AIR's experience of the very poor maintenance of community radio receivers, much simpler to maintain, should cause concern but such difficult questions are brushed aside in the hope that they will disappear!

And finally, programmes of local interest and relevance cannot possibly be transmitted through a satellite. The multiplicity of languages and cultural patterns makes locally relevant programming for a satisfactory duration an imperative. To say a satellite can illuminate the whole of India does not mean satisfying programmes in all languages. Only programmes centrally planned and produced can be fed to the satellite. Therefore, it has to be decided in advance how many terrestrial stations Doordarshan must necessarily have regardless of the satellite.

For all these reasons professional broadcasters consider such technology entirely unsuitable for India's communication needs.

Local radio stations and possibly some local TV stations are what we require. Some students or the subject have suggested that the failure of INSAT (IA) should be turned to our advantage by using the terrestrial transmitters for local broadcasts. They also feel that the acquisition of a third satellite INSAT (1C) would be totally indefensible because in a country of India's size, a hook-up programme is about all that the satellite can provide. If government can be brought to give up its satellite mania, it would realise that low-power TV transmitters which cost less than Rs. 20 lakhs, can cover 300-500 sq kms. One Direct Reception Set (DRS) costs Rs. 30,000. One local transmitter would cost only as much as about sixty-five DRS which can serve only sixty-five villages with all the disadvantages mentioned above.

A hundred ordinary TV receivers cost about Rs. 30,00,000. So the cost of a local station serving 100 villages or so would be only Rs. 50 lakhs. Moreover, local terrestrial transmitters would enable individual homes in urban and rural areas within the range to have TV receivers of their own to pick up the programmes. It is still not too late to reconsider the question afresh.

Two things stand out in this brief review and analysis of rural broadcasting. Firstly, unless listening on radio and TV is extended to many millions more of the people who live in our rural areas the impact of rural broadcasting will be limited. Secondly, unless the programmes are made meaningful to small rural communities by dealing with their specific conditions and problems, ascertained through continuous research, they will continue to be regarded as something imposed from above and will not become a vital force in the regeneration of rural life.

TELEVISION AS AN INSTRUMENT OF SOCIAL CHANGE IN INDIA AND ABROAD

The antennas on the roof tops are increasing day by day all over the world. Today there is scarcely a country which is not utilising television with a view to achieving its cultural, social, political and economic development. TV gives information by transmitting programmes through space satellites to and from people all over the world. Media men often view TV as an electronic magic carpet, the 20th century's creation of the technological revolution, the great instrument of persuasion, and the most powerful weapon for social change. Things which were considered as luxuries in the past have become sheer necessities today. TV is treated as their constant companion by people in advanced countries. This indicates the tremendous mark it has made on world civilization. A unique combination of commercial, political, academic and cultural programmes is the main characteristic feature of TV. The scope of TV programmes can be broadly visualised from three angles, *i.e.*, information, education and entertainment. With communication satellites the task of realising its basic functions has become much easier and the purpose more effective.

Men of many lands contributed to the development of TV. TV was made possible by electronic discoveries in the late 19th century and early 20th century. In 1884 Paul Njpkow, a German, patented a scanning disc for transmitting pictures by wireless. Charles F. Jenkins a German again began his study of the subject around 1880. The English physicist, E.E. Fournier d'Albe conducted experiments in the 1900s. In 1915, Marconi predicted "visible telephone." In 1923 physicist Vladimir Zworykin, a Russian-born American, applied for a patent on the iconoscope camera tube. In the years that followed, there were more experiments by E.F.W. Alexanderson and Philo T. Famsworth of Russia and by John L. Baird in England. An experimental TV programme was sent by wire between New York and Washington by the Bell Telephone Laboratories in 1927. The next year Bell experimentally televised outdoor programmes. The Federal Radio Commission reported that "a few" broadcast stations were experimenting with video in 1923. In the same year WGY Schenectady, N.Y., broadcast the first TV drama. A large screen TV was demonstrated by Radio Corporation of America, at a New York theater in the year 1930. Radio Corporation of America (RCA) tested outdoor TV pickup at Camden, N.J., in 1936. By 1937 there were 17 experimental TV stations operating.

Many advanced countries in the world have tried to fully utilise the potentialities of TV for their political and socio-economic development. Extensive research has been conducted to assess the impact of TV on the minds of the people. In the light of these studies, many developing countries have realised the need for a sophisticated technology like TV which could bring revolutionary changes especially among illiterate masses. Presently, many countries are utilising the satellite facility for live telecasts. Satellite communication system is effectively binding the World with its threads of sight and sound. Today, one can sit at home and simultaneously watch the events that are taking place even in very remote corners of the world. Applying space technology in the communication system is one of the world's recent developments. It strengthens the social, political and economic fabric of the world. Mere invention of technology will not accomplish the task of effective communication. Its value is decided on the way it utilised. In spite of technological development, a major portion of the population in underdeveloped countries is not fully aware of the events that are taking place, and are also deprived of effective enjoyment of their right to information. For example, a poor Indian peasant knows little or nothing about his counterpart in a foreign country. Unless this gap is bridged, development of any sort is not possible. These facts have lead to the idea of using satellites for the purpose of broadcasting. Mass communication technology accelerates the interaction among various cultures of the world. Especially in countries with high population the majority of which being illiterates, this technology can bring about certain radical and imperative changes.

Population, illiteracy and poverty are the three major problems faced by a developing country today. Television, which has shown a tremendous result in advanced countries, can be used as a major instrument in solving these problems and bring about changes in the long run. Considering these possibilities, a worldwide satellite Television experiment called SITE (Satellite Instructional Television Experiment) was initiated for the upliftment of the rural masses. In September 1969, a memorandum of understanding was signed between ISRO (Indian Space Research Organisation) and the NASA (National Aeronautical and Space Authority) of the United States of America. This memorandum lead to the development of the satellite instructional TV experiment (SITE). It is an agreement between the two countries to co-operate in undertaking an experiment in instructional Television via satellite. The USA had the responsibility of providing an application technology satellite (ATS) and placing it in orbit in such a way that it would be available to India for a whole year. India had the responsibility of production of earth stations, receiving stations, microwave transmitters—and receiving sets, of programmes for education, instruction and entertainment. The social benefit of satellite television was expected to break all barriers between nations and also to help promote an understanding among them. There is a relationship between the economic development and social change in a country. Communication plays an important role in bringing social change. Hence a country which needs to develop itself requires the assistance of communication system.

India is a developing country. Therefore, the significance of mass media in this country needs no exaggeration. It can have great impact. Government of India has been taking several steps in educating the masses and bringing awareness through modern media. A majority of our population is living in rural areas. According to the provisional totals of 1981 census, 2331 per cent of the 685 million people live in urban areas and the remaining 76.68 per cent in rural areas. While the urban population is concentrated in 4029 towns, the rural population is spread over 6.05 lakh villages (including 48,087 uninhabitated villages).

In spite of tremendous strides in urbanization, industrialization and mechanization India is still for behind in many aspects. If it has to compete with other countries of the world in economic development and overall progress, India has to start from the village level in its nation building programme. The backwardness of our rural folk chiefly lies in their poverty, innocence, ignorance, illiteracy and inhibitions. The planners desire to give them higher aspirations, with the intention of individual self-development that ultimately leads to national development. The existing formal education system is not able to cater to the needs of the present situation. Hence a medium like television should be made thoroughly extensive in its use for mass educational programmes. Here it may be questioned why TV when there are more formal institutions and other media? The major problem here is that the rural folk is too poor to engage their grown up children in long years of schooling which in their opinion fetches nothing in the end. Being ignorant of the advantages of the small family system, the poor have many children and undergo several hardships to even feed them. This may be due to the feeling that daily labour gives them daily bread and is by far the best solution to their problem. Coming to the print media, it appeals to people who can read and understand and as such it is popular only among a limited sections of the people. Next, the radio is more popular even among illiterates including women and children. Though Radio is still very popular among the villagers, the TV with its additional quality of colour vision is attracting the masses. Here it can be said that the audio and visual combination of TV is a capable medium if the programmes of rural mass education are to be meaningful. The broadcast media provides an opportunity for rural participation in their programmes. The kind of individual participation which brings the media to the masses may be more interesting way of presentation than the monotony of listening to routine talks and lectures. Then, if the broadcast media, especially the TV, is so powerful as to give our poor village rural folk individual self-recognition, then why not exploit it more fully for their own benefit?

The invention of communication satellites has given us a chance to experiment on this basis. Utilization of TV for socially purposive programmes is not limited to India alone. It was experimented even in some advanced countries also. The ATS-6 satellite in USA and Anik Satellite in Canada are used to provide programmes for isolated communities and for tribal people. The Communist countries score in promoting the widest access to media like Radio and TV. The most extensive test of TV as a vehicle of literacy teaching has been made in Italy. Illiteracy is a major obstacle for the fast growth and development of a nation. Countries like Japan and Russia have promptly recognised this as a serious problem and have taken it as a challenge to completely eradicate illiteracy in order to build up a new society. In Japan within less than 40 years of Meiji restoration the transformation of an illiterate mass into literate and enlightened people was achieved. Similarly, the Soviet Union after the Socialist revolution mobilized all the instruments of state and society for eradication of illiteracy in the shortest period of time. In the light of the experience of other countries and in of the dangers ahead by neglecting the issue, the Government of India has recognised the magnitude of the problem and accordingly formulated various schemes to educate the masses. A comparative study with other nations reveals that our efforts are not enough for the magnitude of the problem. Use of sophisticated technology like TV has already been introduced in different fields like agriculture, education etc., but, we are still far behind.

The development of a country sometimes depends on the type or system of the government it adopts. The requirements of a democratic country may differ from a communist country or a totalitarian state. Public opinion is the basis for the democratic form of government. When people are involved in the formation of the government and its policy making, an awareness of the rights and responsibilities and duties of citizens becomes the first and foremost necessity. The role of political parties and their leaders is as important as the role of citizens, for the effective functioning of a democratic society. Formal and non-formal political education that is being imparted by institutions must be supplemented by political leaders from time to time. In a democracy it is upto the elected leaders to provide an environment which makes every common man feel that he is an important citizen. A basic knowledge about politics becomes imperative when it comes to the people choosing a leader. The right understanding of the body politic helps to choose good and efficient leaders without any pressure or influence. Political education teaches what is democracy, the difference between democracy and totalitarianism, the rights and principles of democratic citizens and also the purpose of national policies. Communication researchers observed TV as a potent medium in forming public opinion and illuminating the political fabric of a nation. Describing how politicians can effectively reach the unknown voters through this channel, they say that when a particular medium is popular among the public there is little chance of their accepting a political leader who is not well-acquainted to them through that media. A politician can impress a majority of people with a TV speech than going round the comer of every village and explaining his policies.

The power of the mass media in familiarising and enhancing the personal charisma of a leader is another aspect to be considered. As Wilbur Schramm argues, in a developing country where the media are relatively scarce and the stream of the names in the news is smaller, this power of the media may be even greater than it is in economically developed countries and may provide a way to build leadership. Development of TV has facilitated many political leaders to reach millions of voters without moving from their place. It is evident from the history that they have gained access to the public through televised political campaigns. President Kennedy used live televised conferences and debates in American presidential elections. Many political observers believe that his performance in the campaign debates on TV with Richard Nixon was the decisive factor in his election to the Presidency. Subsequently, Carter and Reagan also concentrated on their TV programmes to impress the public. Considering the role of TV in political affairs, especially in a developing country where the rural population is more, the present study attempts to know the influence of TV on villagers with reference to their levels of political awareness. To convert the ignorant village folk into intelligent thinking citizens the first step should be to provide them an atmosphere of social and political awareness. Especially in a democracy where the policies of the government are the needs of the people, a basic knowledge of this system becomes necessary. To educate the mass of population in this area must naturally start with political education. This is already being done by formal institutions as well as by mass-media. In view of the effectiveness of TV when compared to other media in shaping public opinion it was intended to study the impact of television on the rural masses and the role it plays in creating political consciousness among them. Ten villages in Andhra Pradesh have been selected as the sample and the political programmes telecast over Hyderabad TV were taken to study the impact. Before proceeding to the details of the study a brief account of TV in the world as well in India and a few aspects pertaining to TV may need to be mentioned here.

Impact of Television Worldwide

At present many countries in the world are trying to project their profile through TV. In doing this, they are not only having a common medium but are also having common objectives and definite goals. Nations like Sri Lanka that have hesitated to introduce TV in the beginning are now utilizing the services of TV. However, there are countries like Tanzania which did not go for TV since it has other priorities like health and universal literacy. In 1975 UNESCO reported that 30 countries of Africa and Asia had no TV. During the past decade there was a rapid expansion of TV in the world.

An examination of the broadcasting systems in a global perspective reveals the following features:

Except in a few countries all advanced countries enjoy autonomy in broadcasting. But even while full autonomy exists, commissions and special committees restrict superfluous expression and misuse of the media. In developed countries, while a few channels are continuously engaged in educating the public, a few others orient them on matters of home and foreign policies. Regarding entertainment, a twenty-four hour up-to-date multiform service is being made available by private broadcasting corporations. In developing countries due to lack of funds and a limited channel system there is comparatively less effective transmission; non-availability of multiple channel system has over burdened the programme planners with much to do under severe limitation. As AED (Academy for Educational Development) reports, the programmes in these countries are largely imported, much of it from the United States. The report notices a trend towards the emergence of National TV production centres such as in Egypt and Mexico which produce programmes of increasing appeal to neighbouring countries. It further states that few nations can invest the money required to produce entertaining TV programming. The appetite of TV system for new programming requires a market of many millions to finance production. Therefore, for most countries TV will continue to be an international medium with a high degree of foreign cultural influence.

The revenue for this medium comes in three ways, the licence fee, the commercial revenue and the government aid. The form of revenue varies from one country to another. Commercial advertising brings in the bulk of the income in most of the countries, except where advertizing is limited or totally banned. For example, Indonesia had discontinued commercials on its Television in 1981 after finding that they were having a destablizing effect on Indonesian society by promoting wants in the form of luxury goods and services which the common people have no means to acquire. It is observed that TV has dominated the other media in some of the countries. The circulation of newspapers, Radio listening and movie going have been heavily affected due to TV in advanced countries including Japan. The results of a comparative study done between India and Japan in 1970 are presented in Table 3.1. In Colombo a drastic drop in movie house attendance for locally produced films has been reported by the presidential committee of inquiry. According to the report the decline which began in 1980 has registered a loss of 20 million seats for Simhala films. This trend shows that TV may superceds all the other media when it becomes available to each and every person. However, the high cost of TV set may be an obstacle in this direction. Considering the fact that TV is a costly medium, it is doubtful in the first place, that the common man, a poor villager can afford to purchase himself a set and feel the desired impact of TV. With growing demand for entertainment among urban viewers, there is a possibility of programmes following a commercial pattern. It is also observed that the present day programmes are in-keeping with this trend.

Table 3.1: Comparative Study of Growth of Different Media in India and Japan

Sl. No.	*Newspaper Circulation*		*Film Audience*		*Number of Radios*		*Number of Television Sets*	
	India	*Japan*	*India*	*Japan*	*India*	*Japan*	*India*	*Japan*
1.	21.7 crores (1965)	4.4 crores (1965)	310 crores (1971)	73 crores (1946)	15.59 lakhs (1958)	57 lakhs (1945)	6.2 thousand (1962)	91 lakhs (1958)
2.	29.3 crores (1970)	5.3 crores (1970)	372 crores (1975)	112.7 crores (1958)	53.99 lakhs (1965)	91.6 lakhs (1950)	37 thousand (1971)	68.6 lakhs (1961)
3.	37.4 crores (1977)	5.86 crores (1975)	420 crores (1979)	86 crores (1961)	64.84 lakhs (1966)	1.46 crores (1958)	6.77 lakhs (1977)	2.28 crores (1971)
4.		21.6 crores (1970)	2.06 crores (1979)	22 lakhs (1967)				

Note: Figures in respect of Radio subscribers of Japan are not available after 1971.

Source: Mass Media in India 1980-81, Published by Ministry of Information and Broadcasting, New Delhi, 1982, p. 78.

Then why should the developing countries invest crores of rupees on this luxury entertainment when there are other immediate problems of urgent priority to be tackled? Similar doubt was expressed when Radio programmes were started in India. But now, the Radio has reached even the remotest areas of our country. This is largely due to the transistor revolution. But the cost of TV is not comparable to the transistor Radio. Due to the above facts providing TV sets to rural areas has been undertaken by the governments as a part of development of TV. For example, China could achieve progress in supplying TV sets in its programme of rural mass education.

It is evident from the above discussion that the organization of TV medium is not an easy task especially in developing countries. However, with all the difficulties TV continues to grow in all these countries including India.

History of Television in India

TV transmission started in India (1959) long before SITE was even thought of. The major aim and objective in introducing TV in India was rural development. In view of its backwardness it was intended to utilize TV for the upliftment of rural masses by creating social awareness among them. For doing this India faced, and is still facing, a unique obstacle. The uniqueness of our country's problem lies in the multilingual nature of its people. We do not have enough financial strength to counteract this problem. Though the hardware technology was readily available in the market, introduction of TV in India was not possible because of lack of trained personnel and knowledge in the software aspects and also due to the huge financial implications. In 1959 with the help of UNESCO's grant, a study was conducted in India to test the use of TV, as a medium of education, rural uplift, and community development. The result of the study conducted after an year's transmission of special educational programmes proving positive and encouraging, the next stage of educational programmes for Delhi schools was taken up in 1961. Six years later *i.e.,* in 1967 came the pilot project of agricultural communication initiated by late Dr. Vikram Sarabhai which was primarily aimed at demonstrating the effectiveness of TV as a medium for propagating improved farming practices. With the introduction of agricultural programmes a number of telecasts were organized in rural areas. Earlier from 15th August, 1965 onwards, a daily one hour transmission was introduced in the evening. The second TV centre in the country was commissioned in Mumbai in 1972. The Srinagar and Amritsar centres were inaugurated in 1973 while Kolkata, Chennai and Lucknow found place on the TV map two years later, making it a network of seven centres including the relay station at Pune. In the meanwhile, at international forums on space communication, suggestions were being made for pilot project for assessing the practical uses of space communication technology. India was selected for the experiment. SITE transmissions were inaugurated on August 15, 1975 reaching 2,400 villages in the backward areas in Andhra Pradesh, Bihar, Karnataka, M.P., Orissa and Rajasthan representing a wide range of linguistic, cultural, climatic and agricultural regions of the country. The growth of TV in India was slow in the beginning. Since the necessary technology was at the stretch of the hand and due to the experience gained during SITE, the development of Indian TV was rapid after SITE.

The significant events that took place in the history of TV in India and the other information such, as number of TV transmitters etc., is as below:

Introduction of commercials in TV	:	1st January, 1976
TV separated from All India Radio	:	1st April, 1976
Operationalisation of INSAT (1A) and inauguration of National programmes and colour telecast	:	1st August, 1982
INSAT (1A) abandoned	:	8th September, 1981
Launching of INSAT (1B)	:	30 August, 1983
Operationalization of INSAT (1B)	:	15th October, 1983
Inauguration of 2nd Channel in Delhi	:	17th September, 1984
Morning transmission inaugurated	:	23rd February, 1987
News bulletins for hearing impaired	:	15th October, 1987

Number of TV Transmitters

Total TV transmitters	:	221
Main centres	:	12
Relay centres	:	8
INSAT centres	:	6
HPTs/LPTs linked with Delhi	:	153
HPTs/LPTs linked with Mumbai	:	25
HPTs/LPTs linked with Hyderabad	:	17

Coverage

Total population in lakhs	:	4843 (72%)
Total area (in '000 sq. kms)	:	1519 (48%)

TV Sets: The first indigenous black and white TV receiver was produced in India in 1969. From a production level of a few thousand sets in 1970, the industry had grown to produce 3 million sets in 1986. Of this, 21,50,000 were black and white and 8,50,000 colour sets. This is expected to go upto 29.2 million by 1990 and 45.6 million by 1992.

Policy Guidelines

The Television medium is based on psychological principles. According to the mass communication theories, people take the assistance of mass-media to confirm their ideas, beliefs and convictions. The psychological effects may be positive or negative depending on the individuality of the viewer. Hence, the Ministry of Information and Broadcasting has formulated certain policy guidelines for the proper functioning of radio and TV.

Coverage to government's programmes, publicity to developmental programmes, importance to rural population programmes to eradicate social evils, balanced coverage of news and other features and coordination between different media units are some of the important guidelines. While giving free hand in its programming the policy guidelines imposed certain restrictions and also make it clear that the broadcast media has to operate very cautiously. The AIR Code, which also applies to Doordarshan, was adopted in 1968 and revised in 1970 states that Broadcasts on All India Radio by individuals will not permit:

1. Criticism of friendly countries.
2. Attack on religion or communities.
3. Anything obscene; or defamatory.
4. Incitement to violence or anything against maintenance of law and order.
5. Anything amounting to contempt of court.
6. Aspersions against the integrity of the President, Governors and Judiciary.
7. Attack on political party by name.
8. Hostile criticism of any state or the centre.
9. Anything showing disrespect to the Constitution or advocating change in the Constitution by violence; but advocating changes in a constitutional way should not be debarred.

Committees—Recommendations

The media under government's control is certain to face a lot of problems and complications. The discharge of functions may not be so efficient with limited resources and multiple restrictions. Keeping in view the possibility of probable difficulties in the functioning, the government has constituted different advisory committees under the chairmanship of eminent people and experts in the field of broadcast media. Accordingly in 1964 the government appointed a committee on information and broadcasting under the chairmanship of Sri Ashok K. Chanda. This was the first enquiry committee appointed at the initiative of late Smt. Indira Gandhi the then minister for Information and Broadcasting who felt that Broadcasting needed a fresh look. The Chanda Committee made three major recommendations in its report which was published in 1966. It suggested that AIR be converted into a corporation run by a Board of Governors on the BBC model: that television be separated from Radio and given a twenty-year development plan; and that the Vividh Bharati channel be commercialised and its profits ploughed back into radio for the improvement of programmes. After four years, the government rejected the first recommendation on the ground that the time was not ripe for AIR to be converted into a corporation. While Government did not prepare a long-range plan for the development of TV, it did agree that the country needed TV and that it should be expanded within the available resources. Separation was affected only a decade later. The Chanda Committee's proposal to commercialise the Vividh Bharati channel was accepted and brought into effect in 1967, though here also it took nearly ten years before the profits were actually made available to AIR. In 1978, the Verghese Committee submitted its report on autonomy. The recommendations of the above committee will be discussed under 'AUTONOMY'. With the increase in the number of transmitters all over the country, the necessity for the software development of Doordarshan has grown. So the government appointed a committee under the Chairmanship of Dr. P.C. Joshi to give recommendations on the software aspects of our television. In a report submitted in 1985 the Committee expressed doubt about the rural orientation of the present TV programming. Criticizing the commercial attitude adopted by TV, the committee advised the restructuring of its programme pattern. As observed by P.C. Chatterji, the three enquiry committee reports are Comprehensive documents which have made on an average two hundred and thirty recommendations each covering almost every aspect of broadcasting. They are spaced over a period of nearly twenty years and it is remarkable that they agree on several of their recommendations.

Advisory Committees

Doordarshan gets guidance from various advisory committees consisting of eminent non-officials and experts in the field. There are eight Advisory Committees functioning for the benefit of Doordarshan which includes the Media Advisory Committee at the Centre, the Central Advisory Committee for the utilisation of INSAT, Programme Advisory Committees at the Doordarshan Kendras, Advisory Committees on various categories of programmes such as family, welfare programmes, science programme and the like. Special attention is paid to maintaining contact with agricultural universities, and in certain cases programmes are produced jointly by stations and universities. Though Doordarshan maintain contact with a large number of non-official bodies such as academic institutions, social welfare groups etc., such contacts are informal and no official procedure has been laid down for maintaining them.

Autonomy

Invention of modem technology has changed our life pattern to a great extent. The impact of modern technology on our lives has been seriously viewed by the futurologists. Along with the research and development in scientific areas, man has to follow some ethics and code of conduct for his own welfare. The full use of modern technology had to become restricted for the sake of peaceful living. This may be applicable to communication system also where the usage of modern technology is increasing day by day. History says that from the beginning the political systems have invented communication structure to meet their needs such as getting support to their policies etc. Starting from smoke signals, drummers and runners to present day television, the communication system is being utilized to get backing to the purposes and policies of the government. The exploitation of media is also observed from the beginning such as giving selected information to the people. The United Nations Commission on Human Rights has called information as one of the basic rights. One cannot deny the right to information. Knowledge has to be communicated from one person to another. But at the same time the media cannot be used without considering the evil effects. To quote Nehru "Freedom from ignorance is as essential as freedom from hunger. The mass-media which are very useful have an element of danger in them in that they may be distorted for private gain. The rich group or the rich nation can flood the country and the world through the mass-media with its own view of things which may or may not be the correct one".

The electronic media are highly powerful. Autonomy to electronic media has been under debate since broadcasting started in India. The issue has been viewed from different angles. According to the Indian Constitution Broadcasting together with Posts and Telegraphs, Telephones, Wireless and other like forms of communication are in the union list and, therefore, are the exclusive responsibility of the Union or Central Government. According to K.S. Duggal:

"When Radio was introduced in India in the late thirties the then rulers tried as far as possible to keep the radio free from political controversy. The media advisors Lionel Fielden and Ahmed Shah Bokhari have convinced their masters that once Radio loses its credibility with the listeners it would cease to have any meaning."

"When India became independent, Nehru seriously considered according of autonomy to AIR on the lines of BBC. However, he could take no concrete steps towards relaxing the control over the media. Mrs. Gandhi when she came into power as Information and Broadcasting Minister and later as Prime Minister announced that the old practice would continue. She said 'It is important that the channels should not be subject to political and economic control which could constrain the flow of information.'"

The Chanda Committee recommended among other things the setting up of two autonomous corporations for Radio and Television. This, however, was not acceptable to the government. It was argued that as the press and films were in the private sector, Radio and TV must remain with the government to build its image.

Submitting its report on autonomy, the Verghese Committee recommended a single National Broadcast Trust instead of autonomous regional corporations or even a federation of state government corporations. There will be a large measure of power delegated to the regional and local levels, so that the organisation enjoys the advantages of quick decision-making, sensitivity to local problems, familiarity with local customs and taste, and close linkages with various governments and institutions. As K.S. Duggal further observes:

"The Verghese Committee recommended that the freedom of the Press and Broadcasting is derived from Article 19(1)(a) of the Constitution which guarantees freedom of speech and expression to every citizen. Accordingly the National Broadcasting Trust has proposed it to be a national trustee of the collective right of the Indian people to freedom of speech and expression through the broadcast media. To this end it suggested that the proposed corporation be defined as 'a corporate citizen of India' so that it might exercise and enjoy all the fundamental rights and obligations given to individual citizens.

The Prasar Bharathi bill that was introduced in Parliament by the Janata Government diluted the recommendations made by the group, while rejecting the proposed constitutional amendment altogether. With the collapse of the Janata Government, even this bill lapsed.

When the Congress (I) came into power again, one of the earliest announcements it made was that Radio and TV would continue to function as departments of government. They would however, have functional autonomy."

But many political thinkers and media experts view government's control as monopoly over the media. In this connection Ashok Mitra says that the constitution gives the centre the right to control, but not the right to monopoly over the media. In a country of India's diversities and complexities. Television and Radio offer the quickest and widest reach. The monopoly of the media is the most precious weapon which the ruling party possesses in the battle for winning the people's mind. Explaining the unsatisfactory performance of TV and the problems it has under government's control. Ramesh Thaper states that "The tasks of transformation, of building the alternative vision, are too complex for bureaucratic communication. The freeing of the electronic media will free the mind of India."

Autonomy for broadcasting is a critical issue. In countries where illiteracy is not a problem, people can receive information through the media with objectivity. But in our country the condition is quite contrary, especially in the rural areas, which are backward in all aspects. It is easy to influence the rudimentary thoughts of the people with a powerful medium and this is the kind of exploitation that is taking place today in the fields of free press and movies. Political and business motives have dominated our free press and films giving room to perversion. Hence it is unthinkable to leave the electronic media in the hands of a vested few in the name of autonomy. At the same time free flow of correct information cannot be arrested in the name of control. A judicious method has to be identified and adopted while using this sophisticated technology. Even though full autonomy was given to broadcast media in some advanced countries, there is a constant check on their functioning from time to time. For example, the BBC which is considered as impartial and independent broadcasting authority is also under fire from its government. Thatcher herself has in the past publicly criticized the BBC for corrupting, the morals of the young by broadcasting too much sex and violence. Keeping the above arguments and practical implications in mind the government must formulate a policy where both the programmes of the government as also the public views are given a due place.

Economics of Television

Financing for Broadcasting is wholly made from the consolidated fund of India. The budget for AIR and Doordarshan is presented as part of the expenditure of the Ministry of Information and Broadcasting. A major portion of the revenue for television comes from the commercials. The Revenue from commercials continues to increase over the years. There is substantial increase in revenue from 77 lakhs during 1976-77 to 74 crores during 1987-88 (*i.e.*, upto October 1987 only). The yearly license fee has been abolished since March 1985. Now only one time excise duty of Rs. 100 per TV set is levied at the time of purchase.

The growth of television is very high during Sixth Five Year Plan period. The expansion was so rapid that from July 1984 onwards till the end of the year almost everyday one transmitter was commissioned in some corner or other of the country. This shows that the expenditure was more on hardware side than on software. This fact has been recognised in the Seventh Five Year Plan and the policy makers have therefore placed greater emphasis on the development of software facilities.

Seventh Plan Schemes

An outlay of Rs. 700 crore has been approved in the Seventh Plan for the developmental schemes of Television in the country. The plan includes replacement of all black and white equipment which has completed its useful life, establishment of regular studio centres at 12 places and programme, generation facilities at 12 more places. Coupled with the proposed extension of microwave network,

Doordarshan will be able to provide primary service in each state in the local language. The total number of production facilities would be 47 and the coverage would extend to 80 per cent of the population.

The long-term objective of television is that the largest number of people in the country should have access to three TV programmes.

1. The primary service in the language of the state and originating within the state.
2. The national service available on domestic receivers to all viewers in addition to the primary service.
3. The educational service which again has to be available on all domestic receivers and ultimately provide educational programmes on various subjects at primary, secondary and university levels at times convenient to the target audience and in the language in which education is being imparted in that area.

Besides the above, it is also desirable that programmes for special audiences be made available but these need not be on domestic receivers nor necessarily in the language of the state.

Programme Pattern

Education, information and entertainment are the three major aims of TV programming. Sometimes entertainment is mixed with information *i.e.*, humour is used wherever possible to drive home a point. Dialogues, discussions, playlets and other folk forms like Burra Katha are use to present the programmes which involves the participation of the villagers. Music is a part and parcel of every programme. Sometimes a small beat of the drum or a flick of a string may convey much more than words. Scripts for the programmes are prepared by experts in the particular fields and presented by trained artists. As far as possible visual aspect is given importance in the programmes. Sometimes suitable pictures with commentry are substituted whenever films are not available. Though the format of the programmes on Television is fixed, it varies depending upon the occasional, seasonal and other special programmes. For example, major sports events, political conventions etc.

At present the following three types of programmes are available on TV.

(i) *Regional Programme*: This is transmitted in local languages from the respective programme production centres generally between 6.00 p.m. and 8.40 p.m. These include programmes of information, education inbuilt with entertainment addressed to general and specific audiences including farmers, women, children, youth, industrial workers and others.

(ii) *National Programme*: A common national programme for a duration of 155 minutes between 8.40 p.m. and 11.15 p.m. on all days of the week except Saturdays when it goes upto midnight is telecast from Delhi which is carried by all the transmitters in the country. The national programme is relayed after the regional telecast. However, Chennai receives the National from 9.00 p.m. This programme aims at fostering social, economic and cultural awareness, promoting the spirit of national integration and projecting the progress made by the country in various fields. Besides, two news bulletins—one in Hindi and another in English—are also telecast. Other items in the national programmes include art, music, dance and programme based on literary work in various Indian languages and important features/ discussions on Current Events. Programmes of entertainment sponsored privately and produced by eminent producers are also telecast.

In addition to National programme, Network programme is also being organised on Saturday afternoons and Sunday-full day. Saturday afternoon service is mainly meant for the housewives and children. The service is on the air from 1.45 p.m. On Sundays from 9.00 a.m. to 12.15 p.m. a number of sponsored serials and Doordarshan's own programmes are telecast for the entertainment of viewers. From 1.15 p.m. to 4.00 p.m. a feature film in regional language is telecast. In its Sunday network, Doordarshan has recently introduced a 15 minutes news bulletin in sign language with narration in English under the title News for the Hearing Impaired.

Morning Transmission is also being aired on the entire

network for a duration of 45 minutes, starting from 7.30 a.m. Besides, two news bulletins—one each in Hindi and English—the programme includes visual presentation of 'Vande Mataram' followed by items of physical exercise and entertainment. The transmission also includes programmes like 'Money matters' providing information on the latest trends in economy. Important personalities are also interviewed.

(iii) *Area specific and development oriented programmes* for the INSAT clusters are telecast for a duration of 35 to 40 minutes. Programmes on National Integration and Communal Harmony are telecast both in National Network as well as by the various programme producing Kendras in the local languages. These programmes are telecast in various entertaining formats, including mushairas, quawalis, documentaries, sponsored programmes, plays and quiz programmes.

INSAT based Doordarshan Kendras make programmes in a different way. For programmes intended for rural people via satellite it conducts research in the beginning known as formative research. The plan of the programme is first given to the viewers. Opinions are called for and then the programmes are prepared. Sometimes the programmes are prepared in advance keeping in view the requirements of the viewers and the feedback is analysed.

Objectives of the Programmes

Agriculture

Programmes on agriculture, animal husbandry, forestry irrigation, cottage and small scale industries, health, hygiene and sanitation etc., of varying duration bard core items pertaining to these aspects are telecast supported by suitable visuals of film in order to promote greater agricultural production. In respect of these programmes special chunks are assigned taking into account the viewing habits of the rural audience. The entertainment aspect is not neglected. For making these programmes more palatable folk songs, folk dances, playlets and special features on festive occasions are also in the day to day programmes. Family welfare has been one of the important themes where the thrust has been for limiting the size of the family and bringing about qualitative changes in the standard of life of the people. These programmes received promotional publicity in various forms and formats. Doordarshan utilized the funds provided by the Ministry of Health and Family Welfare for the production of documentaries on the advantages of FP of varying durations and in different languages to make an impact on the people.

Special Audience Programmes

Children, adolescents, youth, women, industrial workers, intellectuals, elderly persons, and the general citizens at large—A large number of programmes keeping in view the varied interests and need of these audience groups are produced with their involvement and participation.

Music and Dance

To reflect cultural heritage, tradition and to entertain people a substantial percentage of transmission is devoted to music programmes. These include, vocal and instrumental music (classical, folk and modern).

The dances of India also find a place of pride in the Doordarshan's programmes. Folk and modern dance are also encouraged and their votaries invited to perform.

Drama

Produce and telecast drama on various social themes almost every week.

Feature Films

A number of good feature films in Hindi and other regional languages are telecast. Since TV is a family medium the suitability of films for family viewing is taken into consideration for selection of films.

Sports

Cultivation of interest in and promotion of sports has been one of the major objectives of Doordarshan.

News and Current Affairs: The aim and objective of the news and current affairs programmes telecast from Doordarshan are to widen the awareness of the people about the major events and developments within and outside the country and to deepen their understanding of current social, economic and political events and issues.

Audience Research

Doordarshan in it's approach for progressive planning relies heavily on the feedback received from the people, by way of letters, views individual or collective expressed in meetings or critical reviews made in the press. In addition, through the scientific system of surveys, audiences reactions are analysed by the Audience Research Units which are in-built in the Doordarshan organisational setup. The Audience Research Unit of All India Radio conducts over 120 field surveys and nearly 1,000 panel surveys during the course of a year. In the field surveys some 44,000 radio and TV households are contacted to assess the quantum of listening/viewing and to determine demographic and other characteristics. Doordarshan has fourteen units attached to its main Kendras and post-SITE centres. They attempt to monitor the quantitative viewing of programmes through field surveys, panel surveys, analysis of viewers' letters and the like. Some studies conducted by them have been on subjects such as the impact of TV on children, surveys on Family serials etc. The Indian Institute of Mass Communication (IIMC) functions in New Delhi as an autonomous body under the Ministry of Information and Broadcasting. Among other things it conducts studies on the impact of media on audiences. Some studies have concerned themselves with AIR/Doordarshan programmes. The two departments co-operate with the IIMC and take note of its findings. Research work has also been conducted by private organisations such as the Operations Research Group (Baroda), the Public Opinion Quarterly and some university departments of communication.

Commercial Service

Commercial service of Doordarshan was started in January 1976 from seven Kendras and later extended through more Kendras. The scheme of sponsored programmes was introduced in 1983 enabling various organizations, business houses etc., to sponsor either programmes produced by them or imported programmes or programmes produced by Doordarshan. The advertisements are telecast as per the provisions of the code for commercial advertising. The code prohibits advertising of tobacco, liquor and gambling, including betting on horse-racing and other sports. The booking of commercials, static or film spots and the sponsored programmes is done through the advertising agencies and in some cases directly by the advertisers. As a matter of policy upto 10 per cent of the total transmission duration can be utilised for commercial advertisements.

The revenues from commercials increased to Rs. 74 crore (upto October 1987) from a meagre Rs. 77 lakh in 1976-77. The steady increase in the revenues is evident from the following:

Year	*Revenue Earnings (in crores)*
1976-77	Rs. 0.77
1977-78	Rs. 2.20
1978-79	Rs. 4.97
1979-80	Rs. 6.16
1980-81	Rs. 8.09
1981-82	Rs. 11.60
1982-83	Rs. 15.89
1983-84	Rs. 19.79
1984-85	Rs. 31.43
1985-86	Rs. 60.20
1986-87	Rs. 93.31
1987-88 (Upto Oct. 1987)	Rs. 74.49

International Relations

In accordance with the policy of the Government of India cultural agreements have been signed with some 20 countries which include Yugoslavia, France, USSR, Hungary and Czechoslovakia. These agreements include a section which deals with broadcasting. Exchange of programmes, co-operation in the field of technology, assistance to visiting news correspondents of other countries, and training and exchange of personnel are included in the agreements. Programme exchange has been largely confined to music but AIR and Doordarshan have also supplied scripts of plays (in English translation) to foreign organisations. There is programme exchange and co-operation in different fields, though no cultural agreement has been signed with USA. In the area of training AIR and

Doordarshan have both benefited from and made considerable contributions to the Asian Institute of Broadcast Development (AIBD) in Kuala Lumpur.

Training

In service training for Television staff is provided at the Film and Television Institute of India at Pune. The Institute was set up initially for films in 1960 and a television section was added in 1974. Courses at the FTII have varied between six and four months depending on the pressure to open new TV centres.

Annual Awards for TV Programmes

Awards for TV programmes are given annually for the best programmes produced and telecast by Doordarshan during each calendar year. The aim of these awards is to promote the art of TV as a medium of communication and means of self-expression and to raise the standards of Doordarshan production. The awards are of two types: best production Awards and individual excellence Awards. Television being a central government organisation its distribution system and functioning is uniform throughout the country. Doordarshan, Hyderabad (the sample district selected is located around the city of Hyderabad) which is part and parcel of central TV network is also functioning on the similar lines as discussed earlier. However, some specific aspects about Hyderabad TV needs to be mentioned here since the same was choosen for the present study.

History of Television in Andhra Pradesh

In Andhra Pradesh, Television transmission commenced from the Capital city of Hyderabad in 1977. Earlier in 1975-76, Andhra Pradesh was one of the states which benefitted by the SITE experiment. The role played by Hyderabad TV as a part of the experiment is worth mentioning. Since the software aspects and other arrangements have to be looked after by India, every state here was fully prepared for the experiment. The SITE programme was so organized that it would be received simultaneously by 24,000 villages located in six different states in India each with its own regional language. These states were selected partly for technological reasons based upon satellite location and partly for reasons of relative economic backwardness. Approximately 400 villages were selected for SITE in each state. Rangareddy, Medak and Mahaboobnagar districts in Telangana area and Kurnool district in Rayalaseema area of Andhra Pradesh are covered under the above scheme. A Total of five hundred and fifty-five community TV sets (VHF sets) have been installed under Hyderabad Transmitter Range out of which 407 sets are installed by the Government of India and the remaining by Andhra Pradesh Government. Under INSAT direct reception scheme in Mahaboobnagar and Kurnool districts the Government of India installed 375 community TV sets. Audience (men, women and children) on a daily-average are in the range of 200-400 per community TV set. It is understood that this figure usually more than doubles on feature film days. The SITE is a historical event. For the first time a satellite has been used for transmitting TV programmes at international level. The findings of the research done after the experiment says that the rural masses of A.P. have responded with enthusiasm and motivation and in some areas people showed more interest compared to other states. The regional programmes for the evening broadcast were produced mainly at the base production centres located in 4 cites of Hyderabad, Cuttack, Ahmedabad and Delhi which took responsibility for 4 days in a week. The research and development work for hardware was done primarily at ISRO at Ahmedabad and the ECIL at Hyderabad. Three years were spent on planning by ISRO. The satellite was lifted into the space in May 1974. A few endings given in UNESCO report about Andhra Pradesh during SITE experience are worth looking before proceeding to know the structure of TV in the state.

Audience Size

A comparison of the audience size in the six clusters shows that except in the states of Andhra Pradesh and Orissa, in all other states the audience tended to decrease as the programme proceeded. However, in the states of Andhra and Madhya Pradesh the programme continued to draw a steady number of viewers. The Hyderabad programmes were broadcast in two states Andhra Pradesh and Karnataka. With regard to presentation and comprehension the most frequently occurring comment was that the programme presentation was interesting and good.

Regularity in Attendance

Between adults and children the latter were found to be more regular in attendance in Andhra Pradesh and in Madhya Pradesh. The response was highest in A.P. with 71 per cent return of cards and, the lowest in Bihar with only 28. The response from the other states was around 60 per cent. The above information speaks that the television impact on the villagers of Andhra Pradesh is satisfactory. With the provision of TV service all over the state recently, people of Andhra Pradesh both urban and rural are enjoying the programmes.

Area and Population

The area of A.P. is 2,75,068 sq. kms. The population of the state as per the 1981 census provisional figures is 5,35,49,673. The state has a rural population of 410.62 lakhs and urban of 124.87 lakhs—Andhra Pradesh is the fifth largest state in the country both in area and population. There are 23 districts in the state. A.P. is primarily an agricultural state.

Capital	Hyderabad
Principal languages	Telugu and Urdu
Literacy	29.94 per cent
Number of Newspapers	1071 (dailies 62)
Radio Stations	Hyderabad, Vijayawada, Vishakhapatnam Cuddapah and Adilabad.

Hyderabad Television (Upagraha Doordarshan Kendra, Hyderabad) is primarily a rural centre catering to community TV villages in the surrounding districts. It has been doing so since 1975 when the SITE programmes commenced. It was in October 1977 that Hyderabad transmitters became operational. Andhra Pradesh is the second states where in all the relay centres were linked with the regional Kendra via INSAT B. Maharashtra being the first one. Since the SITE covered only Telangana and Rayala-Seema areas the Andhra area was totally deprived of the enjoyment of TV for a long time. With the installation of transmitters and satellite relays this deficiency was covered to some extent from 14th January, 1986. The programmes that are telecast from Hyderabad are now feeded throughout A.P. The total area covered by Hyderabad Doordarshan Kendra is approximately 95,009 sq. kms. The total population covered is 254.63 lakhs, out of which 95.29 lakhs is urban population and 159.34 lakhs is rural. Andhra Pradesh like many other states is noted for diversities in culture. In addition to Telugu which is the main language, Urdu is also widely spoken especially in Telangana areas. This calls for special attention on the part of the programme makers to satisfy the needs of the programme viewers. It is very difficult to satisfy the different tastes of people at one and the same time. The massiveness of the medium poses a challenge to the broadcasters. Before trying to teach a concept through projection the programme makers attempt to create an interest for leading in the minds of the viewers. The medium has to maintain a balance between urban demand and the rural needs. Hence, the task is not an easy one in practical terms with limited technical resources, inadequate training in software aspects and financial drawbacks. An overall view of the TV was discussed hitherto with a sociological perspective. TV, like a tree, has various branches related to different subjects. Each branch needs detailed study. Political broadcasting which is concerned with the present study is one among them. This area has some background which requires special attention. The next chapter has been devoted for the main focus of the study *i.e.*, political broadcasting and the research work done in the field of political communication.

The television networks, which can sell everything from soap to automobiles to a complacent public in large quantities, have had their troubles in establishing equal acceptance for news and public affairs. A fairly convincing case can be made out against some of the elements in top management for not having tried very hard, but the same accusation can scarcely be documented against the zealots of broadcast journalism. They have tried, sometimes at excessive cost to themselves. But on the whole they have not been too successful.

The Federal Communications Commission, which is supposed to worry about such things, has scarcely been noted in its history for taking bold and forthright positions in support of the need for stronger, larger, and more independent broadcast journalism services. "Public service programming, particularly in the entertainment and news fields, is often the most expensive and the least profitable. It is not much of an excuse, particularly when it is put forward by a federal regulatory agency. Since when has public service been supposed to show a profit?

It is not lack of talent or ideas in broadcast journalism, but an almost continual carnival atmosphere on television that has caused a substantial proportion of local stations to reject some well-intentioned network news specials on major topics. There should be no surprise, consequently, over the decline during much of the 1960s in the network offerings of scheduled public affairs material. Thus, particularly in foreign affairs, the same kind of a news blackout that has existed for years in areas serviced by the purely local-minded daily press has spread to a large section of the local electronic media. Under such circumstances, a mass audience does not often have an alternative between show business and the news except for all but most of the compelling events. But in the current atmosphere of television, it takes very real journalistic statesmanship to embark on such ventures.

The Scope of Television News

True, the all-sponsored major network Monday—Friday news programmes have had wide acceptance on local stations, primarily because the early evening news has no fixed commercial competitors in most areas. However, the principal network commentators have generally been the first to concede that they are obliged to deal with bulletin-type news, supplemented by filmed reports when available, and can neither explain nor interpret for more than a minute or two at a time on a scheduled programme.

Thus, news coverage in depth is seldom possible during one of the regularly scheduled network programmes of news. For this, there is no substitute today except a good newspaper but these, too, are in short supply. Confronted with what amounts to a considerable local radio, television, and newspaper censorship of world and even national news in some parts of the nation, the serious-minded citizen who wants to keep informed has no alternative but to wait for the news magazines, a responsible Sunday newspaper, or specialized publications. And this in a nation that so often boasts it is the best-informed in the world.

It is a dangerous illusion, moreover, that the networks, for all their vast expenditures and claims of large editorial staffs, originate a great deal of their own news. Even at the time of the escalation of the Vietnam War in early 1966, when American bombers were ordered to blast North Vietnam for the first time, the indifference of the irresponsible part of the local electronic media was matched only by the supine performance of an important segment of the strongly local daily press. Six days later, the use of another Vietnam War news special was only a little better. In other words, approximately half of the network affiliates of each chain refused to break into the evening's routine entertainment (and advertising) to show the American public a vitally necessary programme. These were superior jobs by television correspondents and cameramen, covering their first war, and merited full-scale public attention instead of a selfish and self-serving local censorship.

Just as is the case with the daily press, television has its stalwarts in the area of public affairs who make up in part for the negligence of the majority. All the network news and public affairs programmes in the 1966 survey showed fewer than half such programmes that were being offered. It is clear that advertising on sponsored programmes counts for far more with many local stations, regardless of merit, than public interest on unsponsored programmes.

This was the background for the widely publicized internal argument in CBS that led to the resignation of Fred W. Friendly as president of CBS News. No mere local station was the issue here, but a great national network with a major responsibility to the public that transcended considerations of advertising and entertainment.

The new president of CBS Television, who also had been made responsible for news policy, was John A. Schneider, who had previously been a local station manager and was schooled in the value of dollars and cents. He had been interposed between the CBS top management, William S. Paley and Frank Stanton, and the volatile and dedicated Friendly. To newspaper reporters, Schneider made various explanations for curtailing the marathon coverage of the Senate hearings. "We just didn't feel it was the kind of thing to carry," he told one newspaperwoman. "Nobody's looking at it, not even housewives." Another reporter quoted Schneider as saying that the CBS-TV audience had fallen 50 per cent on two previous days, although NBC for the same programmes reported an audience of 27 million. In effect, what Schneider had decided to do was condense the whole business for showing in compact form later in the day, or in the evening.

It was undoubtedly a source of dour satisfaction that the three networks cancelled all regular entertainment programmes and commercial announcements for more than four hours of prime time on the night of June 6, 1967 to carry the United Nations Security Council debate on the six-day Middle East war. If it cost television millions of dollars in revenue, it also did much to make up for the instances of negligence that have cost the electronic media dearly in public confidence in the past. For this is what television public service is really all about and this is television's job; no other medium can bring national and world issues before a mass public with such immediacy and impact.

Public Television

The nationwide discussion of public television, which Friendly among others has helped to stimulate, undoubtedly has played a part in the willingness of network television as a whole to pay more attention to its responsibilities to the nation. It would, of course, be both uncharitable and unfair, and very probably untrue, to ascribe the motivation for the pooled United Nations coverage to such pressures on commercial television. However, it cannot help but play a part in the thinking of the principal television proprietors as they contemplate the situation in which they find themselves today.

They have control of what is without doubt the most powerful of all instruments of mass communications, properly used, and a source of income of consistently high potential because it is a business with a limited possibility for competitive entry. Unlike published material, which in theory anybody with the means and the desire can issue in the United States, the number of usable broadcasting signals that can be transmitted in any given area at a particular time is now limited; moreover, there are competing uses for the radio spectrum. Thus, while Congress under the Bill of Rights may make no law restricting the freedom of the press, it has in effect subscribed to some sharp limitations on the electronic media that have been imposed by the Federal Communications Commission. In many populous areas of the country, the number of television signals that may be decently received is restricted to as few as two or three, and sometimes only one; in other places, such as the Los Angeles area, for example, a dozen television stations are authorized.

"Although this same physical limitation and governmental restraint does not make networking... necessarily oligopolistic," the FCC has pointed out, "the economies of scale in programme distribution have conspired with the restraints on numbers of stations to produce only three national television networks and four national radio networks. While the importance of networking to radio has declined greatly since the rise of television, the networks have continued to dominate television production and distribution. This has meant that three large corporations are responsible for the bulk of the television programming which goes into American homes."

It was inevitable that such power in private hands would be challenged, particularly after a period of rising complaints against inadequate public service programming. A number of ingenious ideas were put forward, the first being the McGeorge Bundy—Fred Friendly proposal for the Ford Foundation which would have financed non-commercial television out of the partial proceeds of a system of domestic satellites to cut the costs of commercial television. Friendly also provided the inspiration, and the Ford Foundation put up the money, for an experimental series of Sunday night programmes over National Educational Television, the Public Broadcast Laboratory, which got off to an indifferent start late in 1967. But it remained for the Carnegie Commission on Educational Television to take the big leap away from private television and propose to put the government behind what it called public television. This has since become the generic term for educational and all other forms of non-commercial television.

Conceivably, both commercial and public television may be radically altered in the foreseable future by the swift pace of technological innovation. The growth of Cable Television (CATV), and the enormous power that it places in the hands of private operators to offer or shut out whatever programmes they wish regardless of the desires of subscribers, is one facet of television that requires constant surveillance. Another is the increase in satellite transmission with its promise of greater efficiency and scope for television as well as the prospect that it will reduce operating costs eventually. Just what the broadening of ultrahigh frequency transmission and reception will do to television can only be guesswork at this stage in its development. Beyond that lies the imponderable influence of the laser (light beam) and other techniques that are now in the laboratory stage. Certainly, the electronic media are poised on the threshold of an age of monumental change that will add immeasurably to their opportunities as well as their problems.

Conflicts of Interest

No sensible person will argue that television companies should not diversify; nor can it be contended that newspapers or news magazines should have no outside financial interests whatever. That is flying in the face of reality. What does matter very much, however, is that any proprietor who deals in news and opinion must realize his outside investments will be carefully scrutinized by a discerning public to determine if they are influencing the quality or presentation of his news. The big objection to government operation of, or substantial power over, the news media is precisely the fear that it will slant, twist, or directly change the quality of news reporting to suit its own ends. The danger is no less grave in the privately operated news media when proprietors, either innocently or willfully, let their financial interests sway their responsibilities to the public.

In the diversification process in television, some very large questions have been raised over the sponsorship within the electronic media of various amateur and professional sports, particularly big money football. The practice of having-sports announcers paid by sponsoring television interests has also led to considerable criticism, as has the television "time out" to permit the insertion, of. But it is part of a pattern that has scarcely added to the stature of television.

If public suspicions of journalistic probity are thus confirmed in so seemingly innocent a field as sports, the work of television in the far more complicated areas of labour relations, civil rights, national affairs, and foreign policy is also likely to be questioned from time to time. It is no answer to point to polls that show the particular respondents are impressed by the basic fairness of television in covering the news, presumably, they are a part of the audience that can also be sold cigarettes in ever larger quantities despite the federally imposed warnings that are stamped on each package. Moreover, it should never be forgotten that the pressures for regulating news that arise within journalism are very small compared to the tremendous influence that is so often brought to bear from outside the profession.

There is still another source of difficulty in television's handling of the news that is somewhat more common to the news media as a whole. These are the cases of conflict of interest, which very often differ in intent from the rather pitiable efforts to promote rather than report sports. A Wolper production entitled "Wall Street: Where The Money Is" shows the embarrassment that can result in television, even when those involved are people of unquestioned integrity.

In defense of the networks, it may be said in such cases that they are doing no more—and probably not really as much—as the newspaper that puts out a special section for an advertiser and stuffs it with editorial matter about the company's interests. However, the ills that newspapers have developed over two centuries can scarcely justify the practices that have been adapted to television in a little more than two decades. Both the special puff section and the puff documentary are commercial ventures, undertaken primarily to benefit an advertiser, and are morally indefensible as journalism.

TV and Editorial Opinion

The electronic media, however, have done something more than merely pick up bad habits from their older contemporaries. As a primary force in the development of public service, the slow and careful evolution of editorialization in broadcast journalism provides the basis for hope and promise of better things to come. For example, the editorial leadership of WMCA Radio in New York as a champion of such causes as better housing and legislative reapportionment has been outstanding. Stimson Bullitt, operator of several Pacific Northwest television stations, did not hesitate to broadcast editorial criticism of the conduct of the Vietnam War when he thought it justified.

This is still just a trend and not a movement, for the broadcast editorialist has many built-in handicaps that do not affect his associates in print. While the FCC encourages the broadcast of opinion in theory, it actually inhibits such work in practice under the equal opportunities provision of Section 315 of the Communications Act. What this means, in effect, is that time must be given to opposing opinions if a station takes an editorial position that arouses controversy. Consequently, at regular intervals, any station with strong editorial opinions has no choice but to provide time for rebuttal, whether the opposition is qualified or not.

In recognition of this troublesome situation. Congress partially suspended Section 315 in the 1960 Presidential campaign but only 62 stations broadcast editorials for or against candidates. In the next national election, in 1962, the total rose to 148 and it has been slowly increasing since despite the continual threat that someone will have to be granted equal time for response. The FCC in effect has held to its position "that licensees devote a reasonable percentage of their broadcasting time to the discussion of public issues of interest in the community... and that such programmes be designed so that the public has a reasonable opportunity to hear different opposing positions on the public issues of interest and importance to the community."

Without doubt there is wisdom in the continued insistence on time for rebuttal in the electronic media, where the power to influence public opinion may be more easily abused than in the press. But what constitutes a "reasonable opportunity" is something that defies precise definition. This is the heart of the controversy over Section 315 and it is not likely to be settled very quickly. It does not excuse the sanctimonious TV editorial, picked up from a spineless section of the press, that comes out four-square against dope addicts, prostitution, and crime, and celebrates the virtues of home, mother, and the flag. But it also scarcely justifies a position of neutrality in broadcast journalism toward the issues of the day. The licensing authority of the FCC is, of course, a constant threat to the freedom of expression of the electronic media in cases involving the interest of the government, but it should not be permitted to cow the broadcast journalist into abject silence when the public interest is involved.

Radio, which exerted a tremendous influence on American public opinion during the campaign for intervention preceding World War II, may well do as much as television—and perhaps even more—in developing the potential of the electronic media for broadcasting news and opinion. The FCC rule, which requires commonly owned AM and FM stations in large cities to offer different programmes at least 50 per cent of the broadcast day, places more pressure on radio to delve into public service journalism on both the fact-finding and opinion levels. In addition, despite the boredom of the "grind" all-day news programmes of some of the pioneering radio stations, it has proved a ready source for the dissemination of news in capsule form. The steady training of radio news staffs and the efforts of editors to diversify the news "grind" have yielded some improvements, though not many. For as long as proprietors and advertisers are willing to support the "all news" station experiment, it is bound to be a laboratory for the trial of all manner of electronic innovations in public service journalism. The pity is that so few of the "all news" stations are trying to grasp the opportunity.

Neither radio nor television is consigned indefinitely to a diet of news and entertainment geared for the most part to the lowest intelligence. The strength of broadcast journalism is growing in the United States. The need for it is demonstrable. What remains to be supplied is the determination to broaden and deepen current practice, particularly among local stations in television, and provide the public at all times with the news, opinion, and relevant background it must have if self-government is to be anything more than a carefully nurtured delusion in the United States.

TELEVISION AND VIDEO FLOW INTO INDIA

Background

The main purpose of conducting the studies of international television flows is the assumption that these flows imply cultural and economic effects on countries, regions or groups of viewers (Sepstrup, 1990). Several terms like 'international,' 'transnational' 'internationalisation' and 'transnationalisation' are used by different researchers. The terms are often used interchangeably and without being defined properly. Mowlana's (1984) definition as quoted by Sepstrup (1990), International flow of information is defined here as the movement of message across national boundaries between and among two or more national and cultural systems' is favoured by the author.

Channels of Flow

The international flow of "supply" of foreign television programmes is possible in three different ways:

1. Imported programmes shown over the national television network, e.g. Doordarshan telecasting 'I Love Lucky' or 'The Vanity Fair' or the Agatha Christie serials.

2. Foreign programmes telecast through foreign satellites and beamed towards a specific country or countries, e.g. programme of STAR TV and CNN seen in India.
3. Foreign programmes seen in a country because of 'spillover' in the neighbouring country, e.g., Pakistan or Bangladesh television programmes seen in some parts of India or vice versa.

This 'supply' is a necessary condition for viewing the programmes, but it is not a sufficient condition for 'consumption' of these programmes. The term 'consumption' refers to the actual viewing of the supplies programmes by the viewers. The viewing behaviour is dependent on several factors other than the supply of the availability of the programmes. Whether the 'supply' and 'consumption' have a social, cultural or political impact is a more interesting issue but is a 'second' level study. The 'first' level study is to empirically find out the extent of international programme supply, the pattern of supply, the channels of supply and the consumption thereof. This is tedious, less 'glamorous' out necessary step before studying the 'substantial' effects of the 'second' level (Sepstrup, 1990). This paper focuses only on the 'first' level.

International TV and Video Flow Study

It is in the light of this background that a study of the international flow of television programmes was conducted in four Asia-Pacific countries. A similar study was earlier conducted in Western Europe. The study used a common research agenda and a common strategy. It covered three aspects:

- Television landscape—Viewers' actual and technical access to content and households' access to television sets/ programmes.
- Programme supply—analysis of programmes actually transmitted in terms of duration, classification of programmes according to subject/format, proportion of national and foreign programmes transmitted per day per channel.
- Programme consumption—analysis of programmes actually viewed in terms of duration, subject/format/ national vs, foreign programmes by age, education, sex and the level of urbanisation.

Television Landscape

The experimental transmission of television programmes in India started in 1959. In 1975-76 India conducted the Satellite Instructional Television Experiment (SITE), the world's largest techno-social experiment in direct satellite broadcasting. However, the expansion of television continued to be slow and halting till 1982. A phenomenal growth in the number of both television sets and television viewers was observed thereafter (see Table 3.2 and Table 3.3). The major reason for this was the operationalisation of India's INSAT system.

Table 3.2: Percentage Expansion of Doordarshan Area and Population Covered between 1959-91

Year	*Area in sq. kms*	*Total No. of Transmitters*	*Percentage Expansion*	*Population Covered in Millions*
1959-1964	14,300	1	0	10.0
1964-1969	14,300	1	0	10.0
1969-1974	37,700	5	400	25.9
1974-1979	1,60,400	16	225	118.8
1979-1984	4,71,000	180	1,025	348.6
1984-1991	18,70,000	523	290	663.0

Note: Data are taken at mid-points of the year.
The percentage growth has been calculated using the previous year's figure as a base.
Source: Modified from the earlier table of Agrawal (1987: 3).

Table 3.3: Decennial Distribution of Television Sets in India between 1962-1992

Sl. No.	*Year*	*Total Television Sets**
1.	1962	41
2.	1972	84,114
3.	1982	20,95,537
4.	1992	3,00,00,000

* Figure upto 1984 are based on the actual licences issued by Post and Telegraph Department. Thereafter the system of licensing has been abolished. Rest are estimated figures.
Source: Television India 1991 (1991: 36).

The growth was phenomenal in terms of the absolute number as well as the rate of growth. However, it is small in terms of the percentage of the total population having access to television sets. Only about 20 per cent of India's population has actual access to television. Compared to the other three countries included in the study, India was poorest in terms of access provided (see Table 3.4). Ninety-nine per cent or more households in Australia and South Korea had access to television; in the Philippines 51 per cent of the households had access.

Table 3.4: Description of Countries According to Population and TV Households

Country	*Total Population*		*Total TV Household*	
	Household	*Persons*	*Household*	*Persons*
Australia	53,43,000	1,72,10,800	52,89,570 (99% of total)	1,70,38,692 (99% of total)
India	17,00,00,000	84,39,30,861	3,40,00,000 (20% of total)	17,00,00,000 (20% of total)
Philippines	1,07,73,300	6,14,39,000	54,94,383 (51% of total)	3,13,33,890 (51% of total)
Korea	1,13,57,160	4,35,20,000	1,13,54,80 (99% of total)	4,34,76,480 (99% of total)

Source: Based on A Survey of Transnationalisation of Television in Four Asian Countries, Goonasekera (1992).

A more recent phenomenon has changed the television landscape of the country both qualitatively and quantitatively. There has been a spurt in satellite-based international television transmission. It began with the CNN channel telecasting during the 1990 Gulf War. But it really grew at a remarkable rate with the launch of STAR TV. The Hong Kong based STAR television—giving 24 hour television fare of five channels, in addition to the limited duration Hindi service channel—has been the most noticeable development in recent times. It is estimated that 400,000 Indian households are already hooked on to STAR TV (*Times of India*, February 21, 1992).

The spread of Video Cassette Recorders (VCRs) in India has also been significant. Binod C. Agrawal (1989) estimated that there were about two million VCRs in the country. The number has gone up significantly since then. It is estimated that two per cent of Indian households have a VCR. But the actual access to the video programmes is much greater, due to the prevalence of 'cable television.' The term cable television in India means distribution of video programmes from a centrally located VCR in a residential complex.

The same 'cable television's is now used for the distribution of television programmes received directly from satellites through a dish antenna. The channel selection very often rests not with the subscriber but with the cable operator who controls the centrally-operated dish antenna and VCR. There has been a manifold increase in the number of dish antenna and cable television subscribers but the precise number is not known. In a small sample survey, S.R. Joshi (1991) found that out of 54 television viewing households in Ahmedabad 14 subscribed to cable television, while none of the 54 rural households in two villages near Ahmedabad subscribed to cable television. In another nation-wide study S.R. Joshi and K.M. Parma (1992) found that out of 483 respondents 59 respondents subscribed to cable television and that all of them resided in metropolitan or urban areas. In short, one can say that, in spite of a substantial growth in the number of television sets and cable subscribers, a large majority of India's population does not have access to television and that the dish or cable television is largely an urban semi-urban phenomenon.

Television Programme Supply

The mode of programme transmission in India is different from that of the other countries have multiple channels and very often there are specialised channels. For example, there is an entertainment channel a music channel, a sports channel, a new and current affairs channel and so on. In India, there are only two channels, both managed by Doordarshan. The 'second' channel is restricted to the four metros. The 'first' channel is the primary channel in the sense that it is a nation-wide channel. This channel is utilised for different purposes of a time-sharing basis. The same channel is used for local, regional and national transmission and for entertainment, new education/sports, etc., all on a time-sharing basis.

Since the four countries differed in the number of channels, the data were normalised on the basis of minutes transmitted per day per channel to make cross-country comparison possible. Data regarding the programmes actually transmitted were gathered for two randomly selected two-week periods—that is, for 28 days of transmission. The data were analysed to see, among other things, the proportion of national to foreign programmes. A programme was defined as 'foreign programme' when it originated in a foreign country and it was transmitted without any change in its content of video or audio. Table 3.5 shows that over 90 per cent of the programmes transmitted by Doordarshan were Indian programmes. The Indian situation was very similar to the Korean one but it was very different from the situation in Australia and the Philippines, where the foreign programme component was 54 per cent and 67 per cent respectively.

Table 3.5: Internationalisation of National Programme Supply (Per Day Per Channel)

Country	*Australia*		*India*		*Philippines*		*Korea*	
	Minutes	*%*	*Minutes*	*%*	*Minutes*	*%*	*Minutes*	*%*
Domestic Supply	549	46	722	91.7	634	67.3	687	91.1
Foreign Supply	649	54	65	8.3	311	32.7	67	8.9
Total Supply	1198	100	787	100.0	945	100.0	754	100.0

Source: Based on Survey of Transnationalisation of Television in Four Asian Countries, Goonasekera (1992).

Table 3.6 gives the breakup of national and foreign programmes in the different countries according to UNESCO-defined programme categories. An earlier UNESCO study conducted in Europe had shown that the drama/movie programme category totally dominated the foreign programmes shown on national television. The situation is somewhat different in the Asia-Pacific countries. In Australia and South Korea drama and movies dominate, with 66.8 per cent and 51.3 per cent of foreign programme respectively. In India the figure is 31.1 per cent and in the Philippines it is 44.3 per cent, sports (54.9%) and educational programmes (0.9%) are the other two categories with significant foreign programme inputs. While making comparisons between different countries one should keep in mind than the total component of foreign programmes varied a great deal. It was less than nine per cent in India and Korea, but it was more than 50 per cent in Australia and Philippines.

Table 3.6: National Supply, Foreign Supply, Total Supply on National Channel by Programme Categories

Programme Category	Australia			India			Philippines			Korea		
	Nat. %	*For.* %	*Total* %	*Nat.* %	*For.* %	*Total* %	*Nat.* %	*For.* %	*Total* %	*Nat.* %	*For.* %	*Total* %
Dramamovies	8.2	66.8	40	24.9	31.1	25.4	22.2	44.3	29.4	12.5	51.3	15.8
Light Enter	22.3	13.4	17.5	2.2	0.0	2.0	26.0	26.0	25.9	14.3	21.2	14.9
Music	10.4	0.9	5.5	9.9	0.0	9.1	3.5	5.4	4.1	0.7	0.0	0.7
Sports	16.5	3.5	9.5	9.2	54.9	13.0	6.4	1.4	4.8	12.0	1.5	11.1
News	8.9	5.5	7.1	14.6	0.0	13.4	10.5	2.0	8.0	16.8	6.0	15.9
Information	21.2	0.0	9.7	20.1	3.1	18.7	11.9	10.2	11.2	27.9	2.4	25.6
Arts	3.2	0.7	1.9	0.7	0.0	0.6	0.3	3.0	1.1	3.2	17.6	4.5
Education	7.6	9.0	8.4	12.9	10.9	12.7	5.1	0.6	3.6	12.1	0.0	11.0
Religious	1.5	0.0	0.7	0.0	0.0	0.0	10.6	7.5	9.6	0.2	0.0	0.2
Others	0.0	0.0	0.0	5.5	0.0	5.1	3.1	0.0	2.3	0.4	0.0	0.4
Total (%)	100	100	100	100	100	100	100	100	100	100	100	100
PR Channel	549	787	1198	722	65	787	634	311	945	687	67	754
All Channels	2745	3245	5990	722	65	787	3170	1555	4725	3433	335	3768

Source: Based on A Survey of Transnationalisation of Television in Four Asian Countries, Goonasekera (1992).

It is clear that the proportion of foreign programmes supply in India has been very small. However, one should remember that when this study was conducted, STAR TV had barely made its entry through the Indian sky and there was hardly the proliferation of dish antennae that one sees today. The study was primarily based on Doordarshan supply since that was practically the only source of programme supply. The situation has definitely changed today.

Programme Consumption

The pattern of consumption of the programmes also varies from country to country. Table 3.7 gives the country-wise break up. It is lowest in India (1.9 %). It may be recalled that while the supply of foreign programmes was almost the same in India and South Korea, the consumption was much higher in South Korea (11.7 %). But in Australia and Philippines, where more than half the programme supply was foreign, more than one-third of the programmes consumed were foreign programmes.

Table 3.7: Internationalisation of Consumption of National Programme Supply (Per Person Per Day)

Country	*Australia*		*India*		*Philippines*		*Korea*	
	Minutes	*%*	*Minutes*	*%*	*Minutes*	*%*	*Minutes*	*%*
Domestic	108	62.9	87	98.1	62	60.8	132	88.3
Foreign	66	37.1	2	1.9	40	39.2	18	11.7
Total Consumption	178	100	89	100	102	100	150	100

Source: Based on A Survey of Transnationalisation of Television in Four Asian Countries, Goonasekera (1992).

The consumption of foreign programmes varies according to sex age, education and the level of urbanisation of the viewers. If one were to draw the profile of the Indian viewer who watches more foreign in programmes, the profile would be that of a young, educated, male residing in a metropolitan area. The consumption of foreign programmes is almost negligible amongst children, females and those residing in rural areas and those having minimal education. Language ability seems to be playing an important role in determining whether a person would watch a foreign programme or not.

Table 3.8 indicates that in India, the maximum consumption of foreign programmes falls in the category of sports and the rest is equally distributed in drama, light entertainment and information-related programmes. It is of interest to note that while a little over 10 per cent of the total foreign programmes supplied consisted of educational programmes, there is no consumption of the same. The pattern for consumption of national programmes was quite different. The maximum consumption fell in the drama/ movies category followed by news and music programmes.

Table 3.8: Internationalisation of Total Consumption of National Programme Supply by 10 Programme Categories (Per Person Per Day)

Programme Category	*Natioinal*	*Foreign*	*Total Consumption*	*As % of Programme Category*
1. Drama/Movie	67.8	8.3	66.6	0.2
2. Light Enter	2.1	8.3	2.3	7.1
3. Music	11.3	0.0	11.1	0.0
4. Sports	1.3	75.0	2.7	52.9
5. News	12.5	0.0	12.3	0.0
6. Information	3.9	8.3	4.0	4.0
7. Arts	0.8	0.0	0.0	0.0
8. Education	0.2	0.0	0.0	0.0
9. Religious	0.0	0.0	0.0	0.0
10. Others	0.0	0.0	0.0	0.0
Total	100	100	100	1.9
Total Minutes	87	2	89	

Note: NAT= National Origin FOR = Foreign Origin
Foreign as % of Total = Foreign Origin Consumption Minutes/Total Consumption Minutes (For One Programme Category)

Source: Based on a Survey of Transnationalisation of Television in Four Asian Countries, Goonasekera (1992).

Coefficient of Utilisation

Table 3.9 presents data on coefficients of utilisation of programmes in different countries. The coefficient is calculated according to the following formula:

$$\text{Coefficient} = \frac{\text{Consumption per person per day}}{\text{Supply of all channels per day}} \times 100$$

Table 3.9: Coefficients of Utilisation of National Programme Supply

Origin	*Australia* %	*India* %	*Philippines* %	*Korea* %
Domestic	3.9	12.0	1.9	3.8
Foreign	2.0	3.1	2.6	5.4
Total Supply	3.0	11.3	2.2	4.0

Formula coefficient (Consumption per person per day/supply all channels per day)

Source: Based on a Survey of Transnationalisation of Television in Four Asian Countries, Goonasekera (1992).

The coefficient is the ratio of supply to consumption stated in percentage terms. It was seen that India had the highest coefficient of utilisation. It was also observed that the coefficient of utilisation was much higher for Indian programmes as compared to the foreign programmes. It was observed that in India the highest coefficient of utilisation was in the category of information (7.1 %) followed by sports (3.6 %).

Analysis of cable television and video programme viewing also indicated that there was very little viewing of foreign programmes in India. As mentioned earlier, out of 483 respondents, only 59 respondents subscribed to cable television and all of them resided in the metropolitan or urban areas. These 59 respondents reported viewing of 153 programmes in a one week period. Of these, 57 programmes (37.2 %) were foreign programme, mostly transmitted through foreign satellites. Significantly, out of 483 respondents, only 22 or 4.55 per cent respondents watched these foreign programmes. The most predominant use of cable television was to watch Indian movies or other film-based programmes.

Conclusions

While the number of television sets has increased enormously in the last 10 years, there is still a long way to go for providing the Indian population with access to television. At present only 20 per cent of households in India has access to television.

- Indian television shows a very small percentage of foreign programmes and the consumption of foreign programmes is also very low.

- The use of foreign satellites is mainly restricted to upper middle class, young, educated persons residing in urban or metropolitan areas. However, the situation appears to be changing fast.
- The main use of television as well as cable television is entertainment. However, there is also a significant use of television for news and information.
- The coefficient of utilisation is highest in India.

A great deal of anxiety is often expressed about the onslaught of foreign satellites and programmes. The anxiety is about the cultural, social, political and economic impact of these. There is also the anxiety that viewers will be lured away from Doordarshan. My view is that there is no reason to take a negative or pessimistic view of the situation. There are certain technological developments which cannot be wished away. There is no reason to believe that Indians will mainly view foreign programmes. On the contrary, many foreign satellite channels, like Zee TV and ATN have started showing Indian programmes. This will only mean more Indian programmes, even if they are on a foreign satellite channel. Competition will increase, foreign programmes will be watched, but most Indians will continue to watch Indian programmes.

The Crucial Question

Since the Sixth Plan there is a definite move on the part of the government to give higher funding to the Communication Sector. Now the question arises whether in its enthusiasm to expand the communication network, there has been a reshuffling of priorities by the government. Has the higher allocation, to this sector been achieved at the cost of other basic sectors, such as health, education, water and sanitation? The fundamental issue is whether the government is morally justified in diverting huge funds to the communication sector in the face of growing poverty in the country. The Seventh Plan clearly states that over 300 million people in India live below the poverty line. It is a sad irony that over Rs. 12,000 crores have been earmarked to develop a network, which benefits less than 25 per cent of the population, thus depriving hundreds of millions of people of their basic right to food, clothing and shelter. (Media Development, 1989).

STRATEGY FOR MAKING VIDEO PROGRAMME PACKAGES

Television holds tremendous potential as a means of educating and making the viewers conscientious about problems pertaining to their own health, in particular, and the environmental wholesomeness, in general. It is pertinent to recognise, however, that health and nutrition, important ingredients of life as they are, cannot be looked at in isolation from the socio-cultural and economic aspects of the human populace, urban and rural, both. Dealing with health problems piecemeal, devoid of the interacting process of life, minimises, the effectiveness of such programmes in generating a positive, rationalistic and scientific attitude towards solving these problems. Such a fragmentary approach becomes a dilutory effort leading to vague generalities, inconsequential in mobilising the viewers to desired action.

Before starting with the more concrete process of producing these programmes, it is important to arrive at a more in-depth analysis and understanding of the interlinkages in human affairs as well as the underlying causes at the root of diseases, both social and physiological in nature. Consequential upon a whole lot of factors, the changes (subtle and obvious) that have occurred in the social situation in as far as the lifestyle, level of consciousness and value systems of the people are concerned, require to be studied to enable use to view and deal with these issues in a wider perspective. The technological developments, more specifically in the area of medicine and surgery, the effects and influences they have on the well-being or otherwise of the people, cannot be ignored. The potentials and limitations of the on-going medical systems, availability of an accessibility to the resources of care and good health for the average population, are other factors that need to be pondered over and taken into account. The ever-increasing gap between the growing infrastructural facility on the one side and constantly multiplying numbers that need them on the other, makes in imperative to arrive at alternatives that can help maintain a reasonable balance between the two.

Besides, the commercialisation of medical system renders the proper use of such facilities beyond the means and reach of the larger chunk of our population. The culture of over-dependence on the modern and more sophisticated techniques of medical process have almost wiped out the localised systems of curing—

even the most common and conventionally manageable ailments; notwithstanding the hazards of potentially dangerous drugs when used more frequently and without proper medical guidance and supervision. In such a state of affairs identifying the local resources and means, educating the viewers regarding the advantages of preventive measures, emphasising the need for proper nutrition and planned family size, and demonstrating the possibilities of domestic cure, can lessen dependence on outside assistance and supplies, and go a long way in providing answers to the general health problems of the people who themselves happen to be the most valuable resource for their own health.

With this backdrop we may now proceed to work out a strategy for preparing video-programme packages—both for transmission as well as non-transmission use.

Scope and Objectives

The general objectives of such a programme-package should be to:

(*i*) Sensitise the viewers towards the problems and needs pertaining to their health, nutrition, family size and their inter-relationship with the environmental realities—with a view to generate a more scientific and rationalistic attitude and approach in dealing with these problems (both immediate as well as long-term) and finding practically manageable solutions to tackle them effectively.

(*ii*) Stressing on self-help as one of the best ways to good health and helping the viewers to develop a sense of collectiveness and responsibility towards one another and encouraging them to be involved in the decisions about health.

The specific objectives would be as under:

(*i*) To apprise the viewers about the hazards of over-dependence and blind faith in any of the prevailing medical systems, emphasising the damage that indiscriminate use of drugs can do.

(*ii*) To sensitise the viewers about the environmental influences on their health, and the need for a clean and healthy environment.

(*iii*) To demonstrate the positive advantages of preventive measures as well as suggesting simple and effective means of coping with common, symptomatic ailments like diarrhoea, cold, indigestion etc.

(*iv*) Giving the viewers skills to promote good health and to treat minor illness and injuries by themselves.

(*v*) To make the viewers conscious about the maladies of malnutrition and unhygienic diet and suggest a more balanced diet system, possible within the average income-status.

(*vi*) To educate the audience about the possible ill-effects of some of the taboos and superstitions pertaining to prenatal as well as post-natal problems among women and also the process of child-rearing (this shall be done in such a manner that their deep-rooted cultural feelings do not get hurt) and suggest scientific means of dealing with these issues.

Note: It may be emphasised that children and women shall form the core attention-group inasfar as the priorities in the selection of diseases and problems as also some practically possible suggestions regarding health and well-being, are concerned.

The Pedagogical and Communications Approach

In order to attain the set objectives to the optimum possible level, we may adopt what can be termed as the integrated approach.

The integrated approach is the total approach, wherein the varied aspects of life that influence the human situation, are taken into account. "Too often health professionals and governments have tried to tell the people what was wrong, rather than encouraging the people to be involved in the decisions about health" (Lowell Levin, *World Health*).

On the media side, our experience shows that when it comes to making health programmes, it is generally the diseases, their symptoms, their causes and effects, possible remedies and preventive measures, that are taken up. Such single slot disease centred approach does perhaps have its meaning, but it only scratches the surface. While the need for specific and detailed information cannot be overemphasised, by itself it does not suffice the cognitive requirements of the viewers in as far as their active involvement is concerned. The disease lies much deeper.

"There are social causes for much sickness and death, not just biological ones" (Lowell Levin). Focus on symptomatic aspects of diseases keep the human element in the background, reducing it to the secondary status, which in effect alienates the viewers from their problems. The viewer response to such programmes is only casual. While they gain information, the will to take to new ideas, and apply the acquired knowledge in practice is not sufficiently stimulated. The gains as opposed to media efforts made as such are only peripheral. Not without reasons though. The practical difficulties of treading on non-conventional paths are manifold and it becomes easier to stick to tested routes, however, inadequate they might be.

While it becomes necessary to evoke the need for change, it is equally important to work out the modalities for such desired change within the framework of real situations as they exist, the pre-occupations of the people that are being addressed, and practically of the suggestions put forward through these programmes. Some of the traditional values that are detrimental to development and change have to be cautiously and carefully questioned, taking the sensitivities of the viewers pertaining to their beliefs and customs into full cognisance. The approach should be such as can generate confidence among the viewers inasfar as their personal security (physical as well as psychological) *vis-à-vis* the subject-matter and presentation of these programmes is concerned.

Emphasising self-dependence and help, should form the main thrust inasfar as the pedagogical aspects of these programmes are concerned.

As for the portrayal of characters and the events associated with them, the overall approach will have to be of positive attitude-building taking up both negative and positive elements that happen to be a part of the existent realities. The purpose is not showing, things, just as they are but also showing how they ought to be, or could be. The ultimate goal is not to frighten the viewers about the grimness of the situation, but letting them realise that grim and different though the situation is, it is possible to find ways of improving it to our benefit within the resources at our disposal as of now. One may call it an idealistic approach, but it is required as a part of the pedagogical process to make people more confident in themselves, in their own potentials. There is no Utopia, but there are pragmatic practical possibilities within the reach of human effort. The totality of the situation when taken care of in the process of designing, planning, executing and transmitting these programmes will go a long way in optimising positive viewer response and helping them to acquire the status of "praxis" the process of reflection and action—each leading to other.

As is evident, the integrated approach implies a wider canvas, a broader frame of reference. Our emphasis is on the people—their lives with its sweet and bitter experiences, their dreams and aspirations, their potentials and shortcomings, their varied day-to-day as well as long term problems. Blended with all these will be the problems of their health—their minor and major ailments, an analysis of the clinical and underlying causes of these diseases and the pros and cons of the current practices that they follow tackling these problems. All this will be coupled with suggestions regarding the possibilities of approaching these problems and seeking solutions in a scientific and rationalistic manner.

Social life in terms of events, interactions between people at different levels, concerns caused by historical as well as the ongoing influences and also the philosophic content of each individual life have a certain continuity; physical and abstract. It is therefore, necessary that the spirit of these linkages and continuity gets reflected through these programmes.

PRASAR BHARATI RECRUITMENT RULES

Public broadcaster Prasar Bharati is in the process of finalising recruitment rules and service conditions of its employees, Rajya Sabha was told today.

The finalisation of the recruitment rules and service conditions will give the option to the employees of Prasar Bharati for absorption as per the provisions of Prasar Bharati Act 1990, S. Jaipal Reddy, the Minister for Information and Broadcasting, told Rajya Sabha in written reply to a question.

The government had allowed deemed deputation status to the employees working in the Prasar Bharati Corporation and this was done to clarify the state of the government servants in the Corporation and enable Prasar Bharati to exercise necessary powers of a borrowing authority, he said.

Reddy said National Federation of Akashwani and Doordarshan Employees had submitted a memorandum in

September 2004 urging upon the government to ensure proper funding of Prasar Bharati through the grants-in-aid and ensure that they continue to receive the facilities to which they are entitled as government employees.

BECIL

Broadcast Engineering Consultants India Limited (BECIL), a Government of India enterprise, established in the year 1995, provides consultancy services and also undertakes turnkey jobs in the specialised fields of Broadcast Engineering and Information Technology. BECIL has a vast reservoir of experts who come from the premier broadcasting organizations of the country.

BECIL Strength

BECIL provides rapid response to customer needs with quality-driven, attractively priced propositions. It has flexible, tailor-made solutions to every customer's unique requirements. A total quality approach with frequent reviews and monitoring facilitates efficient and cost-effective completion of every project on schedule.

BECIL Field of Activities

BECIL provides consultancy services including turnkey jobs in the specialized fields like Acoustics, Audio-Video Systems (SRS/conferencing/recording/production and post-production systems), Terrestrial & Satellite Broadcasting, Data Broadcasting, MMDS and CATV Network.

BECIL Services

BECIL consultancy and turnkey services range from system design, planning, specifications, site selection, installation and commissioning to projecting running costs, staffing and in service operations regardless of location.

INDIAN RADIO AND TV CHANNELS

- AVS TV—Telecasts Indian movies and songs in USA.
- Adhikari Brothers Television Network—TV programme production.

- All India Radio—Sound broadcasting service operated by Government of India.
- Asian Entertainment TV—Entertainment channel catering Asian community.
- Asianet TV—Asian channel on cable TV network in the United Kingdom.
- Broadcast Engineering Society—Dissemination of Radio and Television broadcast knowledge.
- DD India—News, live telecast, programme schedule and more.
- Delhi FM—Online radio and music channel.
- DesiGrooveRadio—Internet radio channel for Hindi and Bhangra music.
- Doordarshan—Major TV channel in India.
- Doordarshan Jaipur—Rajasthan state television channel.
- Gemini TV—Telugu satellite channel.
- ITBC Radio—Canadian International Tamil radio.
- Ilaignan.com—Tamil Internet radio.
- India Guide—Guide on Indian TV programmes & channels.

RADIO NETWORKS
Site Listings

Most Popular

- Voice of America@.
- National Public Radio (NPR) (46).
- BBC Radio@.
- Radio France Internationale (RFI)—variety of frequencies and programmes on cable, FM, and short wave.
- Radio Free Europe/Radio Liberty—US government funded network with multilingual broadcasts on shortwave, AM and FM bands.
- Air America Radio (13).
- Pacifica Radio (6).

Alphabetical

- ABC Radio Networks (2).
- Air America Radio (13).

- BBC Radio@.
- Birach Broadcasting—operates a network of radio stations encompassing the midwest, northeast portions of the United States and Ontario.
- Caracol Cadena Basica—Colombian radio network.
- CNNRadio—provides news, sports, business, and feature reports to affiliate radio stations worldwide.
- Emmis Communications (Nasdaq: EMMS).
- ESPN Radio Network@.
- Great Lakes Radio Consortium—produces environmentally focused radio and news features heard on more than 100 public radio stations.
- Islamic Broadcasting Network—IBN—offers family programmes, news, and current affairs. Aims to meet the religious and cultural needs of American Muslim youth, as well as dispel myths and stereotypes about Islam and Muslims.
- Learfield Communications. Inc.
- Michigan Radio Network—programmed daily news service for commercial radio stations, including both data and audio news properties.
- Minnesota Public Radio@.
- Monitor Radio—Monitor Radio programming is heard on countless Public Radio International stations and by shortwave listeners worldwide. Now, Monitor Radio is available via the global Internet computer network.
- National Public Radio (NPR) (46).
- New Dimensions Broadcasting Network—in-depth dialogues seeking positive ways to meet personal, social, spiritual, and cultural challenges.
- North Carolina News Network—news, hurricane tracking and sports.
- Pacifica Radio (6).
- Prairie Public Broadcasting—providing free information and discussion throughout North Dakota and northwestern Minnesota.
- Premiere Radio Networks—features programming covering sports, health, politics, music, entertainment and more.

- Public Radio International (PRI) (6).
- Radio America—the 24-hour conservative radio network.
- Radio Bakwaas—Indian talk and music radio network.
- Radio Disney.
- Radio France Internationale (RFI)—variety of frequencies and programmes on cable, FM, and short wave.
- Radio Free Europe/Radio Liberty—US government funded network with multilingual broadcasts on shortwave, AM and FM bands.
- Radio Left—the Anti-Rush, Anti-GOP Antidote. Driving the right wing nuts.
- Radio Sawa—communicating directly in Arabic with the peoples of the Middle East by radio.
- Red River Radio Network—public radio network offering programming information, community information and more.
- TARBS—World TV—Television and Radio Broadcasting Services. Operates within Australia and internationally as a multicultural subscription TV and radio broadcaster.
- Tribune Radio Networks—carries agribusiness programming and Chicago Cubs broadcasts.
- Voice of America@.
- WestStar TalkRadio Network—broadcast syndicator produces The Kim Komando Radio Show, An American Christmas, and The Komando Computer Minute.
- Westwood One (NYSE:WON)—provides news, sports, weather, traffic, video news services, and other local content to the radio and television industries.
- Yellowstone Public Radio—listener supported public radio in Montana and northern Wyoming.

India Television

- Doordarshan India—Doordarshan India network.

Hindi Entertainment

- Zee Television—One of India's prime Hindi Channels.
- Sony Entertainment Television—Another mainly Hindi Channel' shows dubbed English serials and some Hindi programmes.

Movie Channels

- Star Movies.
- Zee Cinema—The official website of the different Zee Cinema around the globe from Asia to the Americas.

Guides

- Indian television—India's cable, satellite terrestrial broadcasting portal.
- Indian television dot com is the online destination of all professionals wanting to be in touch with the Indian television industry, television news, information, research, programming and profession databases, and E-commerce related to the television business.
- theindiaguide.com is India's first website for personalized TV.

Music

- Channel V—Star Networks Music channel.
- MTV Asia—Asia transmission of MTV.
- Music Asia—Music Asia Hindi Songs.

News

- British Broadcasting Corporation.
- CNN—Cable News Network. The News channel.
- Star News Channel—A new 24 hour channel on Star, guided famous political analyst Prannoy Roy.

Sports

- 10 Sports.
- DD Sports—Cricket A Doordarshan site that hosts cricket related information. Occasionally broadcasts live games as well.
- ESPN-Star.

Others

- CNBC Asia—The Asian version of the American CNBC channel.

- Pakistan Television.
- Siti Cable.
- Star Television—The TV network that kind of started the satellite revolution in India.

Radio

- AIR—All India Radio.
  This is the official website of All India Radio. Yeh Aakashwani hai.
- India Network Radio.
- Radio of India—Website that broadcasts Songs and other programmes in numerous languages such as Hindi, Tamil and Telugu.
- Radio Mirchi—Radio Mirchi is an organization that broadcasts programmes over FM from different cities in India such as Mumbai, Delhi, Ahmedabad, Pune and Indore.

INDIAN CINEMA

If India attained a pre-eminent position in any single visual art after Independence it was film making. It shot up to become the top in the world and still retains that pinnacled position. In 1983, over 800 feature films were certified for public exhibition mostly in colour and a few in black and white. This number was nearly four times what India was producing immediately after Independence. Language-wise, Telugu topped the list followed by films in Hindi and Malayalam. Trailing behind were films in Bengali, Gujarati and Marathi. Within the film industry the most significant development that has taken place during this period is the acceleration of film making in south India. Both in terms of the number of cinema halls, and in respect of the number of pictures produced, the south has forged ahead to take the lead from the well-entrenched traditional centre of Mumbai. Over the years more than 17,000 films have been produced in India. More than 13 million Indians go to the movies everyday, sometimes trudging miles to the nearest movie hall.

Yet this enormous structure caters essentially for urban and suburban people, who represent only one-fifth of the total population. The number of cinema houses where films can be screened are 11,682 including the touring talkies. These cinema houses are unevenly distributed and obviously well below the world average.

Milestones in the Growth of Cinema

Many milestones marked the overall growth of cinema in the country since Independence. The government showed concern about the balanced development of the cinema which had become a money bag and multi-star industry. To this end, it appointed the Film Enquiry Committee whose recommendations resulted in the foundation of some basic institutions like Films Division of India, Film Finance Corporation and Children's Film Society in the sixties. In their own way these institutions including a growing number of talented producers and directors have cumulatively given a shot in the arm to the film industry.

The Films Division set up by the Ministry of Information and Broadcasting in 1948 gave a boost to documentary films and upgraded it professionally and technically. In 1975 the National Films Development Corporation was constituted, which was activated in 1980 and the Film Finance Corporation and the Indian Motion Picture Export Corporation were amalgamated with it. The Corporation plays a vital role. Its function is to plan, promote and organise an integrated and efficient development of the industry in accordance with the national economic policy and objectives. Its broad range of activities covers the handling of the import and export of feature films, allocation and distribution of raw stock and equipment used by the industry, distribution and exhibition of films through the existing network, and undertaking a programme of construction of a chain of national theatres, promotion of quality films, research and development in film equipment and raw stock. Recently the Corporation has taken an innovative step in deciding to finance the production of features, *i.e.*, films of approximately half an hour to one hour duration. These can be shown on TV networks in India and abroad.

Film as a Change Agent

The film is motion, picture, sound, theatre and school all packed in one. That is why it can communicate effectively, create better impact than other mass media and draw hundreds and thousands of viewers including the illiterates, workers and villagers. Even the elite and urbanites swarm cine halls or glue to their seats at home near video-cum-TV sets. The film being visual reality and a universal language cutting across cultural barriers, film exponents advocate that a socially relevant cinema can prove to be the best activist. Taking the example of India as a developing country where less than five per cent of the population buy or read newspapers and books, the talkie film is perhaps the only popular form of culture available to a large number of the common people. The contact of most of the people with prose is the dialogue that they hear in pictures, the only poetry that enriches their lives is the poetry of film lyrics, and their models for style, fashion and mannerisms are the celluloid heroes. Many experts therefore think that the film can educate and inspire, motivate and change their attitudes. To use the communication language, the film in the hands of good script writers and directors can function not only to spread a common filmy language but act as a social monitor and a gatekeeper as well. Like any magazine or newspaper, it can be effectively investigatory and expository. More than any other media it can tellingly project social angularities and injustices, forcibly portray the moods and attitudes of alienated and wayward youngsters, emotionally and incisively depict what poverty is and how farmers/workers, woman and the poor and down-trodden eke out their existence. Recent feature and TV films show that given wise direction, the film without becoming didactive or ceasing to be an entertainer, can expose the black marketeer, the corrupt politician, the anti-social, industrialist or a trade union *dada,* the 'yes minister' bureaucrat, eve teaser and social parasite. Not only in this respect but positively it can stimulate values of good life and citizenship as also participatory virtues of developmental activities. Through characterisation, demonstration and depiction of scenes and situations, it can even directly help to sell the concepts and norms of national or emotional integration, dignity of labour, the bare-foot doctor or engineer, an understanding spouse and the pulls of extra-marital relations. Documentary experts say that within the constraints of creative reality, even these films can reflect their country's development aspirations and strivings and even the failings and achievements of its people.

In some African, Asian or communist countries there are few individual film makers classified as new-wave film makers, who have set in motion the movement for the socially relevant cinema. This indicate the effort to use the power of the film medium not only to entertain, but to educate and influence the life pattern of viewers. As a change agent its potentiality has started manifesting to reach wider audience, to persuade them and to get their acceptance. The commercial cinema has also started reflecting some of these new trends and offbeat themes of great social significance.

Commercial Cinema

The cinema after Independence in India was predominantly commercial so far as feature films were concerned. The star system, high budgets, escapism, concoction of popular entertainment ingredients, and abundance of music, song and dance were generally the characteristics of this cinema. Circumstances like inflation, overcrowding, dislocated life, social tension, rampant unemployment, disillusionment and youth alienation encouraged film makers to resort to fantasies and escapist or entertaining themes for their pictures. Starting with *Sholay* and graduating from certain films like *Kache Dhage* and *Reshma Aur Shera,* Indian heroes started having an image of a Robin Hood, Garth or Tarzan. The films had revenge as the theme with accompanying attributes of fighting violence. As one critic points out "the dividing lines between art and industry, between north and south, between the moghul and the maverick became hazier than before, movies more than any of the arts provided a spectacle that enthralled, exasperated and appalled in excess." Multi-crore budgeting registered ascendance in *Naseeb* and *Kranti* and reached its culmination in *Razia Sultan,* which also sought to out do any other picture in respect of grandiose of set and costumes.

Reaction to this trend however found a manifestation both in the form of the evolution of a new wave or art cinema and the appearance of new directions in commercial cinema itself.

A new trend in film making was born first in Kolkata and then in sporadic waves in other centres of film production in the south. The impact of international film festivals, the institution of film awards, documentary cinema, and the influence of famous film makers from abroad like Jean Renoir (France), Frank Capra (Hollywood), V.I. Pudovkin (USSR) were some of the forces which contributed to the quest for an alternative cinema. These new trend films were made at low costs, outside the mainstream of commercial cinema. Their dominant characteristics were their social concern, purposefulness, realism, narrative style, exclusion of unrelated song and dance routines and fights and other familiar devices of the commercial package. Their acceptance by the intelligent and cultivated audiences in the country and the high praise which some of the really good new trend films won abroad brought a much needed self-confidence to adventurous or innovative film makers. The Film Finance Corporation and its successor the National Films Development Corporation provided institutional aid to the otherwise individualistic trend among young film makers. Some notable proponents of this new wave cinema, also called socially relevant cinema or alternative cinema, were Satyajit Ray, K.A. Abbas, Balraj Sahni, Raj Kapoor, Shyam Benegal, Mrinal Sen, Basu Chatterjee, M.S. Sathyu, Utpalendu Chakraborty, Pattabhi Rama Reddy, Adoor Gopalakrishnan, Govind Nihalani, Girish Karnad and B.V. Karanth. This trend was, however beset with difficulties. Important among these were lack of finance and exhibition halls, direct confrontation with influential commercial cinema and their monopoly distributors, and extreme individualism in communication appeals and entertainment techniques by sophisticated aesthetics. Yet, with assistance from Film Finance Corporation and other means, some prize winning films like *Ghare Baire* and *Paar* have been produced. Mrinal Sen, who is regarded as one of the Third World's most experienced and internationally renowned radical film makers, has produced new films that win prize after prize. From *Ek Din Pratidin to Khandar* is a saga of laurel winning in film making. He himself says that cinema should not hibernate and many a film maker with his way of thinking besides India's film wizard Satyajit Ray, have been experimenting with the medium to find a new analysis on the growing explosive social situations around them. The films *Chokh* by Utpalendu Chakraborty and *Damul* by Prakash Jha are described as models of possible alternative cinema, for it is cinema of hope. It is advocated that a good film is one that should depict the odds against the best of life and yet seek to transcend them and affirm that these odds should not choke the indomitable spirit of the men, women and children of a society. *Ardh Satya* is considered the new cinema's biggest hit. It deals with the inequitous system of justice through the story of a sadistic policeman. It is heartening that old masters of new cinema continue to work with increasing maturity and younger film makers are exploring newer subjects and styles with growing confidence.

While the movement for the new cinema in India is still on, though with different intensity and dimensions in different regions, there are some discernible new directions manifested in the commercial cinema itself. Reaction against high budgeting was visible when Hrishikesh Mukherjee carried on the New Theatres tradition with some success. The films of Basu Chatterjee, *Rajnigandha* and *Chhotisi Baat* with their humorous insights into the ordinary daily life of people, proved that such movies could also attract crowds. Films like *Love Story* and *Ek Dujje Ke Liye,* costing one-tenth of the high price-tagged pictures, almost shattered the concept that multi-crore and multi-star pictures would essentially be box-office hits. A change in acting style seemed to be obvious. A new line of heroes and heroines have started emerging who seek to play their roles as actors and actresses and not just stars. Another thing that has emerged is the return of love stories and adoption of offbeat themes including women's lib, extra-marital relations, estrangement between parents and children and the lives of coal miners. Pictures like *Arth, Souten, Dard Ka Rista, Talaq, Mandi, Do Dishayen, Devta, Mayuri* and *Kalka* have proved that such pictures have started having more appeal to the changing tastes and moods of cine goers. Film makers have stopped depicting women as objects of sex exploitation or male chauvinism. A set of films dubbed as feminine genre are gaining popularity. These films present women as equal citizens and individuals in their own right. In *Arth,* two women, a wife and a lover, move from emotional dependence on a man to the freedom of rebuilding their lives on their own. *Subha* sought to find justification for a woman to seek fulfilment in her career even at the cost of her marital security. The movie *Mujhe Insaf Chahiye* depicts the story of a liberated woman in all her trials and turbulations, including her angry cry for justice.

Yet another trend visible in the commercial cinema is an occasional effort at light comedies like *Chupke Chupke, Khatta Mitha, Naram Garam* and *Kissi se na Kehna.* These efforts only show that reasonable thematic experimentation or innovativeness in film-making in India can be tried without box-office debacle.

The taste of cinema goer's seems to be changing also in respect of over padding of chaotic song and dance sequences. This is discernible in cinema halls when viewers walk out when such scenes are being shown.

Some of the film critics today maintain that the real trend centres in the commercial cinemas are the regional films. While the previous monopoly of artistic Bengali films and of the commercial Hindi films has gone down, the regional cinema in Malayalam, Kannada, Telugu and other southern languages is coming into its own. Young directors and new stars are emerging in these regions. Even in competitions the winners are dominantly from regional cinema. However, a recent avalanche of semi-pornographic and blue films from the south, adroitly side-stepping the censor's regulations, constitute an alarming trend.

Documentary in India

India is forging ahead even in the field of documentary films, news reels, cartoon films and quickies which are all different visual instruments of public information, education and instruction, motivation and attitude changes. Defined originally as creative treatment of actuality, today documentary and information films include those which deal with significant historical, social, scientific or economic subjects, photographed in actual occurrence or reenacted, and the emphasis is more on factual content than on entertainment. These films record contemporary history and present filmic reports on the social and economic progress of a country.

Starting modestly when the Films Division of the Ministry of Information and Broadcasting was set up in 1948, India is currently having an annual production of 104 short films. In 1983-84 the Films Division produced 143 documentary films including 40 produced by independent producers.

In India the State governments, public undertakings and private enterprises can also produce documentaries. If they are within the maximum length of 2000 feet, these films can be released on theatrical circuits only through the Films Division. Production assignments can be also given to independent producers, and annually about 40 to 50 films are produced that way.

India has many well-known documentary film makers both

in the public and private sectors. They have made both individually and collectively, significant contributions to the development of Indian documentaries and animated films. Produced by Films Division many of these films have obtained international and national awards. Many independent producers outside Films Division have also made documentary films of merit and received awards for their films.

Documentaries and news reels are exhibited in all cinema houses and at each performance; the rental is one per cent of the average weekly collections. Every week one news reel and two short films are released at all important centres. The Films Division also supplies prints on loan to government departments, semi-government educational and charitable institutions, hospitals, social welfare organisations and individuals. This is done through its distribution branch offices as well as through the regional and field publicity units of the Directorate of Field Publicity. For non-commercial shows films are loaned free of charge.

The documentary film movement has a bright future in India. Other than the number of good film makers in the country, there are also sponsoring organisations which realise the importance of documentary films as a powerful and effective visual medium for depicting creative actuality of our changing social scenes and ecology. The government on its own part is looking forward to having more such films on technology, science, environment, ecology, places of pilgrimage, hill stations, sports, folk music, folk dances and other varieties of art and culture from various parts of the country.

Many Miles to Go

Whatever may be the quality of our motion pictures, they continue to be popular. The video and TV boom has further-boosted their importance and craze. TV films have added a new dimension and it is significant that the first TV film *(Sadgati)* was made by Satyajit Ray and more such films are being produced by other eminent film makers. Good films for children is another branch which needs to be further activised and diversified. To this end, the Children's Film Society, the main producing agency, is being keyed up.

India is an exporter of films especially to those areas where Indians or Asians live in fairly large numbers. It is heartening that package marketing interests and tastes of the internal audience has started being reflected in the widening range of current themes and their improving treatments. Participation in various national and international film festivals is helping to infuse new trends and techniques among the more professionally alert film makers, actors and technicians. Yet, some communication experts still believe that apart from popular entertainment ingredients, creativity and aesthetics, Indian films should become more socially purposeful. They should rid of their irrelevant paddings or trappings and professionally unedifying constituents to have a more ennobling impact on the youth and illiterate persons, without becoming pedantic or shedding individual creativity or professional merit.

At present there are, however, some inbuilt handicaps in the films industry. Apart from the firmness of censors and the new danger from video piracy, the most important hurdle in the way of this popular visual medium reaching a vast majority of people is scarcity of cinema houses and exhibition facilities. Very few of the existing cinema theatres have proximity. Very few of the existing cinema theatres have proximity to deep and distant places of rural India. Although Field Publicity units of the Central and State Governments do try to fill in the gap, the total number of cinema seats is much less than 2/5th of UNESCO's minimum norm. From the point of view of adequate and sophisticated technology the 16 mm, 8 mm super and wide screen technologies need to be improved. The position in respect of raw material and studio equipment also needs to be further geared up. Government activisation and the efforts of the National Films Development Corporation and other media organisations as also innovative film makers both in the field of commercial and new cinema, have pushed the medium and industry well ahead. But our films have many miles to go as yet in the direction of professional, communication and technical excellence, creative visual impact, wholesome entertainment, aesthetics and international marketability.

This task of the Indian cinema, in becoming a booming industry, a more persuasive and socially relevant change agent, technically well-equipped and a decent package offering wholesome entertainment and good music, places at tremendous responsibility upon the industry and on those who operate and direct it, as also on the governing media institutions and censors.

POLICY FOR IMPORT OF CINEMATOGRAPH FILMS AND OTHER FILMS

In exercise of powers conferred under Paragraph 4.11 of the Export and Import Policy 1997-2002, as notified in the Gazette of India extraordinary, Part II, Section 3, sub-section (ii) vide S.O. No. 283(E) dated 31.3.1997 and in supersession of Public Notice No. 4(PN)/9702 dated 31.3.1997, as amended from time to time, the Director General of Foreign Trade hereby notifies the policy for import of cinematograph films and other films (including film on video tape, compact video disc, laser video disc or digital video disc).

(*i*) Import of cinematograph feature films and other films (including film on video tape, compact video disc, laser video disc or digital video disc) shall be allowed without a licence.

(*ii*) The importer of the film shall comply with the provisions of all applicable Indian laws governing the distribution and exhibition of films, including the requirement of obtaining a certificate of public exhibition prescribed under the Cinematograph Act, 1952.

(*iii*) Import of any unauthorized/pirated films shall be prohibited.

(*iv*) import of foreign reprints of Indian films shall not be permitted without the prior permission in writing from the Ministry of Information and Broadcasting, Government of India.

(*v*) The Ministry of Information and Broadcasting, Government of India, on being satisfied that it is necessary or expedient in public interest to do so, may waive or relax the above requirements.

This issues in the public interest.

SHOOTING OF FOREIGN FEATURE FILMS IN INDIA

The Government of India invites foreign film teams to shoot their films in India—a country with locations of untold beauty. We have also simplified the procedure for shooting of films by foreigners in India and the ensuing paragraphs, we hope, will answer all your questions regarding the procedure to apply for shooting permission.

What should Accompany your Application?

- You need to send us a simple letter, telling us of your intention to shoot in India, mentioning the dates of shooting, particulars of the cast and crew, and you chosen locations. Please address your letter to the relevant address a month before your planned shooting schedule, and enclose four copies of the final, detailed shooting script, a draft/cheque for US $200 drawn in favour of Pay & Accounts Officer, Ministry of I&B, (MS), New Delhi (that is a fee for scrutiny of the script), detailed shooting locations and particulars regarding the cast and crew coming to India. *No fee is required for shooting documentaries in India.*
- Should you wish to bring your own shooting equipment, please send us a list of the equipment to be temporarily imported. This will enable us to make a recommendation to the customs authorities to exempt the temporary import from customs duty.
- Your permission to shoot will normally not take more than three weeks to process. The permission letter issued by the Government of India will facilitate your permission from other local authorities, which may, in some cases, need to be obtained directly from these authorities.
- In case any living personality is portrayed in the film as a Character, we suggest that you share the script with that personality or his/her legal heirs, before beginning the shooting, and obtain a 'No Objection Letter'. This letter will expedite the clearance of your application, and also guard against the possibility of any defamation or libel suits.
- If you propose to shoot your film as a co-production, a copy of the agreement between your company and the Indian party, indicating the role of each party, its responsibilities and liabilities, must accompany the application.
- If your film requires shooting in the scenic but sensitive areas of Jammu & Kashmir, the North Eastern India or border belts, and your application will be considered for specific approval in consultation with the Ministry of Home Affairs. In such cases, you would need to allow more time to process your application.

4

India's Information Technology: Law and Action Plan

COMPILATION OF CYBER LAWS IN INDIA

The Information Technology Act, 2000 (No. 21 of 2000) [9th June, 2000]

An Act to provide legal recognition for transactions carried out by means of electronic data interchange and other means of electronic communication, commonly referred to as "electronic commerce", which involve the use of alternatives to paper-based methods of communication and storage of information, to facilitate electronic filing of documents with the Government agencies and further to amend the Indian Penal Code, the Indian Evidence Act, 1872, the Bankers' Books Evidence Act, 1891 and the Reserve Bank of India Act, 1934 and for matters connected therewith or incidental thereto.

Whereas the General Assembly of the United Nations by resolution A/RES/51/162, dated the 30th January, 1997 has adopted the Model Law on Electronic Commerce adopted by the United Nations Commission on International Trade Law;

And whereas the said resolution recommends *inter alia* that all States give favourable consideration to the said Model Law when they enact or revise their laws, in view of the need for uniformity of the law applicable to alternatives to paper-cased methods of communication and storage of information; and

And whereas it is considered necessary to give effect to the said resolution and to promote efficient delivery of

Government services by means of reliable electronic records.

Be it enacted by Parliament in the Fifty-first Year of the Republic of India as follows:

Chapter I

PRELIMINARY

1. Short Title, Extent, Commencement and Application

1. This Act may be called the Information Technology Act, 2000.
2. It shall extend to the whole of India and, save as otherwise provided in this Act, it applies also to any offence or contravention hereunder committed outside India by any person.
3. It shall come into force on such date as the Central Government may, by notification, appoint and different dates may be appointed for different provisions of this Act and any reference in any such provision to the commencement of this Act shall be construed as a reference to the commencement of that provision.
4. Nothing in this Act shall apply to—
   (*a*) a negotiable instrument as defined in Section 13 of the Negotiable Instruments Act, 1881;
   (*b*) a power-of-attorney as defined in Section 1A of the Powers-of-Attorney Act, 1882;
   (*c*) a trust as defined in Section 3 of the Indian Trusts Act, 1882;
   (*d*) a will as defined in clause (h) of Section 2 of the Indian Succession Act, 1925 including any other testamentary disposition by whatever name called;
   (*e*) any contract for the sale or conveyance of immovable property or any interest in such property;
   (*f*) any such class of documents or transactions as may be notified by the Central Government in the Official Gazette.

2. Definitions

1. In this Act, unless the context otherwise requires:

(*a*) "access" with its grammatical variations and cognate expressions means gaining entry into, instructing or communicating with the logical, arithmetical, or memory function resources of a computer, computer system or computer network;

(*b*) "addressee" means a person who is intended by the originator to receive the electronic record but does not include any intermediary;

(*c*) "adjudicating officer" means an adjudicating officer appointed under subsection (1) of Section 46;

(*d*) "affixing digital signature" with its grammatical variations and cognate expressions means adoption of any methodology or procedure by a person for the purpose of authenticating an electronic record by means of digital signature;

(*e*) "appropriate Government" means as respects any matter:

(*i*) Enumerated in List II of the Seventh Schedule to the Constitution;

(*ii*) Relating to any State law enacted under List III of the Seventh Schedule to the Constitution, the State Government and in any other case, the Central Government;

(*f*) "asymmetric crypto system" means a system of a secure key pair consisting of a private key for creating a digital signature and a public key to verify the digital signature;

(*g*) "Certifying Authority" means a person who has been granted a license to issue a Digital Signature Certificate under Section 24;

(*h*) "certification practice statement" means a statement issued by a Certifying Authority to specify the practices that the Certifying Authority employs in issuing Digital Signature Certificates;

(*i*) "computer" means any electronic magnetic, optical or other high-speed data processing device or system which performs logical, arithmetic, and memory functions by manipulations of electronic, magnetic or optical impulses, and includes all input, output, processing, storage, computer software, or communication facilities which are connected or related to the computer in a computer system or computer network;

(*j*) "computer network" means the interconnection of one or more computers through—

(*i*) the use of satellite, microwave, terrestrial line or other communication media; and

(*ii*) terminals or a complex consisting of two or more interconnected computers whether or not the interconnection is continuously maintained;

(*k*) "computer resource" means computer, computer system, computer network, data, computer data base or software;

(*l*) "computer system" means a device or collection of devices, including input and output support devices and excluding calculators which are not programmable and capable of being used in conjunction with external files, which contain computer programmes, electronic instructions, input data and output data, that performs logic, arithmetic, data storage and retrieval, communication control and other functions;

(*m*) "Controller" means the Controller of Certifying Authorities appointed under sub-section (l) of Section 17;

(*n*) "Cyber Appellate Tribunal" means the Cyber Regulations Appellate Tribunal established under sub-section (1) of Section 48;

(*o*) "data" means a representation of information, knowledge, facts, concepts or instructions which are being prepared or have been prepared in a formalised manner, and is intended to be processed, is being processed or has been processed in a computer system or computer network, and may be in any form (including computer print-outs, magnetic or optical storage media, punched cards, punched tapes) or stored internally in the memory of the computer;

(*p*) "digital signature" means authentication of any electronic record by a subscriber by means of an electronic method or procedure in accordance with the provisions of Section 3;

(*q*) "Digital Signature Certificate" means a Digital Signature Certificate issued under sub-section (4) of Section 35;

(*r*) "electronic form" with reference to information means any information generated, sent, received or stored in media, magnetic, optical, computer memory, micro film, computer generated micro fiche or similar device;

(*s*) "Electronic Gazette" means the Official Gazette published in the electronic form;

(*t*) "electronic record" means data, record or data generated, image or sound stored, received or sent in an electronic form or micro film or computer generated micro fiche;

(*u*) "function", in relation to a computer, includes logic, control arithmetical process, deletion, storage and retrieval and communication or telecommunication from or within a computer;

(*v*) "information" includes data, text, images, sound, voice, codes, computer programmes, software and databases or micro film or computer generated micro fiche:

(*w*) "intermediary" with respect to any particular electronic message means any person who on behalf of another person receives, stores or transmits that message or provides any service with respect to that message;

(*x*) "key pair", in an asymmetric crypto system, means a private key and its mathematically related public key, which are so related that the public key can verify a digital signature created by the private key;

(*y*) "law" includes any Act of Parliament or of a State Legislature, Ordinances promulgated by the President or a Governor, as the case may be—Regulations made by the President under Article 240, Bills enacted as President's Act under sub-clause (a) of clause (1) of Article 357 of the Constitution and includes rules, regulations, bye-laws and orders issued or made thereunder;

(*z*) "license" means a license granted to a Certifying Authority under Section 24;

(*za*) "originator" means a person who sends, generates, stores or transmits any electronic message or causes any electronic message to be sent, generated, stored or transmitted to any other person but does not include an intermediary;

(*zb*) "prescribed" means prescribed by rules made under this Act;

(*zc*) "private key" means the key of a key pair used to create a digital signature;

(*zd*) "public key" means the key of a key pair used to verify a digital signature and listed in the Digital Signature Certificate;

(*ze*) "secure system" means computer hardware, software and procedure that—

(*a*) are reasonably secure from unauthorized access and misuse;

(*b*) provide a reasonable level of reliability and correct operation;

(*c*) are reasonably suited to performing the intended functions; and

(*d*) adhere to generally accepted security procedures;

(*zf*) "security procedure" means the security procedure prescribed under Section 16 by the Central Government;

(*zg*) "subscriber" means a person in whose name the Digital Signature Certificate is issued;

(*zh*) "verify" in relation to a digital signature, electronic record or public key, with its grammatical variations and cognate expressions means to determine whether:

(*a*) the initial electronic record was affixed with the digital signature by the use of private key corresponding to the public key of the subscriber;

(*b*) the initial electronic record is retained intact or has been altered since such electronic record was so affixed with the digital signature.

Any reference in this Act to any enactment or any provision thereof shall, in relation to an area in which such enactment or such provision is not in force, be construed as a reference to the corresponding law or the relevant provision of the corresponding law, if any, in force in that area.

Chapter II

DIGITAL SIGNATURE

3. Authentication of Electronic Records

(1) Subject to the provisions of this section any subscriber may authenticate an electronic record by affixing his digital signature.

(2) The authentication of the electronic record shall be effected by the use of asymmetric crypto system and hash function which

envelop and transform the initial electronic record into another electronic record.

Explanation: For the purposes of this sub-section, "hash function" means an algorithm mapping or translation of one sequence of bits into another, generally smaller, set known' as "hash result" such that an electronic record yields the same hash result every time the algorithm is executed with the same electronic record as its input making it computationally infeasible:

(*a*) to derive or reconstruct the original electronic record from the hash result produced by the algorithm;
(*b*) that two electronic records can produce the same hash result using the algorithm.

(3) Any person by the use of a public key of the subscriber can verify the electronic record.

(4) The private key and the public key are unique to the subscriber and constitute a functioning key pair.

Chapter III

ELECTRONIC GOVERNANCE

4. Legal Recognition of Electronic Records

Where any law provides that information or any other matter shall be in writing or in the typewritten or printed form, then, notwithstanding anything contained in such law, such requirement shall be deemed to have been satisfied if such information or matter is:

(*a*) rendered or made available in an electronic form; and
(*b*) accessible so as to be usable for a subsequent reference.

5. Legal Recognition of Digital Signatures

Where any law provides that information or any other matter shall be authenticated by affixing the signature or any document shall be signed or bear the signature of any person then, notwithstanding anything contained in such law, such requirement shall be deemed to have been satisfied, if such information or matter is authenticated by means of digital signature affixed in such manner as may be prescribed by the Central Government.

Explanation: For the purposes of this section, "signed", with its grammatical variations and cognate expressions, shall, with reference to a person, mean affixing of his hand written signature or any mark on any document and the expression "signature" shall be construed accordingly.

6. Use of Electronic Records and Digital Signatures in Government and its Agencies

(1) Where any law provides for:

(*a*) the filing of any form, application or any other document with any office, authority, body or agency owned or controlled by the appropriate Government in a particular manner;

(*b*) the issue or grant of any license, permit, sanction or approval by whatever name called in a particular manner;

(*c*) the receipt or payment of money in a particular manner,

then, notwithstanding anything contained in any other law for the time being in force, such requirement shall be deemed to have been satisfied if such filing, issue, grant, receipt or payment, as the case may be, is effected by means of such electronic form as may be prescribed by the appropriate Government.

(2) The appropriate Government may, for the purposes of sub-section (1), by rules, prescribe:

(*a*) the manner and format in which such electronic records shall be filed, created or issued; and

(*b*) the manner or method of payment of any fee or charges for filing, creation or issue any electronic record under clause.

7. Retention of Electronic Records

(1) Where any law provides that documents, records or information shall be retained for any specific period, then, that requirement shall be deemed to have been satisfied if such documents, records or information are retained in the electronic form, if:

(*a*) the information contained therein remains accessible so as to be usable for a subsequent reference;

(*b*) the electronic record is retained in the format in which it was originally generated, sent or received or in a format which can be demonstrated to represent accurately the information originally generated, sent or received;

(*c*) the details which will facilitate the identification of the origin, destination, date and time of despatch or receipt of such electronic record are available in the electronic record:

Provided that this clause does not apply to any information which is automatically generated solely for the purpose of enabling an electronic record to be dispatched or received.

(2) Nothing in this section shall apply to any law that expressly provides for the retention of documents, records or information in the form of electronic records.

8. Publication of Rule, Regulation, etc., in Electronic Gazette

Where any law provides that any rule, regulation, order, bye-law, notification or any other matter shall be published in the Official Gazette, then, such requirement shall be deemed to have been satisfied if such rule, regulation, order, bye-law, notification or any other matter is published in the Official Gazette or Electronic Gazette:

- Provided that where any rule, regulation, order, bye-law, notification or any other matter is published in the Official Gazette or Electronic Gazette, the date of publication shall be deemed to be the date of the Gazette which was first published in any form.

9. Sections 6, 7 and 8 not to confer right to insist document should be Accepted in Electronic Form

Nothing contained in sections 6, 7 and 8 shall confer a right upon any person to insist that any Ministry or Department of the Central Government or the State Government or any authority or body established by or under any law or controlled or funded by the Central or State Government should accept, issue, create, retain and preserve any document in the form of electronic records or effect any monetary transaction in the electronic form.

10. Power to Make Rules by Central Government in Respect of Digital Signature

The Central Government may, for the purposes of this Act, by rules, prescribe:

(*a*) the type of digital signature;
(*b*) the manner and format in which the digital signature shall be affixed;
(*c*) the manner or procedure which facilitates identification of the persoffixing the digital signature;
(*d*) control processes and procedures to ensure adequate integrity, security and confidentiality of electronic records or payments; and
(*e*) any other matter which is necessary to give legal effect to digital signatures.

Chapter IV

ATTRIBUTION, ACKNOWLEDGEMENT AND DISPATCH OF ELECTRONIC RECORDS

11. Attribution of Electronic Records

An electronic record shall be attributed to the originator—

(*a*) if it was sent by the originator himself;
(*b*) by a person who had the authority to act on behalf of the originator in respect of that electronic record; or
(*c*) by an information system programmed by or on behalf of the originator to operate automatically.

12. Acknowledgement of Receipt

(1) Where the originator has not agreed with the addressee that the acknowledgement of receipt of electronic record be given in a particular form or by a particular method, an acknowledgement may be given by—

(*a*) any communication by the addressee, automated or otherwise; or

(*b*) any conduct of the addressee, sufficient to indicate to the originator that the electronic record has been received.

(2) Where the originator has stipulated that the electronic record shall be binding only on receipt of an acknowledgement of such electronic record by him, then unless acknowledgement has been so received, the electronic record shall be deemed to have been never sent by the originator.

(3) Where the originator has not stipulated that the electronic record shall be binding only on receipt of such acknowledgement, and the acknowledgement has not been received by the originator within the time specified or agreed or, if no time has been specified or agreed to within a reasonable time, then the originator may give notice to the addressee stating that no acknowledgement has been received by him and specifying a reasonable time by which the acknowledgement must be received by him and if no acknowledgement is received within the aforesaid time limit he may after giving notice to the addressee, treat the electronic record as though it has never been sent.

13. Time and Place of Despatch and Receipt of Electronic Record

(1) Save as otherwise agreed to between the originator and the addressee, the dispatch of an electronic record occurs when it enters a computer resource outside the control of the originator.

(2) Save as otherwise agreed between the originator and the addressee, the time of receipt of an electronic record shall be determined as follows, namely:

(*a*) if the addressee has designated a computer resource for the purpose of receiving electronic records:

  (*i*) receipt occurs at the time when the electronic, record enters the designated computer resource; or

  (*ii*) if the electronic record is sent to a computer resource of the addressee that is not the designated computer resource, receipt occurs at the time when the electronic record is retrieved by the addressee;

(*b*) if the addressee has not designated a computer resource along with specified timings, if any, receipt occurs when the electronic record enters the computer resource of the addressee.

(3) Save as otherwise agreed to between the originator and the addressee, an electronic record is deemed to be dispatched at the place where the originator has his place of business, and is deemed to be received at the place where the addressee has his place of business.

(4) The provisions of sub-section (2) shall apply notwithstanding that the place where the computer resource is located may be different from the place where the electronic record is deemed to have been received under sub-section (3).

(5) For the purposes of this section:

(*a*) if the originator or the addressee has more than one place of business, the principal place of business, shall be the place of business;

(*b*) if the originator or the addressee does not have a place of business, his usual place of residence shall be deemed to be the place of business;

(*c*) "usual place of residence", in relation to a body corporate, means the place where it is registered.

Chapter V

SECURE ELECTRONIC RECORDS AND SECURE DIGITAL SIGNATURES

14. Secure Electronic Record

Where any security procedure has been applied to an electronic record at a specific point of time. Then such record shall be deemed to be a secure electronic record from such point of time to the time of verification.

15. Secure Digital Signature

If, by application of a security procedure agreed to by the parties concerned, it can be verified that a digital signature, at the time it was affixed, was:

(*a*) unique to the subscriber affixing it;

(*b*) capable of identifying such subscriber;
(*c*) created in a manner or using a means under the exclusive control of the subscriber and is linked to the electronic record to which it relates in such a manner that if the electronic record was altered the digital signature would be invalidated, then such digital signature shall be deemed to be a secure digital signature.

16. Security Procedure

The Central Government shall for the purposes of this Act prescribe the security procedure having regard to commercial circumstances prevailing at the time when the procedure was used, including:

(*a*) the nature of the transaction;
(*b*) the level of sophistication of the parties with reference to their technological capacity;
(*c*) the volume of similar transactions engaged in by other parties;
(*d*) the availability of alternatives offered to but rejected by any party;
(*e*) the cost of alternative procedures; and
(*f*) the procedures in general use for similar types of transactions or communications.

Chapter VI

REGULATION OF CERTIFYING AUTHORITIES

17. Appointment of Controller and Other Officers

1. The Central Government may, by notification in the Official Gazette, appoint a Controller of Certifying Authorities for the purposes of this Act and may also by the same or subsequent notification appoint such number of Deputy Controllers and Assistant Controllers as it deems fit.
2. The Controller shall discharge his functions under this Act subject to the general control and directions of the Central Government.
3. The Deputy Controllers and Assistant Controllers shall perform the functions assigned to them by the Controller

under the general superintendence and control of the Controller.

4. The qualifications, experience and terms and conditions of service of Controller, Deputy Controllers and Assistant Controllers shall be such as may be prescribed by the Central Government.
5. The Head Office and Branch Office of the office of the Controller shall be at such places as the Central Government may specify, and these may be established at such places as the Central Government may think fit.
6. There shall be a seal of the Office of the Controller.

18. Functions of Controller

The Controller may perform all or any of the following functions, namely:

(*a*) exercising supervision over the activities of the Certifying Authorities;

(*b*) certifying public keys of the Certifying Authorities;

(*c*) laying down the standards to be maintained by the Certifying Authorities;

(*d*) specifying the qualifications and experience which employees of the Certifying Authorities should possess;

(*e*) specifying the conditions subject to which the Certifying Authorities shall conduct their business;

(*f*) specifying the contents of written, printed or visual materials and advertisements that may be distributed or used in respect of a Digital Signature Certificate and the public key;

(*g*) specifying the form and content of a Digital Signature Certificate and the key;

(*h*) specifying the form and manner in which accounts shall be maintained by the Certifying Authorities;

(*i*) specifying the terms and conditions subject to which auditors may be appointed and the remuneration to be paid to them;

(*j*) facilitating the establishment of any electronic system by a Certifying Authority either solely or jointly with other Certifying Authorities and regulation of such systems;

(*k*) specifying the manner in which the Certifying Authorities shall conduct their dealings with the subscribers;

(*l*) resolving any conflict of interests between the Certifying Authorities and the subscribers;

(*m*) laying down the duties of the Certifying Authorities;

(*n*) maintaining a data base containing the disclosure record of every Certifying Authority containing such particulars as may be specified by regulations, which shall be accessible to public.

19. Recognition of Foreign Certifying Authorities

1. Subject to such conditions and restrictions as may be specified by regulations, the Controller may with the previous approval of the Central Government, and by notification in the Official Gazette, recognize any foreign Certifying Authority as a Certifying Authority for the purposes of this Act.
2. Where any Certifying Authority is recognized under sub-section (1), the Digital Signature Certificate issued by such Certifying Authority shall be valid for the purposes of this Act.
3. The Controller may, if he is satisfied that any Certifying Authority has contravened any of the conditions and restrictions subject to which it was granted recognition under sub-section (1) he may, for reasons to be recorded in writing, by notification in the Official Gazette, revoke such recognition.

20. Controller to Act as Repository

1. The Controller shall be the repository of all Digital Signature Certificates issued under this Act.
2. The Controller shall:

   (*a*) make use of hardware, software and procedures that are secure from intrusion and misuse;

   (*b*) observe such other standards as may be prescribed by the Central Government, to ensure that the secrecy and security of the digital signatures are assured.

3. The Controller shall maintain a computerized data base of all public keys in such a manner that such data base

and the public keys are available to any member of the public.

21. License to Issue Digital Signature Certificates

1. Subject to the provisions of sub-section (2), any person may make an application, to the Controller, for a license to issue Digital Signature Certificates.
2. No license shall be issued under sub-section (1), unless the applicant fulfills such requirements with respect to qualification, expertise, manpower, financial resources and other infrastructure facilities, which are necessary to issue Digital Signature Certificates as may be prescribed by the Central Governments
3. A license granted under this section shall:

   (*a*) be valid for such period as may be prescribed by the Central Government;
   (*b*) not be transferable or heritable; and
   (*c*) be subject to such terms and conditions as may be specified by the regulations.

22. Application for License

1. Every application for issue of a license shall be in such form as may be prescribed by the Central Government.
2. Every application for issue of a license shall be accompanied by:
   (*a*) a certification practice statement;
   (*b*) a statement including the procedures with respect to identification of the applicant;
   (*c*) payment of such fees, not exceeding twenty-five thousand rupees as may be prescribed by the Central Government;
   (*d*) such other documents, as may be prescribed by the Central Government.

23. Renewal of License

An application for renewal of a license shall be:

(*a*) in such form;

(*b*) accompanied by such fees, not exceeding five thousand rupees;

as may be prescribed by the Central Government and shall be made not less than forty-five days before the date of expiry of the period of validity of the license.

24. Procedure for Grant or Rejection of Licence

The Controller may, on receipt of an application under sub-section (1) of Section 21, after considering the documents accompanying the application and such other factors, as he deems fit, grant the license or reject the application:

- Provided that no application shall be rejected under this section unless the applicant has been given a reasonable opportunity of presenting his case.

25. Suspension of License

(1) The Controller may, if he is satisfied after making such inquiry, as he may think fit, that a Certifying Authority has:

(*a*) made a statement in, or in relation to, the application for the issue or renewal of the license, which is incorrect or false in material particulars;
(*b*) failed to comply with the terms and conditions subject to which the license was granted;
(*c*) failed to maintain the standards specified under clause (b) of sub-section (2) of Section 20;
(*d*) contravened any provisions of this Act, rule, regulation or order made thereunder, revoke the license:

- Provided that no licence shall be revoked unless the Certifying Authority has been given a reasonable opportunity of showing cause against the proposed revocation.

(2) The Controller may, if he has reasonable cause to believe that there is any ground for revoking a license under sub-section (1) by order suspend such license pending the completion of any inquiry ordered by him:

- Provided that no license shall be suspended for a period exceeding ten days unless the Certifying Authority has been given a reasonable opportunity of showing cause against the proposed suspension.

(3) No Certifying Authority whose license has been suspended shall issue any Digital Signature Certificate during such suspension.

26. Notice of Suspension or Revocation of Licence

(1) Where the license of the Certifying Authority is suspended or revoked, the Controller shall publish notice of such suspension or revocation, as the case may be, in the data base maintained by him.

(2) Where one or more repositories are specified, the Controller shall publish notices of such suspension or revocation, as the case may be, in all such repositories:

- Provided that the data base containing the notice of such suspension or revocation, as the case may be, shall be made available through a website which shall be accessible round the clock.
- Provided further that the Controller may, if he considers necessary, publicise the contents of data base in such electronic or other media, as he may consider appropriate.

27. Power to Delegate

The Controller may, in writing, authorize the Deputy Controller, Assistant Controller or any officer to exercise any of the powers of the Controller under this Chapter.

28. Power to Investigate Contraventions

(1) The Controller or any officer authorized by him in this behalf shall take up for investigation any contravention of the provisions of this Act, rules or regulations made thereunder.

(2) The Controller or any officer authorized by him in this behalf shall exercise the like powers which are conferred on Income-tax authorities under Chapter XIII of the Income-tax Act, 1961 and shall exercise such powers, subject to such limitations laid down under that Act.

29. Access to Computers and Data

(1) Without prejudice to the provisions of sub-section (1) of Section 69, the Controller or any person authorized by him shall, if he has reasonable cause to suspect that any contravention of the provisions of this Act, rules or regulations made thereunder has been committed, have access to any computer system, any apparatus, data or any other material connected with such system, for the purpose of searching or causing a search to be made for obtaining any information or data contained in or available to such computer system.

(2) For the purposes of sub-section (1) the Controller or any person authorized by him may, by order, direct any person incharge of, or otherwise concerned with the operation of the computer system, data apparatus or material, to provide him with such reasonable technical and other assistance as he may consider necessary.

30. Certifying Authority to Follow Certain Procedures

Every Certifying Authority shall:

(*a*) make use of hardware, software and procedures that are secure from intrusion and misuse;

(*b*) provide a reasonable level of reliability in its services which are reasonably suited to the performance of intended functions;

(*c*) adhere to security procedures to ensure that the secrecy and privacy of the digital signatures are assured; and

(*d*) observe such other standards as may be specified by regulations.

31. Certifying Authority to Ensure Compliance of the Act, etc.

Every Certifying Authority shall ensure that every person employed or otherwise engaged by it complies, in the course of his employment or engagement, with the provisions of this Act, rules, regulations and orders made thereunder.

32. Display of Licence

Every Certifying Authority shall display its licence at a conspicuous place of the premises in which it carries on its business.

33. Surrender of Licence

(1) Every Certifying Authority whose licence is suspended or revoked shall immediately after such suspension or revocation, surrender the licence to the Controller.

(2) Where any Certifying Authority fails to surrender a licence under sub-section (1), the person in whose favour a licence is issued, shall be guilty of an offence and shall be punished with imprisonment which may extend up to six months or a fine which may extend up to ten thousand rupees or with both.

34. Disclosure

(1) Every Certifying Authority shall disclose in the manner specified by regulations:

(*a*) its Digital Signature Certificate which contains the public key corresponding to the private key used by that Certifying Authority to digitally sign another Digital Signature Certificate;

(*b*) any certification practice statement relevant thereto;

(*c*) notice of the revocation or suspension of its Certifying Authority certificate, if any; and

(*d*) any other fact that materially and adversely affects either the reliability of a Digital Signature Certificate, which that Authority has issued, or the Authority's ability to perform its services.

(2) Where in the opinion of the Certifying Authority any event has occurred or any situation has arisen which may materially and adversely affect the integrity of its computer system or the conditions subject to which a Digital Signature Certificate was granted, then, the Certifying Authority shall:

(*a*) use reasonable efforts to notify any person who is likely to be affected by that occurrence; or

(*b*) act in accordance with the procedure specified in its certification practice statement to deal with such event or situation.

Chapter VII

DIGITAL SIGNATURE CERTIFICATES

35. Certifying Authority to Issue Digital Signature Certificate

(1) Any person may make an application to the Certifying Authority for the issue of a Digital Signature Certificate in such form as may be prescribed by the Central Government.

(2) Every such application shall be accompanied by such fee not exceeding twenty-five thousand rupees as may be prescribed by the Central Government, to be paid to the Certifying Authority:

- Provided that while prescribing fees under sub-section (2) different fees may be prescribed for different classes of applicants.

(3) Every such application shall be accompanied by a certification practice statement or where there is no such statement, a statement containing such particulars, as may be specified by regulations.

(4) On receipt of an application under sub-section (1) the Certifying Authority may, after consideration of the certification practice statement or the other statement under sub-section (3) and after making such enquiries as it may deem fit, grant the Digital Signature Certificate or for reasons to be recorded in writing, reject the application:

- Provided that no Digital Signature Certificate shall be granted unless the Certifying Authority is satisfied that:

(*a*) the applicant holds the private key corresponding to the public key to be listed in the Digital Signature Certificate;
(*b*) the applicant holds a private key, which is capable of creating a digital signature;
(*c*) the public key to be listed in the certificate can be used to verify a digital signature affixed by the private key held by the applicant:

- Provided further that no application shall be rejected unless the applicant has been given a reasonable opportunity of showing cause against the proposed rejection.

36. Representations upon Issuance of Digital Signature Certificate

A Certifying Authority while issuing a Digital Signature Certificate shall certify that:

(*a*) it has complied with the provisions of this Act and the rules and regulations made thereunder,
(*b*) it has published the Digital Signature Certificate or otherwise made it available to such person relying on it and the subscriber has accepted it;
(*c*) the subscriber holds the private key corresponding to the public key, listed in the Digital Signature Certificate;
(*d*) the subscriber's public key and private key constitute a functioning key pair;
(*e*) the information contained in the Digital Signature Certificate is accurate; and
(*f*) it has no knowledge of any material fact, which if it had been included in the Digital Signature Certificate would adversely affect the reliability of the representations made in clauses (a) to (d).

37. Suspension of Digital Signature Certificate

(1) Subject to the provisions of sub-section (2), the Certifying Authority which has issued a Digital Signature Certificate may suspend such Digital Signature Certificate:

(*a*) on receipt of a request to that effect from:
  (*i*) the subscriber listed in toe Digital Signature Certificate; or
  (*ii*) any person duly authorized to act on behalf of that subscriber;
(*b*) if it is of opinion that the Digital Signature Certificate should be suspended in public interest.

(2) A Digital Signature Certificate shall not be suspended for a period exceeding fifteen days unless the subscriber has been given an opportunity of being heard in the matter.

(3) On suspension of a Digital Signature Certificate under this section, the Certifying Authority shall communicate the same to the subscriber.

38. Revocation of Digital Signature Certificate

(1) A Certifying Authority may revoke a Digital Signature Certificate issued by it:

(*a*) where the subscriber or any other person authorized by him makes a request to that effect; or
(*b*) upon the death of the subscriber, or
(*c*) upon the dissolution of the firm or winding up of the company where the subscriber is a firm or a company.

(2) Subject to the provisions of sub-section (3) and without prejudice to the provisions of sub-section (1), a Certifying Authority may revoke a Digital Signature Certificate which has been issued by it at any time, if it is of opinion that:

(*a*) a material fact represented in the Digital Signature Certificate is false or has been concealed;
(*b*) a requirement for issuance of the Digital Signature Certificate was not satisfied;
(*c*) the Certifying Authority's private key or security system was compromised in a manner materially affecting the Digital Signature Certificate's reliability;
(*d*) the subscriber has been declared insolvent or dead or where a subscriber is a firm or a company, which has been dissolved, wound-up or otherwise ceased to exist.

(3) A Digital Signature Certificate shall not be revoked unless the subscriber has been given an opportunity of being heard in the matter.

(4) On revocation of a Digital Signature Certificate under this section, the Certifying Authority shall communicate the same to the subscriber.

39. Notice of Suspension or Revocation

(1) Where a Digital Signature Certificate is suspended or revoked under Section 37 or Section 38, the Certifying Authority shall publish a notice of such suspension or revocation, as the case may be, in the repository specified in the Digital Signature Certificate for publication of such notice.

(2) Where one or more repositories are specified, the Certifying Authority shall publish notices of such suspension or revocation, as the case may be in all such repositories.

Chapter VIII

DUTIES OF SUBSCRIBERS

40. Generating Key Pair

Where any Digital Signature Certificate, the public key of which corresponds to the private key of that subscriber which is to be listed in the Digital Signature Certificate has been accepted by a subscriber, then, the subscriber shall generate the key pair by applying the security procedure.

41. Acceptance of Digital Signature Certificate

(1) A subscriber shall be deemed to have accepted a Digital Signature Certificate if he publishes or authorizes the publication of a Digital Signature Certificate:

(*a*) to one or more persons;
(*b*) in a repository, or otherwise demonstrates his approval of the Digital Signature Certificate in any manner.

(2) By accepting a Digital Signature Certificate the subscriber certifies to all who reasonably rely on the information contained in the Digital Signature Certificate that:

(*a*) the subscriber holds the private key corresponding to the public key listed in the Digital Signature Certificate and is entitled to hold the same;
(*b*) all representations made by the subscriber to the Certifying Authority and all material relevant to the information contained in the Digital Signature Certificate are true;
(*c*) all information in the Digital Signature Certificate that is within the knowledge of the subscriber is true.

42. Control of Private Key

(1) Every subscriber shall exercise reasonable care to retain control of the private key corresponding to the public key listed in his

Digital Signature Certificate and take all steps to prevent its disclosure to a person not authorized to affix the digital signature of the subscriber.

(2) If the private key corresponding to the public key listed in the Digital Signature Certificate has been compromised, then, the subscriber shall communicate the same without any delay to the Certifying Authority in such manner as may be specified by the regulations.

Explanation: For the removal of doubts, it is hereby declared that the subscriber shall be liable till he has informed the Certifying Authority that the private key has been compromised.

Chapter IX

PENALTIES AND ADJUDICATION

43. Penalty for Damage to Computer, Computer System, etc.

If any person without permission of the owner or any other person who is incharge of a computer, computer system or computer network:

(*a*) accesses or secures access to such computer, computer system or computer network;

(*b*) downloads, copies or extracts any data, computer data base or information from such computer, computer system or computer network including information or data held or stored in any removable storage medium;

(*c*) introduces or causes to be introduced any computer contaminant or computer virus into any computer, computer system or computer network;

(*d*) damages or causes to be damaged any computer, computer system or computer network, data, computer data base or any other programmes residing in such computer, computer system or computer network;

(*e*) disrupts or causes disruption of any computer, computer system or computer network;

(*f*) denies or causes the denial of access to any person authorized to access any computer, computer system or computer network by any means;

(*g*) provides any assistance to any person to facilitate access to a computer, computer system or computer network in contravention of the provisions of this Act, rules or regulations made thereunder;

(*h*) charges the services availed of by a person to the account of another person by tampering with or manipulating any computer, computer system, or computer network, he shall be liable to pay damages by way of compensation not exceeding one crore rupees to the person so affected.

Explanation: For the purposes of this section:

(i) "computer contaminant" means any set of computer instructions that are designed:

(*a*) to modify, destroy, record, transmit data or programme residing within a computer, computer system or computer network; or

(*b*) by any means to usurp the normal operation of the computer, computer system, or computer network;

(*ii*) "computer data base" means a representation of information, knowledge, facts, concepts or instructions in text, image, audio, video that are being prepared or have been prepared in a formalised manner or have been produced by a computer, computer system or computer network and are intended for use in a computer, computer system or computer network;

(*iii*) "computer virus" means any computer instruction, information, data or programme that destroys, damages, degrades or adversely affects the performance of a computer resource or attaches itself to another computer resource and operates when a programme, data or instruction is executed or some other event takes place in that computer resource;

(*iv*) "damage" means to destroy, alter, delete, add, modify or rearrange any computer resource by any means.

44. Penalty for Failure to Furnish Information Return, etc.

If any person who is required under this Act or any rules or regulations made thereunder to:

(*a*) furnish any document, return or report to the Controller or the Certifying Authority fails to furnish the same, he shall be liable to a penalty not exceeding one lakh and fifty thousand rupees for each such failure;

(*b*) file any return or furnish any information, books or other documents within the time specified therefore in the regulations fails to file return or furnish the same within the time specified therefore in the regulations, he shall be liable to a penalty not exceeding five thousand rupees for everyday during which such failure continues;

(*c*) maintain books of account or records, fails to maintain the same, he shall be liable to a penalty not exceeding ten thousand rupees for every day during which the failure continues.

45. Residuary Penalty

Whoever contravenes any rules or regulations made under this Act, for the contravention of which no penalty has been separately provided, shall be liable to pay a compensation not exceeding twenty-five thousand rupees to the person affected by such contravention or a penalty not exceeding twenty-five thousand rupees.

46. Power to Adjudicate

1. For the purpose of adjudging under this Chapter whether any person has committed a contravention of any of the provisions of this Act or of any rule, regulation, direction or order made thereunder the Central Government shall, subject tc the provisions of sub-section (3), appoint any officer not below the rank of a Director to the Government of India or an equivalent officer of a State Government to be an adjudicating officer for holding an inquiry in the manner prescribed by the Central Government.
2. The adjudicating officer shall, after giving the person referred to in sub-section (1) a reasonable opportunity for making representation in the matter and if, on such inquiry, he is satisfied that the person has committed the contravention, he may impose such penalty or award such compensation as he thinks fit in accordance with the provisions of that section.
3. No person shall be appointed as an adjudicating officer unless he possesses such experience in the field of

Information Technology and legal or judicial experience as may be prescribed by the Central Government.

4. Where more than one adjudicating officers are appointed, the Central Government shall specify by order the matters and places with respect to which such officers shall exercise their jurisdiction.
5. Every adjudicating officer shall have the powers of a civil court which are conferred on the Cyber Appellate Tribunal under sub-section (2) of Section 58, and:

    (*a*) all proceedings before it shall be deemed to be judicial proceedings within the meaning of sections 193 and 228 of the Indian Penal Code;
    (*b*) shall be deemed to be a civil court for the purposes of Sections 345 and 346 of the Code of Criminal Procedure, 1973.

47. Factors to be taken into Account by the Adjudicating Officer

While adjudging the quantum of compensation under this Chapter, the adjudicating officer shall have due regard to the following factors, namely:

(*a*) the amount of gain of unfair advantage, wherever quantifiable, made as a result of the default;
(*b*) the amount of loss caused to any person as a result of the default; and
(*c*) the repetitive nature of the default.

Chapter X

THE CYBER REGULATIONS APPELLATE TRIBUNAL

48. Establishment of Cyber Appellate Tribunal

(1) The Central Government shall, by notification, establish one or more appellate tribunals to be known as the Cyber Regulations Appellate Tribunal.

(2) The Central Government shall also specify, in the notification referred to in sub-section (1), the matters and places in relation to which the Cyber Appellate Tribunal may exercise jurisdiction.

49. Composition of Cyber Appellate Tribunal

A Cyber Appellate Tribunal shall consist of one person only (hereinafter referred to as the Residing Officer of the Cyber Appellate Tribunal) to be appointed, by notification, by the Central Government.

50. Qualifications for Appointment as Presiding Officer of the Cyber Appellate Tribunal

A person shall not be qualified for appointment as the Presiding Officer of a Cyber Appellate Tribunal unless he

(*a*) is, or has been or is qualified to be, a Judge of a High Court; or

(*b*) is, or has been a member of the Indian Legal Service and is holding or has held a post in Grade I of that Service for at three years.

51. Term of Office

The Presiding Officer of a Cyber Appellate Tribunal shall hold office for a term of five years from the date on which he enters upon his office or until he attains the age of sixty-five years, whichever is earlier.

52. Salary, Allowances and other Terms and Conditions of Service of Presiding Officer

The salary and allowances payable to, and the other terms and conditions of service including pension, gratuity and other retirement benefits of the Presiding Officer of a Cyber Appellate Tribunal shall be such as may be prescribed:

- Provided that neither the salary and allowances nor the other terms and conditions of service of the Presiding Officer shall be varied to his disadvantage after appointment.

53. Filling-up of Vacancies

If, for reason other than temporary absence, any vacancy occurs in the office of the Presiding Officer of a Cyber Appellate Tribunal, then the Central Government shall appoint another person in accordance with the provisions of this Act to fill the vacancy and the proceedings may be continued before the Cyber Appellate Tribunal from the stage at which the vacancy is filled.

54. Resignation and Removal

(1) The Presiding Officer of a Cyber Appellate Tribunal may, by notice in writing under his hand addressed to the Central Government, resign his office:

- Provided that the said Presiding Officer shall, unless he is permitted by the Central Government to relinquish his office sooner, continue to hold office until the expiry of three months from the date of receipt of such notice or until a person duly appointed as his success or enters upon his office or until the expiry of his term of office, whichever is the earliest.

(2) The Presiding Officer of a Cyber Appellate Tribunal shall not be removed from his office except by an order by the Central Government on the ground of proved misbehaviour or incapacity after an inquiry made by a Judge of the Supreme Court in which the Presiding Officer concerned has been informed of the charges against him and given a reasonable opportunity of being heard in respect of these charges.

(3) The Central Government may, by rules, regulate the procedure for the investigation of misbehaviour or incapacity of the aforesaid Presiding Officer.

55. Orders Constituting Appellate Tribunal to be Final and not to Invalidate its Proceedings

No order of the Central Government appointing any person as the Presiding Officer of a Cyber Appellate Tribunal shall be called in question in any manner and no act or proceeding before a Cyber Appellate Tribunal shall be called in question in any manner on the ground merely of any defect in the constitution of a Cyber Appellate Tribunal.

56. Staff of the Cyber Appellate Tribunal

1. The Central Government shall provide the Cyber Appellate Tribunal with such officers and employees as that Government may think fit.

2. The officers and employees of the Cyber Appellate Tribunal shall discharge their functions under general superintendence of the Presiding Officer.
3. The salaries, allowances and other conditions of service of the officers and employees or the Cyber Appellate Tribunal shall be such as may be prescribed by the Central Government.

57. Appeal to Cyber Appellate Tribunal

1. Save as provided in sub-section (2), any person aggrieved by an order made by Controller or an adjudicating officer under this Act may prefer an appeal to a Cyber Appellate Tribunal having jurisdiction in the matter.
2. No appeal shall be to the Cyber Appellate Tribunal from an order made by an adjudicating officer with the consent of the parties.
3. Every appeal under sub-section (1) shall be filed within a period of forty-five days from the date on which a copy of the order made by the Controller or the adjudicating officer is received by the person aggrieved and it shall be in such form and be accompanied by such fee as may be prescribed:

- Provided that the Cyber Appellate Tribunal may entertain an appeal after the expiry of the said period of forty-five days if it is satisfied that there was sufficient cause for not filing it within that period.

4. On receipt of an appeal under sub-section (1), the Cyber Appellate Tribunal may, after giving the parties to the appeal, an opportunity of being heard, pass such orders thereon as it thinks fit, confirming, modifying or setting aside the order appealed against.
5. The Cyber Appellate Tribunal shall send a copy of every order made by it to the parties to the appeal and to the concerned Controller or adjudicating officer.
6. The appeal filed before the Cyber Appellate Tribunal under sub-section (1) shall be dealt with by it as expeditiously as possible and endeavour shall be made by it to dispose of the appeal finally within six months from the date of receipt of the appeal.

58. Procedure and Powers of the Cyber Appellate Tribunal

1. The Cyber Appellate Tribunal shall not be bound by the procedure laid down by the Code of Civil Procedure, 1908 but shall be guided by the principles of natural justice and, subject to the other provisions of this Act and of any rules, the Cyber Appellate Tribunal shall have powers to regulate its own procedure including the place at which it shall have its sittings.
2. The Cyber Appellate Tribunal shall have, for the purposes of discharging its functions under this Act, the same powers as are vested in a civil court under the Code of Civil Procedure, 1908, while trying a suit, in respect of the following matters, namely:
   (*a*) summoning and enforcing the attendance of any person and examining him on oath;
   (*b*) requiring the discovery and production of documents or other electronic records;
   (*c*) receiving evidence on affidavits;
   (*d*) issuing commissions for the examination of witnesses or documents;
   (*e*) reviewing its decisions;
   (*f*) dismissing an application for default or deciding it ex pane;
   (*g*) any other matter which may be prescribed.
3. Every proceeding before the Cyber Appellate Tribunal shall be deemed to be a judicial proceeding within the meaning of Sections 193 and 228, and for the purposes of Section 196 of the Indian Penal Code and the Cyber Appellate Tribunal shall be deemed to be a civil court for the purposes of Section 195 and Chapter XXVI of the Code of Criminal Procedure, 1973.

59. Right to Legal Representation

The appellant may either appear in person or authorise one or more legal practitioners or any of its officers to present his or its case before the Cyber Appellate Tribunal.

60. Limitation

The provisions of the Limitation Act, 1963, shall, as far as may be, apply to an appeal made to the Cyber Appellate Tribunal.

61. Civil Court not to have Jurisdiction

No court shall have jurisdiction to entertain any suit or proceeding in respect of any matter which an adjudicating officer appointed under this Act or the Cyber Appellate Tribunal constituted under this Act is empowered by or under this Act to determine and no injunction shall be granted by any court or other authority in respect of any action taken or to be taken in pursuance of any power conferred by or under this Act.

62. Appeal to High Court

Any person aggrieved by any decision or order of the Cyber Appellate Tribunal may file an appeal to the High Court within sixty days from the date of communication of the decision or order of the Cyber Appellate Tribunal to him on any question of fact or law arising out of such order:

- Provided that the High Court may, if it is satisfied that the appellant was prevented by sufficient cause from filing the appeal within the said period, allow it to be filed within a further period not exceeding sixty days.

63. Compounding of Contraventions

1. Any contravention under this Chapter may, either before or after the institution of adjudication proceedings, be compounded by the Controller or such other officer as may be specially authorised by him in this behalf or by the adjudicating officer, as the case may be, subject to such conditions as the Controller or such other officer or the adjudicating officer may specify:

- Provided that such sum shall not, in any case, exceed the maximum amount of the penalty which may be imposed under this Act for the contravention so compounded.

2. Nothing in sub-section (1) shall apply to a person who commits the same or similar contravention within a period of three years from the date on which the first contravention, committed by him, was compounded.

Explanation: For the purposes of this sub-section, any second or subsequent contravention committed after the expiry of a period of three years from the date on which the contravention was previously compounded shall be deemed to be a first contravention.

3. Where any contravention has been compounded under sub-section (1), no proceeding or further proceeding, as the case may be, shall be taken against the person guilty of such contravention in respect of the contravention so compounded.

64. Recovery of Penalty

A penalty imposed under this Act, if it is not paid, shall be recovered as an arrear of land revenue and the licence or the Digital Signature Certificate, as the case may be, shall be suspended till the penalty is paid.

Chapter XI

OFFENCES

65. Tampering with Computer Source Documents

Whoever knowingly or intentionally conceals, destroys or alters or intentionally or knowingly causes another to conceal, destroy or alter any computer source code used for a computer, computer programme, computer system or computer network, when the computer source code is required to be kept or maintained by law for the time being in force, shall be punishable with imprisonment upto three years, or with fine which may extend upto two lakh rupees, or with both.

Explanation: For the purposes of this section, "computer source code" means the listing of programmes, computer commands, design and layout and programme analysis of computer resource in any form.

66. Hacking with Computer System

1. Whoever with the intent to cause or knowing that he is likely to cause wrongful loss or damage to the public or any person destroys or deletes or alters any information

residing in a computer resource or diminishes its value or utility or affects it injuriously by any means, commits hack.

2. Whoever commits hacking shall be punished with imprisonment up to three years, or with fine which may extend upto two lakh rupees, or with both.

67. Publishing of Information which is Obscene in Electronic Form

Whoever publishes or transmits or causes to be published in the electronic form, any material which is lascivious or appeals to the prurient interest or if its effect is such as to tend to deprave and corrupt persons who are likely, having regard to all relevant circumstances, to read, see or hear the matter contained or embodied in it, shall be punished on first conviction with imprisonment of either description for a term which may extend to five years and with fine which may extend to one lakh rupees and in the event of a second or subsequent conviction with imprisonment of either description for a term which may extend to ten years and also with fine which may extend to two lakh rupees.

68. Power of Controller to give Directions

(1) The Controller may, by order, direct a Certifying Authority or any employee of such Authority to take such measures or cease carrying on such activities as specified in the order if those are necessary to ensure compliance with the provisions of this Act, rules or any regulations made there under.

(2) Any person who fails to comply with any order under sub-section (1) shall be guilty of an offence and shall be liable on conviction to imprisonment for a term not exceeding three years or to a fine not exceeding two lakh rupees or to both.

69. Directions of Controller to a Subscriber to extend Facilities to Decrypt Information

1. If the Controller is satisfied that it is necessary or expedient so to do in the interest of the sovereignty or integrity of India, the security of the State, friendly relations with foreign States or public order or for preventing incitement

to the commission of any cognizable offence, for reasons to be recorded in writing, by order, direct any agency of the Government to intercept any information transmitted through any computer resource.

2. The subscriber or any person in charge of the computer resource shall, when called upon by any agency which has been directed under sub-section (1), extend all facilities and technical assistance to decrypt the information.
3. The subscriber or any person who fails to assist the agency referred to in sub-section (2) shall be punished with an imprisonment for a term which may extend to seven years.

70. Protected System

1. The appropriate Government may, by notification in the Official Gazette, declare that any computer, computer system or computer network to be a protected system.
2. The appropriate Government may, by order in writing, authorise the persons who are authorised to access protected systems notified under sub-section (1).
3. Any person who secures access or attempts to secure access to a protected system in contravention of the provisions of this section shall be punished with imprisonment of either description for a term which may extend to ten years and shall also be liable to fine.

71. Penalty for Misrepresentation

Whoever makes any misrepresentation to, or suppresses any material fact from, the Controller or the Certifying Authority for obtaining any license or Digital Signature Certificate, as the case may be shall be punished with imprisonment for a term which may extend to two years, or with fine which may extend to one lakh rupees, or with both.

72. Penalty for Breach of Confidentiality and Privacy

Save as otherwise provided in this Act or any other law for the time being in force, any person who, in pursuance of any of the powers conferred under this Act, rules or regulations made thereunder, has secured access to any electronic record, book, register, correspondence, information, document or other material without the consent of the person concerned discloses such electronic record, book, register, correspondence, information, document or other material to any other person shall be punished with imprisonment for a term which may extend to two years, or with fine which may extend to one lakh rupees, or with both.

73. Penalty for Publishing Digital Signature Certificate False in Certain Particulars

1. No person shall publish a Digital Signature Certificate or otherwise make it available to any other person with the knowledge that:

   (*a*) the Certifying Authority listed in the certificate has not issued it; or

   (*b*) the subscriber listed in the certificate has not accepted it; or

   (*c*) the certificate has been revoked or suspended, unless such publication is for the purpose of verifying a digital signature created prior to such suspension or revocation.

2. Any person who contravenes the provisions of sub-section (1) shall be punished with imprisonment for a term which may extend to two years, or with fine which may extend to one lakh rupees, or with both.

74. Publication for Fraudulent Purpose

Whoever knowingly creates, publishes or otherwise makes available a Digital Signature Certificate for any fraudulent or unlawful purpose shall be punished with imprisonment for a term which may extend to two years, or with fine which may extend to one lakh rupees, or with both.

75. Act to Apply for Offence or Contravention Committed outside India

1. Subject to the provisions of sub-section (2), the provisions of this Act shall apply also to any offence or contravention

committed outside India by any person irrespective of his nationality.

2. For the purposes of sub-section (1), this Act shall apply to an offence or contravention committed outside India by any person if the act or conduct constituting the offence or contravention involves a computer, computer system or computer network located in India.

76. Confiscation

Any computer, computer system, floppies, compact disks, (CDs) tape drives or any other accessories related thereto, in respect of which any provision of this Act, rules, orders or regulations made thereunder has been or is being contravened, shall be liable to confiscation:

- Provided that where it is established to the satisfaction of the court adjudicating the confiscation that the person in whose possession, power or control of any such computer, computer system, floppies, compact disks, tape drives or any other accessories relating thereto is found is not responsible for the contravention of the provisions of this Act, rules, orders or regulations made thereunder, the court may, instead of making an order for confiscation of such computer, computer system, floppies, compact disks, tape drives or any other accessories related thereto, make such other order authorised by this Act against the person contravening of the provisions of this Act, rules, orders or regulations made thereunder as it may think fit.

77. Penalties or Confiscation not to interfere with other Punishments

No penalty imposed or confiscation made under this Act shall prevent the imposition of any other punishment to which the person affected thereby is liable under any other law for the time being in force.

78. Power to Investigate Offences

Notwithstanding anything contained in the Code of Criminal Procedure, 1973, a police officer not below the rank of Deputy

Superintendent of Police shall investigate any offence under this Act.

Chapter XII

NETWORK SERVICE PROVIDERS NOT TO BE LIABLE IN CERTAIN CASES

79. Network Service Providers not to be Liable in certain Cases

For the removal of doubts, it is hereby declared that no person providing any service as a network service provider shall be liable under this Act, rules or regulations made thereunder for any third party information or data made available by him if he proves that the offence or contravention was committed without his knowledge or that he had exercised all due diligence to prevent the commission of such offence or contravention.

Explanation: For the purposes of this section:

(*a*) "network service provider" means an intermediary;
(*b*) "third party information" means any information dealt with by a network service provider in his capacity as an intermediary.

Chapter XIII

MISCELLANEOUS

80. Power of Police Officer and other Officers to Enter, Search, etc.

1. Notwithstanding anything contained in the Code of Criminal Procedure, 1973, any police officer, not below the rank of a Deputy Superintendent of Police, or any other officer of the Central Government or a State Government authorised by the Central Government in this behalf may enter any public place and search and arrest without warrant any person found therein who is reasonably suspected or having committed or of committing or of being about to commit any offence under this Act.

Explanation: For the purposes of this sub-section, the expression "public place" includes any public conveyance, any hotel, any shop or any other place intended for use by, or accessible to the public.

2. Where any person is arrested under sub-section (1) by an officer other than a police officer, such officer shall, without unnecessary delay, take or send the person arrested before a magistrate having jurisdiction in the case or before the officer-in-charge of a police station.
3. The provisions of the Code of Criminal Procedure, 1973 shall, subject to the provisions of this section, apply, so far as may be, in relation to any entry, search or arrest, made under this section.

81. Act to have Overriding Effect

The provisions of this Act shall have effect notwithstanding anything inconsistent therewith contained in any other law for the time being in force.

82. Controller, Deputy Controller and Assistant Controllers to be Public Servants

The Presiding Officer and other officers and employees of a Cyber Appellate Tribunal, the Controller, the Deputy Controller and the Assistant Controllers shall be deemed to be public servants within the meaning of Section 21 of the Indian Penal Code.

83. Power to give Directions

The Central Government may give directions to any State Government as to the carrying into execution in the State of any of the provisions of this Act or of any rule, regulation or order made thereunder.

84. Protection of Action taken in Good Faith

No suit, prosecution or other legal proceeding shall be against the Central Government, the State Government, the Controller or any person acting on behalf of him, the Presiding Officer, adjudicating officers and the staff of the Cyber Appellate Tribunal for anything which is in good faith done or intended to be done in pursuance of this Act or any rule, regulation or order made thereunder.

85. Offences by Companies

1. Where a person committing a contravention of any of the provisions of this Act or of any rule, direction or order made thereunder is a company, every person who, at the time the contravention was committed, was in charge of and was responsible to the company for the conduct of business of the company as well as the company, shall be guilty of the contravention and shall be liable to be proceeded against and punished accordingly:

- Provided that nothing contained in this sub-section shall render any such person liable to punishment if he proves that the contravention took place without his knowledge or that he exercised all due diligence to prevent such contravention.

2. Notwithstanding anything contained in sub-section (1), where a contravention of any of the provisions of this Act or of any rule, direction or order made thereunder has been committed by a company and it is proved that the contravention has taken place with the consent or connivance of, or is attributable to any neglect on the part of any director, manager, secretary or other officer of the company, such director, manager, secretary or other officer shall also be deemed to be guilty of the contravention and shall be liable to be proceeded against and punished accordingly.
   Explanation: For the purposes of this section:

(*i*) "company" means any body corporate and includes a firm or other association of individuals; and
(*ii*) "director", in relation to a firm, means a partner in the firm.

86. Removal of Difficulties

1. If any difficulty arises in giving effect to the provisions of this Act, the Central Government may, by order published in the Official Gazette, make such provisions not inconsistent with the provisions of this Act as appear to it to be necessary or expedient for removing the difficulty:

- Provided that no order shall be made under this section after the expiry of a period of two years from the commencement of this Act.

2. Every order made under this section shall be laid, as soon as may be after it is made, before each House of Parliament.

87. Power of Central Government to make Rules

1. The Central Government may, by notification in the Official Gazette and in the Electronic Gazette make rules to carry out the provisions of this Act.
2. In particular, and without prejudice to the generality of the foregoing power, such rules may provide for all or any of the following mailers, namely:

    (*a*) the manner in which any information or matter may be authenticated by means of digital signature under Section 5;
    (*b*) the electronic form in which filing, issue, grant or payment shall be effected under sub-section (1) of Section 6;
    (*c*) the manner and format in which electronic records shall be filed, or issued and the method of payment under sub-section (2) of Section 6;
    (*d*) the matters relating to the type of digital signature, manner and format in which it may be affixed under Section 10;
    (*e*) the security procedure for the purpose of creating secure electronic record and secure digital signature under Section 16;
    (*f*) the qualifications, experience and terms and conditions of service of Controller, Deputy Controllers and Assistant Controllers under Section 17;
    (*g*) other standards to be observed by the Controller under clause (b) of sub-section (2) of Section 20;
    (*h*) the requirements which an applicant must fulfil under sub-section (2) of Section 21;
    (*i*) the period of validity of license granted under clause (a) of sub-section (3) of Section 21;
    (*j*) the form in which an application for licence may be made under sub-section (1) of Section 22;

(*k*) the amount of fees payable under clause (c) of sub-section (2) of Section 22;

(*l*) such other documents which shall accompany an application for licence under clause (a) of sub-section (2) of Section 22;

(*m*) the form and the fee for renewal of a licence and the fee payable there of under Section 23;

(*n*) the form in which application for issue of a Digital Signature Certificate may be made under sub-section (1) of Section 35;

(*o*) the fee to be paid to the Certifying Authority for issue of a Digital Signature Certificate under sub-section (2) of Section 35;

(*p*) the manner in which the adjudicating officer shall hold inquiry under sub-section (1) of Section 46;

(*q*) the qualification and experience which the adjudicating officer shall possess under sub-section (3) of Section 46;

(*r*) the salary, allowances and the other terms and conditions of service of the Presiding Officer under Section 52;

(*s*) the procedure for investigation of misbehaviour or incapacity of the Presiding Officer under sub-section (3) of Section 54;

(*t*) the salary and allowances and other conditions of service of other officers and employees under sub-section (3) of Section 56;

(*u*) the form in which appeal may be filed and the fee thereof under sub-section (3) of Section 57;

(*v*) any other power of a civil court required to be prescribed under clause (g) of sub-section (2) of Section 58; and

(*w*) any other matter which is required to be, or may be, prescribed.

3. Every notification made by the Central Government under clause (f) of sub-section (4) of Section 1 and every rule made by it shall be laid, as soon as may be after it is made, before each House of Parliament, while it is in session, for a total period of thirty days which may be comprised in one session or in two or more successive sessions, and if, before

the expiry of the session immediately following the session or the successive sessions aforesaid, both Houses agree in making any modification in the notification or the rule or both Houses agree that the notification or the rule should not be made, the notification or the rule shall thereafter have effect only in such modified form or be of no effect, as the case may be; so, however, that any such modification or annulment shall be without prejudice to the validity of anything previously done under that notification or rule.

88. Constitution of Advisory Committee

1. The Central Government shall, as soon as may be after the commencement of this Act, constitute a Committee called the Cyber Regulations Advisory Committee.
2. The Cyber Regulations Advisory Committee shall consist of a Chairperson and such number of other official and non-official members representing the interests principally affected or having special knowledge of the subject-matter as the Central Government may deem fit.
3. The Cyber Regulations Advisory Committee shall advise:
   (*a*) the Central Government either generally as regards any rules or for any other purpose connected with this Act;
   (*b*) the Controller in framing the regulations under this Act.
4. There shall be paid to the non-official members of such Committee such travelling and other allowances as the Central Government may fix.

89. Power of Controller to make Regulations

1. The Controller may, after consultation with the Cyber Regulations Advisory Committee and with the previous approval of the Central Government, by notification in the Official Gazette, make regulations consistent with this Act and the rules made thereunder to carry out the purposes of this Act.
2. In particular, and without prejudice to the generality of the foregoing power, such regulations may provide for all or any of the following matters, namely:

(*a*) the particulars relating to maintenance of data base containing the disclosure record of every Certifying Authority under clause (m) of Section 18;

(*b*) the conditions and restrictions subject to which the Controller may recognise any foreign Certifying Authority under sub-section (1) of Section 19;

(*c*) the terms and conditions subject to which a license may be granted under clause (c) of sub-section (3) of Section 21;

(*d*) other standards to be observed by a Certifying Authority under clause (d) of Section 30;

(*e*) the manner in which the Certifying Authority shall disclose the matters specified in sub-section (1) of Section 34;

(*f*) the particulars of statement which shall accompany an application under sub-section (3) of Section 35;

(*g*) the manner in which the subscriber shall communicate the compromise of private key to the Certifying Authority under sub-section (2) of Section 42.

3. Every regulation made under this Act shall be laid, as soon as may be after it is made, before each House of Parliament, while it is in session, or a total period of thirty days which may be comprised in one session or in two or more successive sessions, and if, before the expiry of the session immediately following the session or the successive sessions aforesaid, both Houses agree in making any modification in the regulation or both Houses agree that the regulation should not be made, the regulation shall thereafter have effect only in such modified form or he of no effect, as the case may be; so, however, that any such modification or annulment shall be without prejudice to the validity of anything previously done under that regulation.

90. Power of State Government to make Rules

1. The State Government may, by notification in the Official Gazette, make rules to carry out the provisions of this Act.
2. In particular, and without prejudice to the generality of the foregoing power, such rules may provide for all or any of the following matters, namely:

(*a*) the electronic form in which filing, issue, grant receipt or payment shall be effected under sub-section (1) of Section 6;
(*b*) for matters specified in sub-section (2) of Section 6;
(*c*) any other matter which is required to be provided by rules by the State Government.

3. Every rule made by the State Government under this section shall be laid, as soon as may be after it is made, before each House of the State Legislature where it consists of two Houses, or where such Legislature consists of one House, before that House.

91. Amendment of Act, 45 of 1860

The Indian Penal Code shall be amended in the manner specified in the First Schedule to this Act.

92. Amendment of Act, 1 of 1872

The Indian Evidence Act, 1872 shall be amended in the manner specified in the Second Schedule to this Act.

93. Amendment of Act, 18 of 1891

The Bankers' Books Evidence Act, 1891 shall be amended in the manner specified in the Third Schedule to this Act.

94. Amendment of Act, 2 of 1834

The Reserve Bank of India Act, 1934 shall be amended in the manner specified in the Fourth Schedule to this Act.

THE FIRST SCHEDULE (See Section 91)

Amendments to the Indian Penal Code (45 of 1860)

1. After Section 29, the following section shall be inserted, namely:

Electronic record

"29A. The words 'electronic record' shall have the meaning

assigned to them in clause (t) of sub-section (1) of Section 2 of the Information Technology Act, 2000."

2. In Section 167, for the words "such public servant, charged with the preparation or translation of any document, frames or translates that document", the words "such public servant, charged with the preparation or translation of any document or electronic record, frames, prepares or translates that document or electronic record" shall be substituted.
3. In Section 172, for the words, "produce a document in a Court of Justice", the words "produce a document or an electronic record in a Court of Justice" shall be substituted.
4. In Section 173, for the words "to produce a document in a Court of Justice", the words "to produce a document or electronic record in a Court of Justice" shall be substituted.
5. In Section 175, for the word "document" at both the places where it occurs, the words "document or electronic record" shall be substituted.
6. In Section 192, for the words "makes any false entry in any book or record, or makes any document containing a false statement," the words "makes any false entry in any book or record, or electronic record or makes any document or electronic record containing a false statement" shall be substituted.
7. In Section 204, for the word "document" at both the places where it occurs, the words "document or electronic record" shall be substituted.
8. In Section 463, for the words "whoever makes any false documents or part of a document with intent to cause damage or injury," the words "whoever makes any false documents or false electronic record or part of a document or electronic record, with intent to cause damage or injury" shall be substituted.
9. In Section 464,:

   (*a*) for the portion beginning with the words, "A person is said to make a false document" and ending with the words "by reason of deception practised upon him, he does not know the contents of the document or the nature of the alteration," the following shall be substituted, namely:

"A person is said to make a false document or false electronic record:

First: Who dishonestly or fraudulently:

(*a*) makes, signs, seals or executes a document or part of a document;
(*b*) makes or transmits any electronic record or part of any electronic record;
(*c*) affixes any digital signature on any electronic record;
(*d*) makes any mark denoting the execution of a document or the authenticity of the digital signature,

with the intention of causing it to be believed that such document or part of document, electronic record or digital signature was made, signed, sealed, executed, transmitted or affixed by or by the authority of a person by whom or by whose authority he knows that it was not made, signed, sealed, executed or affixed; or

Secondly: Who, without lawful authority, dishonestly or fraudulently, by cancellation or otherwise, alters a document or an electronic record in any material part thereof, after it has been made, executed or affixed with digital signature either by himself or by any other person, whether such person be living or dead at the time of such alteration; or

Thirdly: Who dishonestly or fraudulently causes any person to sign, seal, execute or alter a document or an electronic record or to affix his digital signature on any electronic record knowing that such person by reason of unsoundness of mind or intoxication cannot, or that by reason of deception practiced upon him, he does not know the contents of the document or electronic record or the nature of the alteration."

(*b*) after *Explanation* 2, the following *Explanation* shall be inserted at the end, namely:

"*Explanation* 3: For the purposes of this section, the expression "affixing digital signature" shall have the meaning assigned to it in clause (d) of sub-section (1) of Section 2 of the Information Technology Act, 2000."

10. In Section 466:

    (*a*) for the words, "whoever forges a document", the words "whoever forges a document or an electronic record" shall be substituted;

    (*b*) the following *Explanation* shall be inserted at the end, namely:
    "*Explanation*: For the purposes of this section, 'register' includes any list, data or record of any entries maintained in the electronic form as defined in clause (r) of sub-section (1) of Section 2 of the Information Technology Act, 2000."

11. In Section 468, for the words "document forged", the words "document or electronic record forged" shall be substituted.
12. In Section 469, for the words "intending that the document forged", the words "intending that the document or electronic record forged" shall be substituted.
13. In Section 470, for the word "document" in both the places where it occurs, the words "document or electronic record" shall be substituted.
14. In Section 471, for the word "document", wherever it occurs, the words "document or electronic record" shall be substituted.
15. In Section 474, for the portion beginning with the words "whoever has in his possession any document" and ending with the words "if the document is one of the description mentioned in Section 466 of this Code", the following shall be substituted, namely:
    "Whoever has in his possession any document or electronic record, knowing the same to be forged and intending that the same shall fraudulently or dishonestly be used as a genuine, shall, if the document or electronic record is one of the description mentioned in Section 466 of this Code."
16. In Section 476, for the words "any document", the words "any document or electronic record" shall be substituted.
17. In Section 477A, for the words "book, paper and writing" at both the places where they occur, the words "book, electronic record, paper, writing" shall be substituted.

THE SECOND SCHEDULE (See Section 92)

Amendments to the Indian Evidence Act, 1872 (1 of 1872)

1. In Section 3:

   (*a*) in the definition of "Evidence", for the words "all documents produced for the inspection of the Court", the words "all documents including electronic records produced for the inspection of the Court" shall be substituted;

   (*b*) after the definition of "India", the following shall be inserted, namely: "the expressions 'Certifying Authority', 'digital signature', 'Digital Signature Certificate', 'electronic form', 'electronic records', 'information', 'secure electronic record', 'secure digital signature' and 'subscriber' shall have the meanings respectively assigned to them in the Information Technology Act, 2000."

2. In Section 17, for the words "oral or documentary,", the words "oral or documentary or contained in electronic form" shall be substituted.
3. After Section 22, the following section shall be inserted, namely:

When oral admission as to contents of electronic records are relevant

"22A. Oral admissions as to the contents of electronic records are not relevant, unless the genuineness of the electronic record produced is in question."

4. In Section 34, for the words "Entries in the books of account", the words "Entries in the books of account, including those maintained in an electronic form" shall be substituted.
5. In Section 35, for the word "record", in both the places where it occurs, the words "record or an electronic record" shall be substituted.
6. For Section 39, the following section shall be substituted, namely:

- What evidence to be given when statement forms part of a conversation, document, electronic record, book or series of letters or papers.

"39. When any statement of which evidence is given forms part of a longer statement, or of a conversation or pan of an isolated document, or is contained in a document which forms part of a book, or is contained in part of electronic record or of a connected series of letters or papers, evidence shall be given of so much and no more of the statement, conversation, document, electronic record, book or series of letters or papers as the Court considers necessary in that particular case to the full understanding of the nature and effect of the statement, and of the circumstances under which it was made."

7. After Section 47, the following section shall be inserted, namely:

Opinion as to digital signature where relevant

"47A. When the Court has 10 form an opinion as to the digital signature of any person, the opinion of the Certifying Authority which has issued the Digital Signature Certificate is a relevant fact."

8. In Section 59, for the words "contents of documents" the words "contents of documents or electronic records" shall be substituted.
9. After Section 65, the following sections shall be inserted, namely:

Special provisions as to evidence relating to electronic record

"65A. The contents of electronic records may be proved in accordance with the provisions of Section 65B."

Admissibility of electronic records

"65B. (1) Notwithstanding anything contained in this Act, any information contained in an electronic record which is printed on a paper, stored, recorded or copied in optical or magnetic media produced by a computer (hereinafter referred to as the computer output) shall be deemed to be also a document, if the conditions mentioned in this section are satisfied in relation to the information and computer in question and shall be admissible in any proceedings, without further proof or production of the original, as evidence of any contents of the original or of any fact stated therein of which direct evidence would be admissible."

(2) The conditions referred to in sub-section (1) in respect of a computer output shall be the following, namely:

(*a*) the computer output containing the information was produced by the computer during the period over which the computer was used regularly to store or process information for the purposes of any activities regularly carried on over that period by the person having lawful control over the use of the computer;

(*b*) during the said period, information of the kind contained in the electronic record or of the kind from which the information so contained is derived was regularly fed into the computer in the ordinary course of the said activities;

(*c*) throughout the material part of the said period, the computer was operating properly or, if not, then in respect of any period in which it was not operating properly or was out of operation during that part of the period, was not such as to affect the electronic record or the accuracy of its contents; and

(*d*) the information contained in the electronic record reproduces or is derived from such information fed into the computer in the ordinary course of the said activities.

(3) Where over any period, the function of storing or processing information for the purposes of any activities regularly carried on over that period as mentioned in clause (a) of sub-section (2) was regularly performed by computers, whether:

(*a*) by a combination of computers operating over that period; or

(*b*) by different computers operating in succession over that period; or

(*c*) by different combinations of computers operating in succession over that period; or (*d*) in any other manner involving the successive operation over that period, in whatever order, of one or more computers and one or more combinations of computers, all the computers used for that purpose during that period shall be treated for the purposes of this section as constituting a single computer; and references in this section to a computer shall be construed accordingly.

(4) In any proceedings where it is desired to give a statement in evidence by virtue of this section, a certificate doing any of the following things, that is to say:

(*a*) identifying the electronic record containing the statement and describing the manner in which it was produced;
(*b*) giving such particulars of any device involved in the production of that electronic record as may be appropriate for the purpose of showing that the electronic record was produced by a computer;
(*c*) dealing with any of the matters to which the conditions mentioned in sub-section (2) relate, and purporting to be signed by a person occupying a responsible official position in relation to the operation of the relevant device or the management of the relevant activities (whichever is appropriate) shall be evidence of any matter stated in the certificate; and for the purposes of this sub-section it shall be sufficient for a matter to be stated to the best of the knowledge and belief of the person stating it.

(5) For the purposes of this section:

(*a*) information shall be taken to be supplied to a computer if it is supplied thereto in any appropriate form and whether it is so supplied directly or (with or without human intervention) by means of any appropriate equipment;
(*b*) whether in the course of activities carried on by any official, information is supplied with a view to its being stored or processed for the purposes of those activities by a computer operated otherwise than in the course of those activities, that information, if duly supplied to that

computer, shall be taken to be supplied to it in the course of those activities;

(*c*) a computer output shall be taken to have been produced by a computer whether it was produced by it directly or (with or without human intervention) by means of any appropriate equipment:

Explanation: For the purposes of this section any reference to information being derived from other information shall be a reference to its being derived therefrom by calculation, comparison or any other process.

10. After Section 67, the following section shall be inserted, namely:

Proof as to digital signature

"67A. Except in the case of a secure digital signature, if the digital signature of any subscriber is alleged to have been affixed to an electronic record the fact that such digital signature is the digital signature of the subscriber must be proved."

11. After Section 73, the following section shall be inserted, namely:

Proof as to verification of digital signature

"73A. In order to ascertain whether a digital signature is that of the person by whom it purports to have been affixed, the Court may direct:

(*a*) that person or the Controller or the Certifying Authority to produce the Digital Signature Certificate;

(*b*) any other person to apply the public key listed in the Digital Signature Certificate and verify the digital signature purported to have been affixed by that person.

Explanation: For the purposes of this section, 'Controller' means the Controller appointed under sub-section (1) of Section 17 of the Information Technology Act, 2000".

12. Presumption as to Gazettes in Electronic Forms:

After Section 81, the following section shall be inserted, namely:

"81 A. The Court shall presume the genuineness of every electronic record purporting to be the Official Gazette, or purporting to be electronic record directed by any law to be kept by any person, if such electronic record is kept substantially in the form required by law and is produced from proper custody."

13. Presumption as to Electronic Aggrements:

After Section 85, the following sections shall be inserted, namely:

"85A. The Court shall presume that every electronic record purporting to be an agreement containing the digital signatures of the parties was so concluded by affixing the digital signature of the parties.

Presumption as to electronic records and digital signatures

"85B. (1) In any proceedings involving a secure electronic record, the Court shall presume unless contrary is proved, that the secure electronic record has not been altered since the specific point of time to which the secure status relates."

(2) In any proceedings, involving secure digital signature, the Court shall presume unless the contrary is proved that:

(*a*) the secure digital signature is affixed by subscriber with the intention of signing or approving the electronic record;
(*b*) except in the case of a secure electronic record or a secure digital signature, nothing in this section shall create any presumption relating to authenticity and integrity of the electronic record or any digital signature.

Presumption as to digital signature certificates

"85C. The Court shall presume, unless contrary is proved, that the information listed in a Digital Signature Certificate is correct, except for information specified as subscriber information which has not been verified, if the certificate was accepted by the subscriber."

14. Presumption as to Electronic Messages:
After Section 88, the following section shall be inserted, namely:
"88A. The Court may presume that an electronic message forwarded by the originator through an electronic mail server

to the addressee to whom the message purports to be addressed corresponds with the message as fed into his computer for transmission; but the Court shall not make any presumption as to the person by whom such message was sent.

Explanation: For the purposes of this section, the expressions 'addressee' and 'originator' shall have the same meanings respectively assigned to them in clauses (b) and (za) of sub-section (1) of Section 2 of the Information Technology Act, 2000."

15. Presumption as to Electronic Records Five Years Old

After Section 90, the following section shall be inserted, namely:

"90A. Where any electronic record, purporting or proved to be five years old, is produced from any custody which the Court in the particular case considers proper, the Court may presume that the digital signature which purports to be the digital signature of any particular person was so affixed by him or any person authorised by him in this behalf.

Explanation: Electronic records are said to be in proper custody if they are in the place in which, and under the care of the person with whom, they naturally be; but no custody is improper if it is proved to have had a legitimate origin, or the circumstances of the particular case are such as to render such an origin probable.

This *Explanation* applies also to section 81A."

16. For Section 131, the following section shall be substituted, namely:

    Production of documents or electronic records which another person, having possession, could refuse to produce.

"131. No one shall be compelled to produce documents in his possession or electronic records under his control, which any other person would be entitled to refuse to produce if they were in his possession or control, unless such last-mentioned person consents to their production."

INFORMATION TECHNOLOGY ACTION PLAN

Preamble

In the history of civilization, no work of science has so comprehensively impacted on the course of human development as Information Technology (IT). Undoubtedly, IT has been the greatest change agent of this century and promises to play this role even more dramatically in the coming decades. IT is changing every aspect of human life—communications, trade, manufacturing, services, culture, entertainment, education, research, national defence and global security. IT is breaking old barriers and building new interconnections in the emerging Global Village. IT has also become the chief determinant of the progress of nations, communities and individuals.

For India, the rise of Information Technology is an opportunity to overcome historical disabilities and once again become the master of one's own national destiny. IT is a tool that will enable India to achieve the goal of becoming a strong, prosperous and self-confident nation. In doing so, IT promises to compress the time it would otherwise take for India to advance rapidly in the march of development and occupy a position of honour and pride in the comity of nations.

The Government of India has recognised the potential of Information Technology for rapid and all-round national development. The National Agenda for Governance, which is the Government's policy blueprint, has taken due note of the Information and Communication Revolution that is sweeping the globe. Accordingly, it has mandated the Government to take necessary policy and programmatic initiatives that would facilitate India's emergence as an Information Technology Superpower in the shortest possible time.

This commitment to Information and Communication Technology in the National Agenda for Governance has been forcefully articulated by Prime Minister Shri Atal Bihari Vajpayee on a number of occasions. In his first televised addresss to the Nation on March 25, the Prime Minister declared that promotion of Information Technology would be one of his Government's five top priorities.

In his speech at the CII Annual Session on April 28, 1998, the Prime Minister said: "This is one area where India can quickly establish global dominance. India can be fully competitive in this area with tremendous pay-offs in terms of wealth creation and generation of high quality employment."

The Prime Minister announced at the CII Annual Session the Government's resolve to set up, within 30 days, a National Task Force on Information Technology, which would formulate the draft National Informatics Policy.

Accordingly, the Office of the Prime Minister issued a Notification on May 22, 1998 constituting a National Task Force on Information Technology and Software Development. This Task Force is chaired by Shri Jaswant Singh, Deputy Chairman, Planning Commission and co-chaired by Shri N. Chandrababu Naidu, Chief Minister of Andhra Pradesh and Dr. M. G. K. Menon, former Minister of State for Science and Technology. Its members include eminent representatives from the Government, industry and academia.

The Prime Minister has given five main tasks and 15 terms of reference to the IT Task Force (see Annexure). The tasks include recommending, within one month, immediate steps that the Government needs to take to remove bottlenecks in the path of rapid development of IT in India and give a big boost to Indian IT and software industry.

The Task Force has completed its deliberations on this immediate task and is pleased to submit its first report to the Prime Minister. This report, called the Information Technology Action Plan, contains 108 recommendations covering both bottleneck areas and broad promotional measures that are crucial for boosting IT in India.

These recommendations cover a wide spectrum of issues relating to telecommunications, finance, banking, revenue, commerce, electronics, human resource development, defence and rural development. They address critical national needs in the areas of information infrastructure, Internet access, software development and exports, hardware manufacture, electronic commerce, R&D in IT, manpower training and education.

Software exports has received much attention of the Task Force. Recognising India's competitive advantage in this area, the Action Plan has made many recommendations aimed at enabling Indian exporters to capture a large share of the global software market in a short time.

A unique promotional campaign suggested in the report is OPERATION KNOWLEDGE, which aims at universalising IT and IT-based education at all levels of the education pyramid in India.

A notable feature of these recommendations is the conscious effort of the Task Force to give Information Technology a pro-people and pro-development thrust. These recommendations flow from a perspective that India can become a strong IT power only if information technology reaches out to the masses in rural areas and in small towns and if its use in Indian languages can also be given major encouragement.

Taken together, the recommendations in the Information Technology Action Plan significantly broaden and deepen the process of economic reforms by encouraging competition, entrepreneurship and innovation—the three priniciples which are cardinal for India's progress in the emerging knowledge-driven global economy.

The Task Force is confident that the implementation of these recommendations will send a strong signal to people within India and abroad that India can swiftly ride on the Information Superhighway.

Activities of the Task Force till Date

The Office of the Prime Minister issued a Notification on May 22, 1998 constituting a National Task Force on Information Technology and Software Development. Dr. M.G.K. Menon, Co-Chairperson of the Task Force, Dr. N. Seshagiri, Member-Convener, and Shri Sudheendra Kulkarni of the PMO met Shri Jaswant Singh, Deputy Chairman, Planning Commission and Chairperson of the Task Force on May 26, 1998 for finalising the guidelines regarding the deliberations of the Task Force.

The Task Force created a Website on the Internet, with a web-letter from the Chairman, inviting suggestions from IT professionals around the world. On the basis of a number of useful reports on the topic prepared earlier by various organisations like the Planning Commission, Ministry of Commerce, Department of Electronics, NIC, Government of Andhra Pradesh, as well as industry associations like NASSCOM, MAIT and ESC and the suggestions given by the various members of the Task Force, the Member-Convener prepared a Basic Background Report (BBR-1) and hoisted the same on the Web. More than 3,000 suggestions have been received on the Web from IT professionals around the world.

The Task Force held a number of preparatory meetings, and several formal and informal meetings with the Ministers concerned and their Secretaries and senior officials as per the following schedule:

- 26 May, 1998: Meeting with the Deputy Chairman, Planning Commission and Chair-person of the Task Force.

- 12, 13 and 15 June, 1998: Preparatory meetings in New Delhi under the chairmanship of Professor M.G.K. Menon, Co-Chairperson of the Task Force.
- 16 June, 1998: Meeting in the Department of Telecommunication.
- 18 June, 1998: Meeting with the Chief Minister of Maharashtra, senior officials of the State Government and scientists and academicians and industry representatives in Mumbai.
- 20 June, 1998: Meeting with the Wireless Adviser, Government of India.
- 22 and 23 June, 1998: Meeting with the Minister for Communications.
- 23 June, 1998: Meeting with Chairman, Telecom Commission.
- 24 June, 1998: Meeting with Scientific Adviser to Raksha Mantri & Secretary, Defence (Research).
- 25 June, 1998: Meeting with Finance Minister.
- 25 June, 1998: Meeting with Chief Minister of Andhra Pradesh & Co-Chairperson of the Task Force.
- 26 June, 1998: Meeting with Finance Secretary.
- 27 June, 1998: Meeting with Finance Secretary.
- 29 June, 1998: Meeting with Finance Secretary.
- July 1, 1998: Meeting with Finance Minister.
- July 1, 1998: Meeting with Wireless Adviser & Defence Ministry officials.

This is the first time in India that representatives of so many ministries, departments, industry associations, business houses, educational institutions and State Governments interacted so intensively and in such a short period of time to cover so many bottleneck and promotional areas in Information Technology. It is also the first time that agreement was reached and concurrence received on most of the points in the Action Plan. This, the Task Force believes, augurs well for its early and effective implementation.

Future Activities

After submission of the first report on bottleneck and immediate promotional issues, the Task Force will begin work on the more substantive work of formulating the Draft National Informatics

Policy. Towards this end, it will soon set up Working Groups on various specific subjects, on which representatives from Government, industry, academia and other sections of society from across the country will be represented. A few of the Working Groups have already started their work.

The Task Force also plans to identify a large number of national missions which will be so designed as to make visible and catalytic impact on the use of IT in India.

In order to broadbase its consultations, the Task Force has drawn up a plan to visit Bangalore, Hyderabad, Kolkata and Guwahati in the coming weeks. It has already held one such meeting in Mumbai on June 18, 1998.

Within the next ten days, the Task Force will prepare a Vision Statement whose aim will be to excite and energize the people of India, creating the faith in them that Information Technology vitally aids personal growth and national growth. It will also embark on an awareness creation strategy for the effective articulation and dissemination of that Vision.

The Information Technology Action Plan follows:

NATIONAL TASK FORCE ON INFORMATION TECHNOLOGY AND SOFTWARE DEVELOPMENT

Information Technology Action Plan

The Government of India, recognising that the impressive growth the country has achieved since the mid-Eighties in Information Technology is still a small proportion of the potential to achieve, has resolved to make India a Global IT Superpower and a front-runner in the age of Information Revolution. The Government of India considers IT as an agent of transformation of every facet of human life which will bring about a knowledge based society in the twenty-first century. As a first step in that direction, the following revisions and additions are made to the Existing Policy and Procedures for removing bottlenecks and achieving such a pre-eminent status for India.

The revisions and additions are aimed at accomplishing the following basic objectives:

(*i*) *Info-Infrastructure Drive*: Accelerate the drive for setting up a world class Info-Infrastructure with an extensive spread of Fibre Optic Networks, Satcom Networks and Wireless Networks for seamlessly interconnecting the Local Informatics Infrastructure (LII), National Informatics Infrastructure (NII) and the Global Informatics Infrastructure (GII) to ensure a fast nation-wide onset of the INTERNET, EXTRANETs and INTRANETs.

(*ii*) *Target ITEX—50:* With a potential 2 trillion dollar Global IT industry by the year 2008, policy ambiance will be created for the Indian IT industry to target for a $ 50 billion annual export of IT Software and IT Services (including IT-enabled services) by this year, over a commensurately large domestic IT market spread all over the country.

(*iii*) *IT for all by 2008:* Accelerate the rate of PC/set-top-box penetration in the country from the 1998 level of one per 500 to one per 50 people along with a universal access to Internet/Extranets/Intranets by the year 2008, with a flood of IT applications encompassing every walk of economic and social life of the country. The existing over 600,000 Public Telephones/Public Call Offices (PCOs) will be transformed into public tele-info-centres offering a variety of multi-media Information services. Towards the goal of IT for all by 2008, policies are provided for setting the base for a rapid spread of IT awareness among the citizens, propagation of IT literacy, networked Government, IT-led economic development, rural penetration of IT applications, training citizens in the use of day-to-day IT services like tele-banking, tele-medicine, tele-education, tele-documents transfer, tele-library, tele-info-centres, electronic commerce, Public Call Centres, among others; and training, qualitatively and quantitatively, world class IT professionals.

I. Info-Infrastructure Drive

With a target of 30 per cent of annual growth rate from the 1998 level of Fibre Optic backbone of 75,000 route kilometers, VSATs of aggregate capacity of over 300 Megabit Per Second, Satellite Transponders of aggregate capacity of more than 3000 Megahertz and in the corresponding 'last mile' Wireless Communication as well as Data Communication based value added services, the Data and Multimedia Info-Infrastructure Policies are liberalised as under:

1. Inernet access nodes will be opened by DoT and authorised ISPs at all District Headquarters and local charging areas by January 26, 2000. As an interim measure, and till nodes are provided in all local charging areas, access to nearest INTERNET access nodes will be on local call rates with effect from August 15, 1998. ISPs will be responsible for ensuring that this facility is not misused for telephone traffic.
2. Voice & Data Communication is permitted for IT Software Development and IT Services on dedicated or leased circuits, but no telephone traffic is permitted. Surcharge on 64 Kbps and higher capacity circuits for voice-cum-data applications is withdrawn with effect from August 15, 1998.
3. Doubling of the lease rental charged by DoT for high speed data circuits leased by Closed User Group (CUG), Licensees of Basic Service, Cellular Service and other Value Added Services and users shall be reduced to single normal lease rental charge.
4. Requests made by public sector Software Technology Parks (STPs) or Private Sector STPs or IT promotional organisations approved by the Government for release of bandwidth shall be acted upon by the VSNL by intimating INTELSAT within two weeks of receipt.
5. Setting up of central call centres by IT Service Providers shall be permitted for which DoT and other Basic telecom Service Providers will make available bandwidth.
6. Intelligent Network (IN) Services including free phone and premium Service (e.g. 1-800 and 1-900) Services shall be introduced by DoT by 31 December, 1998 in several cities over an Intelligent Network (IN) Platform.
7. For setting up ISP operations by companies, there shall be no license fee for first-five years and after five years a nominal license fee of one rupee will be charged.
8. The monopoly of the VSNL on International Gateway for INTERNET shall be withdrawn and authorised public/ government organisations will be allowed to provide INTERNET Gateway access directly without going through VSNL Gateways. Private ISPs are allowed to provide such Gateways after obtaining defence clearance. Suitable

monitoring mechanisms will be put in place to take care of security considerations.

9. The Railways, Defence, State Electricity Boards, National Power Grid Corporation as well as organisations like ONGC, GAIL and SAIL who have rights of way shall be allowed to host fibre optic backbone. These organisations shall be allowed to provide service to the public based on this backbone by having an interface with the existing or new public networks, but without necessarily having to go through DoT network.
10. Networks such as NICNET, STPs, as well as private networks shall be allowed inter-connectivity without necessarily having to go through the DoT's INET network.
11. Providing access to INTERNET through authorised Cable TV shall be permitted to any service provider without additional licensing.
12. The 'last mile' linkages shall be freely permitted either by fibre optic or radio communication for IT application enterprises, IT promotional organisations and ISPs. In case of radio linkages, coordination by the Wireless Adviser will be observed to avoid frequency interference.
13. The radio frequency band in the range of 2.4-2.483 GHz shall be open as 'public wireless' for any Government organisation or PSU or Private Sector Company to set up Spread Spectrum based non-interference type Wireless data/multi-media communication equipment subject to a maximum of 4 Watt EIRP; WPC will periodically issue a district-wise directory of two or three selected sub-bands of 10 MHz each for each of the districts on the criteria of least congestion and reserve these sub-bands maximally for the exclusive use of Spread Spectrum Communication as above. The use of the band will be on the basis of non-interference, non-protection and non-exclusiveness. Private Sector, Public Sector and Government operators shall bilaterally obtain Defence Clearance for location, the area covered and the frequency sub-band: The Private Sector Units will be required to obtain MHA clearance directly; The security agencies shall convey their decision within 30 days of application failing which the application would be deemed to have been cleared from the security angle. If

cleared, the Private and Public Sector operators shall be required to obtain a registration and automatic license directly from WPC by producing the copies of security clearances; the Government operators will directly register with WPC; WPC will be empowered to monitor the violation of the above conditions and impose penalties on defaulters in three stages: Written warning, monetary penalty and debarring for two years. A Public Wireless Technical Audit Unit comprising a representative each from the Defence, DoT, NIC and from NASSCOM for the limited purpose of representing private user interests, shall monitor the implementation of the above policy.

14. Data communication requirements for Electronic Commerce (EC/EDI) shall be met by DoT in a liberal framework by assigning the highest priority under their priority classification if the EC/EDI requirement is certified by authorities in Government authorised by the Ministry of Commerce.
15. Public Tele-Info Centres (PTIC) having multi-media capability specially ISDN Services, Remote Database Access, Government and Community Information systems, Market Information, Desk Top Video-conferencing, Tele-Info and INTERNET/Web Access Services shall be permitted and encouraged by the Government. DoT and other Basic Service Providers, Value Added Service Providers and authorised IT promotional organisations shall be permitted to promote these services on non-exclusive basis. No license fee will be charged for operating these services and the usual tariff, where applicable, will be payable by the PTIC Service providers/franchisees. Efforts will be made by DoT and other Service Providers to upgrade STD/ISD/PCOs to convert them into these powerful PTICs for which ISDN or other digital facilities shall be provided on priority without necessarily having to make additional investment on this account.
16. DoT shall take suitable action to delicense Multi-media services, including FAX, provided by PCOs.
17. To enhance the pace of PC and INTERNET penetration in remote and far flung areas in the country, the Defence Services shall enable provisions of connectivity for ciivilian applications to their communication backbone.

18. Existing Software Centres by themselves may not be able to fulfill the high targets now set for the IT industry by the year 2008. International experience has shown that hi-tech industries flourish essentially in the rural hinterland adjacent to cities with modern telecom and communication infrastructure and top class hi-tech educational/research institutions. India will promote such 'Hi-tech Habitats' in the rural hinterland adjacent to suitable cities. For this purpose suitable autonomous structures will be designed and progressive regulations will be framed to facilitate infrastructurally self-contained self-financed Hi-Tech Habitats of high quality. Initially, five such Hi-Tech Habitats shall be planned and implemented in the rural hinterland of the cities: Bangalore, Hyderabad, Pune, Delhi and Bhubaneswar. It is estimated that progressively 50 such Hi-Tech Habitats can be viably set up by empowering the State Governments to autonomously nucleate them within a technologically progressive and administratively liberal set of guidelines to be prepared by a special Working Group on Hi-Tech IT Habitats to be set up by the Task Force.

II. Target ITEX-50

For creating a congenial ambiance for exporters of IT Software and IT Services (including IT enabled services) to reach the export target of US $ 50 billion by the year 2008, the following incentives shall be provided:

19. (*a*) *Definition*: IT Software means any representation of instructions, data, sound or image, including source code and object code, recorded in a machine readable form, and capable of being manipulated or providing interactivity to a user, by means of an automatic data processing machine falling under heading 'IT Products', but does not include 'non-IT products'. 'IT service' is defined as any service which results from the use of any IT software over a system of IT products for realising value addition. The term 'IT Industry' shall cover development, production and services related to IT Products. The term 'IT Software' shall be substituted in place of 'Computer Software' in all notifications.

(*b*) Finance Ministry (CBEC) shall introduce a new classification called, 'Information Technology (IT) Products' including Computer, Digital/Data Communication and Digital/Data Broadcasting products, by recognising the progressive technological convergence of these three categories and in line with the classification list in Attachment A (Sections I and II) of the WTO (ITA) Agreement and, additionally, Data Communication equipment.

(*c*) IT Software shall be entitled for zero customs duty and zero excise duty.

20. A revised Notification giving the following new schedule for the Government of India acceding to the WTO-ITA Ministerial Declaration of 13 December, 1996 at Singapore shall be issued by the Ministry of Finance:

In Attachment A, Sections I and II of WTO-ITA:

(*a*) Duty shall be brought down to zero by 1 January, 1999 on the following items: Parts and components excluding populated PCBs in HSN 8473.30, all storage devices in HSN 8471.70, ICs above Rs. 1000 in HSN 8542, Stepper Motors in HSN 8501.10, Colour Graphic Display Tube in HSN 8540.40 and Deflective components for Colour monitor in HSN 8504.

(*b*) Out of the 217 items listed in ITA-I, 94 items which were proposed earlier for zero duty by 1st January, 2000 shall now be advanced to 1st January, 1999.

(*c*) The remaining items earlier proposed for zero duty by the 1st January, 2003/04/05 shall now be advanced to 1 January, 2002.

Concomitantly, the following schedule will be adopted:

(*d*) Duty on Capital Goods for the manufacture of items in (*c*), wherever applicable, becomes zero by 1 January, 2000. Inputs/raw materials for the manufacture of the items in (*c*), wherever applicable, becomes zero by 1 January, 2001. Dual purpose items will be taken care of, wherever applicable, by allowing duty drawback benefits or by treating the supplies to the IT industry as deemed export.

Zero excise duty is concomitant with zero Customs duty with in-phase reduction.

Additionally, other suitable supportive measures shall be taken to encourage Indian hardware industry to become globally competitive in the light of the revised WTO-ITA schedule.

21. Customs duty on import of CD-ROMs or Optical Disc Media or Magnetic Media containing text, data or multi-media as content shall be charged only on the media and not on the contents.
22. Imported IT Products shall be permitted to be taken out of bonded offices or out of Electronics/IT Units under EOU/EPZ/STP/EHTP Schemes after a period of 2 years from the date of import if these are donated to recognised educational institutions, Government organisations and registered charitable hospitals, etc., as defined in the Clause 9.19 of the Handbook of Procedures (Volume I) of the EXIM Policy through a customs notification.
23. IT Software and IT Services companies, being constituents of the knowledge industry, shall be exempted from inspection by Inspectors like those for Factory, Boiler, Excise, Labour, Pollution/Environment etc.
24. With technological advancements in Wide Area Computer-Communication networks, which have brought about 'Virtual Technology Parks' in which IT Software and IT services are developed through online integration of software and services sub-systems from widely separated locations in the country, the concept of physical bonding has become obsolete. Accordingly, Software developers/exporters are exempted from Customs bonding at various export promotion schemes including STP/EOU/EPZ, etc. The export obligation shall be the same value as given under the EPCG scheme. Existing bonded units under the various Software Export Promotion schemes will also be considered under the above scheme.
25. A clarification shall be issued by CBEC that Service Tax is not applicable on computer software development industry.
26. The Ministry of Civil Aviation shall issue the following notifications/amendments in the regulations:

— Export shipment time for air cargo will be reduced to less than 24 hours.
— "Known Shipper" will be introduced to avoid delays on account of cooling off period.
— Cargo companies and other associated agencies to allow consolidation of export air cargo.

27. Section 80 HHE of the Income Tax Act provides for income tax exemption to profits derived from software and services exports. This section shall be amended as follows:

    — The existing formula will be so changed that tax on profits shall not have any relation to domestic turnover.
    — The definition of software and export turnover will be changed so as to include IT services exports.
    — The benefits of this section for income tax exemption to profits from exports will be extended to supporting IT Software and IT Services developers.

28. IT software and IT services shall be deemed as manufacturing activity for the limited purpose of applicability of Section 10 (15) (iv) of the Income Tax Act.
29. IT Software and IT Services shall be exempted from withholding tax through amendments in the 'explanation' of Section 9 of the Income Tax Act.
30. For individuals buying IT products including computer, the expenditure shall be deductible under Section 88 of the Income Tax Act.
31. No gift tax shall be charged for the giver or Income Tax for the receiver on PCs upto Rs. 30,000 of the original purchase price.
32. For any investment made in IT products and IT software 100 per cent depreciation shall be allowed in two years for which Ministry of Finance shall take suitable action.
33. As the traditional method of asset-based funding of working capital would not meet the adequate and timely requirements of fund of the software sector, a differential and flexible approach shall be adopted by giving special dispensation towards working capital requirements of this sector in view of the unique nature of the industry. Accordingly, RBI shall issue, by 15th August, 1998, new

guidelines with regard to working capital requirements for the IT software and services sector which would be based on simple criteria such as turnover. Banks shall be advised to give 25 per cent of the contract value for 18 months, with the first-six months as term loan (without collaterals) and from the 7th month onwards annualized Cash Flow Statements shall be accepted instead of collaterals.

34. IT software and services industry shall be treated as a Priority Sector by banks for the next five years. This would help to meet the requirements of IT software and services exports, and also the IT industry and applications within the country. Major banks will be advised to create specialised IT financing cells in important branches, where IT Software and Services units are sufficiently large in number. Performance in this dimension will be monitored by the Ministry of Finance.
35. Against the present estimate of Rs. 400 crore of working capital for the industry, the amount shall be increased to around Rs. 1200 crore by the year 2000 subject to the broad criteria of pro-rata increase for the prospective requirements 24 months ahead as compared to the actuals of the current requirements at any given time. As quantitative targeting is not appropriate, a system will be put in place which would enable substantial increase in working capital provided by the banks.
36. Bank lending to IT Software and Services exporters shall be made eligible for RBI refinancing with sufficiently low interest rates.
37. The banks shall be allowed to invest in the form of equity in dedicated venture capital funds meant for IT industry as part of the 5 per cent of increment in deposits currently allowed for shares.
38. Banks/FIs like ICICI, IDBI, UTI and SBI shall set up joint ventures with Indian or foreign companies for setting up of at least four different venture capital dedicated funds of a corpus of not less than Rs. 50 crore each to cater to the credit need of the industry. Such venture capitalists may be allowed to set off losses in one invested company and profit in another invested company during the block of years for the purpose of income tax.

39. The Company's Act shall be amended to facilitate issuance of Sweat Equity to employees. A new definition No. (66) will be added after definition No. (65) in Clause 2 as under: "(66) Sweat Equity means equity allotted to promoters, Directors or employees for providing any intellectual property or value addition to the Company."
40. Ministry of Finance shall include IT software and IT service sector while issuing general guidelines for dual listing of companies, as well as while considering two-way fungability for ADRs/GDRs.
41. Dollar Linked Stock Options to employees of Indian Software companies were announced in the 1998 Budget and detailed guidelines on this have been issued by DEA, Ministry of Finance. This shall be modified in accordance with the definition of IT Software and IT Services given under (19)(*a*) and (*b*) above.

    Employee Stock option schemes for stock listed in India would also be encouraged. Also, clarification shall be issued that income tax is applicable only at the time of sale and not at the time of excise of option.
42. Recognising the high velocity of business, high degree of competition and fast technological obsolescence faced by the IT software and IT service exporters, RBI shall be maximally accommodate the following:
    - (*a*) A blanket approval for overseas investment for acquisition of software/IT companies across the board for software exporters with previous three years cumulative actual export realisation in excess of US $ 25 million to be given up to 50 per cent or US $ 25 million, whichever is lower, out of the cumulative actual export earning of the previous three years. This is subject to submission of a certificate of software industry by appropriate authorities.
    - (*b*) For FERA approvals beyond this limit, RBI would set up a mechanism for expeditious processing of applications from this sector. This shall be announced by 15 August, 1998.
    - (*c*) For overseas ventures, a dispensation shall be given for allowing the capitalisation of both goods and services; RBI shall accordingly notify this in

consultation with Commerce Ministry by 15 August, 1998.

(*d*) As the present allowable limit of 70 per cent of the contract amount for expenditure abroad does not provide flexibility for utilisation for the purpose of general corporate objectives or for business growth purposes, RBI shall permit IT exporters to freely spend upto 5 per cent of the export proceeds abroad (out of the total 70 per cent) for miscellaneous/sundry purposes to give full flexibility. Also, a new list of allowable expenses under the 70 per cent limit would be worked out by RBI in consultation with NASSCOM.

(*e*) RBI shall issue revised EEFC guidelines to eliminate restrictions on staggered remittance, second and higher generation subsidiaries and also to allow 20 per cent of the EEFC balances for the use on the following:

(*i*) Advance remittances for downloading software (upto US $ 1 lakh per transaction).

(*ii*) Purchase of equipment and related expenditure.

(*iii*) Miscellaneous expenses not detailed in EEFC guidelines (upto 5%) of EEFC balances. Such EEFC accounts shall be permitted for making payments from offshore branches of Indian banks directly.

(*f*) Use of International Credit Cards (ICC) abroad for a variety of purposes required by the IT Software and IT Services sector shall be permitted, the detailing of which will be carried out by RBI and notified by 15 August, 1998, in particular:

(*i*) All payments currently made under Exchange Earnings Foreign Currency (EEFC) Account shall also be allowed to made through International Credit Cards (ICC). Advance payment for IT software and IT services shall be permitted to be done through ICC for which RBI will issue a notification. Notification shall be issued that ICC may also be used for paying for IT Software and

IT services purchased over INTERNET or EXTRANET and also for registering domain names.

(*ii*) RBI shall issue a modified and simplified SOFTEX form required for IT Software and IT Services export by 15 August, 1998.

43. In the EPCG scheme a system of self-declaration shall be introduced with 100 per cent post-checking subject to punitive penalty for default.
44. The value limit for import of IT Products including personal computers shall be reduced from Rs. 1.50 lakhs (c.i.f.) to Rs. 70,000 (c.i.f.).
45. Private and public organisations providing IT infrastructure shall be included for duty exemption for importing capital goods. Such service providers, in view of such capital goods imported, shall undertake the export obligations as provided for import of capital goods in the EPCG Scheme.
46. The India Brand Equity Fund Scheme operated by the Ministry of Commerce shall be made available for Software companies with lower interest and longer interval.
47. On-site IT Services should be made easier by combating Visa regulations of the recipient countries through a planned diplomatic strategy by the Ministry of External Affairs and the Indian Missions abroad for which MEA will create a suitable dedicated structure. This will also include signing of totalisation agreements, wherever necessary so as to maintain the competitive advantage of Indian companies.
48. Returns from package software development shall be increased by enabling Indian Marketing companies to set up wholesale companies abroad. They shall also be given maximum flexibility in organising the marketing of package software from India through INTERNET.
49. For benchmarking our country with our emerging competitors, a study shall be conducted at Government cost once in two years by internationally reputed consultancy companies.
50. Restrictions on the location of IT software and IT Services

(including IT training) companies in residential areas shall be removed.

51. To enable organisations and companies to identify, explore and plan strategies for Large Niche Markets like Y2K and Euro, nationally and corporate wise, all applicable provisions shall be made applicable on higher priority basis. Through MOC and DOE funds 'India Pavilions' shall be set up in several major IT exhibitions around the world through the initiative and coordination of ESC and NASSCOM.
52. Recognising the catastrophic effect of the Y2K problem for solving which a few hundred billion dollars are being spent around the world, an immediate investment of Rs. 700 crore as corpus funds shall be mobilised to control the crisis in critical government, public and private organisations and services; efforts to sensitise such organisations in the country facing the crisis shall be taken up by the Government immediately including issuance of government orders for strict compliance in a time bound manner; a high level empowered Task Force with respresentatives from the Government, Industry Associations, Banks and Financial Institutions, Defence Services, Utility and other Public Service organisations, Railways, among others, shall be constituted by the Government of India.
    - 'Mega Websites' shall be created on Internet for promoting marketing and encouraging Indian Software products and packages under multiple initiatives.
    - Creation and hosting of websites on servers located in India will be encouraged.
54. Under DEPB Rupee trade arrangement, IT Software, IT Services and IT product export to Russia shall be permitted with promotional support given by the Electronics and Software Export Promotion Council (ESC), STP, etc.
55. All promotional and liberalisation policy instruments available to IT Software and IT Services shall be made available to IT enabled services including the Information Content Industry by classifying IT enabled Services as tantamount to IT Software and IT Services.

56. For promoting Indian Software Packages (system as well as application software) users shall be given fiscal incentives for buying Indian packages. A special screening mechanism will be worked out for identifying the more promising packages developed in India and giving consistent support by the Government as well as the industry for ensuring acceptance in international markets.
57. Private STPs shall be encouraged to be set up by combining the provisions under (4), (7), (8), (12), (13), (24), (43), (45), (54) and (55), among others.

IT for All by 2008

For enabling a proactive drive for 'IT for all by 2008', the following new policy instruments shall be devised and activated.

Operation Knowledge

Recognising Information Technology to be a frontier area of knowledge, and also a critical enabling tool for assimilating, processing and productivising all other spheres of knowledge, the Government shall launch 'OPERATION KNOWLEDGE'. The aim of this national campaign will be to universalise computer literacy and also to spread the use of computers and IT in education. 'OPERATION KNOWLEDGE' shall be developed into a comprehensive policy within the next three months. However, the following initiatives shall be taken for the immediate implementation of some of its key objectives:

58. The Government shall soon launch three schemes—*Vidyarthi Computer Scheme, Shikshak Computer Scheme* and *School Computer Scheme*—to enable every student, teacher or school respectively desirous of buying computers to do so under attractive financial packages. These schemes will be supported by a suite of initiatives such as lowering the cost of PCs, easy-instalment bank loans, computer donations by IT companies and other business houses, bulk donations of computers by NRI organisations, large-volume bargain price imports, multi-lateral funding, etc.

59. Computers and Internet shall be made available in every school, polytechnic, college, university and public hospital in the country by the year 2003.
60. All universities, engineering colleges, medical colleges and other institutions of higher learning in the country as well as Research and Development Organisations shall be networked for a supplementary programme of distance education for improving the quality of education before year 2000.
61. The seven national level institutions (IITs, IISc) shall be encouraged to triple their output of students in IT by suitably restructuring the programme.
62. A National Council of IT Education comprising experts from both the industry and the academicia, shall be set up for defining courses and their content in the light of rapid developments taking place in Information Technology. The Council will also initiate a *Teach the Teachers* (3T) programme for upgrading on a regular basis the IT knowledge and skills of teachers.
63. An IT Course Module shall be made a compulsory component of all Degree Courses within a short period.
64. The setting up of *Indian Institutes of Information Technology (IIIT)* shall be implemented with urgency to make up for the lost time. Hi-tech institutions like the Indian Institute of Information Technology (IIIT) will be given the Deemed University status without insisting upon the mandatory three-year stipulation.
65. The Government shall promote the pairing of our Universities with centres of excellence in IT in developed countries.
66. Specific courses shall be launched in association with the Software Industry and IIMs to provide Project Management skills and develop specialised courses on Software Marketing.
67. The concept of SMART Schools where the emphasis is not only on Information Technology in Schools, but also on the use of skills and values that will be important in the next millennium, shall be started on a pilot demonstrative basis in each State.

68. An Institute for Computer Professionals of India shall be set up on the pattern of the Institute of Chartered Accountants of India; the Institute will be nucleated by NASSCOM with initial financial support from the industry and the Government. The Institute will be given the responsibility as an Accreditation Body for IT Education and Training Programmes with full Government recognition in addition to the DOEACC Programme of the Department of Electronics.
69. To enhance the knowledge base of IT related education at all levels the Government shall establish Information Technology, System Engineering and IT Security Institutes from within existing manpower of the Armed Forces. The Centres of Excellence in IT Software and System Engineering in the Defence Services will be utilised to the national advantage.
70. Virtual Institutes in different parts of the country shall be set up to achieve excellence in distance education.
71. The talent and expertise of IT-trained ex-servicemen shall be utilised for IT penetration in rural India and Government will fully support this offer of the Armed Forces. A Plan will be prepared and implemented for utilising the services of the large number of IT literate defence personnel retiring every year for propagating the IT culture at sub-district levels.
72. A 'National Qualification Framework' shall be established for computerised online objective system of knowledge acquisition; An 'Educational Credit Bank' shall be implemented for giving flexibility to integrate credits earned in different institutions/systems towards the eligibility for diplomas and degrees.
73. A specialised sub-committee of this Task Force shall coordinate the setting up of National and State level Digital Libraries Projects.
74. A pilot project under the aegis of the National Task Force on Information Technology shall be launched in some lead districts which have already attained universal literacy, with the aim of achieving universal computer literacy in all the secondary schools in these districts. Alongside, the network of educational institutions in these districts will

be assisted to maximise the induction of IT in order to create world-class talent at the top-end of the education pyramid. These pilot projects will be joint initiatives of the local educational institutions, respective State Governments and the Centre. In the first instance, such a pilot project will be launched in Dakshin Kannada and Udupi Districts in Karnataka on a substantive self-financing basis. Within a short time, the same will be extended to suitable districts in other States.

75. In view of the lower-than-national-average levels of technical and IT education facilities in Uttar Pradesh, Bihar, Madhya Pradesh and Rajasthan, several educational centres will be identified with a view to making them models for IT-based education and training at all levels. The aim of this initiative will be to promote IT education and awareness in Hindi-speaking States and thereby revitalise the Hindi heartland in all the fields of knowledge and knowledge-based enterprises. Allahabad shall be developed as the first such model IT-based education-cum-business centre. Within a short time, this initiative will be extended to other States which are underdeveloped in IT.

IT Penetration and IT Awareness

76. Government shall encourage the setting up of value-added network services including ATMs, Electronic Kiosks, Telephones, Smart Cards, etc., for providing a 'One-Stop Non-Stop' service to the public.
77. To make IT a mass movement, an awareness creation strategy shall be worked out within two months and the structures for implementing the same shall be put in place.
78. A major promotional campaign shall soon be launched to boost IT in Indian languages. This campaign will be based on a multi-pronged approach, involving fiscal and other incentives for R&D, production, marketing and popularisation of IT products in Indian languages. This recommendation addresses the reality that India can become a major IT power only if IT penetration in the country deepens and widens-which in turn, is dependent on large-scale use of IT in Indian languages.

79. The Government shall take all the necessary steps to boost IT for agricultural and integrated rural development. Towards this end, a number of demonstration projects will be devised in each State taking into account the specific strengths and needs at the local level. A unique *'WIRED VILLAGES'* pilot project has been launched under the aegis of the National Information Technology Task Force on Information Technology at the Warananagar Cooperative Complex in Kolhapur District in Maharashtra. Efforts will be made to quickly replicate such projects in other states.
80. The Government shall take necessary measures to develop, productivise and use, in domestic and global markets, indigenous technologies in wireless telecommunication such as CorDECT, remote access switch, etc., to achieve the national objective of rapid, low-cost expansion of telephone and Internet connectivity in rural and remote areas. Similarly, promotional measures shall be taken to encourage technologies that bring IT and Internet to the masses through the vast network of Cable TV houses.
81. For promoting electronic commerce in a time-bound manner, a strict directive shall be given to Sea Ports, Airports Authority of India, DGFT, Banks, Container Services, Customs and Indian Railways in accordance with the programme approved in the tenth Export Promotion Board meeting.
82. Bar Coding of every item sold in the country shall be made compulsory within a five-year period.
83. The Armed Forces shall integrate far-flung and remote areas (Ladakh, North-East, Andaman and Nicobar Islands, Kutch, Lakshadweep and Minicoy Islands, border areas of Himachal and Rajasthan) with mainstream India, through IT penetration as part of their Civic Action Programme. The funds for this initiative shall be provided through the Government/Venture/Seed Capital.

Citizen IT Interface

84. The Cabinet has approved NIC's proposal to make government Information, other than that having a bearing on security, available to the public. This decision shall be

implemented by suitably empowering NIC to do so. This recommendation addresses the felt need for easy availability and extensive transparency of government information.

85. District Information System (DISNIC) Plan Programme shall be made widespread and databases updated online, shall be made available to the public and Panchayats, among others. Courts Information System (COURTIS), Parliament Information System (PARLIS), Computerised Rural Information System Programme (CRISP) and other such databases shall be updated online over NICNET and access to public facilitated.
86. A Citizens Charter for effective and responsive administration in terms of time-bound service to the public shall be framed and implemented under the coordination of the Department of Administrative Reforms and Public Grievances and hoisted on the official Internet Website 'India Image' of the Government of India.

IT in Government

87. Each Department/Agency in the Central Government and State Governments shall be required to prepare a Five Year IT Plan.
88. 1-3 per cent of the budget of every Ministry/Department shall be earmarked for applying IT in the Department/sector; this investment will include not only the purchase of IT products, IT Software, but also for training and IT services; Reappropriation of the Department's budget for the IT sub-budget head shall be within the delegated powers of the Head of the Department.
89. NIC, at the national level, and technology service organisations at the State level, shall establish 'Framework Contracts' with reputed suppliers to provide a wide range of IT consultancy, specialist services and IT products to Government agencies to reach the benefit of lower costs through bulk purchases.
90. India shall participate in international projects like 'Government Online' Project of G-8 countries so as not only learn from the experience of others but also to contribute

to the global experience in planning and implementing projects to promote IT in Government.

91. Tele commuting is recognised as a new modality of doing work in an office and labour laws accommodating the same shall be enacted. An option shall be given to employees, where feasible and efficient, to accomplish part of their work through telecommuting in the framework of 'Management by Objectives' (MBO).
92. The Government of India shall set up a central repository of data elements in Government with the NIC and make it accessible through NICNET.
93. The recommendations of the TG-MAP Committee for Map and GIS Data Policy approved by the Committee of Secretaries under the Cabinet Secretary, shall be notified by the Ministry of Defence expeditiously.
94. A computerised National Inventory of Training pertaining to different areas shall be maintained.
95. A computerised Inventory of Government best practices for electronic access shall be maintained.
96. Government shall stipulate IT literacy as an essential requirement for all future Government and public sector employment; in the Annual Confidential Reports of government employees, a column shall be introduced regarding contribution to IT utilisation in the department/organisation.
97. A National Institute of Smart Government shall be set up to focus on all issues concerning IT-supported governance.
98. State Institutes of Public Administrations shall be re-engineered to help bring about IT-responsive State Governments.
99. Suitable floor space in Government buildings, which are not utilised during non-office hours, could be given to private educational institutions for IT training purposes in return for a proportionate number of free nominations of Government employees for IT training.

Data Security Systems and Cyber Laws

100. A National Computerised Records Security Document shall be prepared within three months for enforcing security requirements by consulting similar documents prepared

by SAG, JCB, WESEE, etc.

101. An Information Security Agency shall be set up at the National level to play the role of Cyber Cop.
102. A National Policy on Information Security, Privacy and Data Protection Act for handling of computerised data shall be framed by the Government within six months.
103. Cyber infractions shall be addressed within the legal framework by the Ministry of Law, Justice and Company Affairs.
104. The cryptology and Cyber Security knowledge and experience developed by the Defence establishments shall be suitably transferred to the civilian information security agencies for wider dissemination in the country to increase information security, network security and bring about a greater degree of secure use of EFT, Digital Signature, etc.
105. The procedure of keeping records in paper form in public and private STPs shall be restricted to a maximum duration of two months after which the records shall be kept only in the Electronic/Magnetic/Optical media.
106. The Indian Telegraph Act of 1885, the Indian Post Office Act of 1888 and the Indian Wireless Telegraphy Act of 1993 shall be suitably modified in the light of the growing predominance of IT in day-to-day life. Suitable changes will also be made in other Laws/Acts, wherever necessary.
107. The draft set of Cyber Laws prepared by the Cyber Law Committee set up by the Committee of Secretaries, shall be approved by the Government with suitable modifications and implemented, as a first step, within six months.
108. All necessary instructions, notifications and amendements to procedures/Law shall be issued by the respective Ministries/Departments within three months.

5

Broadcasting Services Regulation Bill

CONSULTATION PAPER ON THE PROPOSED DRAFT OF BROADCASTING SERVICES REGULATION BILL

The Ministry of Information and Broadcasting has been examining the issue of introducing a legislation to regulate the operation of broadcasting services consequent upon the judgement of the Supreme Court in the Cricket Association of Bengal case delivered in 1995 that airwaves are public property and have to be controlled and regulated by public authority in the interests of the public.

The Broadcasting Bill of 1997 was introduced in the Parliament but lapsed. The Communication Convergence Bill, 2001 was introduced but even this lapsed due to the dissolution of the 13th Lok Sabha. In 1995, the Cable Television Networks Act was brought into regulate the cable business and their operations. Most of the other required regulations in the sector were being accomplished by issuing guidelines such as those for Uplinking TV channels, DTH, FM Radio, Community Radio and Downlinking etc.

The proposed Broadcasting Services Regulation Bill seeks to achieve the following:

(*i*) To provide legislative sanction retroactively to Government guidelines on various regulatory aspects such as television channels' Uplinking/Down linking, private FM Radio and Community Radio, LTH, Teleport, etc.

(*ii*) To set up a new Broadcasting Regulatory Authority of India and delegate the regulatory functions presently being performed by the Ministry of I&B to this new authority.

(*iii*) To incorporate the provisions of the existing Cable

Television Networks Regulation Act in the new legislation through appropriate repeal and savings clauses and provide for licensing of cable operators

(*iv*) To make enabling provisions on the following:

(*a*) Cross media ownership and restrictions on accumulation of interests to provide for competition and plurality of views.

(*b*) Minimum domestically sourced content in foreign channels to promote indigenous media/entertainment industry, particularly in the field of animation and gaming etc.

(*c*) Minimum obligations on all channels for public service broadcasting in their programme and advertising content.

The Ministry of Information and Broadcasting proposes to consult the media and the broadcasting industry organizations to obtain their response to some of the major issues proposed to be covered in the Broadcasting Services Regulation Bill. Accordingly, the draft of the proposed legislation, indicating the current thinking in the Ministry of Information and Broadcasting is put on the Ministry's website. It is to be appreciated that these are not the final views of the Ministry or the Central Government. These will be further refined after the process of consultation with the media and the broadcasting industry as well as concerned Ministries is over and thereafter the Cabinet will consider the final contours of the proposed legislation. Some of the important features are presented below:

1. Definitions

The definition of broadcasting is wide enough to cover not only traditional broadcasting but also internet broadcasting as well as mobile broadcasting. However, the broadcasting services listed in the Bill are traditionally under the administrative and regulatory control of the Ministry of I & B. Depending on the final decision of the Central Government on the issue of 'convergence', flexibility has been provided to list new services. Further, since many of the provisions of guidelines differentiate channels on the basis of news and current affairs content, it is proposed to define a 'news and current affairs channel.'

2. Legislative Validation

While stipulating that, in future, it shall be unlawful for any person to provide broadcasting services without a proper license from the competent authority, it is also proposed to provide legislative backing for all the past guidelines issued by the Central Government from time to time, and validate all consequential actions by taken by all concerned. This has become necessary because of challenge to some of the guidelines. While the Central Government is firmly of the view that all its past decisions/actions are completely legal and valid and drew their support from other relevant statutes and judicial pronouncements, it is proposed to set the record beyond the scope of interpretation by specifically providing for retroactive validation under the proposed Bill.

3. Content

Presently content in cable services is regulated by the Programme Code and Advertising Code under Rules 6 and 7 respectively of the Cable Rules 1994. These codes are made applicable to broadcasters/DTH operators under the relevant Guidelines mentioned above and through specific provisions in the license/ permission agreements. Similarly the AIR code is made applicable on the private radio companies. The Central Government is directly responsible for ensuring compliance with these codes. The Government desires to involve the media and the broadcasting industry in self-regulation of content in the first place, failing which the proposed Broadcast Regulatory Authority of India would step in (instead of the Central Government) to take suitable action.

The Ministry of I&B has already appointed a committee under the chairmanship of Secretary I&B with representatives from the media/industry, civil society and regulatory Ministries to design a more detailed and specific 'Content Code' that can be easily understood and used as a guide by the public as well as the broadcasters to self-regulate content in their respective programmes. This committee will also suggest suitable institutional mechanism for self-regulation by the media/ industry. In order to facilitate the implementation of the above course of action, it is proposed to have enabling provisions in the proposed BSR Bill.

4. Broadcast Regulatory Authority of India (BRAI)

Presently, the regulatory functions are being performed by the Ministry of Information and Broadcasting in respect of the broadcasters under several guidelines issued from time to time. On the other hand, the cable operators only need to register themselves with the local post office. The authorized officers perform some of the regulatory functions in respect of cable operators. It is proposed to set up BRAI on the lines of Telecom Regulatory Authority of India (TRAI). In order to function in a coordinated manner with clear roles and responsibilities, it is proposed to specify respective powers and functions of the Central Government, the BRAI, the licensing authorities and the authorized officers.

5. Digital Addressable Systems

The Central Government introduced CAS in 2003 and had to withdraw the scheme in the face of certain deficiencies. The scheme is attempted to be introduced again with certain modifications as per Delhi High Court directive. In the proposed legislation, it is provided to introduce digital addressable systems in a time bound manner, but with adequate safeguards to ensure that all stakeholders are fully prepared and the scheme actually delivers value to the subscribers and is in their interest.

6. Public Service Broadcasting Obligations

It is considered desirable to provide a minimum level of public service oriented content in all private channels and networks in addition to public broadcasters so as to reach the maximum number of viewers in the country. Also it is considered desirable to lay down certain obligations of foreign channels to encourage domestic entertainment and media related industry e.g., animation, gaming and visual effects industry and provide certain minimum domestic content. While the detailed policy guidelines and their implementation procedures may be developed in close consultation with the media and the broadcasting industry, it is proposed to provide enabling provisions in the proposed legislation for the time being.

7. Intellectual Property Rights

In order to ensure that the name and logo of the channel is not misused to convey undesirable content or mislead the public or get unfair commercial advantage, certain provisions for registration of channels are proposed in the draft Bill. Another aspect of the IPR regime is the denial of legitimate use of content for broadcasting purposes even after the content has been published/reproduced or performed in public: The present Copyright law provides for compulsory licensing for only one complainant while the problem is being faced by most of the broadcasters. It is, therefore, proposed to provide for compulsory licensing for more than one complainant.

8. Accumulation of Interest

There are three types of restrictions on accumulation of interest in the media. These are restrictions on: (*a*) Cross media ownership among different segments of media such as print/television/radio. (*b*) Consolidation including 'vertical integration' within a media segment such as television or radio. (*c*) Market share in the city/ state/country within each media segment. It is proposed to incorporate enabling provisions in the BSR Bill:

9. Offences and Penalties

A clear-cut differentiation is proposed to be maintained between civil and criminal offences. Unlicensed broadcasting or breach of national security or integrity etc., are treated as criminal offences and proposed to be made punishable by the courts of criminal jurisdiction under the normal laws of the land for which prosecution will be filed by the 'Authorized Officers, i.e. District and Sub-Divisional Magistrates or Commissioners of Police. The authorized officers have been given the power to inspect search and seize equipment etc., under proposed Section 24. However this power is limited to only against those who commit a criminal offence under the proposed Bill i.e. run an unlicensed broadcasting service or telecast an unregistered channel or violate directions under Section 5 above. Even in these cases, the authorized officers will file cases before regular courts with criminal jurisdiction. On the other hand, violations of the policy guidelines or regulations or license conditions are treated as civil offences and proposed to be made punishable by the Licensing Authorities and BRAI for which appeals will lie before TDSAT or FCAT.

10. Repeal of Cable Act, 1995

Since all the provisions of the Cable Television Networks (Regulation) Act, 1995 *are being* subsumed in the proposed legislation, including the introduction of licensing of cable operators, it is proposed to repeal the said Act and provide for continued validation of all actions done under it through the following 'repeal and saving' section.

11. Relationship with other Laws

While the proposed legislation will prevail over other existing laws, specific exemption has been provided for the Indian Telegraph Act, 1885 and Indian Wireless Telegraphy Act, 1933.

12. Key Issues

The above narration highlights the key areas covered by the proposed legislation. However, the draft of the proposed legislation is also attached herewith, and also placed on the Ministry's web-site to elicit focused response from the stakeholders. However, it is once again re-iterated that the above proposals represent current thinking in the Ministry of Information and Broadcasting and are subject to modification in the light of comments received from the media and the industry as well as various concerned Ministries. Each subject area discussed above may raise several key issues that need to be addressed before final views can be formulated. The stakeholders are, therefore, requested to submit their views on key issues in respect of the areas covered above as also any other related areas that they consider important enough. Anyone desirous of submitting his comments and views is requested to do so by within a period of one month from the date of putting this consultation paper on the website of the Ministry of Information and Broadcasting.

A DRAFT OF THE PROPOSED BROADCASTING SERVICES REGULATION BILL, 2006

- To promote facilitate and develop in an orderly manner the carriage and content of Broadcasting
- To provide for regulation of broadcasting services in India for offering a variety of entertainment, news, views and

information in a fair, objective and competitive manner and to provide for regulation of content for public viewing and matters connected therewith or incidental thereto

- To provide for the establishment of an independent authority to be known as the Broadcast Regulatory Authority of India for the purpose of regulating and facilitating development of broadcasting services in India
- Whereas airwaves are public property and it is felt necessary to regulate the use of such airwaves in national and public interest, particularly with a view to ensuring proper dissemination of content and in the widest possible manner
- Whereas Government has issued guidelines from time to time, with the approval of the Union Cabinet, for regulating the Broadcasting Services and it is felt necessary to give a statutory effect to these guidelines with retrospective effect.

Be it enacted by Parliament in the Fifty-Eighth Year of the Republic of India as follows:

Chapter 1

PRELIMINARY

1. Short Title, Extent and Commencement

(*i*) This Act may be called the Broadcasting Services Regulation Act, 2006.
(*ii*) It extends to the whole of India.
(*iii*) It shall come into force with immediate effect.

2. Definitions

In this Act, unless the context otherwise requires:

(*a*) "Authority" means the Broadcasting Regulatory Authority of India established under Section 12;
(*b*) "Authorized Officer" means, within his local limits of jurisdiction:

— A District Magistrate, or
— A Sub-Divisional Magistrate, or
— A Commissioner of Police.

And includes any other officer notified by the Central Government or State Government or the Authority, to be an authorized office for such local limits of jurisdiction as may be determined by that Government or Authority.

(*c*) "Broadcaster" means any person who provides a content broadcasting service and includes a broadcasting network service provider when he manages and operates his own television or radio channel service.

(*d*) "Broadcasting" means assembling and programming any form of communication content like signs, signals, writing, pictures, images and sounds, and either placing it in electronic form on electro-magnetic waves on specified frequencies and transmitting it through space or cables to make it continuously available on the carrier waves, or continuously streaming it in digital data form on the computer networks, so as to be accessible to single or multiple users through receiving devices either directly or indirectly; and all its grammatical variations and cognate expressions.

(*e*) "Broadcasting Service" means assembling, programming and placing communication content in electronic form on the electro-magnetic waves on specified frequencies and transmitting it continuously through broadcasting network or networks so as to enable all or any of the multiple users to access it by connecting their receiver devices to their respective broadcasting networks, and includes all the content broadcasting services and the broadcasting network services.

(*f*) "Broadcasting Network Service" means a service, which provides a network of infrastructure of cables or transmitting devices for carrying broadcasting content in electronic form on specified frequencies by means of guided or unguided electromagnetic waves to multiple users, and includes the management and operation of any of the following:

- Teleport/Hub/Earth Station
- Direct-to-Home (DTH) Broadcasting Network
- Multi-System Cable Television Network
- Local Cable Television Network

— Satellite Radio Broadcasting Network
— Such other Network Service as may be prescribed by the Central Government.

(*g*) "Cable Operator" means any person who manages and operates, or is otherwise responsible for, a multi-system or a local cable television network.

(h) "Cable Television Channel Service" means the assembly, programming and transmission by cables of any broadcast television content on a given set of frequencies to multiple subscribers.

(*i*) "Cable Television Network" means any system consisting of closed transmission paths and associated signal generation, control and distribution equipment, designed to receive and re-transmit television channels or programmes for reception by multiple subscribers.

(*j*) "Carrier" means the electro-magnetic waves that can travel on air or cable and are capable of carrying communication content in electronic form on specified frequencies.

(*k*) "Chairperson' means the Chairperson of the Authority appointed under Section 13.

(*l*) "Channel" means a set of frequencies used for transmission of a programme.

(*m*) "Competent Authority" means the Authority designated by the Government for the purpose of this Act.

(*n*) "Community Radio Service" means terrestrial radio broadcasting intended and restricted only to a specific community and within specified territory.

(*o*) "Content" means any sound, text, data, picture (still or moving), other audio-visual representation, signal or intelligence of any nature or any combination thereof which is capable of being created, processed, stored, retrieved or communicated electronically.

(*p*) "Content Broadcasting Service" means the assembling, programming and placing content in electronic form and transmitting or re-transmitting the same on electro-magnetic waves on specified frequencies, on a broadcasting network so as to make it available for access by multiple users by connecting their receiving devices to the network, and includes the management and operation of any of the following:

— Terrestrial television service
— Terrestrial radio service
— Satellite television service
— Satellite radio service
— Cable television channel service
— Community radio service
— Such other content broadcasting services as may be prescribed by the Central Government.

(*q*) "Decoder" means an equipment for decoding an encrypted channel to facilitate its intelligible reception.

(*r*) "Direct-To-Home Broadcasting Service" means a service for multi-channel distribution of programmes direct to subscriber's premises without the help of a local delivery system by uplinking to a satellite system specified for the purpose by the Competent Authority.

(*s*) "Downlinking" with reference to satellite broadcast or DTH Broadcasting service means reception of programmes transmitted from a satellite to an earth station or a receiving device.

(*t*) "Encrypted" means treated electronically or otherwise for the purpose of preventing intelligible reception by unauthorized persons.

(*u*) "Frequency" means frequency of electro-magnetic waves used for transmission of broadcasting service.

(*v*) "Foreign Satellite Broadcasting Service" means a broadcasting service provided by using a satellite, up linked from a foreign country and receivable in India.

(*w*) "Free-To-Air Broadcasting service" means a non-encrypted broadcasting service made available for reception by receiving apparatus commonly available to the public without requiring payment of a subscription fee.

(*x*) "License" means a license issued for any of the broadcasting services by the relevant Licensing Authority prescribed by the Central Government under this Act.

(*y*) "Licensing Authority" means an officer of the Central Government or the Authority, so notified by the Central Government in respect of any of the broadcasting services and for such limits of jurisdiction as may be determined by the Government.

(*z*) "Licensed Service" means a broadcasting service licensed by the Central Government or the Authority, as the case may be, under this Act.

(*aa*) "Local Cable Operator" means any person who manages and operates or is responsible for the management and operation of a cable television network to provide a cable television service to multiple subscribers in a particular area.

(*bb*) "Local Delivery Service" means a service for multi-channel downlinking and distribution of television programmes by a land based transmission system using wired cable or wireless cable or a combination of both for simultaneous reception either by multiple subscribers directly or through one or more local cable operators.

(*cc*) "Member" means a Whole-time Member or a Part-time Member, as the case may be, of the Authority referred to in Section 13 and includes the Chairperson.

(*dd*) "Multi-System Cable Television Network" means a system for multi-channel downlinking and distribution of television programmes by a land-based transmission system using wired cable or wireless cable or a combination of both for simultaneous reception either by multiple subscribers directly or through one or more local cable operators.

(*ee*) "Multi System Operator (MSO)" means any person who manages and operates a multi-system cable television network to provide a cable television service to multiple subscribers, which may or may not include other value added services including telecommunications and Internet.

(*ff*) "Network Operator" means any person who provides a broadcasting network service.

(*gg*) "News and Current Affairs Channel" means a channel that broadcasts programmes containing reports and comments on recent events, ideas, individuals and institutions dealing with political, social, economic and such other subjects as are of general interest to the public at large, but does not include a channel that exclusively broadcasts scientific, cultural, educational or entertainment programmes including news relating thereto.

(*hh*) "Notification" means a notification published in the official Gazette or posted on the official website of the Ministry of

Information & Broadcasting or of the Authority, as the case may be, and the expression "notified" to be construed accordingly.

(*ii*) "Prescribed" means prescribed by rules notified under this Act.

(*jj*) "Private Communication" means:

— a communication between two or more persons that is of a private or domestic nature;

— an internal communication of a business, government agency or other of a business, government agency or other organization for the purpose of the operation of the business, agency or organization; and

— communication in such other circumstances as may be prescribed.

(*kk*) "Programme" in relation to broadcasting service, means:

— any matter the purpose of which is related to entertain, educate or inform public; or

— any advertising or sponsorship matter, whether or not of a commercial kind.

But does not include any matter that is wholly related to or connected with any private communication.

(*ll*) "Public Service Broadcaster" means any entity whose primary objective is to provide broadcasting content to the public that is socially and culturally relevant and in public interest and welfare.

(*mm*) "Registered Channel" means a broadcasting channel registered under this Act.

(*nn*) "Regulations" means regulations made by the Authority under this Act.

(*oo*) "Satellite Television Service" means a television broadcasting service provided by using a satellite, and received with or without the help of a local delivery system but does not include Direct-to-Home (DTH) delivery service.

Explanation: Decision of the Authority whether a particular service falls in the category of a satellite broadcasting service or a Direct-to-Home delivery service shall be final.

(*pp*) "Satellite Radio Service" means a radio broadcasting

service provided by using a satellite and directly receivable through receiver sets by multiple subscribers in India.

(*qq*) "Secretary" means the Secretary appointed under sub-section (1) of Section 20.

(*rr*) "Service Provider" means provider of a broadcasting service.

(*ss*) "Subscriber" of a service means a person who receives the service at a place indicated by him without further transmitting it to any other person.

(*tt*) "Subscription Fee" means any form of consideration given by subscriber.

(*uu*) "Terrestrial Television Service" means a television broadcasting service provided over the air by using a land-based transmitter and directly received through receiver sets by the public but does not include a local delivery service.
Explanation: Decision of the Authority whether a particular service falls in the category of a terrestrial television service or a local delivery service shall be final.

(*vv*) "Terrestrial Radio Service" means a radio broadcasting service for provided over the air by using a land-based transmitter and directly received through receiver sets by the public.

(*ww*) "Whole-time Member" means a Whole-time Member of the Authority appointed under Section 13.

(*xx*) "Wireless Cable" means a land-based wireless transmission system used for multi-point multi-channel distribution of programmes on frequencies designated for the purpose by the Competent Authority.

(*yy*) "Uplinking" with reference to satellite broadcast or Direct-to-Home service means uplinking of programme transmission from an earth station or a transmitting device to the satellite.

(*zz*) "Year" means the financial year.

Chapter 2

REGULATION OF BROADCASTING SERVICES

Broadcasting Services not without License

(1) No person shall, after the commencement of this Act, provide

any broadcasting service, or broadcast any programme or channel, without obtaining a license for such service or permission for such programme or registration of such channel, in accordance with the policy guidelines prescribed under this Act for regulating such broadcasting service, programme or channel.

- Provided that the cable operators registered under the Cable Television Networks (Regulation) Act, 1995 may continue to provide cable services in accordance with the conditions laid down in section 49 of this Act.
- Provided further that the permissions issued, license agreements signed with private operators, and registration of channels done, by the Central Government, from time to time under respective guidelines listed under Sub-section (3) of this section, read with Indian Telegraph Act, 1885, prior to the commencement of this Act shall be deemed to be licenses issued under the provisions of this Act from the respective dates of issue of such permission or signing of such license agreement, or registration of such television channel, and shall be valid till the date of expiry of the original permission or license agreement or registration, as the case may be, or till the expiry of one year from the date of commencement of this Act, whichever is earlier, notwithstanding anything contained in this Act or any other law for the time being in force.
- Provided further that the Central Government may, by notification, exempt a Public Service Broadcaster or such other category of broadcasters, as may be specified, from all or any of the provisions of this Act.
- Provided further that the Government may, by notification, exempt such non-commercial establishments under common ownership from obtaining a license for a Local Delivery Service without using wireless cable, for the purpose of providing such service for the exclusive use of their members subject to such conditions and restrictions as may be specified.

(2) Notwithstanding anything contained in this Act or any other law for the time being in force, the guidelines issued by the Central Government, as specified in Sub-section (3) below, and orders issued there under shall be deemed to have been issued as Rules

under this Act and all actions taken by Central Government or any other person in pursuance of these guidelines, shall be deemed to have been taken under this Act.

(3) The following guidelines issued by the Central Government from time to time shall be deemed to have been issued as Rules under this Act:

(*i*) Uplinking Guidelines of 2000
(*ii*) FM Radio Policy for private agencies of 2000 (Phase 1)
(*iii*) DTH Policy Guidelines of 2001
(*iv*) SNG/DSNG Use Guidelines of 2002
(*v*) Community Radio Policy of 2002
(*vi*) Revision of Uplinking Policy Guidelines of March 2003
(*vii*) Revision of Uplinking Policy Guidelines of August 2003
(*viii*) FM Radio Policy Phase 2 of July 2005
(*ix*) Downlinking Guidelines of November 2005
(*x*) Consolidated Uplinking Guidelines of December 2005.

Registration of Channels and Compliance with the Content Code

1. Every service provider shall register his television or radio channel with the Authority in the manner prescribed.
2. The Authority may refuse to register a channel, or cancel the registration of a channel, if it is of the considered opinion that the content of the channel is likely to threaten the security and integrity of the State or threaten peace and harmony or public order in the whole or a part of the country, or if the name or logo or symbol of the channel, either in part or full or abbreviated form, is:

   (*a*) Obscene or vulgar.
   (*b*) The same or similar to that of a terrorist or terrorist organization, either in full or in abbreviated form.
   (*c*) The same or similar to that of any name or brand or symbol of a product, or a company making such a product, that is prohibited from being promoted or advertised, directly or indirectly, by any law for the time being in force.
   (*d*) The same or similar to that of any other registered channel in India or any well-known channels outside

India, whether registered in India or not, except where valid permission is obtained from the owner of the original name or symbol or logo, as the case may be, provided that any such permission shall not be treated as valid if the said owner does not have more than 26 per cent equity in the applicant company, or contributes or agrees to contribute from the original channel with the same or similar name or logo or symbol, as the case may be, more than 50 per cent of the content of the proposed channel of the applicant company.

- Provided that no such order of refusal or cancellation of registration shall be issued without giving a reasonable opportunity to the applicant company or the service provider of being heard.

3. No service provider shall provide any broadcasting content that is not in conformity with the broadcasting content certification and regulation rules, hereafter referred to as 'the Content Code', as may be prescribed by the Government under this Act.

- Provided that till such time as the Content code is notified under this Act, all service providers shall adhere to the Programme Code and the Advertising Code prescribed under the Cable Television Network Rules, 1994.

Central Government to Exercise Certain Powers in Public Interest

The Central Government may at any time, if it appears necessary or expedient to do so in public interest, in respect of any broadcasting service, which is considered prejudicial to friendly relations with a foreign country, public order, communal harmony or security of the State, direct the Licensing Authority to suspend or revoke its license or direct the service provider to stop broadcasting its service or transmit in its broadcasting service such announcements in such manner as may be considered necessary, and the service provider shall immediately comply with all or any such directions.

Mandatory Sharing of Certain Sports Broadcast Signals

For the purpose of ensuring the widest availability of broadcast signals for viewing in India, no content rights owner or holder and no television or radio broadcasting service provider shall carry a live television broadcast on any cable or DTH network or radio commentary broadcast in India of such national or international sporting events, held in India or abroad, as may be notified by the Central Government to be of national importance, unless simultaneously, it shares the live broadcast signal, without its advertisements, with the public service broadcasters i.e. Doordarshan and All India Radio of Prasar Bharti, in such a manner as to enable them to re-transmit the same on their respective terrestrial networks and DTH networks, on such terms and conditions as may be prescribed.

Compulsory Transmission of Public Broadcasters' Channels

1. Every cable operator shall carry Lok Sabha and Rajya Sabha channels and at least two Doordarshan terrestrial channels and one regional language channel of a state in the prime band, in satellite mode on frequencies other than those carrying terrestrial frequencies.
2. The channels referred to in Sub-section (1) shall be re-transmitted without any deletion or alteration of any programme transmitted on such channels.
3. The Prasar Bharti (Broadcasting Corporation of India) established under Sub-section (1) of Section 3 of the Prasar Bharti (Broadcasting Corporation of India) Act, 1990 may, by notification in the Official Gazette, specify the additional number and name of every Doordarshan channel to be re-transmitted by the Cable Operators in their cable service and the manner of reception and transmission of such channels.

Introduction of Digital Addressable Systems (DASs) in Broadcasting Network Services

1. Where the Central Government is satisfied that it is necessary in public interest to do so, it may, by notification, make it obligatory for every broadcasting network service

provider in the country to transmit or re-transmit content of any or all channels provided by him, through a digital addressable system with effect from such date as may be specified in the notification.

2. With a view to ensuring that the broadcasting network service providers comply with the obligation under Sub-section (1), the Central Government may, by notification, prescribe a transitional scheme for introduction of Digital Addressable Systems (DASs) by service providers, with effect from such date as may be specified in the notification, and different dates may be specified for different types of service providers in different States, cities, towns or areas, which may, inter alia, provide for the following:

(*a*) Policy guidelines, transitional arrangements and the time frame within which the service providers in different areas shall complete the process of providing the DASs to all their viewers.

(*b*) Obligations of the broadcasters in terms of declaration of prices of their registered channels, commercial arrangements with their distributors and networks service providers etc.

(*c*) Obligations of the Multi-service Operators (MSOs) and Local Cable Operators (LCOs) who introduce DASs in terms of their supply, maintenance, quality of service standards, subscriber management system etc.

(*d*) Obligations of the MSOs and LCOs who continue for the time being with the existing non-addressable systems in terms of declaration of the available number, names and prices of channels, maintenance of subscriber registers and furnishing periodical information etc.

(*e*) Rights and obligations of the viewers in terms of getting quality of service, options to choose channels, making payments for the DASs and monthly subscriptions for the channels, proper upkeep and use of DASs etc.

(*f*) Powers and functions of the Authority in terms of regulation of, and adjudication on, the commercial arrangements among various service providers, prescribing quality of service standards, enforcement of license conditions and other obligations under the scheme on the service providers and the viewers etc.

(*g*) Such other terms and conditions of the scheme as are considered necessary and desirable for ensuring the successful transition from the existing technology to the digital addressable systems within the time frame prescribed under Sub-section (1).

(3) Notwithstanding anything contained in Sub-sections (1) and (2) or any other law for the time being in force, the Central Government shall have the power, for reasons to be recorded in writing, to postpone or advance any specified date or dates, or by notification, modify, suspend or revoke a notification already issued or any other order or direction issued by it or the Authority.

- Provided that any order issued or action taken by the Central Government or the Authority or by any other person in pursuance of the earlier notification or order shall, unless specified otherwise, be deemed to be valid and continue to be in operation as if the earlier notification had never been modified, suspended or revoked, as the case may be.

Powers and Functions of the Central Government

The Central Government shall have the authority to:

(*i*) Prescribe policy guidelines and procedures for the grant, refusal or revocation of licenses/registration for all types of broadcasting services.

(*ii*) Designate and notify such officers of the State Governments or the Authority as may be considered necessary, as the Licensing Authorities to grant, refuse or revoke licenses/registration in respect of such broadcasting services and for such limits of jurisdiction as may be prescribed.

(*iii*) Prescribe the terms and conditions of licenses/registration to service providers and procedures to ensure their compliance by the service providers.

(*iv*) Prescribe license fees and processing fees for grant of licenses/permissions/registration for different types of broadcasting services.

(*v*) Prescribe policy guidelines, including transitional arrangements, to facilitate the introduction of digital addressable systems in broadcasting services throughout the country in a time-bound manner.

(*vi*) Prescribe guidelines and norms to evaluate and certify broadcasting content and the terms and conditions of broadcasting different categories of content by the service-providers.

(*vii*) Prescribe policy guidelines and institutional arrangements for self-regulation of broadcasting content by the service providers in conformity with the prescribed norms.

(*viii*) Prescribe guidelines and institutional arrangements for complaint/grievance redressal against violations of the prescribed norms of broadcasting content code by service providers.

(*ix*) Prescribe policy guidelines to facilitate competition and promote efficiency in the operation of broadcasting services so as to facilitate growth in such services.

(*x*) Exercise, or authorize other existing institutions to exercise, any or all the powers and perform any or all the functions of the new institutions, pending their creation and operationalisation.

Restrictions on Accumulation of Interest

1. The Central Government shall have the authority to prescribe such eligibility conditions and restrictions with regard to accumulation of interest in the print and broadcast segments of the media as may be considered necessary from time to time, to prevent monopolies across different segments of the media as well as within the broadcast segment, to ensure diversity of news and views.
2. No content broadcasting service provider and its associated companies shall have more than 20 per cent share of paid up equity or have any other financing or commercial arrangement that may give it management control over the financial, management or editorial policies of any broadcasting network service provider.

3. No broadcasting network service provider and its associated companies shall have more than 20 per cent share of paid up equity or have any other financing or commercial arrangement that may give it management control over the financial, management or editorial policies of any content broadcasting service provider.
4. No content broadcasting service provider and its associated companies shall have more than the prescribed share of the total number of channels in a city or a state subject to the overall ceiling of 15 per cent for the whole country.

Public Service Broadcasting Obligations

(1) Every broadcasting service provider shall discharge such public service broadcasting obligations as the Central Government may prescribe from time to time in accordance with the limits indicated below:

(*a*) The share of content produced in India shall not be less than 15 per cent of the total content of a channel broadcast during every week.

(*b*) The share of public service/social messaging through advertisements and such other promotional materials/ messages shall not be less than 10 per cent of the total commercial time of a channel broadcast during every week.

(*c*) The share of public service/socially relevant programme content shall not be less than 10 per cent of the total programme content of a channel broadcast during every week.

(2) In the event of failure to comply with the public service obligation, every content-broadcasting service provider shall be liable to pay such amount as may be prescribed by the Central Government towards its public service obligation.

(3) The Central Government shall formulate detailed guidelines and institutional arrangement for evaluation of every television and radio broadcaster in respect of its public service broadcasting obligation.

Chapter 3

BROADCASTING REGULATORY AUTHORITY OF INDIA

Establishment and Incorporation of the Authority

1. With effect from such date, as the Central Government may by notification appoint in this behalf, there shall be established for the purposes of this Act an Authority, to be known as the Broadcast Regulatory Authority of India.
2. The Authority shall be a body corporate by the name aforesaid, having perpetual succession and a common seal with power to acquire, hold and dispose of property, both movable and immovable, and to contract, and shall by the said name sue and be sued.
3. The Authority shall consist of one Chairperson and not more than six whole-time Members, to be appointed by the Central Government.
4. The head office of the Authority shall be New Delhi.

Qualifications for Appointment of Chairperson and Members

The Central Government shall, by notification, appoint a whole-time Chairperson and six whole-time members of the Authority at the rate of one each from amongst persons who have special knowledge of and professional experience in, the fields of:

(*a*) Television, Radio, Cinema, Advertising, Audio-Visuals, Fine Arts etc.
(*b*) Journalism, Mass Communication, Literature, Social Sciences etc.
(*c*) Finance, Commerce, Audit, Accountancy etc.
(*d*) Electronics, Telecommunication, Information Technology etc.
(*e*) Consumer Affairs, Social Work/Service, Civil Society Organizations etc.
(*f*) Law, Judiciary etc.
(*g*) Public Administration, Management etc.

Term of Office, Conditions of Service etc. of the Chairman and Other Members

1. Before appointing any person as the Chairperson or a whole-time member, the Central Government shall satisfy

itself that the person does not have any such financial or other interest as is likely to affect prejudicially his functions as such member.

2. The Chairperson and other whole-time members shall hold office for a term of five years from the date on which they enter upon their offices or till they attain the age of sixty-five years, whichever is earlier.
3. The Chairperson or a member shall not be eligible for a second term but a member will be eligible for appointment as Chairperson of the Authority for the remaining part of his term.
4. The Chairperson or a whole-time member shall not take up any commercial employment in the organizations that fall within the operational jurisdiction of the Authority, after demitting office within a period of one year without the prior permission of the Central Government.
5. The salary and allowances payable to and other conditions of service of the Chairperson and other whole-time members shall be such as may be prescribed.
6. A person having commercial employment or interest, direct or indirect, in any broadcasting services provider, advertising or programme producing agency shall not be eligible for appointment or continuation as Chairperson or a whole-time member.

Powers of the Chairperson

The Chairperson shall have powers of general superintendence and direction in the conduct of the affairs of the Authority and he shall, in addition to presiding over the meetings of the Authority, exercise such powers of the Authority, and shall discharge such functions of the Authority, as may be prescribed.

Removal, Suspension or Resignation of Chairperson and Members

(1) The Central Government may remove from office or suspend the Chairperson or any member of the Authority who:

(*a*) ceases to be a citizen of India; or
(*b*) is adjudged an insolvent; or

(*c*) is convicted or any offence involving moral turpitude; or

(*d*) is, in the opinion of the Central Government, unfit to continue in office by reason of infirmity or body or mind; or

(*e*) engages during his term of office in any paid employment outside the duties of his office;

(*f*) acquires such financial or other interest as is likely to affect prejudicially his functions as a Chairperson or member;

(*g*) abuses his position so as to render his continuance in office prejudicial to public interest.

(2) The Chairperson or any other member may resign his office by giving notice thereof in writing to the Central Government and on such resignation being accepted, the Chairperson or the member shall be deemed to have vacated his office.

Meetings of the Authority or its Committees

1. The Authority may constitute committees of the Authority for specific purposes, and make regulations for the transaction of business at the meetings of the Authority as well as its committees.
2. The Authority or its committee shall meet at such time and place and shall observe such procedure in regard to the transaction of business at its meetings as may be provided by regulations.
3. The Chairperson shall preside at the meetings of the Authority or its committee, and if for any reason he is unable to attend any meeting, any other whole-time member elected by the members present at such meeting, shall preside at the meetings.
4. A member shall be deemed to have vacated his office if he absents himself for three consecutive meetings of the Authority without the leave of the Chairperson.
5. All questions which come up before any meeting of the Authority shall be decided by a majority of the votes of the members present and voting and, in the event of an equality of votes, the Chairperson, or in his absence, the person presiding, shall have and exercise a second or casting vote.

Vacancies not to Invalidate Proceedings

No act or proceedings of the Authority shall be invalid merely by reason of:

(*a*) Any vacancy in, or any defect in the constitution of, the Authority; or
(*b*) Any defect in the appointment of a person acting as a member; or
(*c*) Any irregularity in the procedure of the Authority not affecting the merits of the case.

Regional Offices of the Authority

The Authority may, with the prior approval of the Central Government set up Regional Offices at Delhi, Chennai, Kolkata and Mumbai, and such other regional offices at places to be notified by the Government and to perform such functions and with such jurisdictions as may be prescribed. At each such Regional Offices there shall be one Regional Director to be appointed by the Central Government to discharge the functions delegated to him by the Authority.

Secretary and other Officers and Employees of the Authority

1. Secretary of the Authority shall be the Chief Executive Officer of the Authority. Subject to the provisions of Section 15 of the Act, the Secretary shall exercise such powers and discharge such functions of the Authority as may be delegated to him by the Authority.
2. The Central Government shall make available to the Authority, a panel of not less than three officers of the rank of the Additional Secretary to the Government of India, and the Authority may select one of them and recommend his appointment as Secretary of the Authority to the Government.
3. The Central Government shall make available a panel of not less than three officers of the rank of Joint Secretary to the Government of India for each of the five Regional Offices at Delhi, Chennai, Kolkotta, Mumbai and Guwahati, and the Authority may select one from each

panel and recommend his/her appointment to the Government. As and when more regional offices are opened, the Authority may seek officers of the rank of Joint Secretary or Director to the Government of India, as the case may be, for appointment as their Regional Directors.

4. The Authority may appoint such officers and other employees, as it considers necessary for the efficient discharge of its functions under this Act in the manner as provided by the regulations.
5. The salary and allowances payable to and other conditions of service of the officers and other employees of the Authority shall be such as may be determined by regulations.

Powers and Functions of the Authority

(1) Authority shall exercise the following powers and functions:

(*a*) Notify the terms and conditions of licenses for various categories of service providers, in accordance with the policy guidelines prescribed by the Government.

(*b*) Recommend to the Central Government, guidelines or norms or amendments of prescribed guidelines or norms, in the light of its experience in the discharge of its functions, as well as on such other issues as may be referred to it by the Government.

(*c*) Grant registration to TV and Radio channels as provided under Section 4 of the Bill.

(*d*) Lay-down the standards of quality of service to be provided by the service providers and conduct the periodical survey of such service provided by the service providers so as to protect interest of the consumers of broadcasting service.

(*e*) Notify detailed regulations to implement the policy guidelines prescribed by Government and take all necessary legal and administrative actions to ensure their compliance by the service providers.

(*f*) Formulate and determine conditions for fair, equitable and non-discriminatory access to broadcasting services.

(*g*) Consider and publish its findings for wider public debate on issues of public importance relating to broadcasting services and their programme content.

(*h*) Facilitate competition and promote efficiency in the operation of broadcasting services so as to facilitate growth in such services.

(*i*) Advise the Central Government in the matters relating to the development of broadcasting technology and any other matter relatable to broadcasting industry in general.

(*j*) Evolve codes and practices in respect of such other services which are neither licensed nor registered under this Act as may be notified by the Central Government from time to time and lay down obligations on service providers for such codes and practices in a manner as may be prescribed.

(*k*) Ensure effective compliance of public service broadcasting obligations, and in the event of failure of a licensed service provider to meet such obligations, levy and collect such fees and in such manner as may be prescribed.

(*l*) Hear appeals against the orders and directions of the Licensing Authorities.

(*m*) Adjudicate on disputes between two or more Licensing Authorities or between a licensing authority and one or more service providers under jurisdiction of other licensing authorities, or between two or more service providers under jurisdiction of more than one licensing authority.

(*n*) Certify content in respect of such categories of programmes or advertisements or promotional materials as require certification before broadcast, as may be prescribed in the Content Code.

(*o*) Adjudicate between licensing authorities or consumers or complainants and the service providers in respect of violations of the Content Code, and impose penalties in accordance with prescribed norms.

(*p*) Perform such other functions including such administrative and financial functions as may be entrusted to it by the Central Government or as may be necessary to carry out the provisions of this Act.

(2) The Authority may, for the discharge of its functions under Sub-section (1) of this section, issue such directions from time to time to the service providers, as it may consider necessary.

(3) The Authority may by general or special order, delegate to its Chairperson or a Member or Secretary or Regional Officers or any other officer of the Authority or to any "Authorized Officer", subject to such conditions and limitations, if any, as may be specified therein, such of its powers and duties under this Act as it may deem fit.

Powers and Functions of the Licensing Authorities

(1) Subject to such directions as the Central Government or the Authority may issue from time to time, the Licensing Authorities shall exercise all or any of the following powers and functions:

(*a*) Grant, refuse or revoke licenses/registration in respect of such broadcasting services and for such limits of jurisdiction as may be prescribed.

(*b*) Inspect, enquire or supervise, or direct an "authorized officer" to inspect, enquire or supervise all or any of the service providers to ensure compliance with the terms and conditions of their respective licenses.

(*c*) Ensure technical compatibility and effective inter-connection between service providers.

(*d*) Arbitrate between service providers in respect of commercial arrangement mandated by the Central Government or the Authority for sharing their revenue derived from providing broadcasting services.

(*e*) Ensure effective compliance of such public service broadcasting obligations as may be prescribed for its licensees.

(*f*) Perform such other functions including such administrative and financial functions as may be entrusted to it by the Central Government or as may be necessary to carry out the provisions of this Act.

(*g*) Impose in accordance with prescribed norms, all or any of the penalties, individually or in combination, in case of breach of any terms and conditions of the license/permission/registration, after providing an opportunity to the concerned service provider of being heard.

Provided that the violations of the Content Code shall be punishable only by the Authority, and the licensing authority shall have the power to enforce compliance with such punishment by the service provider.

(*h*) Adjudicate between consumers and service providers licensed by it, in respect of complaints and disputes regarding the quality or standards of service and payments by the consumers.

Powers and Functions of the 'Authorized Officers'

Subject to such directions as may be given from time to time by the Central Government or the Authority, every Authorized Officer shall have the following powers:

(*i*) to inspect, search and seize equipment etc. under Section 24 of this Act;

(*ii*) to prosecute, on a written complaint by the concerned Licensing Authority, such licensed service providers or other persons as are found to have committed offences under the Act;

(*iii*) to co-ordinate with the Licensing Authorities to ensure that the terms and conditions of the licenses are not violated by any service provider;

(*iv*) to receive and enquire into complaints from the District Monitoring Committee or consumer groups or individual consumers regarding content or quality of service and report to the Licensing Authority for appropriate action; and

(*v*) any other powers and functions as may be delegated to him by the Authority as deemed necessary.

Seizure and Confiscation of certain Equipment

1. If any authorized officer has reason to believe, or is directed by the Licensing Authority or the Authority or the Central Government, as the case may be, that the provisions of Sub-section (1) of Section 3, or sub-section (1) of Section 4, or of Section 5 of this Act have been or are being contravened by any person, he may seize the equipment being used by such person for operating such unlicensed service or broadcasting such unregistered channel or programme or for failure to comply with the directions under section 5 of the Act.

- Provided that the authorized officer shall not retain such equipment for a period exceeding 30 days from the date of its seizure without the approval of the District Judge, within the local limits of whose jurisdiction such seizure has been made.

2. The equipment so seized under Sub-section (1) above shall be liable to confiscation unless the person operating such service or channel complies with the provisions of the Act within a period of sixty days from the date of such seizure.
3. The District Judge shall not pass any order adjudicating confiscation unless the person operating such service or channel has been given a reasonable opportunity in writing to make his representation against the proposed confiscation.

Finance, Accounts and Audit

1. The proceeds of the license/registration/permission fees in respect of broadcasting services shall be credited to the Consolidated Fund of India.
2. The Central Government may for enabling the Authority to discharge its functions efficiently, after due appropriation made by Parliament by law in this behalf, pay to the Authority in each financial year such sums of money as the Government considers necessary by way of grants-in-aid.
3. The Authority shall have its own fund and all the receipts of the Authority shall be credited to the fund and all payments by the Authority shall be made there from. All money belonging to the fund shall be deposited in one or more Scheduled Banks in such manner as the Authority may decide and Authority may spend such sums as it thinks fit for performing its function under this Act.
4. The Authority shall prepare, in such form and at such time each year as may be prescribed, a budget in respect of the financial year next ensuing showing:

   (*a*) The expenditure which is proposed to be met from the internal resource of the Authority; and

   (*b*) The sums required from the Central Government to

meet other expenses, and copies thereof shall be forwarded to the Central Government.

5. The Authority shall maintain proper accounts and other relevant records and prepare an annual statement of accounts in such form and in such manner as may be prescribed.
6. The accounts of the Authority shall be audited by the Comptroller and Auditor General of India at such intervals as may be specified by him and any expenditure incurred in connection with such audit shall be payable by the Authority to the Comptroller and Auditor General.

- Provided the matters relating to the adjudication by the Authority, manner and number of issue of licenses and quantum of license fee, levied by the Authority or the nature and quantum of penalties imposed by the Authority on any service provider, shall lie outside the purview of such Audit.

7. The Comptroller and Auditor General of India and any person appointed by him in connection with the audit of the accounts of the Authority shall have the same rights and privileges and authority in connection with such audit as the Comptroller and Auditor General has in connection with the audit of Government accounts and, in particular, shall have the right to demand the production of books, accounts, connected vouchers and other documents and papers and to inspect any of the offices of the Authority.
8. The accounts of the Authority as certified by the Comptroller and Auditor General of India or any other person appointed by him in this behalf together with the audit report thereon shall be forwarded annually to the Central Government and that Government shall cause the same to be laid before each House of Parliament.
9. The Authority shall, after the end of each financial year, shall submit to the Central Government a report on their activities during the preceding financial year and containing such information relating to the proceedings and policy of the Authority, as the Government may prescribe from time to time.

10. The Central Government shall cause such report to be laid before each House of Parliament.

Furnishing of Returns, etc. to the Central Government

1. The Authority shall furnish to the Central Government at such time and in such form and manner as may be prescribed or as the Central Government may direct, such returns and statements and such particulars in regard to any proposed or existing programme for the promotion and development of the broadcasting services, as the Central Government may, from time to time, require.
2. The Authority shall prepare once every year in such form and at such time as may be prescribed, an annual summary of its activities during the previous year and copies of the report shall be forwarded to the Central Government.
3. A copy of the report received under Sub-section (2) shall be laid, as soon as may be after it is received, before each House of Parliament.

Power of the Authority to Make Regulations

(1) The Authority may, by notification, make regulations not inconsistent with this Act and the rules made thereunder, for enabling it to perform its functions under this Act.

(2) Without prejudice to the generality of the foregoing power, such regulations may provide for all or any of the following matters, namely:

(*a*) The manner of appointment of officers and other employees of the Authority under Sub-section (4) of Section 20;

(*b*) The salary and allowances payable to and other conditions of service of the officers and other employees of the Authority under Sub-section (5) of Section 20;

(*c*) The terms and conditions, fees and procedure to be followed for granting licenses /registration under clause (a) of Sub-section (1) of Section 21;

(*d*) The times and places at which meetings of the Authority and its committees may be held and, the procedure to be followed in regard to the transaction of the business at such meetings under sub-section (l) and Sub-section (2) of Section 17;

(*e*) The technical and other quality standards and the reasonable quality of reception under clause (d) of Sub-section (1) of Section 21;

(*f*) The places and types and quantity of equipment to be provided, free of cost, by the licensee service provider for monitoring of content and the quality of technical standards of service, and the manner in which such monitoring may be carried out by the licensing authorities or authorised officers under clause (e) of Sub-section (1) of Section 21;

(*g*) The delegation of powers and functions to the Chairman, members and other officers of the Authority under sub-section (3) of Section 21;

(*h*) The documentary record and transmission schedule to be maintained by the licensees under Sub-section (1) of Section 40;

(*i*) The manner in which broadcasters shall establish and operate the system of self-certification of broadcasting content under Sub-section (vii) of Section 9;

(*j*) Any other matter in respect of which provision is, in the opinion of the Authority, necessary for the performance of its functions under this Act.

Provided that the regulations under clauses (a), (b) and (c) shall be made with the prior approval of the Central Government.

Chapter 4

OFFENCES, PENALTIES AND APPEALS

Punishment for Offences under this Act

(1) A person who in contravention of the provisions of this Act, provides, distributes or receives any broadcasting service which is not licensed under Sub-section (1) of Section 3 or broadcasts a channel which is not registered or a programme which is not permitted under Sub-section (1) of Section 4, or abets or assists transmission or distribution of such service or content, as the case may be, in any manner which may include collection of subscription

for his principal, issuing of advertisements to such service, dealing in or distribution of decoders, shall be guilty of committing an offence of illegal broadcasting, and on conviction, shall be punishable with imprisonment which may extend up to three years, or with fine which may extend up to rupees twenty-five lakh or both, and for subsequent offence and conviction such imprisonment may extend to five years or fine up to rupees fifty lakh, or with both.

> Provided that unauthorized decoding or receiving of a programme that is not permitted or of a channel that is not registered or dealing in or distribution of equipment for the purpose shall also constitute an offence of illegal broadcasting and shall be dealt with accordingly.

(2) Whoever contravenes the provisions of Sections 5 of this Act shall be punishable:

(*a*) For the first offence, with imprisonment for a term which may extend to two years or with fine which may extend to rupees ten lakh or with both,

(*b*) For every subsequent offence, with imprisonment for a term which may extend to five years and with fine which may extend to rupees twenty-five lakh.

Offences by Companies

1. Where an offence under this Act has been committed by a company, every person who, at the time the offence was committed, was in charge of, and was responsible to, the company for the conduct of the business of the company, as well as the company, shall be deemed to be guilty of the offence and shall be liable to be proceeded against and punished accordingly.

   Provided that nothing contained in this sub-section shall render any such person liable for such punishment, if he proves that the offence was committed without his knowledge or that he had exercised all due diligence to prevent the commission of such offence.

2. Notwithstanding anything contained in Sub-section (1), where an offence under this Act has been committed by a company and it is proved that it has been committed with the consent or connivance of, or is attributable to the negligence on the part of, any director, manager, secretary or other officer of the company, such director, manager, secretary or other officer shall also be deemed to be guilty of that offence and shall be liable to be proceeded against and punished accordingly.

   Explanation: For the purpose of this section:

   (*a*) "Company" means any body corporate and includes a firm or other association of individuals; and

   (*b*) "Director" in relation to a firm, means a partner in the firm.

Cognizance of Offences

1. No court shall take cognizance of any offence punishable under this Act except upon a complaint made in writing by any authorized officer.
2. No Court inferior to that of a Chief Metropolitan Magistrate or a Chief Judicial Magistrate of First Class shall try any offence punishable under this Act.

The Authority to Prescribe Penalties for Violations of License Conditions etc.

The Authority may prescribe the penalties to be imposed for violation of various terms and conditions of the license/permission/registration subject to the condition that such penalties shall not exceed a fine of rupees fifty lakh, besides suspension or revocation of such license/permission/registration, subject further to the condition that no penalty shall be imposed unless and until a reasonable opportunity has been given to the service provider to explain its position.

The Licensing Authorities to impose Penalties

(1) Subject to the provisions of Section 31 of this Act, every licensing authority shall have the power to impose any of the following penalties, individually or in combination, on its licensee service providers, in case of breach of any terms and conditions of the license or permission or registration, as the case may be, namely:

(*i*) Direct the licensee to broadcast a correction or an apology or not to repeat a programme; and/or
(*ii*) Impose a fine which may extend up to rupees twenty-five lakhs;
(*iii*) Suspend the license for a specified period; or
(*iv*) Curtail the period of the license; or
(*v*) Revoke the license.

Provided that no such penalty shall be imposed without giving a reasonable opportunity to the concerned service provider of being heard in person or through a legal representative.

Provided that the violations of the Content Code shall be punishable only by the Authority, and the licensing authority shall have the power to enforce compliance with such punishment by the service provider.

(2) Pending disposal of the case, the Licensing Authority may, if it considers it expedient or desirable in public interest to do so, direct the concerned service provider to stop the repeat broadcast or broadcasts of a particular programme or portion thereof which is under investigation or enquiry, and the service provider shall immediately comply with such a direction.

Provided that no such interim direction shall be issued without giving a reasonable opportunity, as far as practical, to the concerned service provider of being heard in person or through a legal representative.

Appeals against the Orders of the Licensing Authorities

An aggrieved person may prefer an appeal against an order or direction of any of the Licensing Authorities to the Authority within a period of thirty days of such an order or direction.

Appeals against the Orders of the Authority

An aggrieved person may prefer an appeal against the order or direction of the Authority before the Film Certification Appellate Tribunal (FCAT) in respect of cases of violations of the Content Code, and before the Telecom Disputes Settlement and Appellate

Tribunal (TDSAT) in respect of cases of all other violations of the terms and conditions of license.

Appeals before the Supreme Court

1. Notwithstanding anything contained in the Code of Civil Procedure or in any other law, an appeal by either party to the dispute shall lie against any order, not being an interlocutory order, of the TDSAT or FCAT, as the case may be, to the Supreme Court on one or more of the grounds specified in Section 100 of that Code.
2. No appeal shall lie against any decision or order made by the TDSAT or FCAT, as the case may be, with the consent of the parties.
3. Every appeal under this section shall be preferred within a period of 90 days from the date of the decision or order appealed against.

   Provided that the Supreme Court may entertain the appeal after expiry of the said period of 90 days if it is satisfied that the appellant was prevented by sufficient cause from preferring the appeal in time.

Transfer of Pending Cases to the Authority

1. On the date to be notified by the Central Government, after the establishment of the Authority, all proceedings pending before the Telecom Regulatory Authority of India (TRAI) shall be deemed to be pending before the Authority and shall be disposed off in accordance with the provisions of this Act.
2. On the date to be notified by the Central Government, after the establishment of the Authority, all proceedings pending before the Ministry of Information and Broadcasting, Government of India shall be deemed to be pending before the Authority and shall be disposed of in accordance with the provisions of this Act.

Civil Court not to have Jurisdiction

No Civil Court shall have jurisdiction to entertain any suit or proceedings in respect of any matter which the Authority or the

Licensing Authority, as the case may be, is empowered by or under this Act to determine and no injunction shall be granted by any civil court or other authority in respect of any action taken or to be taken in pursuance of any power conferred by and under this Act.

Chapter 5

MISCELLANEOUS

Power of the Central Government to Issue Directions

1. The Central Government may, from time to time, issue to the Authority such directions as it may deem necessary in the interest of the sovereignty and integrity of India, the security of the State, friendly relations with foreign countries, public order, decency or morality.
2. Without prejudice to the foregoing provisions, the Authority shall, in exercise of its powers or the performance of its functions, be bound by such directions on questions of policy as the Central Government may give in writing to it from time to time.

   Provided that the Authority shall, as far as practicable, be given an opportunity to express its views before any such direction is given under this sub-section.

3. The decision of the Central Government whether a question is one of policy or not shall be final.

The Authority to Follow Principles of Natural Justice

(1) The Authority shall not be bound by the procedure laid down by the Code of Civil Procedure, 1908, but shall be guided by the principles of natural justice and, subject to the other provisions of this Act and of any rules, the Authority shall have powers to regulate its own procedure including the fixing of places and times of its enquiry.

(2) The Authority shall have, for the purposes of discharging its functions under this Act, the same powers as are vested in a civil court under the Code of Civil Procedure, 1908, while trying a suit, in respect of the following matters, namely:

(*a*) Summoning and enforcing the attendance of any person and examining him on oath;
(*b*) Requiring the discovery and production of documents;
(*c*) Receiving evidence on affidavits;
(*d*) Issuing commissions for the examination of witnesses or documents;
(*e*) Requisitioning any public record or document or a copy of such record or document, from any office;
(*f*) Reviewing its decisions;
(*g*) Dismissing an application for default or deciding it, ex-party;
(*h*) Setting aside any order of dismissal of any application for default or any other passed by it, ex-party;
(*i*) Any other matter, which may be prescribed.

Service Providers to maintain Records

1. Every service provider shall maintain such documentary records and transmission schedules as may be specified in the policy guidelines, notified under this Act and allow inspections of the facilities and such documentary records and transmission schedules by any person authorized by the Authority.
2. The Authority may call for any information from the service provider, which is necessary for transparency and ascertaining the true ownership of the service provider.
3. The Authority or any officer authorized by the Authority shall have power to inspect and obtain information wherever necessary, from programme producers, distributors and advertising agents.
4. For effective enforcement of restrictions on holding of licenses, as provided under Section 10, the Authority or any officer authorized by the Authority for that purpose, shall have all the powers of an inspecting officer as provided under Section 209-A of the Companies Act, 1956.
5. It shall be the duty of every service provider to carry out the directions of the Authority given under this section.
6. If default is made by a service provider in complying with the provisions of Sub-section (5), the Authority may take such action as provided under Section 32 (1) after providing him an opportunity of being heard.

Members and Employees of the Authority to be Public Servants

The Chairman, every member, every officer or other employee of the Authority, shall be deemed to be a public servant within the meaning of Section 21 of the Indian Penal Code.

Protection of Action taken in Good Faith

No suit or other legal proceeding shall lie against the Government, Authority, or any Member or Officer or other employee thereof for anything which is in, good faith done or intended to be done in pursuance of this Act or of any rules or regulations made there under.

Exemption from Tax on Wealth and Income

Notwithstanding anything contained in the Wealth Tax Act, 1957, the Income Tax Act, 1961, or any other enactment for the time being in force relating to wealth, income, profit or gains, the Authority shall not be liable to pay wealth tax, income tax, or any other tax in respect of their wealth, income, profit or gains derived.

Over-riding Effect

1. This Act shall have overriding effect over provisions of any other law for the time being in force and shall be given effect to, notwithstanding anything contained in any other law for the time being in force and notwithstanding any rights claimed under contract or created under any other law for the time being in force.
2. Notwithstanding anything contained in Section 31 or Section 37 of the Indian Copyright Act, 1957, where one or more persons have made complaints in respect of a work which has been published or performed in public or which has already been broadcast or whose licensed reproductions have already been made available in public, licenses shall be granted to all such complainants under Sub-section (1) of Section 31 of the Indian Copyright Act 1957.

Power of the Central Government to make Rules

(1) The Central Government may, by notification, makes rules for carrying out provisions of this Act.

(2) In particular and without prejudice to the generality of the foregoing power, such rules may provide for all or any of the following matters, namely:

(*a*) To determine other circumstances for communication under sub-clause (c) of clause (ii) of Section 2;

(*b*) To notify the sporting events and to lay down the procedure to be followed for enabling their being shared with Prasar Bharti under Section 6;

(*c*) The policy guidelines, designate licensing authorities, specify terms and conditions, and procedures for grant of the licenses/permissions/registration to the service provider under clauses (i) to (iv) of Section 9;

(*d*) To lay down a time frame for change over to digital addressable networks for broadcasting content, and commercial and technical arrangements during the transition phase under clause (v) of Section 9;

(*e*) The lay down the Content Code and procedures to be followed for content certification by the service providers, adjudication of complaints against content certification and appeals against imposition of penalties, under clauses (vi) to (viii) of Section 9;

(*f*) The norms of public service broadcasting obligations, rates and procedures for levying and collection of fees, and setting up institutional arrangement and norms for managing and operating the public service broadcasting obligation fund under clauses (x) and (xi) of Section 9;

(*g*) The eligibility conditions and restrictions to prevent accumulation of interest in licensed services and restrictions on controlling interest in print media and electronic media as well as within different segments of the electronic media under Section 10;

(*h*) The salaries and allowances payable and other conditions of service of the Chairperson and whole-time members under sub-section (5) of Section 14;

(*i*) The places where the Regional Offices may be set up and the functions to be performed by such offices under Section 19;

(*j*) The form in which and the time at which in each year the Authority shall prepare a budget under Sub-section (4) of Section 25;

(*k*) The form and the manner in which the annual statement of accounts shall be prepared under Sub-section (5) of Section 25;

(*l*) The information relating to the proceedings and policy of the Authority to be contained in a report to be submitted by the Authority under Sub-section (9) of Section 25;

(*m*) Any other matter which is required to be or may be prescribed.

Rules and Regulations to be Laid before Parliament

Every rule and every regulation made under this Act shall be laid, as soon as may be after it is made, before each House of Parliament, while it is in session for a total period of thirty days which may be comprised in one session or in two or more successive sessions, and if, before the expiry of the session immediately following the session or the successive sessions aforesaid, both Houses agree in making any modification in, the rule or regulation, or both Houses agree that the rule or regulation should not be made, the rule or regulation shall thereafter have effect only in such modified form or be of no effect, as the case may be; so, however, that any such modification or annulment shall be without prejudice to the validity of anything previously done under that rule or regulation.

Application of Certain Laws

The provisions of this Act shall be in addition to the provisions of the Indian Telegraph Act, 1885 and Indian Wireless Telegraphy Act, 1933 and, in particular, nothing in this Act shall affect any jurisdiction, powers and functions required to be exercised or performed by the Telegraph Authority in relation to any area falling within the jurisdiction of such Authority.

Power to Remove Difficulties

1. If any difficulty arises in giving effect to the provisions of this Act, the Central Government may, by other published in the Official Gazette, make such provisions, not inconsistent with the provisions of this Act, as it may deem necessary, for the removal of the difficulty.

   Provided that no such order shall be made after the expiry

of a period of three years from the commencement of this Act.

2. Every order made under this section shall be laid, as soon as may be after it is made before each House of Parliament.

Repeal and Saving

1. The Cable Television Networks (Regulation) Act, 1995 is hereby repealed.
2. Notwithstanding such repeal any cable operator registered under that Act as on the date of repeal, may continue to provide his services, provided he makes an application to the Authority for the grant of a license for any of the broadcasting network services within six months from the date of the commencement of this Act or where he has made such an application, till the disposal of such application, whichever is later.
3. The Authority may on receipt of an application under Sub-section (2) grant a license for any of the broadcasting network services subject to fulfillment of such eligibility and other terms and conditions as may be prescribed.
4. The cable operators operating under Sub-section (2) above shall continue to be regulated as if the Cable Television Networks (Regulation) Act, 1995 has not been repealed during the interregnum i.e., the period from the commencement of this Act and disposal of his application for the license or a period of six months, whichever is later.
5. Notwithstanding such repeal, all cable operators registered under that Act as on the date of repeal, shall continue to comply with the provisions of the Programme Code under Rule 6 and the Advertising Code under Rule 7 of the Cable Television Networks Rules, 1994 prescribed under that Act, till the said Codes are replaced by the new guidelines and norms (the Content Code) provided for under Sub-section (vi) of Section 9 of this Act.

6

An Overview of Laws and Policies Regarding Indian Broadcasting

THE INDIAN BROADCASTING REGULATIONS FORUM: CASE STUDY OF VIEWS AND OPINIONS

The Indian Government has announced that it wants a Broadcasting Act enacted within the next six months. It has the old broadcasting bill draft and the report of the Sharad Pawar Committee which reviewed the draft as reference points. But it is seeking the opinion of the satellite channels and cable TV industry once again later this month. You, as a television or media executive, can share your opinions on what shape Indian broadcasting regulations should take by posting them in indiantelevision.com's Indian Broadcasting Regulations Forum. One can air one's views on:

- The limits for foreign equity in Indian broadcasting and on cross-media holdings. On what should these restrictions be based.
- Whether DTH television should be allowed and in what form.
- Whether a broadcasting regulator is needed or not and what shape should it take, what powers should it have.
- Whether a television license fee is needed.
- Whether a Prasar Bharsti is needed and should it be autonomous or government-controlled.
- Whether the current unorganised nature of the cable TV business should be allowed to continue or whether licensing should be brought in and in what form.

- Whether uplinking from India should be made mandatory for all channels including foreign ones.
- Whether wireless cable should be permitted.
- Whether private firms should be allowed to enter terrestrial television broadcasting.

Inclusion of Community Broadcasting in the Broadcasting Bill, 1997

Recommendations to the Ministry of Information and Broadcasting on non-profit community broadcasting. Prepared by VOICES in consultation with broadcasting and development professionals and the National Law School of India, Bangalore. VOICES is a development communication organization. One of our key thrust area is Community Radio and we have been working in this issue for the past four years. This includes, Bangalore Declaration on Radio, Airing community related programmes from AIRs Chitradurga FM station, and lobbying for promotion of CR at ministerial and local level. Respected Honourable Minister with the ongoing technological revolution, information plays a crucial role in bringing people together and enables them to make informed choices. The right of free speech and expression includes the right to receive and impart information. For ensuring the Indian citizens' right to free speech and information, it is necessary that they have the benefit of plurality of views and access to range of options to public issues.

(1) The national goals of an Indian Broadcasting Policy have to be unique keeping in mind the diverse citizenary and the need for the peoples participation in a democracy. The Joshi Commission (1982) recommended a decentralized system of broadcasting, stressing upon the need for access, participation, local autonomy and control training and public service as the basis for broadcasting future of India. Thus any broadcasting policy must carry with it the onus to safeguard the citizen's right be informed, transmit varied programmes to awaken, inform, enlighten, educate, enrich and entertain all sections of the people and serve the rural and urban illiterate and underprivileged populations, keeping in mind the special needs and interests of the young women, social and cultural minorities, the tribal populations and those residing in the backward areas.

(2) The Broadcasting Bill, 1997 must be analyzed in this light to see if it fulfils these national objectives. Analysis of the Provisions

of the Broadcasting Bill Section 16 (2) talks about granting licensee to institutions which provide education, environment protection and community service under a restricted bid system as notified by the regulations. There is some ambiguity in the terms used here: What type of institutes can be considered eligible? Private institutions, non-profit institutions or community broadcasting services? The South African Independent Broadcasting Authority Act 153 of 1993 defines a community broadcasting service as—one which is fully controlled by non-profit entity and operated for non-profitable purposes: serves a particular community: encourages members of the community served by it to participate in the selection and provisions of the programmes to be broadcast: may be funded buy donations, grants, sponsorship or advertising or membership fees.

(3) This kind of clarity of definition is required. There must be cogent differentiation between a private broadcasting service operated for profit and non-profit community broadcasting which can fall under Section 16(2). Suggested Amendments to Clauses DEFINATIONS Section 2 of the Bill should therefore include of both running thus: 2(zt) "Private Broadcasting Service" means a broadcasting service operated for profit and controlled by an entity which is not a public broadcasting licensee. 2(zu) "Community Broadcasting Service" means a non-profit broadcasting service which caters to the needs of geographically bounded group of persons having a definite ascertainable common interest, subject to Section 25(2) and which is permitted to raise funds to meet operational costs through donations, grants, sponsorships, membership fees, advertising or a combination of aforementioned.

Functions of the Authority

Section 7 of the Bill deals with the Functions of the Authority. This section lays no positive obligation on the Authority to promote a diverse range of services on national, local, and regional level which would cater to the different cultural language groups and communities. It must be seen that a healthy balance is maintained between the different electronic media so that it does not lead to the marginalization of radio which is the only medium of information for 70 per cent of rural India and covers 90 per cent of the geographical area. Promotion of community-based non-profit developmental radio, which is characterized by active participation of the community the process of creating news, information, entertainment, and culturally relevant material with emphasis on local issues and concerns, should be one of the responsibilities of the Authority. An addition should be included under Section 7 to come after 7(iii) to read as: 7(iv). To promote broadcasting through low cost terrestrial radio and protect the interests and concerns of local communities.

Grant of Licenses

Section 16(2) may read as: Notwithstanding anything contained in sub-section(1), the Authority may grant licenses to such institutions as may be notified for terrestrial broadcasting services through restricted bids or on payment of nominal fee that may be determined by the regulations. The Proviso 16(2) should be broadened in the public interest, to read: Provided that no institution shall be notified under this sub-section unless the object of such institutions is to promote education, community service, environment protection, health awareness, women's empowerment or cultural expression.

Restrictions on Holding Liscenses

Part I Clause 4 of the schedule disqualifies publicly funded bodies from obtaining license. This brings under its purview universities and other educational institutions as well as co-operatives. These should be exempt, bearing in mind the need for youth participation in media and deployment of media for promoting education. The Varadan Report (1991) had in fact enunciated that preference to be given to public bodies like universities, co-operative institutions etc., if they apply for licenses. The Proviso to Clause 4 here should read as:

— Provided that this disqualification does not apply to the universities and other educational institutions and co-operatives.

— Provided that the disqualified under this clause shall not apply to a community broadcasting service.

Statement of Objects and Reasons

One of the objects of this Bill is to meet the challenges proposed by the invasion of the skies by direct satellite broadcasting by foreign entities and it has addressed this issue. However, the main object remains to keep India's democratic traditions alive and keep its diverse citizens well-informed and this issue needs a closer look. For instance deregulation in the USA is not synonymous with the total abrogation of government regulation: media laws can liberate this neo-liberal communication policy initiative by not ignoring matters vital to public interest and community participation in India. The last sentence of the statement number 3 of this section should read as:

This can be provided by facilitating private broadcasting and broadcasting services which enable access and participation by the citizens of the country. The role of broadcasting is all the more important in providing information and access to media so that people can participate in the process of nation building. In the unique conditions of India, terrestrial radio has the widest audience.

Thus, the Bill seeks to encourage and create conditions for the development of community radio.

Signatories

Ms Sucharita Eashwar, Ex Director-VOICES, Bangalore Dr. K.E Eapen International communication expert and Scholar Mr. N. Kalayan Raman, ASC Enterprises, New Delhi; Dr. Michael Traber United Theological College, Bangalore; Mr. A.R. Pasha Cinematics, Bangalore; Ms Ammu Joseph; Freelance Journalist, Bangalore; Ms M.T. Rukhmini, Family Planning Association of India, Bangalore; Ms N. Lakshmi, Concerned for Working Children; Bangalore; Ms N. Bhatia, Indian Express, Bangalore; Ms Amula Seethanaman, Indian Express, Bangalore; Ms Raji Reddy, Bangalore; Ms Vijayashree Rajaram, Jyothi Nivas College, Bangalore; Ms Preetha, Mount Carmel College, Bangalore; Ms Udaya, Mount Carmel College, Bangalore; Ms Vinaya Mount Carmel College, Bangalore; Ms Puja Mount Carmel College, Bangalore; Ms Bhavana Thakur, National Law School of India, Bangalore; Mr. M.A.S. Rajan I.A.S (Retd.) Formerly Add. Chief Secretary, Karnataka; Ms Indubai Ramesh, Director of Commercial Broadcasting(Retd), AIR, Bangalore; Ms K.E. Eapen Bangalore; Mr. Chandra Mouli, AIR, Bangalore; Mr. Sam Emmanuel, Media Centre, Bangalore; Mr. T.N. Munniswamy; FPAI, Gauribidanur; Mr. Prem James, FEBA, Bangalore; Mr. Simon Verghese, Deccan Herald; Bangalore; Ms

Prachi Bhuchar, Indian Express, Bangalore; Mr. Sowmya Bharadwaj, Jyothi Nivas College, Bangalore; Ms Neerja, Mount Carmel College, Bangalore; Ms Shalini, Mount Carmel College, Bangalore; Ms Winnie, Mount Carmel College, Bangalore; Ms Mayura, Mount Carmel College, Bangalore.

VOICES is Bangalore based non-profit development communication organization.One of our key thrust area is promoting community radio and have been into it for the past four and half years now. We came up with Bangalore Declaration radio in 1996. We also aired programmes exclusively on local issues on FM in Chitradurga, courtesy AIR, in 1999 and plan to set up a CR in Kolar. Our address is:

VOICES,165, 9th Cross, Stage-I, Indiranagar, Bangalore-650 038
Tel# 080-521 3902-3 FAX# 080-521 3901
E-mail voices@vsnl.com.

Mahesh Acharya <voices@vsnl.com>
Bangalore, Karnataka, India
Thursday, February 24, 2000 at 22:36:56 (PST)

I am a cable operator. There is an act to regulate the cable TV networks. But it is not sufficient. There are many youths who may be unemployed and have invested huge amount of money in this business. They are earning their livelihood out of this Cable TV Networks Regulations Act, 1995 does not protect any cable operators from being harassed by the subscribers, pay channels and the bad competitors (fellow cable operators). Major problem we are facing everyday is about our area of operation. I think the unregulated Cable TV industry should be regulated. In most of the places only GOONDAs, Thugs and Dirty Politicians are having ownership of these and they try everything possible to wipe out their law abiding good competitors. New Broadcast Bill should include the area of operation and control over pay channels and the bad pay master subscribers. Braodcast bill should protect the law abiding cable operators and meanwhile Cable TV subscribers also.

R.S. Patilkulkarni <rspk@satyam.net.in>
DHARWAD, KARNATAKA, India,
Saturday, January 22, 2000 at 04:07:59 (PST)

To whom Ever May Concern: One of the main concern regarding growth of broadcasting is the separation of Broadcasting and Distribution. World over in its infancy stage all the progressing countries have not allowed the Cross Ownership of Broadcasting and Distribution. If allowed, a monopolistic distributor can and will ristrict the upstart Broadcasters in their tracks. Take the US as example, it is after over 30 years the cross ownership of two streams is allowed only in last five years. One should study these and formulate any policies regarding this. Even the DTH, if not licensed and not made nutral will surely affect the growth of the Broadcast Media. I think DTH should be looked at in tandem with cable laws. Once again, one needs to really look at the issue of cross ownership of Broadcasting and Distribution. I encourage the policy makers to study the developments in some of the developed markets. Thank you for the opportunity to voice of my opinion.

Vishnu Patel <vishnupatel>
Mumbai, Maharashtra, India.
Monday, November 22, 1999 at 23:31:38 (PST)

I represent an organisation in Bangalore called VOICES. This is a non-profit orgnisation working towards decentralised communication and citizen's access to the media. VOICES has been actively involved in a community radio programmes for the last three years. In 1998, VOICES launched its first community radio show called Namma Dhwani (our Voices) in Holalkere, a village in Karnataka. Since then VOICES has conducted projects in Kolar and Chitradurga in Karnataka. Our request to the Minister is for a separate provision in the Broadcast Bill for Community Radio. We think that a separate provision is necessary since a clear distinction must be made between commercial broadcasting services and community radio. In this respect there should be a separate nominal license fee for community radio broadcasters. Institutions and groups working with developmental and organisational goals must also be made eligible for licenses to set up community radio stations. We hope that the Minister will look into this matter and ensure that Community radio is duly represented in the Broadcast Bill.

Shilpa Jacobie<voices@vsnl.com>
Bangalore, Karnataka, India
Sunday, November 21, 1999 at 22:03:33 (PST)

Prasar Bharati is of no use to the government or the people today. Let us remember that it was thought of, when only AIR and DD were in existance and they were really misused by the then Government. After all the governments as everywhere else in the world, needs a vehicle for propogating its views. Let AIR and DD be with the Government. Let the private operators be given a chance to have their say on their own channels. In a poor country like India, it is essential to have private radio as much as private TV. How come nobody is thinking of that? Small radio stations, owned by communities, to reflect the language, aspirations and music of the community are essential today. The top down pattern of even the private TV opearators will be disliked after a while. Let us have small private radio stations.

Indu Ramesh <ramind@vsnl.com>
Bangalore, Karnataka, India
Wednesday, November 17, 1999 at 06:33:37 (PST)

I would like Cable TV operators to sort out their operations and give me a box which will allow me to watch what I want to watch. The government should make cable operators responsible for this rather than just waiting for the winds of change take it in that direction. I have heard there is this box called an addressable box which can allow us to watch what I want to. This is the box I'm referring to. There should be DTH restrictions excepting pornography should be allowed on the service late into the night and with parental control systems in place. Foreigners should be allowed to come in as partners of Indian companies to upgrade our technology in television. We have very skilled people here but we need the direction which the government and foreigners can give. Let's catch up with the US and UK markets now and get digital television in place, why keep reinventing the wheel everytime; that's the advantage we have of beginning late. We can catch up that much faster. I hope the authorities are listening.

Anirudh Chatterjee <tvlover@mailindia.com>
Calcutta, West Bengal, India
Thursday, November 11, 1999 at 20:32:12 (PST)

I would like to see foreign and Indian broadcasters having some controls on the programming and advertising side. Nobody is really selecting programming responsibility. The basic idea is to broadcast programmes that make pots of money or that hopefully will. A regulator like the TRAI would help TV broadcasters to be less adventorous. But please give it muscle unlike the TRAI is.

Road skater <rs@indiamail.com>
Delhi, India.
Monday, November 08, 1999 at 08:30:46 (PST)

The foreign equity in Indian broadcasting can be allowed upto 49 per cent without any hesitation, since Broadcasting segment also require huge funds as other sector for its growth. There is no relevance in restricting the foreign equity less than 49 per cent for investment proposal.

DTH must be allowed immediately in India. Politicians play dirty game in DTH without understanding the nature of technology, since DTH is already operating in India in c-band for the past 7-8 years. Then, what is the point in banning it in the Ku-band alone. DTH must be allowed in PROPRIETORY TECHNOLOGY formet with a license to 2-3 operators nationally, since the nature of investment is very high and returns will take not less than five years to reach break-even. DTH operator must be able to provide Hardware like off-set small dish, LNB and decoders at free of cost to customers along with INTERNET service as value-added service. So that, they can expect to cover good number of customers, otherwise DTH will not be successful in present Indian scenario. Totally, DD is unfit to provide DTH service in any form, it is irrelevant to allow DD for five years as monopoly. It will destory the entire concept of DTH in Indian market.

Cable TV must be regulated to avoid unhealthy competition in the sector. The license to two operator per telecom circle can be a ideal solution to bring down the present controversy.

Even though wireless cable losts its relevance now, it can be allowed on trial basis, since DTH will destroy MMDS sector, if it is opened along with DTH operations. It is like, MOBILE PHONE segment has now reduced the importance of PAGERS everywhere in India.

R. Manoharan <sharcstar@vsnl.com>www.sharcstar.com
COIMBATORE, Tamil Nadu, India.
Saturday, November 06, 1999 at 21:54:08 (PST)

Prasar Bharti is needed and should it be autonomous.We have to give freedom to Broadcasting sector by getting rid of bloody politicans and gondas. Learn something which are good in US than always find bad thing with them. Government has no business in business.

Indian <indian2@hotmail.com>, India
Friday, November 05, 1999 at 09:53:29 (PST)

I think the unregulated Cable TV industry should be regulated. In most of the places only GOONDAs, Thugs and Dirty Politicians are having ownership of these and they try everything possible to wipe out their law abiding good competitors.

Rick Janarthanam <Alert_bodyshoper@hotmail.com>
Chennai, Tamil Nadu, India.
Friday, November 05, 1999 at 07:01:20 (PST)

LEGAL RESOURCES RELATED TO INDIAN BROADCASTING

Goverment Rules and Policies

- *New Telecom Policy*: The New Telecom Policy [NTP, 1999] announced by the government.
- *Media Policy*: The Media Policy announced by the BJP Government as a part of their Election manifesto for the forthcoming Lok Sabha elections.
- *Information Technology Action Plan*: National Task Force on Information Technology and Software Development Information Technology Action Plan.

Acts and Regulations for Cable and Television in India

- *The Cable Television Networks Rules, 1994.*
- *The National Security Act, 1980.*
- *The Cable Television Networks (Regulation) Act*: Almost everybody in the country is familiar with the Cable Television. It has been spreading its wings from the initial urban cities, right to the remote villages. There has been a haphazard mushrooming of cable television networks all over the country due to the availability of signals of foreign

television networks via satellites. To check the screening of undesirable programmes and advertisements which are screened on these channels and to regulate the operation of the cable television networks in the country, so as to bring uniformity in their functioning, the Cable Television Networks (Regulation) Act was passed in both the Houses of the Parliament.

- *The Prasar Bharti Act, 1990*: This Act was passed to provide for the establishment of a Broadcasting Corporation of India, to be known as Prasar Bharti. It says that it shall be the primary duty of the Corporation to organize and conduct public broadcasting services to inform, educate and entertain the public and to ensure a balanced development of broadcasting on radio and television.
- *The Broadcasting Bill, 1997*: The Bill is to provide for an independent authority to be known as the Broadcasting Authority of India which is for the purpose of facilitating and regulating broadcasting services in India.
- *The Indian Telegraph Act, 1885*: This Act came into force on 1st October, 1885. "Telegraph" means any appliance, instrument, material or apparatus used or capable of use for transmission or reception of signs, signals, writing, images, and sounds or intelligence of any nature by wire, visual or other electro-magnetic emissions, Radio waves or Hertzian waves, galvanic, electric or magnetic means. The Indian Telegraphic Act, 1885 was an Act to amend the law relating to Telegraphs in India.
- *The Copyright Act*:"The importance of copyright was recognized after the invention of the printing press which enabled the reproduction of books in large quantity. The Indian Copyright Act was thus passed in 1914. But, during the last four decades, modern and advanced means of communications like broadcasting, lithophotography, television, etc., made inroads in the Indian economy. It necessitated the fulfillment of international obligations in the field of Copyright. A comprehensive legislation had to be introduced to completely revise the Copyright law. This was achieved by the introduction of a Copyright Bill, 1957 in the Parliament."

- *Guidelines for Uplinking from India*: "The Union Government has taken a decision on 25th July, 2000 to further liberalise its Uplinking Policy and permit the Indian private companies to set up uplinking hub/teleports for licensing/hiring out to other broadcasters. The new policy also permits uplinking of any television channel from India. It also allows the Indian news agencies to have their own uplinking facilities for purposes of news gathering and its further distribution."
- *Latest CAS Amendments of the Cable Television Act*. Television Networks (Regulation) Amendment Bill, 2002. A bill further to amend the Cable Television Networks (Regulation) Act, 1995. The proceedings in the Rajya Sabha Regarding the Passage of The Cable Television Networks (Regulation) Amendment Bill, 2002.

Important Judgements and Committee Reports

- *Judgement for ownership of Air Waves*: Excerpts from the historic judgement in 1995 which stated that the Air waves are not the monopoly of the Indian Government.
- *The Nitesh Sengupta Committee Report*: The Nitesh Sengupta Committee was set up to review the provisions of Prasar Bharti (Broadcasting Corporation of India) Act, 1990 and to make recommendations regarding the restructuring of Prasar Bharti. Read the contents of the report submitted by The Nitesh Sengupta Committee.
- *Recommendations of Verghese Working Group*: Excerpts from 'Major Recommendations' of Shri B.G. Verghese Working Group on Autonomy for Akashvani and Doordarshan, February, 1978.

  "We envisage an autonomous national trust as the authority under which Akashvani and Doordarshan should grow. This we are naming Akash Bharti—the National Broadcast Trust."
- *Recommendations by Ram Vilas Paswan Consultative Committee*: Summary of the recommendations given by the Ram Vilas Paswan Consultative Committee on National Media Policy for the Information and Broadcasting Ministry, 1996.

  "9.1—The Broadcasting should observe a greater degree of responsibility and sensitivity to Indian culture and ethos and cater to the developmental requirement of the country. It should achieve an Indian personality in telecasting/ broadcasting." (Para 6.4.1.1)"

- *Varadan Committee Report*: Summary of the recommendations of the inter departmental committee on electronic media under the chairmanship of Shri K.A.Varadan, Additional Secretary in the Ministry of Information and Broadcasting.
- *Interim Report of the Sub-Group on Convergence*: India's dream of becoming a super-power in Information Technology. India is in a competitive race for investment and it is believed that investment in this new millenium will flow to countries where there is visible evidence of a strong policy framework, supported by clear and precise laws facilitating growth of business in a converged environment.
- *Final Report of the Sub-Group on Convergence*: A complete report presented by Fali Nariman Committee to Cabinet.
- *Draft Communication Convergence Bill, 2000.*
- *Revised Draft Communication Convergence Bill, 2001*: Incorporating comments/suggestions received from interested organisations and individuals on the Draft Bill prepared by the Sub-Group on Convergence in January 2001.
- *Communication Convergence Bill 2001*: This Bill was introduced in Parliament on 31 August 2001 by the then Communications Minister Ram Vilas Paswan.

Policies for Doordarshan

- The DD Notice
- The DD Advertising Code
- The Code for Commercial Advertising on Doordarshan
- Guidelines for Commissioning of Programmes in Doordarshan.
- DD Press Release.

BROADCASTING CONTENT REGULATION

A. Violation of Advertising Code

Ministry of I&B has issued show cause notices to various satellite channels for telecasting the following objectionable advertisements for the year 2005-06. All the satellite television channels are requested not to telecast/re-telecast these advertisements and they are directed to strictly adhere to the Advertising Code prescribed under the Cable Television Networks (Regulation) Act, 1995 and Rules framed thereunder.

S. No.	Name of the Advertisement/Product
1.	Roop Amrit
2.	Gen-X
3.	Frenchie- X
4.	Gilbeys Green Label Pure Aqua.
5.	Hayward 5000 Soda
6.	McDow ell's No.1 Soda
7.	Seagram's Fling Wicked
8.	Mason Summer's Royal Crown Ca
9.	Seagram's 100 Pipers Pure Music
10.	Smirnoff's Cassettes/CD's
11.	Officer's Choice Premium Soda
12.	Old Tavern Mineral Water
13.	Bacardi Blast Cassettes and CD's
14.	Day Night Soda
15.	Royal Stag Cup Ind/Zim 05
16.	Royal Challenge Premium Sparkling Water
17.	Kingfisher Mineral Water
18.	White Mischief Holidays
19.	100 Pipers Cassettes and CDs.
20.	Sand Piper NA Mald Beverage
21.	Kingfisher Model Hunt
22.	Paan Parag Paan Masala
23.	Seagram's Imperial Blue
24.	Mahak Chaini Chaini
25.	Gopal Zarda 132

B. Violation of Programme Code

Similarly, the Ministry has also issued show cause notices to the various satellite television channels for telecasting objectionable programmes for the year 2004-06. They are:

S.No.	Name of the Programme
1.	Final orders giving warning issued to MH1, ETC, Channel [V], B4U, Balle Balle, iTV, MTV for telecasting songs "Bin Tere Sanam", "Chadati Jawani", "Kabhi Aar Kabhi Paar", "Leke Pehla Pehla Pyar", "Meri Beri Ke Ber."

(Contd.)

S. No.	Name of the Programme
2.	SCN issued to Zee News Channel for telecasting a programme titled "Kal Kapal Mahakal".
3.	Final order giving warning issued to India TV for telecasting a programme on private activities of MPs and MLAs.
4.	Final order giving warning issued to India TV for telecasting news item on sexual involvement of priest of the Swaminarayan Temple.
5.	Final order giving warning issued to FTV for telecasting several programmes, which are violative of the Programme Code.
6.	SCN issued to Zoom TV for telecasting a programme titled "Dangerous" telecast from Monday to Thursday at 11:00 p.m.
7.	SCN issued Trendz TV for telecasting programmes namely 'Lingerie Show' etc.
8.	SCN issued to In Digital Channel for telecasting an adult film, i.e. 'A' certified film by CBFC titled "Khawahish".
9.	SCN issued to Teja TV for telecasting a programme "Kamasutra".
10.	SCN issued to Zee TV for telecasting programme "Item Bomb".
11.	SCN issued to FTV for telecasting obscene programme on 09.12.05.
12.	SCN issued to Maa TV for telecasting programmes titled "Kamasutra", "Manmadha Samrajyam", "Samaram Samayam" and "Sarasm".
13.	SCN issued to Zoom TV for telecasting trailers of films titled "Fun, Sheesha, Shabd and Chahat" which are certified as 'A' by CBFC.
14.	SCN issued to ETC for telecasting trailers of films titled "Fun, Sheesha, Shabd and Chahat" which are certified as ' A' by CBFC.
15.	SCN issued to Zee TV for telecast of a news item regarding alleged phone tapping of Justice (Retd.) S.N.Variava.
16.	SCN issued to MTV for telecast of objectionable songs from Hindi film's "Ashiq Banaya Aapne" and "Zeher".
17.	SCN issued to Zee News for telecast of programme "Deshdroh".

REPORT OF THE TASK FORCE ON INTRODUCTION OF CONDITIONAL ACCESS SYSTEM

Introduction

The issue of introduction of an addressability system has been engaging the attention of the Government for some time, keeping in view the problems being highlighted by sections of the broadcasting industry, including Cable operators, MSO's and Content Providers. A large number of complaints had also been received from subscribers, protesting unwarranted and frequent increase in subscription rates by Cable operators. With almost 38 million cable and satellite households in the country and with a household paying on an average Rs. 125 per month, as subscription charges, the revenue generated in the sector is close to Rs. 5,700 crore. Of this, there have been reports of substantial under reporting by different sections depriving the different players of the industry of their entitled revenue/collection and reportage of transparent viewership figures and the Government of tax. To deliberate and decide upon various issues on this topic, it was decided to set up a Task Force, under Joint Secretary (Broadcasting) in the Ministry of Information and Broadcasting (I & B) with representations from the cross section of the industry. The objective, inter alia, was to deliberate in the need for introducing a Conditional Access System for viewing channels through the cable network and to determine the modalities for doing so.

Constitution of Task Force and Terms of Reference

The Task Force was constituted by an order dated 25th September, 2001 and it consists of representatives from Indian Broadcasting Federation, MSOs Content Creators, Cable Operators, Broadcasters, Infrastructure Providers, nominee from the Ministry of Consumer Affairs, representative of Consumer activists and technical experts. The order constituting the committee, with its Terms of Reference, is annexed.

The Committee was empowered to invite experts and to broadbase the representation on the Task Force, technical experts were co-opted from the industry. Other participants who desired to contribute were also invited to attend. The primary issue of concern for the Committee was to establish the need for introducing Conditional Access System in order to provide a choice to the consumer and to examine the feasibility of doing so, to protect the interests of the consumer from additional costs on replacement of the TV receiver or on purchase of the Conditional Access System, and to debate technology issues relating to standardization and performance.

Meetings

The Task Force held three meetings, one each in the month of October, November and December 2001. At each meeting specific issues were identified for discussion and deliberation and decisions were taken there on, at the same meeting. Since the technology issues were more complex and required extensive consultations, a

Sub-committee was constituted under Director (BD), I&B with representations from the industry, equipment manufacturers and technical experts to go into those aspects. This Sub-committee held separate meetings and their recommendations were considered by the Task Force in its last meeting held on 26th December, 2001. At each stage the members were encouraged to send further comments/ observations in writing for the consideration of the Task Force.

After each meeting of the Task Force, the minutes were circulated to the members by post as well as over Internet. Members of the Task Force as well as other representatives of the industry have provided inputs, which were also considered by the Task Force. This included comments, which were received from National Cable and Telecommunications Associations, Cable Operators etc.

Summary of Discussions

It was acknowledged that Cable Television in India was a technology, which had entered in an unbridled manner and had become a reality totally through private investment. A connectivity of over 35 million homes had been achieved in this syndrome. The MSOs were later entrants. Cable and Satellite Television had gradually become an irresistible force in the process of transformation of communication technology and the perceived potential of Cable TV, DTH, DTT etc., was immense. The Cable Operators observed that since demand of content was driving ad revenue and viewership, the Broadcasters and the Content Creators were whimsically levying exorbitant charges for programmes, channels and for bouquets. Arbitrary increases in subscription rates were creating a problem because Cable Operators were left with no option but to pass on this burden frequently to the subscribers.

The Group discussed the problems and alternatives available and was of the view that the consumer needed to exercise a choice of watching what he chose, and that the viewer should be made aware of what it would cost to view 'Pay' Channels. Addressability is a technique, where signals are sent in an encoded from and an equipment, placed at the subscriber's end, decodes the signals, in accordance with the choice exercised by the consumer and authorized by the Service Provider, specifically on the subscriber's request. The

Task Force considered it desirable that the Conditional Access System should be introduced to provide the consumer choice of viewing and an option to pay for what he chose to watch. The consumer should also not be expected to pay unreasonably for the 'Free to Air' channels and must be able to receive the 'Free to Air' channels without any Set Top Box or any need to change the existing receiver.

The Task Force acknowledged the existence of the value chain starting from the Content Maker, to the Content Provider (Broadcaster) to the main Content Distributor, to the last mile Content Distributor (Cable Operator) and finally the consumer household. In the existing arrangement the consumer was paying for all the channels, irrespective of what he actually watched or desired to watch. There was now need to make the system transparent in respect of the Pay Channels /Pay programmes, which can be watched by selective subscribers. The subscribership of all 'Pay ' channels should be fully determinable. This transparency would allow entitled revenue to accrue to the different links in the chain, permit the consumer to have programming of his choice and watch channels according to their affordability, hopefully at a lower cost, and provide realistic and authentic viewership data. The Task Force was unanimous that the Conditional Access System is necessary to bring transparency at different levels, but that it should not add to the financial burden of the consumer. It was decided that the Government should mandate it by law. The Set Top Box, allowing addressability, should be required only for 'Pay' channels; for subscribers who opt to view only 'Free-to-Air' channels, there would be no requirement of a Set Top Box. The Set Top Box shall be supported by the MSOs/Cable Operators through installation of necessary infrastructure like Subscriber Management System etc. It was considered desirable that the Government must be empowered to enter and inspect the premises and operations of the MSOs and Cable Operators to ensure enforcement of the requirements of the Set Top Box, of transparent recording of viewership figures, display of channel rates etc.

The Task Force saw a presentation on the system introduced by M/s Ortel Communications, in Bhubaneshwar, on experimental basis. It is using 'Dalvi', a low cost conditional access scrambling system, which combines security and multi-tiered addressability. It encrypts analogue signals and the system is compatible with any video transmission system. The system has the potential to address

80,000 customers with a subscriber Management System. A total of 4 channels-mix of 'Free-to-Air' and 'Pay'—are presently being routed through the Set Top Box. The cost of the Set Top Box is approximately Rs. 3,500. The system is one way and not interactive. It was informed that the start up costs, for investment in equipment at Head-end Level, was approximately Rs. 50,000 for each channel. The financial implications of introducing the Set Top Box and addressability system, at each level, were discussed against this background. The need to keep the present system intact, at least for those viewers who prefer to watch only 'Free-to-Air' channels, was favoured.

The Task Force felt that the Set Top Box should be mandated only for "Premium Tier"; 'Free-to-Air' channels being taken in a "Basic Tier", receivable by all viewers at a standard subscription rate. The Task Force debated other issues emerging out of the presentation and felt that the price of channels/content for the Cable Operators should be fixed in a transparent manner, by Content Providers and Channel owners, for all operators.

The Task Force was unanimous in its view that there was need for an enabling provision in the legislation for Government to prescribe certain basic minimum standards for the equipment and its performance. In order to consider all issues relating to prescriptions of Standards and Performance Parameters, for the Set Top Box /Conditional Access System, a Sub-Committee made recommendations on the standards and the specifications for Digital Cable TV and Analogue Cable TV, as well as for Digital/Analogue Set Top Boxes. It also recommended that the Cable Operator/ Equipment Provider should declare, in a transparent manner, the capability of the Set Top Box and its inter-operability with other networks. It also recommended that unauthorized viewing/ redistribution of the signal should be made a cognizable offence. The packaging of services, including Value Added Services, should be left to the Operators who should be free to choose the middleware/software/hardware provided that it conformed to basic minimum performance standards. It further recommended that the subscriber management system should provide transparent information to all the players.

The Task Force was of a strong view that there was urgent need to educate the subscribers, by all the stakeholders, on the operation of Cable Television and the cost of various services, including the operation and cost of Set Top Boxes. The Task Force accepted the recommendation of the Sub-Committee, for an enabling provision in the Act to prescribe basic minimum technical standards and performance parameters, through the Bureau of India Standards (BIS). The manufacturers of the equipment must provide full information on the capability of the hardware. It was also considered desirable that BIS may invite comments from the industry and examine internationally acceptable standards before prescribing standards for India. The Task Force was of the view that eventually the Set Top Box would permit migration, by the subscriber, across various delivery media-Satellite, Cable and Terrestrial. The user will thus have the capability to migrate to various delivery media, simply by changing the "Network Interface Module."

The members of the Task Force debated the need for a Conditional Access System base on DVB simulcrypt technology or any other currently acceptable technology but eventually felt it appropriate to leave the issue of technological specifications to the Bureau of Indian Standards, who would ensure that the technology is not proprietary in nature. In order to ensure transparency in the interface between MSOs and the Cable operators, it was decided that the Government be empowered to obtain monthly reports from the MSOs, Broadcasters and Cable operators in the manner prescribed.

The Task Force also debated the issue of "must carry" provision for the content of the Public Service Broadcaster and the pricing of the "Basic Tier" of service and the Set Top Box. The Group felt that the consumer should not be burdened with the cost of changing his television sets on purchasing a Set Top Box, if he wanted to view only Free to Air channels. The Subscriber should exercise choice of viewing the 'Pay' channels through a Set Top Box. However, there was no need to prescribe the cost price of either the Set Top Box or the 'Pay' channels. It was however, considered desirable that the pricing of various channel bouquets, by the Broadcasters, MSOs should be done in a transparent manner. The Group was unanimous that the Government should fix the price of the 'Basic Tier' and therefore legislation should enable the determination of the 'Basic Tier' price, from time to time by the Government. The Pricing/subsidy of the Set Top Boxes, by any player should be left to market forces, as long as the consumer was made fully aware of the availability and capability of the equipment. The equipment suppliers were confident that with larger volume, market forces would drive down the price of Set Top Boxes. The

Group also felt that the Broadcasters, MSOs and Cable Operators should be allowed the freedom to work out their individual business plans to subsidise the Set Top Boxes, in accordance with their own marketing strategy.

The Group acknowledged the fact that with progressive introduction of Digital Video Broadcasting technology, its combination with interactive return path, between the user and the Service operator, will pave the way for other Services, for which the Subscriber should be prepared to pay on the basis of charges fixed.

Recommendations

(*a*) The Conditional Access System and the supportive Subscriber Management System should be mandated under the Cable Television Networks (Regulation) Act, 1995.

(*b*) The Set Top Box shall be required only for "Pay" Channels and the "Free-to-Air" channels shall be receivable by the subscribers in the current mode, without Set Top Box. The encrypted channel should be defined as "Subscription based Channel."

(*c*) The Technical parameters of the Set Top Box shall conform to the Indian standards, to be prescribed by the Bureau of Indian Standards, in accordance with the provisions of the Bureau of Indian Standards Act, 1986. While doing so, the Bureau of Indian Standards may take into account the internationally acceptable standards and obtain recommendations from technologists and manufacturers of equipment.

(*d*) It shall be mandatory for the Equipment Provider/ Manufacturer to declare, in a transparent manner, the capability of the Set Top Box and its interoperability on other networks.

(*e*) In order to ensure transparency in the operations between MSOs, Cable Operators etc., the Government must be empowered to obtain detailed information on regular basis from each level of operation. This may include information on total subscriber base, on individual programmers, viewership of independence channels, subscription rates, charges fixed by the Broadcasters, Content Creators for each channel etc. Each subscriber shall be keep informed in a transparent manner of the subscription rates for each individual 'Pay' channel.

(*f*) Unauthorised viewing/distribution/redistribution of the broadcast signal should be made a cognizable offence.

(*g*) The Government should regulate the price of 'Basic Tier' of the 'Free-to-Air' channels. The Government should also be enabled to revise the cost of the 'Basic Tier' from time to time. The Government will also make a special provision for the channels of the Public Services Broadcaster. No government intervention was considered necessary with regard to the cost of the Set Top Box or the rates of the individual 'Pay' channel.

(*h*) There should be no requirement for change of the receiving set, irrespective of whether the consumer chooses to watch 'Free-to-Air' channels and/or 'Pay' channels.

(*i*) There was an immediate need to educate the consumer on the operation of cable television on the cost of content creation and its distribution upto the households. The Broadcasters, Content Creators and MSOs should not enhance the charges of the 'Pay' channels arbitrarily, it should be done in a transparent manner.

(*j*) The packaging of services includes Value Added Services, as well as the pricing of the paid bouquets would be left to market forces. However, consumer interest needed to be protected by providing efficient and responsive service and through a transparent and accurate billing and collection system. This will also ensure that the revenue accruable to the Government is determined in a fair manner.

CARRYING ILLEGAL TELEVISION CHANNELS IN VIOLATION OF THE DOWN LINKING GUIDELINES IN CABLE/DTH SERVICE

F. No. 2302/1/20H4—BC-III (Part-1) Ministry of Information and Broadcasting, Broadcasting Wing, Dated 29.5.2006

1. The undersigned is directed to inform you that as per the policy guidelines for down linking of television channels' issued on 11.11.2005 by the Ministry all the television channels uplinked from abroad and downlinked into India have to register themselves before the expiry of 180 days from the date of this notification. The

last date for such registration expired on 10.5.2006. The notification of the Cable Television Network (Amendment) Rules 2006 and the amendment to DTH guidelines was issued on 11.5.2006. As per this, a cable operator may continue to carry or include in his cable service any television broadcast or channel only those TV channels which had made an application for registration to the Central Government on or before the date of commencement of the notification for a period of six months from the date of such commencement or till such registration has been granted or refused, whichever is earlier. The details of the 173 television channels permitted to uplink from India, the details of the 65 television channels uplinked from abroad and downlinked in India and notification issued by this Ministry on downlinking guidelines are posted on Ministry's web-site *http/:mib.nic.in*.

2. In the light of the above all MSOs/DTH Operators/Cable Operators with head-ends are directed give the following information within seven days of receipt of this letter:

— to intimate this Ministry the names of the channels that have been disconnected for telecasting, giving specific dates from which these have been disconnected.

— to intimate this Ministry the names of channels that are not permitted/registered by the Ministry of SB and which are still being carried in their networks and reasons for violation of the Cable Television Networks (Regulation) Act, 1995 and the Rules framed thereunder, the notification of the Cable Television Networks (Amendment) Rule, 2006 vide F. No. 2302/1/2004 BC III, dated 11.5.2006 and DTH licence agreement amendment order dated 11.5.2006.

3. Apart from the above, all MSOs/DTH Operators and COFI are directed to sensitized and activate all the Cable/DTH operators about the new regime and inform the action taken to this Ministry within seven days of receipt of this letter.

(Prawin Kumar)
Director

To,

1. All MSO's

2. Smt. Roop Sharma, President, Cable Operators Federation of India (COFI) 13/97, New Rajori Apartments, Subash Nagar, New Delhi 110027.

3. Lt. Col. (Retd.) K.K. Sharma, Publisher and Chief Editor, Cable Quest, 13/97, New Rajori Apartments, Subash Nagar, New Delhi-1100027 (with a request to give a wide publicity in their magazine).

4. M/s ASC Enterprises (Agrani), J-27, South Extension, Part-I, New Delhi-110049. (Shri Rajiv Khattar, President–Projects, FC-19; Sector-16 A; Film City, Noida-201301.

5. DD. Direct Plus, Engineering-in-Chief, DG: Doordarshan, Doordarshan Bhavan, Copernicus Marg, New Delhi-110001.

6. Copy to US (BP X L).

Status at a Glance

Community Radio Stations

—	Total No of applications received	—	200
—	Letter of Intent Issued	—	60
—	License Agreement signed	—	36
—	Operational CRS	—	19

List of Operational Community Radio Stations

1. Anna Malai University, Chennai
2. Sri Manakula Vinayagar Engineering College, Pondicherry
3. India International Engineering of Management, Jaipur
4. Kongu Engineering College, Erode
5. MOP Vaishnav College for Women, Chennai
6. Sunbeam English School, Varanasi
7. Vidya Pratisthan's Institute of Information and Technology, Baramati, Pune
8. City Montessori School, Lucknow
9. Sardar Patel University, Vallabh Vidyanagar, Gujarat
10. AJK Mass Communication Jamia Millia Islamia, Delhi
11. Banasthali Vidyapeeth, Banasthali, Rajasthan
12. P.G. College, Ghazipur
13. Indian Institute of Mass Communication, New Delhi
14. Erode Sengunthar Engineering College, Erode

15. Pune University, Pune
16. Jagan Institute of Management Studies, Rohini, New Delhi
17. DC School of Management and Technology, Kottayam, Kerala
18. Indian Institute of Business Management, Patna
19. Jagannath International Management School, Vasant Kunj, New Delhi.

List of Letters of Intent

1. Indian Institute of Technology, Kanpur
2. Anna Malai University, Chennai
3. Sardar Patel University,Vallabh Vidyanagar, Gujarat
4. DC School of Management and Technology, Kottayam, Kerala
5. AJK Mass Communication Jamia Millia Islamia, Delhi
6. Banasthali Vidyapeeth, Banasthali, Rajasthan
7. Subhalakshmi College of Science, Madurai
8. P.G. College, Ghazipur
9. Sri Manakula Vinayagar Engineering College, Pondicherry
10. Indian Institute of Mass Communication, New Delhi
11. Film and TV Institute of India, Pune
12. Jodhpur Engineering College and Research Centre, Jodhpur, Rajasthan
13. India International Institute of Management, Jaipur
14. Mudra Institute of Communication, Ahmedabad
15. Kongu Engineering College, Erode
16. MOP Vaishnav College for Women, Chennai
17. Mailam Engineering College, Mailam, Villupuram
18. University of Pune, Pune
19. Loyola College, Chennai
20. Erode Sengunthar Engineering College, Erode
21. Indian Institute of Business Management, Patna
22. City Montessori School, Lucknow
23. CMS Degree College, Lucknow
24. Vidya Pratisthan's Institute of Information Technology, Baramati, Pune
25. Sunbeam English School, Varanasi
26. Madurai Kamraj University, Madurai
27. National Law School of India, Bangalore
28. Manipal Academy of Higher Education, Manipal, Karnataka

29. Hyderabad University, Hyderabad
30. Jagan Institute of Management Studies, Rohini, New Delhi
31. St. Xavier's College, Mapusa, Bardez, Goa
32. Dhirubhai Ambani Institute of Information & Communication Technology, Gandhinagar, Gujarat
33. Amrutvahini College of Engineering, Ahmednagar, Maharashtra
34. Vivek High School, Chandigarh
35. IIMT College, Meerut
36. Guru Nanak Girls College, Ludhiana
37. Padamshree Dr. D.Y. Patil Vidyapeeth, Navi Mumbai (MH)
38. Jagannath International Management School, Vasant Kunj, New Delhi
39. Shree Ramana Maharishi Academy for the Blind, Bangalore
40. Satyajit Ray Film & TV Institute, Panchsayer, Kolkata
41. SRM Institute of Science and Technolgy, Kanchhipuram, Tamil Nadu
42. Bangalore University, Bangalore
43. Sinhgad College of Engineering Vadgaon, Pune
44. University of Agricultural Sciences, Dharwad, Karnataka
45. Sri Sidhartha Centre for Media Studies, Tumkur, Karnataka
46. Sri Venketswara Oriental College, Tirupati
47. Peace Industrial School, Dindigul, Tamil Nadu
48. Holy Cross College, Tiruchirappalli
49. University of Calicut, Calicut, Kerala
50. Periar Maniamai College of Technology for Women, Thanjavur
51. University of Mumbai, Mumbai
52. Acharya Arts and Science College, Villianur, Pondicherry
53. Sri Vishnu Engineering College for Women, Bhimavaram, Andhra Pradesh
54. PSG College of Technology, Coimbatore
55. Sri Bhagwan Mahaveer Jain College, Bangalore
56. Jawahar Lal Nehru University, New Delhi
57. Universal College, Vijaynagar Toll Gate Circle, Bangalore
58. Central India Engineering of Science and Technology, M.P. Nagar, Bhopal, Madhya Pradesh
59. Eminent T.T. Girls College, Diggi, Malpura, Distt. Tonk, Rajasthan
60. RKDF Institute of Science and Technology, M.P.Nagar, Bhopal, Madhya Pradesh

List of License Agreements

1. Anna Malai University, Chennai
2. Sardar Patel University, Vallabh Vidyanagar, Gujarat
3. AJK Mass Communication Jamia Millia Islamia, Delhi
4. Banasthali Vidyapeeth, Banasthali, Rajasthan
5. P.G. College, Ghazipur
6. Sri Manakula Vinayagar Engineering College, Pondicherry
7. India International Institute of Management, Jaipur
8. Mudra Institute of Communication, Ahmedabad
9. Kongu Engineering College, Erode
10. MOP Vaishnav College for Women, Chennai
11. University of Pune, Pune
12. Loyola College, Chennai
13. Erode Sengunthar Engineering College, Erode
14. Sunbeam English School, Varanasi
15. Indian Institute of Mass Communication, New Delhi
16. Vidya Pratisthan Institute of Information Technology, Baramati, Pune
17. Indian Institute of Business Management, Patna
18. City Montessori School, Lucknow
19. CMS Degree College, Lucknow
20. Subhalakshmi College of Science, Madurai
21. DC School of Management and Technology, Kottayam, Kerala
22. Jagan Institute of Management Studies, Rohini, New Delhi
23. Film and TV Institute of India, Pune
24. Padamshree Dr. D.Y. Patil Vidyapeeth, Navi Mumbai
25. Jagannath International Management School, Vasant Kunj, New Delhi
26. Satyajit Ray Film and TV Institute, Panchsayer, Kolkata
27. Vivek High School, Chandigarh
28. Sri Venketswara Oriental College, Tirupathi
29. Guru Nanak Girls College, Ludhiana
30. University of Agricultural Sciences, Dharwad, Karnataka
31. Peace Industrial School, Dindigul, Tamil Nadu
32. Holy Cross College, Tiruchirappalli
33. University of Mumbai, Mumbai
34. SRM Institute of Science and Technolgy, Kanchipuram, Tamil Nadu
35. University of Calicut, Calicut, Kerala
36. IIMT College, Meerut

List of Applicant Institutions

1. Indian Institute of Technology, Kanpur
2. Sardar Patel University,Vallabh Vidyanagar, Gujarat
3. DC School of Management and Technology, Kottayam, Kerala
4. AJK Mass Communication Jamia Millia Islamia, Delhi
5. Banasthali Vidyapeeth, Banasthali, Rajasthan
6. University of Jammu, Jammu
7. AVRC, Anna Malai University, Chennai
8. Subhalakshmi College of Science, Madurai
9. P.G. College, Ghazipur
10. District Institute of Education and Training, Pondicherry
11. Sri Manakula Vinayagar Engineering College, Pondicherry
12. Noorul Islam College of Engineering, Kumarcoil, Kanyakumari
13. New Light, Keonjhar, Orissa
14. Indian Institute of Mass Communication, New Delhi
15. State Institute of Education and Technology, Patna
16. S.D. Public School, Muzaffarnagar (U.P.)
17. Janson's School of Management, Coimbtore
18. G.D. Sawant Arts, Commerce and BCS College, Nasik
19. St. Soldier Education Society, New Delhi
20. IITT College of Engineering Pojewal, Nawanshahar, Punjab
21. B.V. Bhumareddi College of Engineering and Technology, Hubli, Karnataka
22. Film and TV Institute of India, Pune
23. Jagatguru Tontadarya College, Gadag-betgeri, Karnatak
24. Great Commission Kids Academy, Dimapur, Nagaland
25. Kashmir University, Srinagar
26. Attam Vallabh Girls College, Sri Ganganagar, Rajasthan
27. Athavale College of Social Work, Bhandara, Maharashtra
28. Kumaon Engineering College, Dwarhat, Distt. Almora, Uttaranchal
29. National Institute of Agricultre Extension Management (MANAGE), Hyderabad
30. Lakshmi Matriculation School, Sirunathur, Tamil Nadu
31. City Montessori School, Gomti Nagar, Lucknow
32. City Montessori School, Station Road, Lucknow
33. CMS Degree College, LDA Colony, Lucknow
34. Jodhpur Engineering College and Research Centre, Jodhpur, Rajasthan

35. Bhaktikala, Mumbai
36. Hindustan College of Engineering, Chennai
37. Buldana Urban Charitable Society, Buldana, Maharashtra
38. India International Institute of Management, Jaipur
39. Godavari Institute of Engineering and Technology, Rajahmundry, Andhra Pradesh
40. G.H. Raisoni College of Engineering, Nagpur
41. Barli Devi Institute for Rural Woman, Indore
42. Jawahar Lal Nehru University, New Delhi
43. St. Xavier's College, Bardez, Goa
44. Vidya Pratisthan's Institute of Information Technology, Baramati, Pune
45. Mudra Institute of Communication, Ahmedabad
46. The Rajaas Engineering College, Tirunelveli
47. Kongu Engineering College, Erode
48. MOP Vaishnav College for Women, Chennai
49. Jagan Institute of Management Studies, Rohini, New Delhi
50. Jagan Institute of Management Studies, Vasant Kunj, New Delhi
51. Mailam Engineering College, Mailam, Villupuram
52. University of Pune, Pune
53. Karunya Institute of Technology, Coimbtore
54. Loyola College, Chennai
55. Erode Sengunthar Engineering College, Erode
56. Indian Institute of Business Management, Patna
57. Sunbeam English School, Lanka, Varanasi
58. Madurai Kamraj University, Madurai
59. National Law School of India, Bangalore
60. Manipal Academy of Higher Education, Manipal, Karnataka
61. Dhirubhai Ambani Institute of Information and Communication Technology, Gandhinagar, Gujarat
62. Amrutvahini College of Engineering, Ahmednagar, Maharashtra
63. Vivek High School, Chandigarh
64. IIMT College, Meerut
65. Hyderabad University, Hyderabad
66. Guru Nanak Girls College, Ludhiana
67. Padamshree Dr. D.Y. Patil Vidyapeeth, Navi Mumbai
68. Bangalore University, Bangalore

69. Mayiladuthurai Community Centre, Mayiaduthurai, Tamil Nadu
70. Sinhgad College of Engineering, Vadgaon, Pune
71. Shree Ramana Maharishi Academy for the Blind, Bangalore
72. Satyajit Ray Film and TV Institute Panchsayer, Kolkata
73. SRM Institute of Science and Technology, Kanchipuram, Tamil Nadu
74. University of Agricultural Sciences, Dharwad, Rajasthan
75. Sri Vishnu Engineering College for Women, Bhimavaram, Andhra Pradesh
76. Sri Sidhartha Centre for Media Studies, Tumkur, Karnataka
77. Aditanar College of Arts and Science, Virapandianpatnam, Tiruchendur, Tamil Nadu
78. Sri Venketswara Oriental College, Tirupathi
79. Indian Institute of Technology, Kharagpur, West Bengal
80. Delhi Public School, Aligarh
81. Holy Cross College, Tiruchirappalli
82. PSG College of Technology, Coimbatore
83. Sri Bhagwan Mahaveer Jain College, Bangalore
84. Periar Maniamai College of Technology for Women, Thanjavur
85. Peace Industrial School, Dindigul, Tamil Nadu
86. Acharya Arts and Science College, Villianur, Pondicherry
87. University of Calicut, Calicut, Kerala
88. University of Mumbai, Mumbai
89. Eminent T.T. Girls College, Diggi, Malpura, Distt. Tonk, Rajasthan
90. RKDF Institute of Science and Technology, M.P. Nagar, Bhopal (M.P.)
91. Brahma Kumaris Educational Society, Mount Abu, Rajasthan
92. Thane Municipal Corporation, Thane (M.H.)
93. Central India Institute of Science and Technology, M.P. Nagar, Bhopal (M.P.)
94. Seraji Secondary School, Bylakuppe, Mysore, Karnataka
95. Universal College, Vijaynagar Toll Gate Circle, Bangalore
96. Institute of Management Studies, Noida, U. P.
97. Municipal Secondary School, Thane (M.H.)
98. Government Girls Higher Secondary School, Cherthala, Distt. Alappuzha
99. Prajapita Brahm Kumaris Ishwariya Vishwa Vidyalaya, Mount Abu, Rajasthan

100. Guru Nanak Fifth Centenary School, Vincent Hill/Shangri-la, Sardar Mehtab Singh Road, Mussoorie (U.A.)

APPROVED ANNUAL PLAN, 2007-08

Ministry of Information and Broadcasting
(Plan Co-ordination Cell)

The Annual Plan 2007-08 in respect of Ministry of I&B has been fixed at Rs. 475 crore (Gross Budgetary Support) by the Planning Commission. The Sectoral break-up has been approved as under:

Sl. No.	*Sector*	*GBS*	*IEBR*	*Total*
1.	Information Sector	042.47	0.00	042.47
2.	Film Sector	041.98	0.00	041.98
3.	Broadcasting Sector	390.55	0.00	390.55
	Total	475.00	0.00	475.00

The approved Media-unit-wise allocation of Annual Plan 2007-08 is indicated in Annexure-I and the schematic break-up is shown in Annexure-II. It may be noted that many new schemes have been introduced in Annual Plan 2007-08 for which only token provisions have been made. Mere inclusion of the schemes in the Annual Plan does not mean formal approval. Before incurring expenditure out of Plan budget/the following steps should be completed:

(*i*) In respect of the new schemes introduced in Annual Plan 2007-08, necessary "in-principle" approval of the Planning Commission should be obtained latest by 31.03.2007. The total requirement of funds for Eleventh Plan in respect of the new schemes should be assessed and indicated while seeking such "in principle" approval.

(*ii*) Necessary approval of SFC/EFC should be obtained at the earliest so that the implementation starts timely.

Relevant orders in this regard are contained under Rule 18 of the DFPRs/1978 and other instructions in this regard.

All the Media Units/Organization should incur expenditure of an amount exceeding 2-3 per cent of their Budget for initiatives relating to furthering the use of Information Technology/including training/acquisition of hardware/software as well as development and maintenance of software. Media Units/Organizations are/ therefore/requested to work out Action Plan for IT and forward the same to the concerned Administrative Divisions in the Ministry with a copy to Plan Coordination Cell latest by 15.3.2007. The progress in this regard will be monitored by the Planning Commission through the Half Yearly Performance Review reports. To facilitate monitoring of progress made in this regard/schematic break up of the outlays allocated for IT may be maintained/shown separately in the HPRs to be submitted.

As Heads of Departments/Media Units are aware/instructions have been repeatedly circulated to ensure phased and balanced Plan expenditure. All concerned are cautioned to ensure timely achievement of the physical and financial targets of Annual Plan 2007-08. Delay/failure on this account will be viewed seriously.

Heads of Department/Media Units are also aware of the instructions relating to Outcome Budget 2007-08 which should be finalized quickly and scrupulously monitored and implemented.

Encl.: Annexures I & II

Sd/-
(C Angrup Bodh)
Director Fin.&PC)

Heads of All Media Units/Organizations [As per list attached] Ministry of I&B's ID No. 4/73/2006—PC/dated 11/02/2007

Copy along with copies of Annexures I and II forwarded to:

1. PS to MIB/PS tc MSIB
2. Sr. PPS to Secretary (I&B)/PPS to AS/PPS to AS&FA
3. JS (P&A)/JS(B)/JS(F)/Economic Adviser.
4. All Directors/Deputy Secretaries
5. All Under Secretaries/Desk Officers/Section Officers/ Administrative Sections.
6. Technical Director/NIC for putting on I&B's website (along with soft copy)

(C Angrup Bodh)
Director Fin. &PC)

GOVERNMENT OF INDIA
MINISTRY OF INFORMATION & BROADCASTING

'A' Wing Shastri Bhawan, New Delhi-110001

Dated: 18-04-2006

To

Shri N.P. Nawani
President
Indian Broadcasting Foundation (IBF)
B-3-4, 3rd Floor, Ansal Plaza, Khel Gaon Road
New Delhi-110049.

Sub: Sharing of Broadcasting rights of sports events with Prasar Bharati—meeting regarding.

Sir,

The undersigned is directed to enclose herewith a copy of the order No. 603/1/2005-BC-III dated 05.04.2006 regarding sharing of sports events between Prasar Bharati and sports channels and sports rights holder companies. This was decided after consultation with Ministry of Sports and Youth Affairs, Prasar Bharati and sports channels and sports rights holders companies as per Para 5.2 of the Policy guidelines for downlinking for television channels issued on 11.11.2005.

It is requested that the same may be disseminated to all the sports TV channels. This order has been posted on the Ministry's website www.mib.nic.in.

Yours faithfully

(G.R. Raghavender)
Under Secretary (BC)

Copy to : All sports channels.

GOVERNMENT OF INDIA
MINISTRY OF INFORMATION & BROADCASTING

'A' Wing Shastri Bhawan, New Delhi -110001

Dated: 5th April, 2006

ORDER

In pursuance of para 5.2 of the policy guidelines for downlinking of television channels issued vide notice no. 13/2/2002-BP&L/BC-IV dated 11th November, 2005 *and after consultations with the Ministry of Sports and Youth Affairs, Prasar Bharati and the Sports Channels and Sports Rights Holders Companies,* it is hereby ordered that live feeds without any advertisements of the sports channel/sports rights holder, of following sporting events of national importance held in India or abroad are required to be shared with Prasar Bharati with immediate effect by sports channels/sports management companies having television broadcasting rights for broadcast on their terrestrial and DTH networks:

A. International Events

— Summer Olympics
— Winter Olympics
— Commonwealth Games
— Asian Games
— Afro-Asian Games

B. (*i*) Tennis

(*a*) *Davis Cup*—All matches featuring India and semi-final/final matches.
(*b*) *Grand Slam Tournaments*—Finals of all tournaments i.e. Men's single, Women's single, mixed doubles, Men's double, Women's doubles. Further that if an Indian plays then all matches featuring him/her in quarter-final and above.
(*c*) *WTA Championships*—Same as for Grand Slam tournaments.

(*ii*) Hockey

(*a*) World Cup—All matches featuring India and semi-finals and finals.
(*b*) Champions Trophy—All matches featuring India and finals.
(*c*) Beighton Cup—Semifinals and final.
(*d*) Indira Gandhi Gold Cup for Women—Semifinals and finals.

(*iii*) Football

(*a*) World Cup—Semi-finals and finals.
(*b*) European Cup—Semi-finals and finals.
(*c*) Asia Cup—All matches featuring India and semi-finals and finals.
(*d*) Subroto Cup—Semi-finals and finals.
(*e*) Santosh Trophy—Semi-finals and finals.
(*f*) Federation Cup—Semi-finals and finals.
(*g*) Durand Cup—Semi-finals and finals.
(*h*) National Women Football Championship—Semi-finals and finals.
(*i*) Junior National Footbal Championship—semi-finals and finals.

(*iv*) Chess

(*a*) World Championship—Finals of the championship and all games featuring an Indian player in quarter-finals and above.
(*b*) Chess Olympiad—Finals of the championship and all games featuring an Indian player in quarter finals and above.

World Championships in Billiard and Snooker

1. Finals of the championships and all games featuring an Indian player in quarter-finals and above.
2. The events in the list shall be firm for five years from the date of issue of this order.
3. In case an event mentioned in the list is not telecast by Doordarshan (except for reasons beyond its control) the event would be considered for deletion in the next annual review, after giving an opportunity to Doordarshan to explain their position.

4. The Ministry shall annually review the implementation of this order and consider new proposals, if any.

(Seema Jere Bisht)
Director (BC)

* * * * *

MINISTRY OF INFORMATION AND BROADCASTING
NOTIFICATION

New Delhi, the 2nd August, 2006

G.S.R. 459(E).—In exercise of the powers conferred by Sub-section (1) of Section 22 of the Cable Television Networks (Regulation) Act, 1995 (7 of 1995), the Central Government hereby makes the following rules further to amend the Cable Television Network Rules, 1994, namely:

1.(*i*) These rules may be called the Cable Television Networks (Amendment) Rules, 2006.

(*ii*) They shall come into force on the date of their publication in the Official Gazette.

2. In the Cable Television Network Rules, 1994—

(*i*) in Rule 6, in sub-rule (1) after clause (0) the following provisions shall be inserted, namely:
"Provided that no film or film song or film promo or film trailer or music video or music albums or their promos, whether produced in India or abroad, shall be carried through cable service unless it has been certified by the Central Board of Film Certification (CBFC) as suitable for unrestricted public exhibition in India."

(*ii*) in Rule 7, for sub-rule (9) the following shall be substituted, namely:—

"(9) No advertisement which violates the Code for self-regulation in advertising, as adopted by the Advertising Standard Council of India (ASCI), Mumbai for public exhibition in India, from time to time, shall be carried in the cable service."

[F. No. 2302/1/2001-BC-III (Part)]
N. Baijendra Kumar, Jt. Secy.

Note: The principal rules were published in the Gazette of India, Part II, Section 3, Sub-section (i) *vide* number G.S.R. 729(E), dated the 29th September, 1994 and subsequently amended by G.S.R. 459(E), dated the 8th October, 1996 and G.S.R. 710(E), dated 8th September, 2000 and G.S.R. 282(E), dated the 11th May, 2006.

* * * * * *

MINISTRY OF INFORMATION AND BROADCASTING
NOTIFICATION

New Delhi, the 9th August, 2006

G.S.R. 469(E).—In exercise of the powers conferred by Sub-section (1) of Section 22 of the Cable Television Networks (Regulation) Act, 1995 (7 of 1995), the Central Government hereby makes the following rules further to amend the Cable Television Network Rules, 1994, namely:—

1.(*i*) These rules may be called the Cable Television Networks (Amendment) Rules, 2006.

(*ii*) They shall come into force on the date of their publication in the Official Gazette.

2. In the Cable Television Network Rules, 1994, in Rule 7, in sub-rule (2), in clause (viii), after sub-clause (A), the following shall be inserted, namely:

"Provided that a product that uses a brand name or logo, which is also used for cigarettes, tobacco products, wine, alcohol, liquor or other intoxicants, may be advertised on cable service subject to the following conditions that—

(*i*) the story board or visual of the advertisement must depict only the product being advertised and not the prohibited products in any form or manner;

(*ii*) the advertisement must not make any direct or indirect reference to the prohibited products;

(*iii*) the advertisement must not contain any nuances or phrases promoting prohibited products;

(*iv*) the advertisement must not use particular colours and layout or presentations associated with prohibited products:

Provided further that all such advertisements shall be previewed and certified by the Central Board of Film Certification suitable for unrestricted public exhibition prior to telecast or transmission or retransmission."

[F. No. 804/3/2005-BC-III/BC-II]
N. Baijendra Kumar, Jt. Secy.

Note: The principal rules were published in the Gazette of India, Part II, Section 3, Sub-section (i) *vide* number G.S.R. 729(E), dated the 29th September, 1994 and subsequently amended by G.S.R. 459(E), dated the 8th October, 1996 and G.S.R. 282(E), dated 11th May, 2006.

भारत का राजपत्र
The Gazette of India

असाधारण

EXTRAORDINARY

भाग II– खण्ड 3–उपखण्ड (i)

Part II—Section 3—Sub-section (i)

प्राधिकार से प्रकाशित

Published by Authority

[सं. 201] नई दिल्ली, बृहस्पतिवार, मई 11, 2006/वैशाख 21, 1928

[No. 201] New Delhi, Thursday, May 11, 2006/Vaisakha 21, 1928

सूचना और प्रसारण मंत्रालय

अधिसूचना

नई दिल्ली, 11 मई, 2006

सा.का.नि. 282(अ).–केन्द्रीय सरकार, केबल टेलीविजन नेटवर्क (विनियमन) अधिनियम, 1995 (1955 का 7) की धारा 22 की उप-धारा (1) द्वारा प्रदत्त शक्तियों का प्रयोग करते हुए, केबल टेलीविजन नेटवर्क नियम, 1994 का और संशोधन करने के लिए निम्नलिखित नियम बनाती है, अर्थात्:–

1.(1) इन नियमों का संक्षिप्त नाम केबल टेलीविजन नेटवर्क (संशोधन) नियम, 2006 है।

(2) ये राजपत्र में इनके प्रकाशन की तारीख को प्रवृत्त होंगे।

2. केबल टेलीविजन नेटवर्क नियम, 1994 के नियम 6 में उप-नियम (5) के पश्चात्, निम्नलिखित अंत:स्थापित किया जाएगा, अर्थात्–

"(6) कोई भी केबल ऑपरेटर अपनी केबल सेवा में किसी भी ऐसे टेलीविजन प्रसारण या चैनल को प्रसारित या शामिल नहीं करेगा जिसको भारत के राज्य क्षेत्र के भीतर देखे जाने के लिए केन्द्रीय सरकार द्वारा रजिस्ट्रीकृत न किया गया हो":

परन्तु, कोई भी केबल ऑपरेटर जिसने इस अधिसूचना के प्रारम्भ की तारीख का

या उसके पूर्व केन्द्रीय सरकार को रजिस्ट्रीकरण के लिए आवेदन किया है, किसी भी टेलीविजन प्रसारण या चैनल को, अधिसूचना के प्रारंभ की तारीख से छह मास की अवधि तक अथवा ऐसे रजिस्ट्रीकरण के मंजूर या अस्वीकृत होने तक इनमें से जो भी पहले हो, अपनी केबल सेवा में प्रसारित या शामिल करना जारी रख सकेगा।

परन्तु, यह और कि दिसंबर, 2005 से पूर्व अपलिंकिंग हेतु प्रदान की गई अनुमति के अनुसार भारत से अपलिंक किए जाने वाले चैनलों को "रजिस्ट्रीकृत" टेलीविजन चैनल माना जाएगा और उनको केबल सेवा में प्रसारित या शामिल किया जा सकता है।

[फा. सं. 2302/1/2004 बी.सी.-III]
प्रवीण कुमार त्रिपाठी, संयुक्त सचिव

पाद टिप्पण: मूल नियम सं. सा.का.नि. 729(अ) तारीख 29 सितम्बर, 1994 के तहत प्रकाशित किए गए थे और सं. सा.का.नि. 459(अ), तारीख 8 अक्तूबर, 1996 और सं. सा.का.नि. 710(अ), तारीख 8 सितम्बर, 2000 द्वारा संशोधित किए गए थे।

भारत का राजपत्र
The Gazette of India

असाधारण

EXTRAORDINARY

भाग II– खण्ड 3–उपखण्ड (i)

Part II—Section 3—Sub-section (i)

प्राधिकार से प्रकाशित

Published by Authority

[सं. 545] नई दिल्ली, शनिवार, नवम्बर 11, 2006/कार्तिक 20, 1928

[No. 545] New Delhi, Saturday, November 11, 2006/Kartika 20, 1928

सूचना और प्रसारण मंत्रालय

अधिसूचना

नई दिल्ली, 11 मई, 2006

सा.का.नि. 697(अ).–केन्द्रीय सरकार, केबल टेलीविजन नेटवर्क (विनियमन) अधिनियम, 1995 (1955 का 7) की धारा 22 की उप-धारा (1) द्वारा प्रदत्त शक्तियों का प्रयोग करते हुए, केबल टेलीविजन नेटवर्क नियम, 1994 का और संशोधन करने के लिए निम्नलिखित नियम बनाती है, अर्थात्:

1.(*i*) इन नियमों का संक्षिप्त नाम केबल टेलीविजन नेटवर्क (संशोधन) नियम, 2006 है।

(*ii*) ये राजपत्र में इनके प्रकाशन की तारीख को प्रवृत्त होंगे।

2. केबल टेलीविजन नेटवर्क नियम, 1994 के नियम 6 में उप-नियम (6) में, पहले परंतुक के स्थान पर निम्नलिखित परंतुक रखा जाएगा, अर्थात्–

"(परन्तु कोई केबल ऑपरेटर, जिसका रजिस्ट्रेशन के लिए आवेदन, केन्द्रीय सरकार को 11 मई, 2006 को या उससे पूर्व किया गया था और वह विचाराधीन है, इस अधिसूचना की तारीख से तीन मास की अवधि के लिए या ऐसा रजिस्ट्रीकरण मंजूर किए जाने या खारिज किए जाने तक, इनमें से जो भी

पूर्वतर हो, किसी टेलीविजन प्रसारण या चैनल में अपनी केबल सेवा जारी रख सकेगा या शामिल कर सकेगा"।

[फा. सं. 1601/71/2006–टीवी (आई)]
एन. बैजेन्द्र कुमार, संयुक्त सचिव

पाद टिप्पण: मूल नियम सं. सा.का.नि. 729(अ), तारीख 29 सितम्बर, 1994 द्वारा प्रकाशित किए गए थे और सं. सा.का.नि. 459(अ), तारीख 8 अक्तूबर, 1996, और सं. सा.का.नि. 710(अ), तारीख 8 सितम्बर, 2000, सा.का.नि. 282(अ), तारीख 11 मई, 2006. सा. का.नि. 452(अ), तारीख 31 जुलाई, 2006, सा. का.नि. 459(अ), तारीख 2 अगस्त, 2006 और सा.का.नि. 469(अ), तारीख 9 अगस्त, 2006 द्वारा संशोधित किए गए।

* * * * * *

MINISTRY OF INFORMATION AND BROADCASTING NOTIFICATION

New Delhi, the 11th November, 2006

G.S.R. 697(E).— In exercise of the powers conferred by Sub-section (1) of Section 22 of the Cable Television Networks (Regulation) Act, 1995 (7 of 1995), the Central Government hereby makes the following rules further to amend the Cable Television Networks Rules, 1994, namely:

1.(*i*) These rules may be called Cable Television Networks (Amendment) Rules, 2006.

(*ii*) They shall come into force on the date of their publication in the Official Gazette.

2. In the Cable Television Networks Rules, 1994, in rule 6 in sub-rule (6) for the first proviso the following proviso shall be substituted, namely:

"Provided that a cable operator may continue to carry or include in his cable service any Television broadcast or channel, whose application for registration to the Central Government was made on or before 11th May, 2006 and is under consideration, for a period of three months from the date of this notification, or till such registration has been granted or refused, whichever is earlier:

[F. No. 1601/71/2006 —TV (I)]
N. Baijendra Kumak, Jt. Secy.

Footnote: The principal rules were published *vide GSR* 729(H), dated the 29th September, 1994 and amended *vide* GSR 459(H), dated the 8th October, 1996, GSR 710(E), dated the 11th September, 2000, GSR 282(E), dated the 11th May, 2006, GSR 452(E), dated the 31st July, 2006, GSR 459(F.), dated the 2nd August, 2006 and GSR 469(E), dated the 9th August, 2006.

* * * * * *

7

India's Media and Broadcast Policies

THE INDIAN MEDIA: AN OVERVIEW

Compared with many other developing countries, the Indian press has flourished since independence and exercises a large degree of independence. British colonialism allowed for the development of a tradition of freedom of the press, and many of India's great English-language newspapers and some of its Indian-language press were begun during the nineteenth century. As India became independent, ownership of India's leading English-language newspapers was transferred from British to Indian business groups, and the fact that most English-language newspapers have the backing of large business houses has contributed to their independence from the government. The press has experienced impressive growth since independence. In 1950 there were 214 daily newspapers, with forty-four in English and the rest in Indian-languages. By 1990, the number of daily newspapers had grown to 2,856, with 209 in English and 2,647 in indigenous languages. The expansion of literacy and the spread of consumerism during the 1980s fueled the rapid growth of news weeklies and other periodicals. By 1993, India had 35,595 newspapers—of which 3,805 were dailies—and other periodicals. Although the majority of publications are in indigenous languages, the English-language press, which has widespread appeal to the expanding middle class, has a wide multicity circulation throughout India.

There are four major publishing groups in India, each of which controls national and regional English-language and vernacular publications. They are the Times of India Group, the Indian Express Group, the Hindustan Times Group, and the Anandabazar Patrika Group. The *Times of India* is India's largest English-language daily, with a circulation of 6,56,000 published in six cities. The *Indian*

Express, with a daily circulation of 5,19,000, is published in seventeen cities. There also are seven other daily newspapers with circulations of between 134,000 and 477,000, all in English and all competitive with one another. Indian-language newspapers also enjoy large circulations but usually on a statewide or citywide basis. For example, the Malayalam-language daily *Malayala Manorama* circulates 673,000 copies in Kerala; the Hindi-language *Dainik Jagran* circulates widely in Uttar Pradesh and New Delhi, with 580,000 copies per day; *Punjab Kesari*, also published in Hindi and available throughout Punjab and New Delhi, has a daily circulation of 562,000; and the *Anandabazar Patrika*, published in Kolkata in Bengali, has a daily circulation of 435,000. There are also numerous smaller publications throughout the nation. The combined circulation of India's newspapers and periodicals is in the order of 60 million, published daily in more than ninety languages.

India has more than forty domestic news agencies. The Express News Service, the Press Trust of India, and the United News of India are among the major news agencies. They are headquartered in Delhi, Mumbai and New Delhi, respectively, and employ foreign correspondents.

Although freedom of the press in India is the legal norm—it is constitutionally guaranteed—the scope of this freedom has often been contested by the Government. Rigid press censorship was imposed during the Emergency starting in 1975 but quickly retracted in 1977. The Government has continued, however, to exercise more indirect controls. Government advertising accounts for as much as 50 per cent of all advertisements in Indian newspapers, providing a monetary incentive to limit harsh criticism of the administration. Until 1992, when government regulation of access to newsprint was liberalized, controls on the distribution of newsprint could also be used to reward favoured publications and threaten those that fell into disfavour. In 1988, at a time when the Indian press was publishing investigative reports about corruption and abuse of power in government, Parliament passed a tough defamation bill that mandated prison sentences for offending journalists. Vociferous protests from journalists and opposition party leaders ultimately forced the government to withdraw the bill. Since the late 1980s, the independence of India's press has been bolstered by the liberalization of government economic policy and the increase of private-sector advertising provided by the growth of India's private sector and the spread of consumerism.

Broadcast Media

The national television (Doordarshan) and radio (All India Radio, or Akashwani) networks are state-owned and managed by the Ministry of Information and Broadcasting. Their news reporting customarily presents the government's point of view. For example, coverage of the 1989 election campaign blatantly favoured the government of Rajiv Gandhi, and autonomy of the electronic media became a political issue. V.P. Singh's National Front Government sponsored the Prasar Bharati (Indian Broadcasting) Act, which Parliament considered in 1990, to provide greater autonomy to Doordarshan and All India Radio. The changes that resulted were limited. The bill provided for the establishment of an autonomous corporation to run Doordarshan and All India Radio. The corporation was to operate under a board of governors to be in charge of appointments and policy and a broadcasting council to respond to complaints. However, the legislation required that the corporation prepare and submit its budget within the framework of the central budget and stipulated that the personnel of the new broadcasting corporation be career civil servants to facilitate continued government control. In the early 1990s, increasing competition from television broadcasts transmitted via satellite appeared the most effective manner of limiting the pro-government bias of the government-controlled electronic media.

Since the 1980s, India has experienced a rapid proliferation of television broadcasting that has helped shape popular culture and the course of politics. Although the first television programme was broadcast in 1959, the expansion of television did not begin in earnest until the extremely popular telecast of the Ninth Asian Games, which were held in New Delhi in 1982. Realizing the popular appeal and consequent influence of television broadcasting, the government undertook an expansion that by 1990 was planned to provide television access to 90 per cent of the population. In 1993, about 169 million people were estimated to have watched Indian television each week, and, by 1994, it was reported that there were some 47 million households with televisions. There also is a growing selection of satellite transmission and cable services available.

Television programming was initially kept tightly under the control of the government, which embarked on a self-conscious effort to construct and propagate a cultural idea of the Indian nation. This goal is especially clear in the broadcasts of such megaseries as the Hindu epics *Ramayana* and *Mahabharata*. In addition to the effort at nation-building, the politicians of India's ruling party have not hesitated to use television to build political support. In fact, the political abuse of Indian television led to demands to increase the autonomy of Doordarshan; these demands ultimately resulted in support for the Prasar Bharati Act.

The 1990s have brought a radical transformation of television in India. Transnational satellite broadcasting made its debut in January 1991, when owners of satellite dishes—initially mostly at major hotels—began receiving Cable News Network (CNN) coverage of the Persian Gulf War. Three months later, Star TV began broadcasting via satellite. Its fare initially included serials such as "The Bold and the Beautiful" and MTV programmes. Satellite broadcasting spread rapidly through India's cities as local entrepreneurs erected dishes to receive signals and transmitted them through local cable systems. After its October 1992 launch, Zee TV offered stiff competition to Star TV. However, the future of Star TV was bolstered by billionaire Rupert Murdock, who acquired the network for US$525 million in July 1993. CNN International, part of the Turner Broadcasting System, was slated to start broadcasting entertainment programmes, including top Hollywood films, in 1995.

Competition from the satellite stations brought radical change to Doordarshan by cutting its audience and threatening its advertising revenues at a time when the government was pressuring it to pay for expenditures from internal revenues. In response, Doordarshan decided in 1993 to start five new channels in addition to its original National Channel. Programming was radically transformed, and controversial news shows, soap operas, and coverage of high-fashion events proliferated. Of the new Doordarshan channels, however, only the Metro Channel, which carries MTV music videos and other popular shows, has survived in the face of the new trend for talk programmes that engage in a potpourri of racy topics.

Analysis of the Government of India's laws and policies regarding television (Doordarshan) provides insight into the concrete realities, rather than professed goals, of India's nation-building in the context of phenomenal class disparities, cultural pluralism and multilingualism. We first explore the development communications paradigm on which Doordarshan was predicated and the evolution of the legal infrastructure into which it emerged in 1959. As examines India's adoption of the development communications paradigm to justify early television experiments, including the largest ever undertaken, the Satellite Instructional Television Experiment of 1975-76. I then turn to the period of greatest threat to democratic media practice in India, the Emergency of 1975-77; the unsuccessful reforms of the Janata interregnum; and the politically driven investment in television made by Mrs. Gandhi upon her return to power. We then examine the unintended consequences of this governmental media monopoly, including the politicization of news programming under Rajiv Gandhi, making television a contentious political issue in the 1989 Lok Sabha (Parliamentary) elections; and the implication of Doordarshan in the rise of communal politics (through state-sponsored serialization of major Indian epics), in increasing consumerism, and in exacerbation of regional anti-Centre sentiments. The final chapter examines the end of the government's monopoly over the airwaves due to the advent of transnational satellite television and the growth of cable systems, and India's attempts to govern these technologies. Based on archival data, memoirs, government documents and numerous interviews with politicians, television officials, producers, advertisers and legal experts, we demonstrate how the development communications paradigm rationalized a governmental television monopoly that was politicized, centralized and hierarchical, creating a widening gap between government rhetoric and programming realities. The result has been a series of lost opportunities, in which Doordarshan undermines its greatest strengths: its wide reach, greater than that of any transnational broadcaster; its public, rather than commercial, rationale; and its extensive infrastructure that, unlike any satellite channel, could contextualize programming for local and regional informational and language needs.

INS Expresses Concern over Government Media Policy

The Indian Newspaper Society's outgoing President Jacob Mathew expressed concern over the government's media policy in view of some provisions of the draft Broadcast Services Regulation Bill, 2006, including the proposed restrictions on cross-media holdings.

The draft bill envisages the creation of a Broadcast Regulatory Authority empowered to administer a content code and to restrict cross-media holdings of media enterprises.

"In a democratic society, content in the media should only be subject to self-regulation. There exists a sufficient framework of laws in the country to ensure that the freedoms guaranteed by the Constitution are not misused by the media", Mathew told the 67th Annual General Meeting of INS.

"The proposed restrictions on cross-media holdings are a cause for concern", he said. Noting that newspaper enterprises had made large investments in broadcast media, in which the investment market had also taken significant positions, he said, "these investments cannot be jeopardised."

"At the present stage in their evolution, newspaper enterprises provide to broadcast media the maturity and the expertise they require for ensuring orderly growth", he said.

On newsprint, Mathew said its prices continued to be a source of anxiety. International and domestic prices rose by over 10 per cent during the year and the current price of newsprint had touched USD 700 per tonne.

Mathew said the Customs Tariff Act had now redefined newsprint to include de-inked and recycled newsprint which might provide "some relief' but there were newer issues to tackle.

The enforcement by the Supreme Court of weight restrictions on container cargo by road transport would push up the delivered cost of imported newsprint "at our doorsteps", Mathew said.

He also observed that through recent changes in the format for applications for import entitlements for newsprint, the government could be trying to introduce administrative control on the quantities of newsprint being imported by INS members.

"The Society believes that the benefits of a liberalised trade policy should not be denied to the newspaper industry."

The INS, he said, continued persuading the Empowered Committee on VAT implementation in favour of 'Zero Per cent' VAT on newsprint and hoped to get a favourable decision on it.

Looking at 2005-06, Mathew said this had been a year of healthy growth for the newspaper industry with a turnover of Rs. 11,800 crore in 2005.

INS' members reported total advertising revenue of Rs. 7,400 crore for 2005, a 23 per cent growth over 2004. "This growth comes after 15.6 per cent growth in 2004, and 16.9 per cent in 2003", he added.

However, the industry's bottomlines were not growing hand in hand with the sales figure, he said, adding one major dampening fact had been the steep rise in international and domestic newsprint prices. Another factor had been potential of taxes to corrode the industry's profits.

> "We have observed a trend towards a hardening of the policy environment with respect to the freedom of the media. Some of the legislative initiatives being considered by the Government appear to be undemocratic. Considering the volatile environment in which we live, the threat to our freedom to report, inform and educate is as serious as the threat to our economic viability," Mathew said.

On the prospects of the newspaper industry, Mathew said a vibrant advertising industry supported by a buoyant economy sustained its business. "But, this business model is under great stress."

Taxation policy towards the industry had to necessarily take into account the current business model of the media industry, he said, emphasising, "we do not recover our costs or make a profit from our readers."

Given the low cover price, the reach and spread or the dispersion of the newspapers in India was nowhere near those of developed countries, he said.

> "We subsidise the reader by selling advertising space—a by-product. The cover price of a newspaper does not even cover the variable cost of producing a newspaper. Our newspapers are the lowest priced in the world, costing even less than a cup of tea or coffee in our cities.
>
> "At some point, therefore, we have to give a serious thought as to what extent, we can afford to subsidise the reader," Mathew told the members.
>
> He said despite competition from television and other media, advertising revenues of the press medium would sustain a healthy rate of growth in the foreseeable future.

"Our own figures, as well as Price Waterhouse projections justify an estimated annual growth of 12-15 per cent over the next five years."

In the long-term, the threat from TV might be more significant as TV channels proliferate in the news area, he said. "We should consider this aspect of the media market, and work on strategies to ensure that the press continues to be a major player in our country's democratic process."

MEDIA AT CROSSROADS IN INDIA: A VIEWPOINT

It has to choose between commerce and credibility. Newspapers, the earliest form of the media, have been around in some sort of a way as long as the printing press. In Elizabethan London, they took the form of pamphlets filled with grisly tales of murder, executions, witchcraft and "monstrous" creatures. Political news was absent as it was considered "dull and boring". The world's oldest surviving headline dated December 2, 1620, said "The new tidings out of Italie are not yet come."

The power of the newspaper in a democracy got unleashed in 1820, when publishers rode on Queen Carolina's trial to garner public support for her. George IV, the then king, was adamant that his wife, Carolina of Brunswick, should not become queen and so sought to divorce her. Newspapers took up her cause to build overwhelming public pressure that enabled Queen Carolina to win—but unfortunately she died a year later suddenly and the great effusion of 1820 was quickly forgotten. However, the trial of Queen Carolina benefited her adopted country. The British people had gained confidence that, even without the franchise, their voice would be heard. Public opinion had arrived in politics, finding outlets wherever it could—on streets, in petitions and in a popular press that, once it had learnt how to annoy rulers, never stopped. In fact, the power of the press, more so the media, grew so fast that during the Russian Revolution, Lenin and Trotsky identified the media as one of the five institutions to gain control of as a means to get ascendancy. The media as an institution has never looked back since and only grown in power, stature and control on the general public. And in a democracy where "freedom of speech" is a fundamental right, the media is the ultimate expression of that right. Clamp down on it, and democracy begins to crumble.

Formal advertising emerged in the late 19th century, taking the form of "salesmanship in print" as defined by an early guru, John Kennedy. It evolved through the 20th century from being just information dissemination to creating desire and engagement, reaching its crescendo in the late 20th century, when it was branded "the want makers." If the the media is representative of "freedom of speech" in a democracy, advertising (and marketing) is the expression for "freedom of choice", the other fundamental right in a democratic world.

Marketing gives consumers choices and advertising enables them to choose more intelligently and freely.

In the branding space, the media is an interesting and complicated category. A media brand has a commercial side—a responsibility to give the market and consumer what they want; yet it also has a conscience side—a responsibility to society and the citizen. And these are not often conciliatory. The content within the media is both the product and its promotion. Its content can ride on social trends; but simultaneously it can influence social trends more powerfully than any other product category can. It has overwhelming power on the public. It is both B2B (business to business) and B2C (business to consumer). B2B—the advertiser—is its source of revenue and sustenance; however, this depends on the brand's power in the B2C segment—viewer, reader, listener. The higher the user figures, the more revenue it can garner from the advertiser because it can deliver more value for the advertising buck. So not surprisingly, there is a symbiotic relationship between advertising and the media.

There has been a media explosion in this country since the economic liberalisation process started in 1991. Our televisions have over 200 channels—international, national, regional and local. And the print media has moved into specialisations like fashion and automobiles. The radio is opening up and growing by the day. And India has always been a big billboard country with larger-than-life cut-outs and messages—used so successfully by political parties and campaigns. The net and mobile are booming new media. The new media and the proliferation of options within the traditional media are putting pressure on media brands in print and television to garner readers and viewers. Television spot rates are today the lowest in this country—which in itself is not a bad thing but does put pressure to generate revenue and audiences. And this is where conflict sets in. The head of a leading television news channel, a few years ago prophetically and rightly, said: "The day editorial and sales merge, that day will spell the death of media."

Two distinct trends emerged in the media in 2006, clearly reflecting the crossroads it is at today. The first: the review of and the conviction of the culprit in the Jessica Lall case. Much like the 1820 trial of Queen Carolina, the media took on the role of the social ombudsman and championed the cause of Jessica Lall in early 2006. The laudable efforts of the media led to the case being reopened and the accused getting convicted by the end of the year. This is the conscience face of the media—activities that build its credibility and strengthen the pillars of democracy.

On the other hand, there has emerged a disturbing new trend in the media—the promotion of "mass voyeurism." Getting into the private lives of people and celebrities and putting them in the public domain. The "supposed impending" marriage of a celebrity couple and the happenings in a celebrity birthday party moving from page three to front page are manifestations of this trend. Vir Sanghvi in a recent piece did say rather mournfully: "Mika Singh today makes better news than Manmohan Singh." This is trivialisation of news at its best. And the oft-repeated claim by media brand managers is that this is what consumers want. The crowning glory of this intrusion into lives is the serial "Big Boss", which is actual legitimisation of mass voyeurism. This is perhaps a return to the "pamphlet world" of the 17th century, when sensational events make for better news than actual reportage.

Simultaneously the continuous pressure from the advertising world to merge commercial brand messages into editorials for a price is another disturbing trend. Some media brands are already into selling editorial space. And a movie promoted itself recently by having its lead stars read the 9 o'clock news on a very reputed news channel. These are, sure, media attempts to garner resources from their advertising brothers. But this leads to a threat to their credibility.

While media brands may argue that it is the yin and yang of its content and both can co-exist, somewhere choices need to be made. If media brands remain apathetic to the credibility of their editorial, they suffer the danger of losing respect and credibility. And that will be a loss for Indian society and citizens. After all, the media needs to be the watchdog of society, a mirror that makes citizens and administrators soul-search and take necessary corrective action. And advertisers and advertising agencies need to recognise their needs as citizens to ensure that their pursuit of consumers does not infringe on the credibility of society's most powerful means of expression—the media.

The BBC is one example that has successfully maintained its credibility in the face of commercialisation of most markets. It can be sought as a source of inspiration. Something worth thinking about.

Indian Government and Media Scare in Recent Times

Fear of government controls came to haunt the Indian media in 2006, a year which saw the much-resisted CAS finally moving toward roll-out and the struggling FM radio sector literally boom.

Just as media rode high on popular public support to sting operations, especially those exposing MPs allegedly accepting money for raising questions or for diverting funds from MPLAD schemes, came a shocker when reports surfaced that the government was working on a bill that would effectively curtail media's independence.

The Broadcasting Services Regulation Bill, 2006, a draft of which came in the hands of the media, was aimed at giving sweeping powers to the Government to take control and manage private broadcasting channels in certain eventualities.

The Bill also gave powers to "authorised officers to inspect, search and seize equipment" of media in case of any violation.

The proposal, for obvious reasons, saw the media cry foul forcing the Government to not only keep introduction of the Bill in abeyance but also invite suggestions from media industry on a new draft bill it issued with some modifications.

Another issue that saw the Ministry on a sticky wicket was related to the issue of on-screen smoking, which Health Minister Ambumani Ramadoss refused to give up. Information and Broadcasting Minister P.R. Dasmunsi clearly looked uneasy in a balancing act, especially as the film industry and Censor Board Chief made a case for what they termed creative freedom.

The issue remains unresolved and going by the magnitude of controversy it could create, the Ministry seems happy with the vagueness associated the matter.

Controversies apart, 2006 was also a year that saw one of the broadcasting sector's most contentious issues—Conditional Access System, infamous as CAS—move toward implementation.

A brainchild of erstwhile BJP-led NDA Government, the roll-out of cable TV delivery system in notified areas of Delhi, Mumbai and Kolkata had been in limbo for last three years or so, except for Chennai where it was implemented with little success.

After Delhi High Court refused to buy government pleas that its implementation should be delayed for some more time, the Government was left with no option but to order its roll-out from the New Year.

A favourable Rs. 5 rate per pay channel, ordered by TRAI for CAS areas also seems to be an enabling factor for roll-out of the new system.

But if any issue for which the Government needs to pat itself, it was the way it sold FM radio stations in second phase of bidding, primarily led by positive policy measures.

After the first round of allotments ended in disaster and losses for the very-few operating FM radio companies, the Government relaxed the policy framework, shifting to a revenue share regime.

In fact, the Government even liberalised the sector and allowed 20 per cent FDI in FM radio, another positive for the industry.

The Government was able to sell about 280 radio stations in around 91 cities across the country, earning a good Rs. 1,145 crore as revenue by way of one-time entry fee from new players and migration fee from those already in operation.

Spread over five rounds, Phase II of licensing saw not only existing players like the Times Group, Music Broadcast and Radio Mid-Day clamouring for new cities, but also new entrants like Adlabs of Anil Ambani and HT Music and Entertainment win licenses.

Another area where Government's efforts in the year were directed was on the issue of ensuring feed of sporting events, especially cricket, to cash-crunched Prasar Bharati.

After some of the private broadcasters refused to share feed with Doordarshan, the Government made clear that it would introduce a Bill in the Parliament that would pave the way for a legislation on the matter, making it binding on private broadcasters to share the feed in events of "national interest."

Talking about cricket, the vexed issue of BCCI's cricket telecast rights—which landed more in courts rather than in a broadcaster's pockets—was finally resolved. Nimbus stumped established players like ESPN-Star and Zee to bag the four-year global media rights for a staggering 612 million dollars, putting an end to constant bickering over the matter.

On the corporate side, 2006 looked like the year for expansion announcements by media companies. NDTV announced plans for expanding beyond news and also beyond India. These included more channels, including entertainment and metro-centric.

Raghav Behl's TV18 network also moved ahead on the path of expansion. The company, which said it will diversify into film production and distribution, also bought a controlling stake in Jagran's Hindi News Channel, that has now been rechristened IBN7.

Toward the end of the year, the company purchased business news wire, Crisil Market Wire, strengthening its news gathering network.

The Zee group, one of the India's oldest media and entertainment group, also was in an expansion mode as the company bought a stake in Dubai-based Taj Television, owners of sports channel Ten Sports. The group also got the telecast rights for Indian cricket team's matches in non-ICC countries.

Zee, through an investment company Media Vest, was also in the news for takeover of domestic news wire United News of India (UNI), though the issue has landed in the Company Law Board after protest from some of the existing shareholders.

A significant development toward the end of the year, on the media side, was the 50:50 joint venture memorandum of understanding between rivals HT Media and The Times of India Group to jointly publish a newspaper in Delhi.

The companies said the joint venture would draw strength from the competencies of both Groups, allowing them to work together to efficiently grow an exciting and nascent market.

Singh said the country was passing through a "difficult phase" and it climed only the BJP was capable of facing and tackling them.

He asked party workers to strengthen the party so that it could tackle these problems and lead the country.

India and Foreign Equity Cap in Media: A Government Viewpoint

India could review the 26 per cent foreign equity cap in news and current affairs publications if stakeholders take a collective view on the matter, Information and Broadcasting Minister Priyaranjan Dasmunsi said in an important declaration.

"Let the industry decide and get back to me. We will then review the policy. We have an open mind, Dasmunsi told a seminar on the future of magazines at the two-day Indian Magazine Congress, referring to both criticism and support over the issue of foreign equity caps.

"Why do you want me to be your enemy? You decide," he said adding that he knows why the foreign publications are interested in entering the Indian market. "The temptation of the market here is too strong."

India presently allows 100 per cent foreign equity—including those by portfolio funds and foreign institutional investors—in non-news and non-current affairs journals but limits it to 26 per cent in news and current affairs publications.

The minister, who was a journalist himself before entering politics, said he believed that print media had a great future in the country. "India is today the biggest media market in the world perhaps after China," he said.

In support of his arguments, he spelt out some statistics. He said despite the growth in the reach of satellite TV channels at 34-40 per cent per annum, the reach of the print media was growing.

"The print media's reach has increased from 179 million in 2003 to 222 million in 2006. Magazines are one of the fastest-growing segments in print media, with 4,000 magazines in English alone with a readership of 100 million," he said.

Dasmunsi said, magazines have kept the old-age traditional habits of reading in both rural and urban India alive.

"An interesting fact I noticed in the National Readership Survey, 2005, is while the reach of the press has fallen in urban India in the last three years from 48 per cent to 46 per cent, it has grown in rural India—17 per cent to 19 per cent."

He said the number of newspapers and magazines in rural India were almost equal to those in urban areas. "As a result of the total of 200 million readers in the country in 2005, as many as 98 million are from rural India."

Dasmunsi said the trend also suggested a proliferation of niche journals—where 100 per cent foreign equity is permitted—in areas like travel, tourism, heritage, popular science, regional literature and health.

"We have approved 78 titles till August last. Many more applications are under process. With further liberalisation, especially 100 per cent equity in special interest publications, we expect foreign investments in this segment to grow."

According to the I & B minister, the advertising market in India has also grown with the share of print media growing at 15 per cent per annum, which, he said, would ensure the financial health of magazines.

"But some unpleasant aspects have to be measured before they assume threatening dimensions. As I see, private media houses use the business model of advertising to sustain the costs of the media product," he observed.

"This has over time led to corporate influence—or, may I say, interference on content—and consequently, affected media freedom. The clear mission ascribed to media to report the truth appears to have been blurred by corporate pressure."

In a democracy like, India such an influence may negate the need for an objective assessment of issues, the minister said, adding: "Media, as we can easily perceive, is a means for corporates to become more powerful within the system."

India to Establish 4000 Community Radio Stations under New Community Radio Policy: A Recent Announcement

In the next few years 4000 community radio stations will have sprung up in India under the new enabling community radio policy announced by the Government says Shri S. K. Arora, Secretary, Ministry of Information and Broadcasting of India.

This was announced during the "National Consultation on Community Radio for practising and potential Community Radio Operators in India", at the Indian Institute of Mass Communication (IIMC), New Delhi, 6-7 March, 2007.

The Ministry of Information and Broadcasting, Government of India in collaboration with the United Nations, led by UNESCO, organised the consulation meeting attended by over 150 representatives from Government of India, bilateral agencies, umbrella NGOs, grassroots community workers, both mainstream media and community radio enthusiasts. The consultation achieved its aims of raising awareness about the processes involved in Community Radio (CR) licensing in India, and taking the dialogue forward.

Based on presentations from Community Radio operators in South Africa, Philippines, Nepal, Sri Lanka and India relating to crucial aspects ranging from policy to operation, organisation and management, programming and technical aspects and sustainability, it showcased different models/experiences in South Asia and other regions and focussed on contextualising them to meet the Indian situation.

The National Consultation, envisaged as a precursor to a series of regional workshops to spread awareness of community radio and encourage community groups to set up community radio stations, was further encouraged by the Government's proposal to follow up with a "touring technical exhibit" of technology options for this purpose.

Other proposals emerging from this meeting related to the establishment of a pro-active national community radio association to build peer pressure for trustworthiness; voluntary mechanisms for dispute resolution that may also form a link to a national broadcast complaints commission; development of mechanism for on-going dialogue on policy; professionalisation of community radio; lowering of entry barriers in an effort to reach the Government target of establishment of 4000 community radio stations by 2008; maintenance of community radio networks for information sharing and capacity building; continued targeted advocacy to involve communities in taking the lead to spread the community radio movement in India; and publication of a source book on technical facilities available in the country.

In his inaugural address, Shri S.K. Arora, Secretary, Ministry of Information and Broadcasting anticipated that in the next few years 4000-5000 community radio stations will have sprung up in India and that it was indeed helpful for community radio operators (practicing and potential) in India to understand different aspects from others' experience. According to him, "The Indian Government has been extremely supportive of NGOs functionning. The mass media factor had been missing in this support. This gap will be filled up by community ratio operations." He further added, "Community radio focuses on low cost and low return pattern of operations, which are aimed at educating and entertaining the community using their own idioms and language in contrast to the private FM radio which is primarily driven by entertainment and business considerations."

W. Jayaweera, UNESCO Director, Division for communication development, Paris in his keynote address reminded one and all that community radio was all about community engagement by harmonizing local potential. "CRS can prove to be an excellent tool for managing plurality in a society and fostering the democracy." In the welcome remarks delivered by Jocelyne Josiah, Adviser in communication and information, the meeting was reminded of the added power of community radio when combined with multimedia devices as practised in the four experimental Community Multimedia Centres (CMCs) in India promoted by UNESCO.

UN Resident Coordinator and UNDP Resident Representative Maxine Olson said that UNESCO is training 150 personnel for Radio Banasthali in Rajasthan. She also referred to the support being lent by United Nations in Andhra Pradesh and Karnataka in the setting up of community radio stations.

This National Consultation comes in the wake of the November 16, 2006 the Union Cabinet clearance of the community radio policy allowing non-profit organizations with a three-year track record to set up and run stations. A modification of an earlier policy that let 'reputed educational institutions' have radio stations, this one permits civil society organizations to have their own transmission. Ownership over transmission was one major point of contention by NGOs; they could use campus radios and buy time on All India Radio (AIR) earlier, but did not own the transmitters.

Radio is the main source of news and entertainment for most of India. AIR is the top tier in radio coverage, as the public service broadcaster. Private FM has now become the second tier. Community radio promises to be the third-tier, closest to the people. Community radio in India has many advantages over AIR and private FM. Programmes, nearly always in the local languages deal with local issues involving ordinary people so that villagers and townspeople understand what they are about. The Government's broadcasting code notwithstanding, audio programmes have exposed corruption. Just hearing themselves on radio is an empowering experience for people, who realize that this, truly, can be their voice and help them get a better deal from the government and other castes. It is the first time Dalits, tribals and women have found an opportunity to speak out.

Bibliography

Alan, Taylor. *We, the media...", The Hollywood Representation of News Broadcasting, 1976-1999, Peter Lang, 2005, p. 418, ISBN 3631518528.*

Barnouw, Erik. *The Golden Web* (Oxford University Press, 1968); *The Sponsor* (1978); *A Tower in Babel* (1966).

Briggs, Asa. *The BBC—The First Fifty Years* (Oxford University Press, 1984).

Briggs, Asa. *The History of Broadcasting in the United Kingdom* (Oxford University Press, 1961).

Covert, Cathy and Stevens John, L. *Mass Media Between the Wars* (Syracuse University Press, 1984).

Douglas, B. Craig. *Fireside Politics: Radio and Political Culture in the United States, 1920-1940* (2005).

Ewbank, Henry and Lawton Sherman, P. *Broadcasting: Radio and Television* (Harper & Brothers, 1952).

F. Leslie Smith, John, W. Wright II, David H. Ostroff. *Perspectives on Radio and Television: Telecommunication in the United States,* Lawrence Erlbaum Associates, 1998.

Gibson George, H. *Public Broadcasting; The Role of the Federal Government, 1919-1976* (Praeger Publishers, 1977).

Gwenyth, L. Jackaway. *Media at War: Radio's Challenge to the Newspapers, 1924-1939,* Praeger Publishers, 1995.

John, Dunning. *On the Air: The Encyclopedia of Old-Time Radio,* Oxford University Press, 1998.

Lazarsfeld, Paul F. *The People Look at Radio* (University of North Carolina Press, 1946).

Maclaurin, W. Rupert. *Invention and Innovation in the Radio Industry* (The Macmillan Company, 1949).

Peers, Frank W. *The Politics of Canadian Broadcasting, 1920-1951* (University of Toronto Press, 1969).

Ray, William B. *FCC: The Ups and Downs of Radio-TV Regulation* (Iowa State University Press, 1990).

Robert, W. McChesney; *Telecommunications, Mass Media and Democracy: The Battle for the Control of U.S. Broadcasting, 1928-1935*, Oxford University Press, 1994.

Rosen, Philip T. *The Modern Stentors; Radio Broadcasting and the Federal Government 1920-1934* (Greenwood Press, 1980).

Scannell, Paddy, and Cardiff, David. *A Social History of British Broadcasting, Volume One, 1922-1939* (Basil Blackwell, 1991).

Schramm, Wilbur, ed. *Mass Communications* (University of Illinois Press, 1960).

Schwoch, James. *The American Radio Industry and its Latin American Activities, 1900-1939* (University of Illinois Press, 1990).

Slater, Robert. *This . . . is CBS: A Chronicle of 60 Years* (Prentice Hall, 1988).

Sterling, Christopher and Kittross, John M. *Stay Tuned: A Concise History of American Broadcasting* (Wadsworth, 1978).

Sterling, Christopher H. *Electronic Media: A Guide to Trends in Broadcasting and Newer Technologies 1920-1983* (Praeger, 1984).

Tim, Crook. *International Radio Journalism: History, Theory and Practice*, Routledge, 1998.

Tom, McCourt. *Conflicting Communication Interests in America: The Case of National Public Radio*, Praeger Publishers, 1999.

White, Llewellyn. *The American Radio* (University of Chicago Press, 1947).

William, A. Rugh. *Arab Mass Media: Newspapers, Radio and Television in Arab Politics*, Praeger, 2004.

Index